WHAT DO YOU SAY TO
A NAKED ROOM?

Books by Catherine Crane

Residential Interiors Today

What Do You Say to a Naked Room?

WHAT DO YOU SAY TO A NAKED ROOM?

A Practical Guide for Translating Your Needs and
Wishes into Personal Home Decorating
Options and Answers

Catherine C. Crane

The Dial Press New York

Published by
The Dial Press
1 Dag Hammarskjold Plaza
New York, New York 10017

Manufactured in the United States of America

9 8 7 6 5 4

Design by James L. McGuire

Library of Congress Cataloging in Publication Data

Crane, Catherine C.
What do you say to a naked room?

Includes index.
1. Interior decoration—Handbooks, manuals, etc.
I. Title.
NK2115.C928   747'.8'83   79-11982
ISBN 0-385-27121-2
ISBN 0-385-27122-0

To Don Gold, who got me into this.

First of all, I want to thank my sister-in-law, Joanne Goward Crane, for the title. Quick-witted as usual, she came up with it during a brainstorming session.

Second, Nancy van Itallie, my editor at Dial, deserves a medal for her perseverance and patience in molding my manuscript into a real live book.

Thirdly, I want to salute Jim McGuire, the book designer. I suspect that most of us read only if we like the look of a book. I'm grateful to Jim for wrapping all these ideas in a pleasing package.

I'm most grateful also to the designers, manufacturers, museums, photographers, and public relations people who have allowed me to present their pictures.

The copy editor, David Frederickson, I congratulate for his thoroughness, professionalism, and—thank God—sense of humor.

I appreciate the work of everyone else associated with Dial who has had anything at all to do with birthing this book.

Maybe most of all I'm thankful to my friends for their emotional support and encouragement. It has meant so much to me. Ruth and Jay Fitzgibbons not only egged me on, but "made a Xerox copy" of my enormous manuscript in its first incarnation. Virginia Dajani had the kindness to look over the first version and offer editorial advice. My brother, Bill, and sister-in-law, Jo, offered constructive suggestions, as did Jim Harper. My dear friends Ellen Parker, Jeannie Layton, Marcia Poston, Mary Gilbert, Purcell Palmer, and Annie Westbrook Fraser have been believers even in my darkest hours and for that words cannot express my gratitude.

CONTENTS

INTRODUCTION

What do you say to a naked room? The first word that's likely to come to mind is "HELP!" Where do you begin? And even if you do take a plunge and begin, do you know where you're going and how to get there? It's all so confusing. And the worst of it is that no part of the room stands alone; everything depends on everything else. If the room is ever to come together, all the elements have to be *orchestrated*. And who ever held a maestro's baton? Most of us are more likely to need a magic wand!

You do know what you want. You do know how you like to live. But it's likely that you don't know how to translate your realities into the home of your dreams. It's a language barrier. Never mind.

This book is a tract of translation. In Parts One and Two you can look up the circumstances of your life and see how they translate into decorating ideas and options. You might well be led to a "look" you like. In Part Three you can look up those key words that describe what you *wish* your room were like and see how those words translate into decorating ideas and options. (Key words are set in SMALL CAPITALS throughout the text.) (As you are reading about a subject you might check the index for other pictures and references.) Part Four will help you pull together all the decorating ideas and options that are appropriate for you and *orchestrate* them into an interior that is what you would have wished all along. Part Five will give you guidance in shopping.

You can converse with your naked room! It can speak to you, and you *can* tell it how to get dressed.

PART ONE

YOUR WHOLE HOME

The character of your whole home should be determined by where you live, who lives with you, and what you do, as well as by the furnishings you have and the money you have to spend. This part of the book will ask you the questions that will lead to answers.

Although you will want variations from room to room, your whole home should have some consistency of character. You won't want to furnish the rooms of your home in widely differing styles. It would make the place seem more like a museum than a home. Your home should have a flowing feeling—with variations on a unified theme. As you read through Part One, write down any of the KEY WORDS that you would want to describe your whole home. These words can lead you to your decorating answers.

Rooms that can be seen together should have compatible plans. If the rooms in your home seem small and choppy, you can smooth them out and make them seem larger by coloring all the walls the same and covering the floors with the same continuous treatment. Pale or neutral colors are particularly effective.

To coordinate adjacent rooms, you might repeat colors or patterns. For example, you might hang patterned draperies in the living room, and in the adjacent dining room, you might paper the walls with the same pattern. The color of the walls in one room might be the color of the accessories in the next.

If your home has a traditional floor plan where individual rooms are entered from halls, the rooms can be more different than in a modern floor plan where the rooms all open into each other. Children's rooms are most often the exception to a flow-through scheme. It is good for a child's developing sense of self to be allowed to select his or her own favorite colors.

1

WHERE DO YOU LIVE?

Just like any animal, we all have to adapt to our environment. The place where you live will force you to compensate for the climate and probably lead you to adopt some of the styles of the natives.

HOW LONG ARE YOU GOING TO BE HERE?

Do you want permanent or portable furnishings? If this is a vacation home, you surely will want it to be EASY TO CLEAN.

PERMANENT If you intend to keep your furniture for a long time, it pays to buy simple styles or classics. They will never seem dated.

If you own your own home and intend to stay, you should do your utmost to make it efficient and comfortable. Structural changes, if appropriate, are worth the investment. They will probably increase the value of your home if you change your mind and want to sell. It would be worthwhile to have things custom made to fit the place.

If you rent your home but intend to stay, you could invest in structural changes if they would really make your family more comfortable. But remember—if you must move, your landlord, not you, gets the benefit of your investment. As an alternative, you might find portable furnishings that work as well as built-ins.

TRANSIENT If you move a lot, it pays to buy portable furnishings you can easily rearrange in different spaces. Modular furniture is a good bet. And neutral colors, such as oatmeal, will mix with almost anything. It's also a good idea to mat and frame your pictures alike so there's no problem in regrouping them.

If you own your home, you can make structural improvements, even if you won't be staying long. These improvements may increase the value of your property and make it more salable.

If you rent your home, you may have to leave the apartment or house just as you found it or pay a penalty to the landlord. Therefore, make sure, whatever you do, that the walls, floor, ceiling, and windows are easily restorable to their original condition, and make your major investments in what you can move with you. Avoid spending money on walls, built-ins, and wall-to-wall carpeting. Instead think of portable area rugs, modular furniture, and walls covered with strippable wallpaper or with fabric stretched between rods hung at the ceiling line and floor line.

If you rent your home and won't want to take your furnishings when you go, forget the "lifetime investment" type of furniture, and buy things that will work for the short term. Don't spend a lot of money. Get furniture from attics or garage sales, and refinish or shape it up yourself. For carpet, buy carpet remnants. For draperies, use sheets.

SEASONAL OR OCCASIONAL—VACATION HOMES Will you use it in all seasons? If so, you have to think of insulating against heat or cold. Will you use this home ultimately for retirement? If so, then you might invest in your future comfort while you have the money.

Just because it is a vacation home, you should invest in things that make it DURABLE and EASY TO CLEAN. Who wants to spend their holidays cleaning?

The decor should be LIVELY. After all you're here to have fun. The scheme should accommodate the climate. Ski houses should have WARM EFFECTS; beach houses should have COOL EFFECTS. Houses by the beach also should be WATERPROOF.

WHAT IS THE CLIMATE?

In order to make your home feel comfortable, you might well have to compensate for the climate.

HOT In a hot climate, you will want to create COOL EFFECTS. Pare things bare, use cool blues, greens, and whites, and keep almost everything slick and smooth.

COLD In a cold climate you will want to create WARM EFFECTS with thick cuddly textures and hot colors.

CHANGEABLE If the climate is changeable with the seasons, you'll want your decor to be CHANGEABLE too.

DO YOU LIVE IN THE CITY, COUNTRY, OR SUBURBS?

You might like to reflect the atmosphere of your locale in your design.

CITY If you live in the city, you might want to reflect the city's sophistication and FORMALity, especially if that's the type of life you lead. Or you might like to do the opposite—create a relaxing INFORMAL atmosphere to contrast with your day of hustle-bustle. For an earthy, natu-

This vacation studio is LIVELY-looking, space-saving, and EASY TO CLEAN. The carpet, woodwork, and countertops are bright red. The platform sofa bed is covered with a punchy pattern and pillows. Counter supports, mesh chairs, and industrial shelving are see-through. (Photo courtesy Fibers Division/Allied Chemical Corporation; design by G. Allen Scruggs, ASID.)

The city sophisticate might slip into a little champagne, and a little Deco drama. The sensuousness of the soft rug and the velvet upholstery set off the sparkle of the mirror and the chrome-and-glass table. The DRAMATIC skyscraper-painted shoji screens give a sense of size. They slide back to provide a grand entrance to the dining room. (Photo courtesy of Selig Furniture and Magee Carpet; design by Elroy Edson, ASID.)

ral effect, many have stripped their walls of plaster to expose old brick and beams. Many city dwellers seem starved for nature. Plants provide a little of God's greenery.

City people have an especially great need for privacy. Thick carpets and wallcoverings help absorb sound. An executive at Bloomingdale's department store says he sells a lot of four-poster beds. He calls them "the metropolitan retreat."

COUNTRY   If you live in the country, you can play up the simplicity of country life by choosing COUNTRY/RUSTIC styles.

You also might like to bring the outdoors in by leaving your windows unobstructed and by repeating nature's colors in your interior.

If the view outside is nothing special, you might create a sense of excitement by giving your walls a DRAMATIC treatment.

SUBURBS   If you live in the suburbs, you might want to blend country calm with city sophistication. Life in the suburbs has its dignified moments and its casual times. Your interior could be SEMIFORMAL, adaptable to all occasions.

Life in the suburbs is also activity-oriented. Your activities and interests can inspire your scheme.

WHAT IS THE ARCHITECTURE OF YOUR HOME?

The architecture of your home can help you choose appropriate furniture styles. Imagine walking into a simple ranch house and finding furniture as elaborate as King Louis's Versailles. It's somehow not suitable, right?

A home and its furnishings should generally be of the same formality. For example, country cottages, mountain lodges, farmhouses, and barns are rustic. They express simplicity and strength. The furnishings should also be COUNTRY/RUSTIC or INFORMAL to carry through the same simple message.

Houses built with symmetrical sides and crafted in fine detail out of expensive materials are formal. These houses express dignity and reserve, and generally so should their furnishings. For example, formal English Georgian and American Colonial houses look just right furnished in the FORMAL GEORGIAN styles of Chippendale, Hepplewhite, and Sheraton. To echo this symmetry, furniture might also be arranged in balanced matching pairs.

Informal houses are not symmetrical in design. If you split them in half, down the center, the sides wouldn't match. Informal homes, including modern ranch and traditional Early English styles, express friendliness and hospitality. Their furnishings also should be INFORMAL and express casual comfort.

Furnishings might be chosen in a style to match the architecture. For example, a tradi-

It is harmonious to repeat the shape of an important architectural feature in the shape of furnishings. Here the backs of the bamboo chairs repeat the appealing arch of the fireplace. The oval of the etched mirror adds another rounded note. (Design by R. Michael Brown; photo by Arie de Zanger.)

tional home is complemented by furnishings of the same tradition. There is a natural harmony between the two because they come from the same roots. Like you and the folks from your own hometown.

If you decide that you want your style of furniture to contrast with the architectural style of your home, you'll have to work on something else besides history to establish a relationship.

You can repeat the shapes of the architecture in the shapes of your furnishings. For example, a round table would look good in a rounded bow window. A rectangular room might have furniture arranged in a rectangular shape. Repetition of shape creates a sense of harmony.

Your furniture can be inspired by the textures of the architecture. For example, with a rough stone wall, furnishings should be rather rough-textured or natural-looking.

Like you and your friends, your home and your furniture have to have something in common.

EARLY ENGLISH These styles include Gothic, Tudor, Elizabethan, Jacobean, and Cotswold or English cottage. Some of these houses are built of stone. Most are made of half timber frames filled in with brick, stone, or wattle, which is usually plastered with clay or stucco and then whitewashed. The plaster is rough and shows natural trowel marks. A modern imitation is made of stucco with a plank overlay. The steep roofs were originally thatched; later they were tiled. The irregularly spaced windows are small with tiny diamond-shaped panes.

Appropriate furnishings: EARLY ENGLISH Tudor and Jacobean furniture is suitable, as well as COUNTRY/RUSTIC and INFORMAL styles.

EARLY AMERICAN The Early American style is an adaptation of the Early English. The early settlers reconstructed as best they could the styles they knew. There is a lot of Early American architecture in New England.

Early American homes often have the second floor projecting over the first, and a plain gable roof might extend lower in the rear to cover lean-to rooms. Exterior walls are covered with clapboards and have small casement windows. The floor plan is symmetrical with a single room on each side of a central chimney, upstairs and down.

Appropriate furnishings: INFORMAL or EARLY AMERICAN styles.

COLONIAL With growing wealth and sophistication, colonists strove to emulate the refinement of English Georgian homes. Colonial homes are rectangular and symmetrical. The doorway is in the center and features a pediment on top and columns on either side. Windows are evenly spaced on each side of the door. There is a chimney in the center or at each end of the house. Colonial houses are usually built of wood, although stone and brick are also used. Like Early American houses, some "garrison" colonials have the second story overhanging the first in the front.

Appropriate furnishings: FORMAL or SEMI-FORMAL furnishings, especially of English ancestry—EARLY COLONIAL/QUEEN ANNE, GEORGIAN, AMERICAN FEDERAL. (QUEEN ANNE pieces are also handsome in a mix with modern.)

CAPE COD The Cape Cod house is a smaller and more simplified version of New England's Colonial houses. The original Cape Cod cottage was usually a story and a half, with a plain gable roof and no dormers. Exterior walls are covered with gray weathered shingles or white clapboard. Typically, one or two windows are located on either side of a central door. They are double-hung, with small panes, and shutters.

Appropriate furnishings: INFORMAL, COUNTRY/RUSTIC or EARLY AMERICAN styles.

GEORGIAN By the time the first Georgian homes were built in America, the early settlers had reached wealth and sophistication. Their homes reflect this. The houses have columns, brick walls, tall chimneys on the end walls, a center doorway with a fancy pediment on top, large, regularly spaced windows, and delicate moldings. The floor plan features a central hall and staircase with symmetrical rooms on each side, both upstairs and down. The restoration at Williamsburg, Virginia, is an excellent example of American Georgian architecture.

Appropriate furniture: Furnishings should be FORMAL and express dignity and restraint. QUEEN ANNE and GEORGIAN styles are perfect. Styles should be light, graceful, mainly rectangular.

FEDERAL After the Revolution, Americans proclaimed the birth of the republic by harking back to the styles of ancient Greece and Rome. In truth, the Europeans of the time were also influenced by the ancients. Napoleon was busy associating himself with the ancient emperors of Rome, while the English were fascinated with the archaeological diggings and discoveries of Pompeii.

Examples of Federal architecture are Thomas Jefferson's Monticello and University of Virginia, and the Boston State House by Charles Bulfinch. Buildings were designed with classical columns with perfect proportions in symmetrical balance. The eagle, trumpet, and thunderbolt—the symbols of our nascent nationalism—were mixed with the motifs of the ancients: the acanthus leaf, saber, cornucopia, lyre, and rosette.

English Adam styles greatly affected the interior architecture. Classical columns and niches in formal symmetry were often part of the wall treatment. Wood paneling was often seen on the fireplace wall, the dado (the lower third of the wall), and the cornice molding.

Appropriate furnishings: FORMAL, light-looking, and classically inspired: some GEORGIAN, FEDERAL, and FRENCH LOUIS XVI.

FRENCH French aristocrats fled the revolution at home in 1789. The French influence has been greatest in Louisiana and South Carolina.

These symmetrical FORMAL homes are notable for their studied proportions and delicate refinement. Characteristic features include a high, steep mansard roof, an elaborate double-front door with curved moldings, and tall French windows.

Appropriate furnishings: FORMAL furnishings, especially the French styles of LOUIS XV and LOUIS XVI, look at home.

If the setting is the country or the mood is informal, you can choose FRENCH PROVINCIAL furnishings.

GREEK REVIVAL A number of Greek Revival homes were built in this country in the first half of the nineteenth century. They can be found as far west as Illinois and as far south as the Gulf of Mexico.

The old plantation homes in the Deep South are versions of the Greek Revival style. The architecture features enormous high porches and porticoes with columns. The gable roof often extends unbroken over the porch. There are central halls, large rooms, high ceilings, and French doors. Greek motifs are often found on mantels, woodwork, cornices, and in plaster rosettes on the ceiling.

Appropriate furnishings: FORMAL, heavy-looking, and classically inspired: GREEK REVIVAL, ENGLISH REGENCY, FRENCH EMPIRE.

VICTORIAN Victorian styles have had a particularly strong influence in the Mississippi River Valley and in San Francisco.

Victorian homes are thought of as picturesque, romantic, rambling. They have high gabled roofs, with corner towers and balconies. They might be covered in shingles, applied in patterns. The rooms are often irregular in shape with circular bow windows. Golden oak is often used heavily in the interior—for parquet floors, for false beamed ceilings, for paneled dadoes, and heavy wooden trim.

Appropriate furnishings: SEMIFORMAL styles. VICTORIAN in a mix with MODERN is appealing. For today's taste, a Victorian interior usually needs to be lightened and simplified. Lighter, brighter colors, fewer patterns, and less clutter will do the trick.

SPANISH (OR MEDITERRANEAN)

The Spanish influence is found mostly in Florida, Texas, Arizona, New Mexico, and California—areas where the climate is sunny and warm.

A typical Spanish home is built around three sides of an open (but private) patio. There is usually an arcade running around between the patio and the enclosed rooms. Walls are tinted stucco. Roofs are low and tiled and overhang the stucco walls. There is usually beautiful ironwork. The interiors feature colorful tiles. All floors are either tile or brick. Ceilings are beamed, and walls can be adobe.

Appropriate furnishings: This is where SPANISH styles look best. Other heavy INFORMAL styles also work well.

INSPIRED BY THE AMERICAN INDIANS

In Arizona and New Mexico, the Spanish colonists built houses inspired by the homes of the Pueblo Indians. Made of adobe, the homes featured flat roofs and parapet walls. Originally, pole ladders on the exterior took the place of stairs.

Appropriate furnishings: INFORMAL furnishings with Pueblo rugs, blankets, and accessories. These Indian artifacts are still to be found in Arizona and New Mexico. The colors of your home might be inspired by the desert scenery.

MODERN HOME INSPIRED BY A TRADITIONAL MODEL

Many modern homes are designed on traditional models, and very successfully so. Your house may be young in years, but have an ancient heritage behind it. Read the above and see if anything seems to describe your home. If so, you might include some appropriate traditional furniture in an ECLECTIC mix. Then your home could say today and still be wise about yesterday.

MODERN

Modern homes are characterized by flowing space. This is called "open planning." Halls are eliminated wherever possible, and walls are often visually eliminated, becoming simply sheets of glass. These window walls help connect the indoors with the outdoors to give even a greater sense of space. There is a sense of light and air spreading around unimpeded.

Walls are often in architectural materials such as concrete blocks, brick, rough plaster, or wood. Floors are often a clean sweep of masonry or carpet.

Appropriate furnishings: MODERN or an ECLECTIC mix of modern with traditional. You could make traditional furnishings look more modern by painting them white or upholstering them in contemporary fabrics. Furniture shapes and colors might echo the outdoors.

Furniture should be placed to take advantage of the view, if there is one. Furniture might

In this MODERN home many of the furnishings look as structural as the architecture. The metal chairs repeat the material of the window frames. The table repeats the wood of the ceiling. An antique Chinese screen provides ECLECTIC excitement. (Photo courtesy of Thayer Coggin, Inc.; design by Milo Baughman; photo by Alexandre Georges.)

be arranged so that different parts of the room can function separately. Rugs, screens, open bookcases, plants, or the backs of furniture might define areas and furniture groupings.

RANCH HOUSE The ranch house is characterized by a single-floor plan, and a low-pitched roof. Halls lead to the main rooms. There is usually an off-center fireplace in the living room. Windows are large and there may be sliding glass doors leading onto a patio.

Appropriate furnishings: INFORMAL styles look at home. Very dressy or elegant styles look out of place.

MODERN CITY APARTMENT BUILDING These are usually so nondescript you can do anything. You might give dimension and interest to a boring, boxy room by using a large mirror or a tall piece of furniture, such as an armoire. You might break out of confinement by placing furniture on the diagonal.

HOW MUCH SPACE DO YOU HAVE?

The size of the overall space will indicate how much you must double up your activities, or how much you can spread them out. It also indicates how much and what kind of furniture you will want.

LARGE SPACE You may have one room for each activity of your home, or you may enjoy the same activity in different places. For example, you might eat in the kitchen, the dining room, the library, the sun porch; you might have breakfast in bed, a snack by the pool. You could have one living room for adults, another for children. You might even have a guest suite.

In a large space you can have decorative furniture as well as functional pieces.

MEDIUM-SIZED SPACE A medium-sized space is not constricting. It gives you a nice latitude. (Also makes you realize how nature abhors a vacuum. Somehow space always gets filled up!)

SMALL SPACE A small space can be claustrophobic unless you discipline yourself to contain clutter. If you want air to breathe, reduce your furnishings to the minimum. Develop an ongoing relationship with a thrift shop, and keep cleaning out your closets and getting rid of articles that are of no use but just take space. You'll not only feel organized, you'll have a tax deduction!

SPACE-SAVING IDEAS

How can you make the most of a small space?

YOU CAN REMODEL You might gain space by putting your attic or basement or garage to work. You might enclose a porch or a breezeway. You might even panel a room to create a storage wall. In many areas of the country, home-improvement loans are easier to come by than mortgage money. And an investment in your home will increase its resale value.

YOU CAN DOUBLE UP ACTIVITIES A room can be used for different activities at different times of day. Simultaneous activities can be grouped according to whether they are noisy or quiet.

USE THE VERTICAL SPACE You might raise an area of the room up on a platform, and use the space under the platform for storage. One clever room I've admired has two trundle beds on casters shoved under an open-ended platform.

Here is an example of ingenious use of vertical space. A platform was built over a chest of drawers to provide a surface for sleeping. All the requirements of the bedroom in one neat package. The mirrored wall, of course, stretches space, and the vertical blinds and contrasting beams emphasize the height of the ceiling. (Photo courtesy of Fibers Division/Allied Chemical Corporation; architectural design by Ari Bahat.)

If your ceiling is especially high, you might build a second-level loft into the room. It could be used for studying, sleeping, and storing.

Use those walls. You could hang shelves and even storage cabinets on the walls. Wall-hung furniture can be inexpensive, but it does mess up the walls a bit. Consider the wall space above the doorway in the kitchen, the closet, or the bath. A shelf there could keep seldom-used items out of the way. Consider the fact that you need only six to eight inches of depth to build a bookcase. One can fit even in a narrow corridor.

Use tall furniture. Tall storage pieces free the floor and leave space for other furniture such as chairs and tables. Tall pieces can also give architectural overtones to boring, boxy rooms, and minimize the size of large, wide pieces, such as beds.

Vertical storage pieces work miracles in small spaces. They can organize and contain an incredible amount of clutter, and if filled with books, plants, or accessories, they can give a room a lot of warmth and personality. The style may be MODERN or TRADITIONAL.

Some modern storage walls incorporate fold-down surfaces for desk work and dining, or pull-down beds. Most have shelves, closed cabinets, and drawers to hold TVs, hi-fis, clothes, or what have you. Traditional armoires are often adapted to store TVs and hi-fis.

Built-in storage walls can contain closets and shelves and create a clean line when their doors are closed. They don't intrude on the decoration of the room. If a bookcase or other storage unit covers a whole wall, it will have the neat architectural look of a built-in. Free-standing furniture has the advantage of being easily moved. If it is finished on the back, it may be used as a room divider as well as against a wall.

USE DUAL-PURPOSE FURNITURE The most obvious piece is the sofa bed for sleeping and sitting. Consider a platform bed with storage drawers built into its base; it can perform as a luxurious lounge during the day. Storage headboards serve simultaneously for support and storage.

The Parsons table is popular because it works for almost anything. It can be used for dining, desk work, or display, for a makeup table or for a table in back of the sofa. This simple, slim-lined design comes in all sizes, and in a variety of finishes from lacquer to laminate.

Storage tables can contain your clutter while serving as surfaces. Cubes, cabinets, chests, and trunks can be found in all sizes to act as end tables or coffee tables. They may be equipped with casters to move out of the way of the sofa bed.

USE FURNITURE THAT FOLDS, STACKS, OR MOVES OUT OF THE WAY *Tables.* There is a wide variety of folding tables on the

This dining el serves as an efficient office by day, an exotic entertainment area by night. The camphor burl tabletop is actually EASY TO CLEAN Formica. The same material covers the countertop under the

window. The chairs of leather, wood, and chrome are also rich in look, but practical in use. (Photos courtesy of Chromcraft Furniture and Formica; design by Tony Moses; photo by Bill Helms.)

market—everything from the old American tilt-top piecrust table to the dropleaf. These tables rise to the occasion of entertaining, and then collapse when the guests go. Expanding tables with leaves do the same trick.

Wall-hung shelves can fold flat. If the shelf is suspended on chains, it can be hoisted up. It also can be hinged to drop down when not in use.

Serving carts on casters can be rolled out of the way. Tray tables and nesting tables are designed to do a disappearing act.

Beds. When you need to bring out the beds, you can resurrect collapsible cots, or search for the sleeping bags. Trundle beds and sleep sofas are more comfortable. Double-deckers are fun for the young, or those not suffering from acrophobia. If your limbs are limber and your carpet is plush, you could sleep on the floor and just bring out your pillows and blankets at night. The Japanese have been using this space-saving trick for centuries.

Seating. Stacking or folding chairs are eas-

ily stored, and are perfect for pulling out when there's company coming. Floor pillows can be stacked and spread out when you want. Ottomans, stools, and backless benches can be tucked under tables when not in use.

ARRANGE FURNITURE STRATEGICALLY

You can place pieces to serve double purposes. For example, a desk can be placed perpendicular to the wall at the end of the sofa and double as an end table. If it isn't too high, you can place your bureau by the bed so it can serve as a night table.

You can place some pieces in front of others. A desk or table can be placed behind a sofa. A sofa can be placed in front of a tall bookcase. The blocked shelves can be used for dead storage.

Use every inch. Don't waste the walls. For example, instead of placing a sofa against a wall, you might place it at a right angle to the wall. Then the wall space would be freed for a wall-hung storage piece, or for a chest or armoire. Two chairs or a love seat might face the sofa, and there could be a coffee table in the middle. A library table or a Parsons table can be placed in back of the sofa to hold a lamp or flowers. It could double as a desk or dining table.

Use those corners. Lounge chairs, love seats, or beds can be placed along adjacent walls, with a square table joining them in the corner. You could build seating into the corner—something similar to the banquettes you see in restaurants. Corners are also good places for hanging shelves and storage, or you might use the traditional corner cabinet. A desk placed in front or to the side of shelves can convert a corner into a study area. Alternatively, you could build a triangular desk into a corner.

CREATE THE ILLUSION OF SPACE The secret to a SPACIOUS effect is to keep everything smooth, sleek, pale, plain, and simple. See Chapter 10.

2
WHO LIVES WITH YOU?

Not only do you adapt to your environment, your environment has to adapt to you! After all, it's your life and your life-style. When thinking about decorating your home, it's a good idea to think about your life-style.

Who lives in your home? What are these people's ages and stages? What size are they? What sex? What are their interests?

WHAT SIZE?

Furniture must be scaled to suit the size of the person using it. Imagine going to a PTA meeting in a third-grade classroom and you'll see what I mean. The seat would be too small and your knees would be under your chin. The setup would be great for a kid, but not for you. Small furniture gives big people cramps, or makes them feel like the proverbial bull in the china shop (or Woody Allen on a date). Huge furniture dwarfs small people, and makes them feel uncomfortable. However, I heard of a calculating woman who chose furniture much bigger than she is so that she would look small and defenseless—and in need of male protection.

If people of vastly different sizes live together, selecting furnishings that are comfortable to all can be a bit of a problem. The acid test is to have everyone wiggle in the seating. You might hit it right and find something comfortable to all, or you might compromise and have each person have his own specific chair. You also might want to consider the comfort of your guests and have something to suit an average person.

WHAT SEX?

The French say, "Vive la différence!" Women's Libbers say something else. It's up to you whether or not you want to play up your sexuality and the sexuality of those you live with. (It just might make it more fun.)

Today people are more oriented toward being themselves than fulfilling sexual stereotypes. But if you want, you can play up the old roles. The room could be MASCULINE, FEMININE, UNISEX, or SEXY. (See Chapter 13.)

WHAT COLORING?

The colors you choose for an individual's special spaces should be flattering to his or her complexion. Most women like pink because it reflects a rosy glow on their skin. Brunettes often prefer warm colors—reds, oranges, yellows. Blonds and gray-haired people often select cool colors—blues and greens. Auburn hair is flattered by salmon, pink, and brown. Some redheads like purples and orange; others like pinks and kelly green. Black-haired people are flattered by bright strong colors as well as neutral browns.

WHAT AGE?

CHILDREN Children are unaware of danger. Rooms where they spend time should be safe. Electric outlets should be covered. Electric cords and breakable objects should be out of reach. Cleaning fluids, medicines, poisons, and sharp instruments should be locked away. Furniture must be accident-proof. Corners and sharp edges at eye level must be eliminated. Furniture must be strong and solidly constructed so a child can't topple it over.

Children may be adorable, but they are messy. A child's areas should be DURABLE and EASY TO CLEAN. Choose furnishings you can wipe clean or throw in the washing machine. Vinyl floors, walls treated with washable paint or vinyl wallcoverings, furniture covered in plastic laminate (such as Formica), and washable curtains, bedding, and rugs are all answers. To provide floor space for play, and to ease cleaning, you might arrange heavy furniture against the walls of a room, and keep any furniture in the center light and movable. To make the room easy for the child to clean, provide easily accessible storage spaces—toy boxes, shelves, closets.

A child isn't a baby forever. He'll soon grow out of baby furniture, so it doesn't make much sense to spend a lot of money on it—unless, of course, you need it to last through a lot of infancies or you want to give it to your pregnant sister-in-law. If you choose simple furniture, it can last from toddler to teenager. Low, squat styles will work through the ages—because children are short and teenagers are oriented toward the floor. After you buy your basic bed, bureau, and shelves, the only thing that might change as the child grows older is the size of the work-table/desk and chairs. Unpainted furniture—cabinets, drawer units, etc.—and Formica-top tables are good bets. You might

Kids need a place to play, especially on rainy days. This room is an invitation to the imagination. It offers opportunities for climbing, hiding, putting on a show, or playing house. It provides beds for two and ample storage for clothes and toys. The rug on the floor helps to absorb sound.

choose to put pattern where you can easily change it to something more sophisticated when the child gets older. Curtains, bedspreads, window shades, rugs, removable decorations for the wall—all give you this freedom. You might well want your basic walls and floor to be simple and durable so they can last through all ages and stages. These large areas could be expensive to change.

Children need support and encouragement. Their rooms should be CHEERFUL and STIMULATING. Children like bright, happy colors, and such colors are good for them. Bright colors are even supposed to improve a child's IQ! (White walls make a wonderful background for these vivid hues.)

Children are developing a sense of independent identity. Their furnishings should be arranged so that they can do things for themselves. Often-used toys should be within easy reach so a child can take them out and put them back. Often-used clothing should be accessible so that the child can dress himself. To support the child's sense of identity, his favorite objects should be around him—be it a teddy bear or a picture of his favorite movie star. Open display shelves and a bulletin board are essential. A child should be encouraged to participate in the decorating decisions for his own room. That will make him feel good about himself and his room. Older children need a private place for entertaining their friends. You might want to arrange their rooms as sitting rooms for conversation, and provide entertainment equipment—such as games, a record player, a TV. (Then you might want to soundproof the room!) It is essential to provide a place for a friend to stay overnight. A double-decker bed or a trundle bed will save floor space. A cot or a sleeping bag can be brought out when needed.

A child eats. For a baby, you'll need a place for bottles and baby food. A high chair in the kitchen would do. Older children may eat earlier than their parents, and they might well prefer to eat in the INFORMAL atmosphere of the kitchen where spills aren't a disaster. A child might also like a spot for snacks in his own room.

A child sleeps—usually longer hours than the parents. He needs an atmosphere insulated from other noise. He also might be sleeping during daylight hours—so he will need a room-darkening window treatment. (A washable room-darkening window shade can be colored to match the room. It may be laminated with a pattern, or be decorated on the bottom with cut-outs, flat braid or fringe.) In the dark, a child often feels more secure with a night-light. If the child is young, he might need rails on his bed so he doesn't fall out. If he has difficulty going to sleep, you might want a rocker in the room—for you! For safety's sake, the nursery should be located within earshot of the parents' room (or if you like gimmicks, you can install electronic eavesdropping).

As far as washing, grooming, and dressing go, babies are known to wet their diapers. You'll need a changing table. You could use a chest of drawers with protective edges around the top, a conventional changing table, or even, if you like antiques, an Early American dry sink. A baby's room should be near a bathroom, for obvious reasons. To bathe the baby, you might need a small rigid or inflatable plastic tub. To dress him, you'll need drawers in which to keep his clothes.

Dressing is a bigger deal for some kids than for others. Some girls yearn for a full-length mirror and the romance of a dressing table. For a child with a lot of clothes, storage units designed to be lined up against the walls (some incorporating desks) give a great deal of storage space without intruding on the floor space. Alternatively, you might have storage closets with folding or sliding doors built in along the walls. They will keep all that storage pleasantly out of sight and not impose any restrictions on the design of the room.

A baby plays. You might begin with a mobile over the crib and advance to a playpen when the child becomes more active. Then grandma will come with the toys and you'll have to find a place to put them. Open shelves and a toy chest will keep the mess under control. Small children seldom play in their rooms. They want to be near mother or other children.

For airing, the child will need a set of wheels. If you're short on space, choose a collapsible stroller. If you have an eight-car garage, you can buy the Rolls-Royce of baby carriages—an English pram.

For playing and hobbies, children need as much floor space as possible. The floor itself must be able to withstand spills and the traffic of toy trucks. Other than the floor, a child might need a work table or desk. It is usually best to plan space for two children to work at once. Besides the floor and a table, any child would love to cavort in a playhouse! You'll need spaces to store hobby collections, records, books, toys. You can use open bookshelves, closed cabinets with shelves, toy chests, plastic trays (like dishpans you can buy at the five-and-dime).

For homework, a child needs a comfortable, well-lit study spot with a large free surface. This could be a regular desk or table, or a desk incorporated into a wall storage system. To create a desk yourself, you could place a sheet of plywood surfaced with plastic laminate on top of two sawhorses or two cabinets. You'll need bookcases and perhaps a good direct reading light over the bed or over a comfortable chair.

Children often have special lessons of some sort. The child will need the equipment and a place to practice where it won't drive everyone else crazy.

TEENAGERS Teenagers want to be independent. They are going through that trying time of getting out from under Mama's wing. It is important to let them make their own decisions on how to decorate their rooms; it will help solidify their sense of identity. Teenagers want to escape the rest of the family. If possible their rooms should be located away from the living room and away from kid brother or sister's room. (You might make up a special teenage suite in the basement, or even over the garage.) Teenagers may become so independent that you barely see them—except for meals. Make the family dining area congenial to your teenager and you may see more of him!

Teenagers are very close to their friends. They usually like to entertain their friends in their rooms. It is a good idea to arrange their rooms like living rooms and make the beds

Do you wonder how your teenager will ever earn a living? You might encourage his or her hobbies. Here DURABLE, EASY TO CLEAN white plastic units stack up for storage and provide a base for a board to work on. Red plastic chairs are comfortable and washable, and a red plastic shelf provides a place for showing off accomplishments. A teenage work space could be built in the basement or attic. (Courtesy of Kartell Furniture by Beylerian Limited.)

look like studio couches. Be sure there is an extra bed to sleep a friend overnight.

Teenagers are active and agile. They will need a place to burn up energy when the weather is bad. They may dance, wrestle, or whatever in their rooms. Their furnishings had better be INFORMAL and DURABLE, and the floor should be free of furniture. Furniture can be arranged against the walls to leave some open space. Since teens still have good knee joints, seating can be low to the ground—seating can be provided by pillows. Teenagers are usually noisy. Most feel that music isn't any good unless it's loud. To protect your sanity and that of the rest of the family, you might want to soundproof your teenager's room. A thick carpet on the floor or even on the walls will help absorb sound.

Teenagers tend to be sloppy. There should be adequate places to store all their stuff. Clothes, records, books, games, sports and hobby equipment need someplace to go besides the floor. Teenagers' rooms should be EASY TO CLEAN, because heaven knows, they don't like to clean!

Teenagers should be studying. Be sure that they have a good, convenient place, with adequate light, to study and write.

ADULTS Adults don't have special requirements because of their age. Look to their interests, size, and sex for inspiration.

ADULTS OVER SIXTY-FIVE Adults over sixty-five aren't usually as limber as they were in their twenties, but they are irritated when their lack of agility is an inconvenience—to them or to others. The considerate thing is to be sure their furnishings are comfortable and convenient for them, so they can maintain their independence.

Furniture should be easy to get into and out of. Chairs should have arms that can be used as support when rising. Seats should be relatively high, and not too soft. Beds should be easy to make up, high enough so the person doesn't have to bend over too much. If beds are against the wall, they should be equipped with casters. Entertainment equipment should be easy to turn on and off. If the radio and TV are across the room, they should have remote controls. Objects used every day should be easily accessible. To see easily, an older person might require a higher level of lighting.

Older people like lives of their own. If an older person is living with a younger family, it would be nice to provide him or her with an escape – a place away from the rest of you. It would be ideal for him to have a separate suite, with living room, bedroom, and bath. Alternatively, his bedroom can be designed like a living room so he can have his own area to entertain his friends. He will want his own personal treasures around him—this might include pictures of the grandchildren, or mementos from his own childhood home.

WHAT INTERESTS?

Hobbies or special interests might inspire the decorative theme.

THE JOB AWAY FROM HOME   Most people come home yearning for creature comforts. They want to kick off their shoes, have a hug, a drink, a good meal, a little entertainment, and a lot of loving. Put food in the larder, take a cooking course, select furnishings that are comfortable to the tired toiler, place his or her favorite objects about, and be affectionate. After that you can worry about decorating.

If the homemaker works during the day, the cooking, cleaning, and laundering routines must be made as simple and efficient as possible. Storage should be designed to keep everything organized.

If during the week the home is enjoyed only in the evening, it must look WARM and CHEERFUL in night light. Choose light sunny colors for the interior. If you have a pretty yard or garden, you might light it up with outdoor spotlights at night to create a refreshing view.

THE FAMILY   If Dad or Mom only gets to spend nights and weekends with the family, there should be places for comfortable communication. Everybody can meet at the refrigerator and then relax and chat over the kitchen table. A family room is a good all-out meeting ground. A kid's bedroom is really his private place, but maybe Dad will be invited in. The parents' bed is Mom and Dad's domain, but sometimes the kid might come in for a cuddle. If kids are encouraged to use the living room, choose INFORMAL and DURABLE furnishings.

If Mom devotes most of her time to the family, the home should be designed to ease her duties and support her psyche. A homebody would probably like unpretentious INFORMAL furnishings and a WARM, COZY atmosphere.

PETS   Pets need a place to eat, sleep, and maybe a place to poop. The space and equipment they require depends on whether they swim, fly, run, crawl, or slither.

Most pets can make a mess. Generally the rooms they use should be DURABLE and EASY TO CLEAN. You also should consider their safety. You don't want your cat eating the poison you put out to kill the ants.

If you have cats, you may prefer to slipcover your furniture rather than to upholster it. Cats love to sharpen their claws on taut upholstery. Slipcovers offer less satisfaction, and therefore less attraction. Avoid real cane seating. Cats love to pull it apart.

Furry animals shed. You might choose a floorcovering or upholstery materials close to their coloring so you can't see their hair.

FRIENDS   Are you outgoing and friendly? If so, you will probably invite friends over often. You might prefer to entertain in a casual, INFORMAL style, making outsiders feel like members of the family.

An inveterate party-giver would love an upbeat atmosphere that puts people in the mood to have a good time. Choose bright, happy colors.

Are you a little distant and reserved? If so, you may invite only a select few home to your castle, and you might entertain even these few in a FORMAL manner, observing all the delicate social graces.

Are you shy and introverted? You might need encouragement to bring anybody home. A bright, CHEERFUL room in warm colors will help lift your spirits.

THE COMMUNITY If you are involved in community responsibilities you might have to have meetings at home. You'll probably want your home to inspire confidence and respect in others.

Since people generally feel secure with the familiar, the community leader might want to choose TRADITIONAL furnishings. But so that the others understand that he or she is with-it and up-to-date, there might be a few MODERN pieces for flair. The budding community leader might also choose furnishings that reflect the climate and heritage of the area, so that he truly looks like he belongs.

The colors should have GENERAL appeal— like blue, gold, green, white, or neutrals.

TRAVEL If you love to travel, you may want to be surrounded with mementos of your trips. If you travel a lot, you'll need a home that's EASY TO CLEAN.

SPORTS Do you like your sports active or passive? If passive, all you need is a TV or tickets to a ballgame. If active, you need the equipment and a suitable place. A sports interest might provide a decorative theme. For example, if your teenage girl is nuts about horseback riding, horses might be the motif of her decor.

SEX Some people are sex maniacs, and some people could live without it, but almost anybody of any age will respond to a home that is pleasing to the senses. Choose materials that are thick, shaggy, soft, pleasant to the touch. These materials not only appeal to

the senses, they create a feeling of warmth, and because they absorb sound, they create a feeling of privacy. Examples of these materials range from Linus's blanket to Mom's mink.

Set off these warm, soft textures with shiny exciting ones—crystal cocktail glasses, glittering mirror, sparkling chrome, a glint in your eye.

Illuminate it all with warm dim lights— firelight or candlelight are ideal. Place hi-fi speakers strategically to permeate the atmosphere with soft music. Who could resist?

NATURE—GARDENING A serious gardener will need a deep sink and a dirtproof area for repotting. You may want a greenhouse or a skylight to let in the sunshine. A person who just wants to achieve a fresh outdoorsy feeling can design a decor to create a garden effect.

A garden effect is particularly appropriate for a porch or sun room. Choose the colors of the outdoors—sky blue, sun yellow, grass green. Choose lattice patterns and tree-and-flower patterns.

For the floor, you might choose a grass, jute, or hemp rug. For the walls, you might choose paper with a floral or lattice pattern. (A coordinated upholstery fabric will give a summery feeling.) The windows might be treated with a lattice, louvered shutters, or bamboo shades.

The furniture should be light-looking. You could choose bamboo, rattan, wicker, or even wrought iron. You might even choose Chippendale's Chinese lattice-pattern sidechairs. Floral upholstery brings up the blooms.

The obvious accessory is plants—lots of them. You can also use a lot of baskets.

One cheerful garden room I know has sky-blue ceilings and white walls. Bright happy colors are supplied by houseplants, birds, and tropical fish.

CULTURE—BOOKS, ART, MUSIC, DRAMA, DANCE Besides buying books, getting tickets, going to shows, taking how-to lessons

This person collects 19th-century dog portraits, pets he doesn't have to feed. For a romantic feeling the paintings are hung from ribbons on the walls, and even in front of the bookcase. Such a display of a collection gives character to a room. (Design by Mario Buatta.)

or courses in cultural appreciation, what else can you do? You can imbue your home with the atmosphere of your interest.

Display Your Books   Glass-enclosed bookcases provide protection for rare or good books. Open bookshelves lend a more intimate charm and invite browsing.

Display Your Art   If you want to emphasize paintings or pictures on the wall, the rest of the room should be rather CALM. The walls should be unpatterned, and the color scheme could be soft and subtle—maybe something like white, cream, and beige. A particular painting can be the focal point of the room. Place it in a prominent position, so it's the first thing you see when you enter the room. Such a painting might also inspire your color scheme.

If you are a music-lover, you can arrange the room for good acoustics. (See Chapter 3, page 29).

If you love the theater, and you are a dramatic person, you can make your home DRAMATIC. You will want to make a splash with bold, assertive colors or patterns. You might paint the walls red or orange and have stark white furniture and black accessories. Or you might paint a screaming supergraphic across the walls and ceiling. If you feel life is as adventurous as a gypsy caravan, you might load the room with a multitude of patterns. Or if you alone are the star, you might dress to the hilt and do the room in neutrals so you're not upstaged.

HOBBIES, COLLECTIONS   Hobbies might be painting, collecting stamps, doing crafts or carpentry—you name it. The person will need the equipment required by the hobby, and the hobby might inspire the decorative theme. Accessories might be the hobby paraphernalia.

Special collections should be featured in your decor. For example, porcelain, old glass, small objects could be placed in locked cabinets to protect them from dust and damage. To set them off, you might put them on glass shelves, and direct hidden lights at them to give special sparkle.

FASHION   If you are interested in being up with the new trends, you should study the latest decorating magazines before making your design decisions.

A new fashion "look" can make you feel up-to-date, fresh, alive, and vital. Fashion can give you a new lease on life, a new way to rethink old problems, an opportunity to discover new aspects of yourself that you may never have explored before. In short, fashion can give you a lift.

However, fashion can be expensive—as we all know from some of the mistakes in our closet. At least with clothes, you can hide your mistakes in the closet. With home furnishings, it's not so easy! So here comes some advice:

Before you buy any furnishings at all, analyze your real needs. (This book aims to help you do that.) You see, fashion is fickle. If, at least, you pick something that fits your real needs, you might still like it when it is out of fashion. As a matter of fact, it might be so "you" that fashion won't matter at all.

Second, if you're spending a lot of money, buy the best *quality* you can afford. Quality lasts. It transcends the transience of fashion.

Third, if you're not spending a lot of money, don't. Inexpensive things can update a room and give it fashion flair—a new tablecloth for a draped table, new pillows, a new print, new accessories. You won't need much. As a matter of fact, if you want to be trendy, it's a good idea to achieve the look with inexpensive items. Today's trend often has a very short life-span, and yesterday's trend is very ho-hum. At least with inexpensive items, you need feel no guilt when you send them off to the Salvation Army.

Some people have a negative view of changing styles. They claim that manufacturers, magazine-makers, and storekeepers invent "fashion" as an insidious plot to keep you spending your money. Well, there is some truth to that. Manufacturers, magazine-makers, and storekeepers have to eat too.

But the times *do* change. Sometimes technological advances allow manufacturers to come up with products that are really new and improved. Think of how the invention of plastic laminates and tufted carpet has changed our lives. You should be open to new things, but be wary. Many things that are advertised as "new and improved" haven't been properly tested, and who wants to spend money to be a guinea pig? Don't rush out to buy the latest thing; wait a while and then see if it's still on the market.

Sometimes changes in life-style cause new products to be invented. If we all had maids, who would care about having a dishwasher? If we all lived in enormous spaces, who would care about vertical storage? Be alert to products that will help you live your way more comfortably.

Some people use fashion to compete with others rather than to enjoy themselves. There are the magazines that tell all the world what's "in" this season, how Mrs. Moneybags has

Fashion is fickle; instead you might want to recreate an atmosphere you have enjoyed in your travels. This tented dining area, with pebbled floor and stuccoed walls, recalls the bazaars of North Africa. The skirted chairs offer a softening sense of comfort. Peach and pink colors (and pretty wine-glasses) lift the spirits. (Courtesy of W & J Sloane; design by Albert Etienne Pensis.)

done her summer estate by the beach. There are some people who are interested, who want to zap Mrs. Moneybags when she visits their old chateau in the south of France. But let's leave such competition to the crazy or to the money-mad. Who needs it? You want a home that is happy and comfortable, that suits you, that fits your personality and your needs. Study this book to find your fit. Then, knowing what you need, look again at the magazines. You will probably find some things in fashion-favor that will work for you.

An interest in fashion might inspire a glamorous look in the home. Glamour is created by glitter—the sparkling effect of focusing a bright light on something shiny. The shiny, slick surface can be crystal, glass, steel, chrome, mirror, gold, bronze, silver, or even a foil wallpaper. Glitter can also be produced directly by tiny clear incandescent bulbs. It's the magic of Christmas trees and of movie stars in sequins.

For an avant garde effect, you can decorate with colored light. There are devices similar to movie cameras that can project pictures or patterns on naked walls and ceilings. It's instant decoration and atmosphere, and changeable at the flick of a finger.

SELF-DISCOVERY TEST

Let's forget logic for the moment and work with your emotions. After all, in your home you need to satisfy your soul as well as solve your practical problems. Get out a piece of paper, and let's get to work on making your dreams come true. Have each person in your household take this test.

GENERAL

1. Close your eyes and think happy thoughts. Where are you? What are you doing? Where do you like to spend your vacation? What do you like most about this place? What is your favorite activity? What do you like most about it?
2. What is your favorite thing about the home you grew up in?
3. What have you admired most about other people's homes?

SPACE

4. If you had to spend a whole weekend locked up in an attractive, but small, apartment, how would you feel on Sunday night?
   Choose one:
   a. Claustrophobic and crazy
   b. Cozy and content
5. How do you feel when riding an elevator?
   a. Stifled
   b. Okay
6. When you go to a restaurant, do you choose to sit in—
   a. An open area
   b. An enclosed booth
7. When standing in an enormous hotel lobby, do you—
   a. Feel grand
   b. Feel like running for cover
8. Say you were on a ship many miles out to sea with no land in sight and a limitless horizon. Would you feel—
   a. Free and wonderful
   b. Small and defenseless
9. After a busy day of work, would you rather—
   a. Get out in the open
   b. Go hide

COLOR

10. Look in your closet. Which color clothes make you feel the best? Write down your answers.
11. What kind of scenery appeals to you the most?
    The sea
    The woods
    The desert
    Snow-covered mountains
12. What season of the year do you like best?
    Spring
    Summer
    Fall
    Winter
13. If you're partial to roses and a friend brought you some, which color would you wish they were?
    Red
    Pink
    Yellow
    White
14. How are your nerves? Are you—
    Excitable/Flighty
    Tense/Rigid
    Placid
15. What do you long for?
    Peace and quiet
    Excitement
    Relaxation and revitalization

STYLE

16. Look in your closet. What are your clothes like?
    Simple and serviceable
    Sophisticated and stylish
    Conservative or timeless
    Dramatic or assertive
    Tailored
    Quietly confident
    Mousy
    Sexy
    Sweet
    Tweedy
    Exotic
    Offbeat or funky
17. If you could wake up tomorrow in any era, when would it be?
    The past
    The present
    The future

ANSWERS TO SELF-DISCOVERY TEST

General   Your home could remind you of a

place or an activity that makes you happy. What does your favorite place look like? What are its characteristic colors, shapes, textures? You could use those same colors, shapes, and textures in your own home to make yourself feel good. For example, I love the ocean; it makes me feel relaxed and refreshed. In my apartment I've brought in the blues and the shimmery silvers of the ocean to make myself feel happy. Try to write a description of a place you love. That description can translate into decorative ideas for you. For instance, if you love Tuscany in Italy, you love its sunshine, serenity, and space. It's possible that you would want your home to be LIGHTER AND BRIGHTER, CALM, and SPACIOUS.

Your favorite activity could inspire the design of your home. When you are doing the thing you most love to do, how does it feel? Soft? WARM? COOL? SPACIOUS? SEXY? You can suggest these same good feelings in your home.

Try to describe your favorite thing about the home you grew up in. Maybe you can recreate this thing in your own home. I loved the sound of the wind in the trees. Maybe I should put a tree by an open window in my apartment.

What have you most admired about other people's homes? You can interpret their idea in your own way. Maybe you like a particular piece of furniture. What is its style? Its size? Its shape? Write down its characteristics. They can give you design direction.

Space *If you consistently chose answer "a"* for these questions, you want to break out of confinement, open up the space around you. The atmosphere of your home should be open and airy. You will want a SPACIOUS feeling in your home. How do you create a SPACIOUS feeling? Make everything smooth, sleek, pale, and simple. Color the walls a continuous pale color; keep your floor covering pale, unpatterned, and continuous. Color large furnishings the same as the walls or floor. Have the minimum amount of furnishings. Don't clutter up your windows; keep an open view out. Put a mirror opposite the view. Then stretch and enjoy your sense of space.

If you consistently chose answer "b," you want the comfort of a COZY cocoon. Choose warm colors, and soft textures like carpeting and comforters. You might even make a nook to nestle in—tuck a bed between bookcases, build a softly upholstered bench in a cozy corner, buy a wing chair or a big wraparound easy chair. Have well-loved familiar objects around.

If you sometimes chose "a," sometimes "b," your home should have pleasing and inviting contrasts between airy open spaces and cozy small places.

Color The colors that you like wearing obviously flatter you and make you feel good. Your home should also flatter you and make you feel good, so you can well consider using some of the same colors. You may have to tone them down to make them livable in large areas, but you can stay within the same color family. The colors that depress you probably make you look pale, green, or like some other day-after disaster. Avoid them!

The scenery you like might set the scene for your home. If you like the sea, choose blues and greens. If you like the woods, choose greens. The desert? Choose browns, oranges, and reds. Snow-covered mountains? Choose whites and ice blues.

Since Mother Nature is the best colorist of all, you can take your color scheme straight from the season. Spring suggests yellow daffodils, tender green grass, blue skies, and white light. Summer suggests flowers in bright full bloom, rich green grass, lots of bright yellow sunshine. Fall suggests the turning of a leaf—from green to orange to burnt orange to brown; the grass goes olive green. Winter suggests the cold colors of ice and snow—snow white and ice blue. The sky and the ground are light and the woods dark. This might translate into light floors and ceiling, and dark walls.

Gertrude Stein said "A rose is a rose is a rose," but they're not all the same. A red-rose-lover might be passionate and DRAMATIC, innovative and adventurous. His or her home might be full of startling surprises and contrasting colors. The pink-lover is a romantic. Mozart, firelight, brandy, a kiss on the earlobe, and it's all over. The yellow-lover also has a soft touch. The mood is gentle, the home a harmony of yellow, white, beige, blue, and green. The white-lover is a purist, waiting for Mr. Clean on a white charger.

How are your nerves? If you're the excitable, flighty type, avoid light warm colors—they are too stimulating. Especially avoid orange and red. Choose green or blue to calm yourself down. Green is supposed to soothe the nerves and relax the eyes. Are you tense and rigid? It is reported that warm colors direct attention away from the self and can help relieve psychic tension. If you are placid, maybe you need a stimulus. Try red.

What do you long for? If you like to come home and tune out, a CALM/PEACEFUL atmosphere would be good for your blood pressure. Choose soft, serene colors, minimize contrasts, and avoid a lot of pattern. Everything should be soft and subtle. If you like to come home and turn on, the home can be DRAMATIC. You can use bright, socko colors, lively patterns, bold contrasts. Maybe you're in search of relaxation and revitalization. To achieve a RELAXING effect, you should have enough pattern and color and contrast to be interesting but not tiring.

Style What are your clothes like? If simple and serviceable, you will probably want unpretentious furnishings, perhaps in a COUNTRY/RUSTIC style. If sophisticated and stylish, you will probably want to read the latest magazines before doing your home. If conservative or timeless, you will probably want more neutral color schemes and classic, perhaps TRADITIONAL, furnishings. If your clothes are dramatic or assertive, you might want a DRAMATIC home, maybe with wild colors and sleek surfaces— lots of metal and mirror. If they are tailored, you might want the look of your home to be neat, crisp, tucked-in, and buttoned-down. If your clothes express a quiet confidence, you can relax a bit about designing your home. You have the assurance to pull it off. If your clothes are mousy, read this book very carefully. It should give you confidence in your decisions. Realize too that a successful home is one where the people are less concerned about "rules" and more concerned about pleasing themselves. If your clothes are SEXY, you might want your home to be, too. Choose warm colors that are flattering to your skin tones. Make everything soft and luscious to the touch—have fur bed throws, thick carpets. You might upholster your furniture in satin and cover your walls in fabric. You might dim the lights and play soft music. You might leave your clothes in the closet. If, alternatively, your clothes are sweet, choose soft pastel colors and dainty designs. If they are tweedy, choose leather or corduroy upholstery, Rya rugs, dark woods and plants. If your wardrobe is exotic, you might choose furnishings from far-away places, or extraordinary styles. Your furniture might be Turkish Victorian or your accessories African. If your duds are offbeat or funky, you could shop for furnishings at Goodwill or the Salvation Army. You might even find something super on the street!

If you could wake up tomorrow in any era, when would it be? If the past, what a clear clue to choose TRADITIONAL styles! The present? The present is the moment between the past and the future, so you might mix traditional and modern styles for an ECLECTIC look. If you chose the future, you can go all-out for space-age MODERN.

How did you do on the test? Do you know anything more about yourself? Before you get nervous about spending a cent on your furnishings, you need to take the time to explore. Explore yourself, your reactions. Don't let anyone tell you what you should like. And absolutely run away from people who start telling you what's "in" this season. What's "in" this season is sure to be "out" next. And unless you intend to redecorate every year, you're going to be stuck living with a foolish fad. Remember, *style* is something different from *fashion*. Style endures, fashion doesn't. And style is your particular expression of your personality and your way of life. That, nobody knows but you.

3

WHAT WILL YOU DO IN YOUR HOME?

Although each of us is individual, most of us do the same old things in our homes. We eat, sleep, read, study, make love, watch TV, and listen to music, for example. To express our personalities and our priorities, most of us like to do these things in our own way. For instance, entertaining could mean having the guys over for poker, or the ladies over for tea. The design of our home should enhance our own style.

Where will you do all the activities of your home? In allocating activities to rooms, think of the convenience of the location and the appropriateness of the lighting and noise conditions. For example, don't put Dad's study right next to the teenage rec (wreck?) room. However, noisy and quiet activities *can* share a space, as long as they occur at different times of day.

The activities in the room will determine the furnishings you need. The convenience of the activity will often dictate the furniture arrangement, and suggest a mood for the room. For example, the room where you do laundry had better be CHEERFUL!

CONVERSING

WHERE? Conversation is usually the primary purpose of the living room. In the family room, watching TV often takes precedence over conversation. The den and the porch are secondary scenes for conversation. Bedrooms may be designed as sitting rooms, convenient for conversation, or if they are large, they may feature a special area for conversation.

HOW? Seating should be comfortably close so people can talk easily. For animated conversation, people should be no more than eight feet apart, and it's nicest to talk face to face. The arrangement should be out of the path of traffic. It's very disturbing to have people marching through ruining your punch line. You can place the back of seating pieces to the traffic.

The seating should be arranged around some center of attraction, or focal point. It's pleasant to face a fireplace in the winter. A good view is a natural attraction. A long wall can be made into a focal point if you hang a prominent painting (or group of pictures) on it, and put some kind of chest, or even your sofa, underneath.

If your room is small, center your sofa on the wall opposite the focal point. If you have the space, you may have two chairs to the sides of the sofa, and two chairs to the sides of the focal point.

If your room is large, you can have a conver-

This conversational grouping is arranged around the fireplace, but on the diagonal for a fresh feeling. It sits in the center of the room on an area rug. Traffic walks around. The modular units are generous in size, but because they are low and unified, they don't crowd the space. Pillows provide extra pull-up seating. (Design by Kelly G. Amen, ASID; photo by Michele Maier.)

sation island, with seating placed out in the middle of the room. It is important to leave enough space so people can navigate around the island. If the back of a sofa faces the entrance, it can look forbidding and unwelcoming to your guests. To soften its effect, put a table of compatible size behind the sofa. The table can hold a reading lamp, interesting accessories, and a cheerful bunch of flowers. If chairs are out in the middle of the room, they should be low-backed so they don't seem to chop up the space.

What to do with empty walls in island arrangements? This is the place for chests, cabinets, stereos, secretaries, breakfronts, bookcases, desks, or even an organ.

Flexible Seating Arrangement for Entertaining It's hard for more than six people to carry on one conversation. If you have a larger group, you will want to break it up. You can rearrange seating to create several sit-down clusters. Seating that allows people to face in a variety of directions is an asset. People can sit any which way on backless, armless stools and ottomans. A chaise longue allows people to sit facing any of three directions. Armless

swiveling chairs allow people to join whichever nearby conversation intrigues them. (After the party is over, check the wreckage to see where people put the seating. It might inspire a new furniture arrangement.)

If you have an enormous group, you will want to rearrange furniture against the walls to allow a large open area for stand-up conversation.

The atmosphere for conversation should be RELAXING. Avoid bright colors in large areas. If you want to use a warm color on the walls or floor, tone it down with gray or white to soften its impact. Socko colors are okay, though, in accessories.

Limit the variety of colors. You might just work with variations of one color, mixed with neutrals. For example, you might carpet your floor in a refreshing and restful blue or green. The walls might be white or a lighter shade of the carpet color. Draperies and large upholstery might be simple styles in a pattern that combines the colors of the floor and the walls. Small furniture might be in wood tones or in brighter tones of the carpet color. Accessories can be snappy black or white. Colors can get brighter as the size gets smaller. If colors are all in the same family, the effect is harmonious.

Avoid wild, jazzy patterns. Simple linear patterns, like stripes, are a good bet. Subtle and soft patterns are also easy to live with. Often draperies and large upholstery are made in matching patterns. If the pattern in the room is limited to small pieces such as ottomans or throw pillows, these can be bold without becoming overwhelming. Patterned walls are usually not appropriate for conversational areas. The focus of interest should be in the foreground, on the conversational grouping—not on the walls.

If the room is essentially one color, you might want to create interest with uneven surfaces. You could have nubby upholstery—say of Haitian cotton. You could have wicker or cane chairs. You could use rough-woven baskets for planters and magazine holders. These will give the room a subtle and appealing variety.

Choosing the Seating Chairs and sofas need not be deeply upholstered to be comfortable, and chairs should not recline so much that people fall asleep in the middle of a conversation. The seating should conform to the proportions of people's bodies. When children sit with the family, they should have chairs that fit their size. If they feel more comfortable, maybe they will squirm less.

Plan enough seats for your normal group of people. Pull-up chairs can accommodate additional occasional guests. Maybe you'll need your sofa or a chair to double as a bed; if so, you can choose a convertible style.

The typical living room has at least one conversational grouping for six to eight people. A smaller room might accommodate a group of from four to six. A large room may have more than one conversational grouping, and it also may have several little groups of two.

You can order a custom-made sofa for much moola or save some cents by making a sofa from a hollow-core plywood door. (Just put a mattress on top, bolsters in back, and legs beneath.) You can also make a twin bed into a sofa if you have big enough bolsters.

If you may be moving, you might want to choose a modular design that you can easily arrange in another space. If you are going to be in this place till you die, you can have things custom-made to fit the space.

Another tip: If you want to slipcover, choose fully upholstered pieces. Seating with wood arms is hard to slipcover.

A seating grouping is often composed of a sofa, upholstered chairs, and occasional chairs. Sofas come in a wide variety of sizes and styles. Upholstered chairs can be purchased in pairs if you like. Occasional chairs are usually light and open in effect—such as a French oval-back armchair, or an open-back bamboo chair with a padded seat, or an inexpensive deck chair.

For extra pull-up chairs for guests, you can use straight lightweight chairs from around the dining table or game table. You could use a desk chair, or chairs that you keep on either side of a doorway or cabinet. Backless poufs, ottomans, and floor pillows are inexpensive

and easy to move around. These pieces are also space-savers, because they are easy to tuck away under a table, and they don't seem to take much space sitting in front of a fireplace, stereo, window, or what-have-you.

Choosing Service Tables by the Seating When you're sitting around talking, you might want a drink or a cup of coffee. Since it's hard to gesture while you're holding a drink, you will want to put it down. There should be a convenient, serviceable surface. Surfaces come in all shapes and sizes. What will you want to choose?

There are several rules to guide you. You have to provide enough surface to do the job. What do the tables by the seating have to hold? Lamps, ashtrays, books, magazines? Be sure the surfaces you select are big enough. The surface has to be within easy reach. Side tables should be about the height of the arms of the seating. (Two inches higher or lower doesn't matter.) Front tables should be about the height of the seat cushions.

The table or tables should look good with

The tables here are perfect for serving the seating. They are ample in size, within easy reach, and about the same height as the seat cushions. The three rectangular tables also allow people to move in and around. (Photo courtesy of Celanese; design by Robert Metzger, ASID.)

the seating. What looks good? It depends on the seating arrangement. When the sofa is against the wall, you'll probably want end tables. End tables don't have to match; if they do, the effect is FORMAL. You can have a chest on one side and a rectangular table on the other. You can have just one large end table, or just one round skirted table to provide a color accent. When the sofa is fronted by a long coffee table, round end tables provide a welcome change of pace.

If your seating arrangement is L-shaped, a round, octagonal, or square coffee table works well. A rectangular coffee table won't work unless it is unusually wide, because the seating at the end will look ignored. Small square tables on each side of the L work well.

If you have chairs or sofas placed facing each other, say on either side of a fireplace or other focal point, choose a round, octagonal or square coffee table. A narrow rectangular coffee table simply cannot serve both sides; you must relate it to one side or the other.

If you have single chairs facing each other, place a small coffee table—not wider than the chairs—between them.

If you have a single chair alone, you can place a little cigarette table by the corner of the chair. If the chair is placed diagonally in a corner, a round table next to it not only looks best, it takes up the least room.

If you are concerned with saving space, tables beside chairs and sofas take less space than tables in front. Folding tables or nesting tables can be brought out as needed. A set of several small matching tables can be used individually or lined up in a row. Chests, trunks, and cabinets of convenient height serve for storage. Remember that a table in front of a convertible sofa bed must be light enough to be moved easily; avoid a big glass coffee table there.

To resist stains and cigarette burns, you might want to cover your tables with glass. There are some modern tables on the market with finishes that can withstand almost anything, but they are a bit pricy.

Choosing Lighting   You need soft general il-lumination so you can see. You don't want brilliant glaring light in your eyes. Even though the police shine light in people's eyes to make them talk, the device doesn't usually inspire conversation.

Lamps on end tables should be high enough to shed light on your lap—anywhere from twenty-eight to forty-four inches high, complete with shade. Thirty-eight inches high is a safe bet. Lamps on matching end tables should match. Lamps on unmatching end tables need not match, but they should be about the same height. The lamps can be centered on the table, or placed toward the back to give more space up front.

EATING

WHERE?   The regular spot for eating should be near the kitchen. You may have secondary eating areas almost anywhere in your home.

The Kitchen   If the kitchen is large enough, it's nice to be able to eat there. For meals on the move, you might like to sit on a stool at a counter in the kitchen. For INFORMAL fun with the family or with friends, you might like to gather around a kitchen table for a hearty meal. The children might prefer the uninhibited informality of meals in the kitchen—so what if they spill? A breakfast nook is an intimate way to begin the day.

The Living Room   If you eat in the living room, the dining furniture must be compatible with the furniture in the conversational grouping. The styles don't need to match, but they do need to blend.

To avoid a cluttered look, it's best to arrange the conversational grouping and the dining grouping at opposite ends of the room. To make serving convenient, the dining table would be best nearest to the kitchen. You might choose a dining table that takes little space—an expandable console, or a dropleaf table, even a Parsons table. When not in use, the table might fold up in back of the sofa, or against a wall. A game table might double for dining.

If you want to demarcate the dining area without chopping up the room, you could place low-backed furniture—a sofa or two chairs—at a right angle to the wall to separate the areas. You could suggest an entrance to the dining area by placing tall étagères, open-backed bookcases, see-through screens, Plexiglas panels, narrow draperies, or tall plants by the side walls. You could change the floor level—raise the dining area on a platform, or sink the conversational area in a pit. You could change the floor treatment—for example, you could have carpeting or an area rug in the conversational area and a plain wood floor or tiles in the dining area. Lighting alone could define a difference. You might keep the dining area darker or dimmer for drama.

If you lack space for a dining area, you might pull out folding tray tables.

Separate Dining Room or Dinette The table is commonly centered in a dining room, but to save space, a rectangular table may be placed with either side or end against the wall.

You can leave at least four chairs pushed up to the table. If you have six, you can fill the empty wall spaces with two. It is most flattering to put the chairs directly against the wall rather than diagonally in corners. If you have a dining el, place extra chairs against the longest wall.

A sideboard looks best centered against a long stretch of wall. A dining el or dining room can often use another small wooden piece near the kitchen door. You could choose a small server, a bar cabinet, a bachelor's chest, or a wall-hung shelf.

A china cabinet, displaying your treasures, might be placed on the end wall of the room, facing the entrance. This position will give it emphasis.

The Hallway or Foyer Using a foyer takes advantage of a little-used space. Use a folding or dropleaf table. You might mirror one wall so the setting seems less crowded.

A Double Closet Romance in a closet. Seriously, a large closet can be an intimate dining spot for two. It's a small, cozy, rather enclosed space. Take off the door. Place a small table in the closet against the wall. Add two chairs and candles. When gatherings are larger, the table can be used as a serving surface for a buffet.

The Bedroom How luxurious and intimate to eat in the bedroom! A Parsons table could double for dining and desk. A round skirted

This dining el establishes a feeling of serenity and space with classic MODERN furnishings. The pedestal table is by Eero Saarinen. The tubular stainless steel and woven wicker chairs are attributed to Mies van der Rohe. The sideboard is a simple board on the side. (Photo courtesy of Harold Imber; design by Sig Udstad; photo by Ben Schnall.)

table could carry on the feeling of softness and comfort. A tray in bed could make you feel like royalty!

The Library Maybe in front of the fire in the library. You could set up a card table, or use a game table or a flat-topped desk.

The Family Room A game table in the family room could double for dining.

Meals Served Far Away from the Kitchen Meals in a garden, on a terrace, by a fire, or by a pool might require a tea cart, a table on wheels, or a large tray as well as a few covered dishes.

HOW? Where there is eating, there is the chance of spilling. The odds improve with age. If you have children, you might want to choose especially DURABLE and EASY-TO-CLEAN materials—glass or plastic laminate surfaces, Naugahyde upholstery, and tile floors. If the dangers are less dramatic, you might buy trivets and hot pads to protect your table and make sure your chair upholstery is stain-proofed. Your flooring should be easily cleaned or wiped up, or at least patterned so it doesn't show the stains.

Lighting depends on whether you're eating or dining. People like to "see what they eat." People also like to "dine by candlelight." In general, lighting for eating need not be strong. A fixture directly over the table, supplemented by lights elsewhere in the room, does fine.

The mood in the eating area can be WARM and STIMULATING. Warm colors tend to stimulate the appetite and create a convivial mood—good for digestion and friendship. Lively colors tend to inspire sparkling conversation.

Be careful to leave enough space around the table for serving and seating. Three feet of open space is ideal. If this allowance is impossible, you might consider placing one end of your table against the wall. Then you would need space only on three sides.

Choosing the Dining Table Buying a dining

table is not a priority. You can eat in the kitchen or on trays in the living room until you can afford to buy dining-room furniture. A dining table is one of those things you are likely to have to your grave, so it's worthwhile to choose one that would last a lifetime. A substantial table that is not too unusual in design will endure many changes in decor and be a good investment.

You need a table that will seat everyone without crowding. If you are going to have guests to dinner, it's a good idea to choose a table that will expand to a suitable size. There are all sorts of expandable tables. Dropleaf tables take little space when their leaves are down. There are tables you can add leaves to. There are ones with tops you can turn and unfold to double their size. There are ones that expand like an accordion. You might even put two tables together for a big banquet. Two tables would give you a great deal of flexibility in entertaining groups of different sizes.

If you're really short on space, you might hinge a table to the wall. It could be folded up against the wall when not in use and take no space at all. The underside might even become decorative when raised—it could be covered in fabric with a finishing molding around its edges. Chains, legs, or brackets could provide stability when it's down. Similarly, you might buy a wall storage unit with a fold-down table. Also remember that a dining table can double as a desk.

Choosing the Dining Chairs Extra dining chairs can act as occasional chairs in the living room. They can flank a doorway or a console. They can do as desk chairs. You can keep them in almost any room of the home. Or you can use chairs from other rooms in the home as dining chairs, as long as the seats are about eighteen or nineteen inches off the floor.

If you want to shave space and save money, you could use stools or backless benches for dining, but they're not comfortable for long dinner conversations.

For Serving and Storage A flat surface to

This small dining room in a Florida condominium accommodates the owners' preference for TRADITIONAL styles and their yearning for a fresh feeling. The furnishings are traditional in style, but smaller in size. The chandelier, mirror, and sideboard are bright white. The screen is a perky print. For parties the sideboard works well as a bar. (Photo courtesy of Hickory Manufacturing Company; design by Pat Plaxico.)

serve from can be almost anything—a suspended shelf, a serving cart, a narrow console, a Parsons table, a sideboard, or a serving unit with storage underneath.

If the group is too large to sit at a table, plan a buffet. Lay the food and utensils out on the table, and let people sit around in the living room. Give people a place to put their plates. Your guests might dump dirty dishes on a serving cart that you can wheel away at will.

To store dishes, glasses, flatware, linens, and table mats, you could use a credenza, a sideboard, a chest of drawers, or cupboards in the kitchen, pantry, or dining room.

DRINKING

WHERE? You can drink anywhere, but unless you want to keep trailing to the kitchen, it's a good idea to set up a bar where you do your drinking. The bar can be permanent or on wheels, or just equipment on a tray on a table.

HOW? Sometimes people like to put their glasses down between sips. Your well-meaning friends could thereby destroy your furniture. Most wood finishes are ringed and ruined by liquor, although a few modern finishes are impervious. Glass is unaffected. You might choose glass-topped tables, or put a sheet of glass over another surface. Formica and other plastic laminates are resistant to staining and damage, and so is ceramic tile.

If you are having a cocktail party, you might want to plan an area separate from the bar for serving food in order to avoid a traffic jam. If your party is large, you might want to rearrange your furniture against the walls to allow more standing room.

WATCHING TV

WHERE? TV and conversation don't mix. You might want to separate these activities if you have the space. If you can't separate the TV from other activities, you might want to choose a portable set, or place the TV in a position where it doesn't attract undue attention. The TV may find a home in the family room, den, living room, or bedroom.

Is Watching TV the Main Activity of the Room? If watching TV is *not* the main activity of the room, you obviously don't have to organize the room around it. You can relegate this activity to a small section of the room.

If TV-watching is the main activity, the TV should be the center of attention. You might choose a TV in a console cabinet, center it on a wall, and place pictures above it. Seating should be arranged to face the TV. This is the perfect place for an extra-long sofa.

The Appearance of the TV in the Room Many people find a blank screen cold

Isn't it lovely to watch TV from bed? This TV is equipped with remote controls, so it's not necessary to get out of bed to avoid the commercials or change the channel. Unified into a wall storage system, the TV doesn't attract undue attention. (Photo courtesy of Harold Imber; design by Sig Udstad; photo by Ben Schnall.)

and objectionable. What can you do about it? You can conceal the TV. You can buy a TV enclosed in a cabinet. You can place a TV in your own cabinet with closing doors. (Be sure to ask an expert about the proper ventilation.) You can build a set into the wall and cover it with a picture on sliding tracks. (Again, check with an expert about ventilation.)

You can place the TV in an inconspicuous position. You can choose a portable set and remove it from sight when it is not in use. You can place it off to the side of the room or mount it high on the wall where it won't attract attention when it is off. You can put it in a bookcase or in a storage wall.

Lastly, you can brazen it out. A modern set in a modern room looks fine. After all, this is an electronic era.

HOW? Your first concern is comfort of vision. You see best when you are sitting almost directly in front of the TV, and when there are no reflections on the screen from either daylight or lamplight. Place the TV out of direct sunlight. Place lamps so they don't reflect on the screen. Lamps to the right and left of the

viewer, approximately at right angles to his line of vision, are effective. Soft lights in the room help avoid eyestrain. Some soft light should reflect on the wall in back of the TV to reduce the glare from the screen.

The TV must be placed for the best reception. Sometimes the picture is better when the TV is turned in one direction rather than another. It depends on your aerial, the intervening walls, and where the broadcast is coming from. The location of electric and aerial outlets, naturally enough, also determines the placement of the TV.

If some people want to watch TV while others nearby want quiet, you may want to soundproof the TV area or get earplugs.

PLAYING MUSIC—FOR LISTENING OR DANCING

WHERE? This depends on who listens to music, for how long, and how loud. Some music-listening should be a private affair in a person's own room. Other music-listening, of general interest, can occur in the communal living room or family room. If you love to be surrounded with music, you might have speakers all over your home.

If music-listening is the main activity of a room, the room arrangement should center around it. If it's not, the equipment can be relegated to a corner.

The Living Room Stereo components can be placed in a bookcase or wall unit, along with the TV. A console can be chosen in a style that coordinates with your furnishings.

The Den This is a nice place for an intimate evening alone with Beethoven.

The Family Room Here you might roll up the rugs and dance to the music.

The Bedroom Can you imagine a nicer place to daydream to Debussy? The kids might have other ideas.

HOW? For good acoustics, position stereo speakers carefully. Seating should face the speakers and be equidistant between them to achieve balanced sound.

Controls must be accessible. If the music is just getting to a passage you hate, you'll want to be able to change that tune without having to climb over the sofa.

Stereo components are adaptable. They can be tucked into a bookcase or storage wall. A stereo cabinet is less flexible, but it can be centered on a large empty wall. With paintings above, it can become a focal point.

You may want to keep your sounds from annoying others. If you live in an apartment building, don't place your stereo on a wall you share with a neighbor. Rugs and wall-hangings will help absorb sound. Wall paneling will provide some sound insulation.

If you want to dance to the music, you'll need a large empty, or emptiable, floor space, and you may well want to dim the lights.

Storing records and tapes can sometimes be a problem. Here they are stored free from dust in closed floor-to-ceiling cabinets edged in brass. The storage units, built out from the wall, act like a wall themselves, enclosing a cozy space, a den with daybed and desk. (Design by Rubén De Saavedra, ASID; photo by Paulus Leeser.)

PLAYING MUSIC— PERFORMING AND SINGING

WHERE? Choose a place to practice where the musician won't drive everyone else crazy.

If you have a piano, where you put it depends on what it looks like. Anything from a grand piano to a spinet in wood tones looks fine in the living room, if there is space. An old upright painted white belongs in the family room; if it must go in the living room, dress it up in a mahogany stain first.

HOW? The instrument should be placed where it will not be injured between uses. Ideally, pianos should be kept away from windows and exterior walls. The sunshine, moisture, and sudden temperature changes can fade and warp the piano, and interfere with the tuning. Smaller instruments might be arranged for display between uses. They might be hung from the walls or placed on well-lit shelves.

Placing a Piano A grand piano should be placed with its curved side toward the room, its straight side parallel to the wall. This is the most graceful arrangement, and it saves space. Fill the curve of the piano with a curved-back upholstered or occasional chair. Add a little round table and you'll have a cozy little seating space. You can place a grand piano on the diagonal. This gives a look of nonchalant elegance.

An upright looks best in a space that seems made for it. An el or alcove, or a length of wall that would leave some space on each side, is ideal. Lacking such luck, you can create a neat nook for the piano by placing bookcases on either side of it. You might connect the bookcases with shelves over the piano. You can hide a light on the bottom side of that shelf, and spotlight the piano.

If the person needs to read the music, place a music stand and light so he can see. For singing, allow plenty of space for people to gather around. If you're not interested in listening to the music, while others are, you might want to insulate the room for sound.

PLAYING GAMES

WHERE? The scene for active play is usually the family room or the children's rooms. Sometimes part of the kitchen can act as a playroom. This is a particularly good idea when Mom wants to keep an eye on the kid while she's cooking.

More sedate games, played at a table while sitting, can take place in more delicately decorated rooms—the living room, the den, the sun porch, the dining room.

If you have the space, it's very pleasant to have a game table and chairs in the living room. You can use the chairs for extra seating when you have a large gathering. And on a cozy, cold winter evening you can use the table for intimate dining by the fire.

You might have a chess or backgammon table set up permanently in the den.

You might use the dining table to play poker, or even bridge, if the table is small.

HOW? Active play is rough. It requires open floor space and indestructible, DURABLE furnishings. An area of active play should incite a merry mood. The decor can be STIMULATING.

Adequate lighting is important to table games. You might have an overhead fixture, or move a floor lamp into an appropriate position. If you are cramped for space, choose a folding table and chairs.

Plan on places to store games and toys. It might be a drawer for a deck of cards, or a whole closet in the kitchen for ice skates, baseball mitts, or what-have-you.

MAKING LOVE

WHERE? You know best what atmosphere pleases you. Most people prefer to mate in private. To create that exclusive intimacy, use whatever can enclose you and cut you off from the rest of the world. You can close doors. You can draw curtains—at the window, between rooms, or around your four-poster bed. You can insulate yourself from sound by surrounding yourself with thick carpets and soft fabrics. You can take your phone off the hook, turn on some music, dim the lights.

HOW? You can make the atmosphere SEXY. Why not?

SLEEPING

WHERE? Typically, the bedroom, but also in almost any other room if the bed is convertible or concealed.

HOW? The atmosphere should be QUIET, CALM, and dark. You should be able to cut off the light when somebody is sleeping, or at least manage to keep it out of his eyes. This includes sunshine, moonglow, and outside streetlights. It's good to place the beds so that the sleepers do not face the windows. If the person sleeps during daylight hours, you'll need a room-darkening window treatment. Children, however, might be comforted by a night-light.

The furniture should be arranged so the bed is easy to make and to get into and out of. A bedside table and light should be within easy reach.

Choosing the Bed Your first budget priority is a good bed or beds. It is worth it to spend money to buy the very best. Your comfort and temperament depend on it. Have the potential user test the bed *by lying on it.*

A lively, multipurpose family room can also serve for sleeping. Simply choose a sofa that can convert to a bed. Here, skinny-slat blinds turn to block out the light for sleeping. Bookshelves provide easily accessible bedtime reading, and a wall-mounted flexible lamp provides the right light. (Photos courtesy of Duo-Sofas.)

Your choice of bed depends on who will use it, where it will be—a bedroom, or another place—and how big the room is.

Determining the size of the bed: Who's going to use the bed? What is this person's size? Anyone needs six inches or so of extra bed length, and nothing less than twin-size width (thirty-nine inches) is really comfortable for adults.

Determining its hardness or softness: What is the user's preference? This is also a matter of body weight and build. A bed should support the body so it is well aligned in any position. It should never sag in the middle. You could choose a conventional box spring and mattress, or a foam mattress over a wooden base, or an orthopedically constructed slatted base.

Determining its style: Appropriate choices for a couple include twin beds, a double bed, a queen-sized bed, and a king-sized bed. Twin beds on a single headboard are a good choice if the individuals are of greatly different weights, and one tends to roll into the other, or if one prefers a harder or softer mattress than the other. The two beds can be made up as one, or the beds can be equipped with casters so that they can be swung apart to be made

up. Avoid buying a king-sized bed unless your room is enormous; a queen-sized bed is a luxurious space of a more workable size.

Children seem to love double-decker beds. Trundle beds provide space for that overnight guest. Guests of the children can be accommodated in anything from a twin bed to a cot to a sleeping bag.

For adult guests, you may not want to waste one whole room on the occasional visitor. Choose a convertible bed and make the room double-purpose. If you do want a guest room, twin beds are more adaptable to a range of guests than a double bed.

If the room is multipurpose, it is a good idea to disguise the sleeping function. You can choose a sofa bed, a convertible chair, a day bed or studio couch, or a wall cabinet that encloses a pull-down bed, or you can disguise an ordinary bed.

You can make an ordinary bed into a sofa. Take a regulation mattress and box spring and put them on legs no more than three or four inches tall. Place cushions or bolsters in back of the mattress to reduce the seating depth to eighteen or twenty inches. A narrow bed needs only a tailored slipcover and bolsters. A wider bed might have wall cabinets built in

Do you want a regal resting place? Do you have a big bedroom? Yes? Well, then do something DRAMATIC with the bed. Buy a big one of some special interest and center it on a wall. Here's one with high-turned posts and a canopy covering, the original made for a monarch. (Courtesy of Baker Furniture; design by John Braden.)

behind the bolsters to reduce the seating depth. In this case, the bed would have to be on gliders or rollers so it is easy to move. However, you don't want to lean over to reach your martini and find that your seat has slipped out from under you! You might put blocks in front of the casters to keep the seat stationary.

You can conceal an ordinary bed. You can hide it in a niche, or close it off with draperies, shutters, folding doors, or a screen.

Placing the Bed   If the room is small, and you have one large bed, shift the bed toward a corner of the room instead of letting it take over the space. If you have two single beds without headboards or footboards, you can place them with their long sides to the wall in order to save floor space. They can form an L-arrangement along adjacent walls. A square table in the corner can link the beds and act as a night table. You might choose a corner table that is high enough and wide enough for one of the beds to be partly shoved underneath when not in use. This will save more floor space. You can put the beds against opposite walls, or end-to-end against one long wall with a night table between. Conventional twin beds with headboards are usually placed side by side extending out from a wall with a night

table between. This arrangement takes up a lot of space. Trundle beds and double-deckers take the floor space of only one bed.

In a large room, you can put the bed against almost any wall that is large enough, and generally the bed can extend well into the room. It is wise to leave a comfortable space on each side of the bed so that there will be room to make up the bed and room to crawl into it at night. Thirty inches is good. If you have a large bed and a large room, the bed is the natural focal point of the room. You should center the bed against one wall, preferably so the bed can be viewed head-on as you enter the room. If you have plenty of space, you can follow the fashion and place your bed diagonally in the room.

Choosing Tables Serving the Bed   The sleeper needs a place to put down a book or a magazine. He might want a radio or a telephone handy, and his alarm clock ought to be in view. Almost anything can serve as a bedside table; just make sure it's big enough to hold everything you want to put on it. Electric blanket controls, an electrifying novel, an electric light, a sardine sandwich—they all take space.

Bedside tables don't have to match each other or the bed. End tables by sofa beds can act as night tables and storage space. Coffee tables in front of convertible beds should be easily movable.

WASHING AND GROOMING

WHERE?   The Bathroom. Most rental homes come equipped with the fixtures, a light, a mirror, a medicine chest, and towel racks. All you have to buy is a shower curtain, towels, and a toothbrush. If you are building a home or remodeling one, you might have to buy fixtures. You should budget for them at the beginning.

If you are buying fixtures, begin by measuring your bathroom so you know precisely how much space you have. Think in terms of aligning the fixtures to make the space work most efficiently. Go to bathroom showrooms with your measuring tape. Measure fixtures to figure out what will fit.

What materials should you choose? Porcelain has been with us a long time and is still popular. Fiberglas is now being used for some fixtures, particularly showers and bathtubs. It has some advantages: It is warm to the touch. It does not chip or crack, and it can be molded into unusual shapes, all in one piece. Because it is all in one piece, it does not have cracks and crevices that will collect dirt. One caution: Do not wash Fiberglas with abrasives; it will scratch.

You used to be able to have any color, as long as it was white. Now you're faced with a flush of rainbow hues. White still might be the easiest color to live with. It will give you great freedom in determining (or changing) your color scheme. If you choose fixtures in other colors, you will have to organize your color scheme around them.

Bathroom fixtures now come in a selection of styles. Choose the size and shape that will best fit the room and its decorative character. The salesperson at the showroom will advise you. There are such things as tubs for two! If you want a sunken tub, you'll need an architect or contractor to help you. You can create the effect of a sunken tub by building up a platform around it.

If you need more storage space, utilize the walls. Decorative shelves of glass or Plexiglas are easily hung on the walls. They are ideal for cosmetics and pretty little knick-knacks. Open or closed cabinets can be mounted on the wall if the room is deep enough to accommodate them. They shouldn't crowd your head space. Shelves can be mounted across a corner or above the toilet to make use of space usually wasted.

Counterspace and cabinets can be built around the washbasin. A counter can be cut to fit around the washbasin. It's useful to have such an area for putting down your toothpaste. Cabinets can be built under the counter. They will hide pipes and provide a place for your bubblebath. All can be made of plywood

panels and covered with plastic laminate.

You can utilize the back of the door. A shallow plywood cupboard, exactly the size of the door, can be mounted on the back of the bathroom door. It could hold finger towels, or whatever. Just be sure things don't fall out when the door opens or closes.

HOW? Where you wash, you splash. The atmosphere should be WATERPROOF/MOISTURE RESISTANT. Ceramic tiles, glass, and all sorts of plastics can weather the wetness—vinyl tiles, vinyl-coated wallcoverings, plastic and Plexiglas furnishings. Avoid wood, or at least keep it away from the shower. It will warp in a wet atmosphere.

People usually like to take care of their bodily needs in private. A lock on the door will

Most of us want to do something to dress up our bathrooms but we don't have much leeway. The fixtures are fixed. A pretty pattern is often the answer. Here a pattern covers the ceiling, forms a valance over the shower and draperies to its sides. The pattern and the fabric have the effect of softening all those hard bathroom textures. (Design by Sandra Merriman; photo by Michael A. Peñalba.)

keep away the invading barbarians. Make sure your window treatment provides you with the privacy you want. Some kind of two-tiered treatment—curtains or shutters—will allow you to close the bottom for privacy, while leaving the top open for sunlight. Opaque glass will also let in the light while obscuring your neighbors' view of you. You might even hang an old stained-glass panel in front of the bathroom window.

Lighting in the bathroom should be bright and clear so you can see the whites of your eyes the morning after. But it shouldn't be harsh—it should show a little mercy, after all. Good lighting is essential on the crucial mirror for fixing your face.

DRESSING

WHERE? Dressing usually occurs in the bedroom and bathroom. If you live in a studio, you'll surely dress there. If you have plenty of room, you might have a separate dressing room. You'll don and doff your outer clothes by the entrance to your home.

The Bedroom Storage pieces do *not* have to match the beds. The bedroom is more interesting if they don't. If you have a great deal to store, and want a clean, uncluttered look, consider having storage closets built in along the walls. They will conceal clutter without influencing the style of the room. Too many separate storage pieces in one room make the place look as crowded as the wardrobe room backstage. A triple dresser may store a lot, but it may present problems—it may be too big for the size of the room. It's usually safer to choose something of more modest size.

Remember that you can make use of the space under your bed. People have always loved hiding things under the bed. It can be your child, your lover, your Christmas presents, or a more mundane flat wooden or cardboard box holding out-of-season clothes. You might have a storage platform built under the bed, or even choose a bed with drawers in its base.

Storage pieces should not be lined up against a wall unless they were designed to be used that way. A normal dresser should have some space on either side of it. It needs room to breathe, visually. Don't shove it into a corner.

A Studio Storage in a studio shouldn't look bedroomy. Clothes storage can be in chest end tables or a trunk coffee table, in the drawers of a wall unit, or in wicker baskets. A mirror may hang over a chest. In a traditional room, you might utilize a large armoire. You could leave stuff at the cleaners.

You can conceal storage in a corner. You can rig up shelves attached to the two adjoining walls in a corner. Hang a tapestry, a window shade, or even a decorative beach towel over it to hide your secret storage.

A Large Bathroom or Dressing Room You might really do it up with mirrors and lounge chairs and a dressing table complete with bot-

Closets built in on either side of the bed provide plenty of storage space while creating a cozy nook for the bed. The room was small and long and narrow. Building the closets on the end wall made the room a more pleasant rectangular shape, and the avoidance of large storage furniture keeps the room from feeling crowded. (Photo courtesy of the Simmons Company; design by Carleton Varney.)

tles of magic lotions. You can have large storage closets built in along the walls.

An Entrance Hall or Foyer Here's where you take your outer wraps on and off. If the climate is wet, the floor should be WATERPROOF and washable. It's handy to have a drawer for gloves and scarves close to the coat closet.

HOW? Often-used clothing should be stored within easy reach. You'll need good lighting by the mirror so you can get a true view.

To make the most of available space, you can inch-pinch in the closets. In addition to hanging your clothes on a rod, you can use the other areas. You can use the space above by having shelves built around the walls near the ceiling. If the closet is high, you can have a double row of shelves. See-through plastic boxes can hold your summer sandals or woolly winter underwear. You can stack stuff up on the floor (again, maybe in plastic boxes) until you reach the height of your hanging clothes. You can stick your shoe in the door—in a hanging shoe bag.

READING

WHERE? You can read anywhere, as long as you have light. I have a friend who used to read in a doorway under the red Exit light while he was on duty with the National Guard.

The Living Room, Family Room, or Porch As long as you have light, you can read in the comfortable seating arranged for conversation.

If you will want to read while others are talking, it's best to make a reading area away from the conversational group. Conversation and reading don't mix. You don't want anyone to talk to you just as you're getting to the juicy part!

Den, Library, or Study Reading and desk work are usually the main activities of the den. Your reading chair might even share the desk

A COZY, CALM retreat for reading, this room features a daybed where you can put your feet up, a bookcase stocked with inviting titles, and a wall lamp placed for good reading light. QUIET is maintained by the carpeting, upholstery, and fabric-covered walls. (Design by Robert Metzger, ASID; photo by Peter Vitale.)

light. For example: Place the desk perpendicular to the wall. Place the desk chair on one side. On the other side, along the length of the desk, you can place a lounge chair and ottoman.

Here is the logical place to store your books.

The Bedroom Good light by the bed should be within easy reach to switch on and off. If two share a bed, make sure there are two lights and two controls, so one can sleep while the other reads.

If there is space, you might have a comfortable chair and ottoman, or a chaise longue with a good reading light by it. This chair might be placed in the corner and share the night table with the bed.

The Bathroom You might have built-in bookshelves, magazine racks, reading lamps, even a comfortable chair. You might have a plastic tray to go over the bathtub so you can prop up your book while soaking.

HOW? Proper lighting will save your eyes.

Place the reading chair where it can take advantage of natural light during the day. At night, place a lamp so it shines down and fully illuminates whatever you're reading. A table should be handy for laying down your book.

Most people find it easier to concentrate in a QUIET environment. Soft things absorb sound—rugs, curtains, upholstery, draped tables. Fabric-covered or carpeted walls really suck up sound.

People often prefer to read in private. It's easier to concentrate when there are no people around. However, having a quiet companion is sometimes the nicest of all. You have the comfort of company, and the freedom from flak. Here is an example of a convenient corner arrangement for two: Put a table with a good reading light in the corner. Put a comfortable chair on either side of the table. One ottoman can serve both chairs. If the table is especially long, a reading chair and ottoman can be placed on the long side, a smaller chair on the short side.

Where Can You Keep Your Books? Bookshelves require so little space, they can be built into the most unlikely places—any niche that is six to eight inches deep. Bookshelves would fit in a narrow corridor, in the entrance foyer, any waste space along the walls. Space between the shelves should range from eight to ten inches or more. To accommodate books of various sizes, it's a good idea to graduate the distance between shelves, or to use adjustable shelves.

Where you put the bookcase depends on what it looks like. Single movable bookcases should be centered in their wall space. Built-in bookcases should extend in width across the

This office can accommodate conferences as well as desk work. A sofa, together with a desk of the same height, occupies the center of the space. QUIET is kept by a luxurious carpet and a sound-absorbent felt wallcovering. The tailored lines of the furnishings together with the primitive sculptures create a mood of efficiency and excitement. (Photo courtesy of Fibers Division/Allied Chemical Corporation; design by Virginia Frankel, ASID.)

whole wall area in order to create a balanced and neat effect. It's handsome to flank a fireplace with bookcases. You could do the same with a sofa, a bed, a desk, or an upright piano.

Books may be lined up solidly, or for a more casual and INFORMAL effect, they may be interspersed with pottery, plants, or art objects. They may flank a radio or a TV. Bookends should be either unnoticeable or terrific.

DOING DESK WORK

WHERE?
The Den Desk work might be the major activity of the den. If so, the desk can sit out in the center of the space and be the center of attention. A big masculine kneehole desk is suitable in the den.

The Bedroom A lot of people like to do their desk work in their own rooms. It gets them away from the others. A man might want a big heavy desk and a woman might want something that looks more like a writing table. A versatile Parsons table can be used in a bedroom for desk work, games, and eating.

Children usually do their homework in their bedrooms. Cornered shelf-and-desk units are especially designed for them.

The Living Room To save space and provide light to the sofa, a table-type desk may be placed in back of the sofa. A wall storage system could include a desk. A traditional secretary could add height and interest to the room while providing a drop-down desk.

The Kitchen If Mom spends most of her time in the kitchen, she might want to do her desk work there. Countertops might be extended to make her a desk, with drawers and storage below, or she might use the kitchen table and adjacent drawers. A handy telephone and appointment calendar increase efficiency.

The Dining Room Desk work can be done at the dining table, provided suitable direct lighting is arranged. Choose a multipurpose

fixture for over the table. Some fixtures are especially designed for this double duty. Flip one switch and they provide diffuse light for dining; flip another and they provide direct downlight for studying, reading, or other close work.

HOW? Most people prefer to study and work in peace and QUIET.

To avoid eyestrain, you should have good direct light. A desk should be as near as possible to natural light for daytime use. For right-handed people, turn the desk so light comes from the left side. That way shadows won't fall on the work. For left-handed people, light should come from the right side. At night, a desk lamp should fully illuminate the entire working surface.

The chair and desk height should be comfortable, and you may need a wastebasket and files, drawers, or shelves for storage.

TALKING ON THE TELEPHONE

WHERE? Where do you spend most of your day? You will want a telephone handy so you don't have to run all over the place each time it rings. You might want extensions in the kitchen, study, and bedroom. (The phone can act as a decorative accessory and be color-coordinated to the room.)

The Kitchen What if the phone rings while you are in the middle of mastering your hollandaise? You won't want to go far.

The Bedroom A bedroom is a good place to have private talks on the telephone. You might want the phone right by your bed, so you won't have to stumble and fumble in the dark to answer it.

The Study It's convenient to have a phone by your desk, close to your appointment calendar.

The Bathroom is certainly a place to be private.

The Corridor might provide easy access from a number of rooms.

Teenager's Bedroom You might want to give a teenager a phone of his own (if only to keep him off yours).

HOW? Do you want to have your conversations in private? If so, place a phone where you can get away from the others. If you can't go to a separate room, you may opt for a long extension cord so you can retire to the closet.

Certainly you will want relative quiet (or quiet relatives) so you can hear.

It's convenient to have a pad and pencil and the telephone directories handy.

MAKING COLLECTIONS/ PURSUING HOBBIES

A collection or a hobby can be the theme of your decorating scheme.

WHERE? If this is a private pursuit, you might do it in your bedroom. If it is a shared activity, you might do it in the family room or the living room.

Where you display a collection depends on what it is. Paintings and sculpture are lovely in the living room. China and glass are handsome in closed cabinets in the dining room. Books can go in the library, the living room, the dining room, the bedroom, the entrance, the hall—almost anywhere. Especially personal collections belong in the bedroom. You might show off your collection by putting it on glass shelves and illuminating it with hidden lights.

HOW? The appropriate atmosphere depends on what the hobby is. For example, if

An interest in sewing and stitchery inspired this cozy corner. An old sewing machine is placed to take the best advantage of daylight. Old samplers entertain the eyes. A nearby chest stores fabrics and threads, and the EASY TO CLEAN quarry-tile floor cannot conceal dropped pins. (Photo courtesy of Ridgeway.)

you paint, a room with a large skylight facing north would be ideal. It would provide a lot of shadowless light and help you see colors. If you collect stamps, you will want to keep your sorted stamps away from the wind. Most hobbies make a mess. You'll want the room to be EASY TO CLEAN. The simplest method for straightening up is to have enormous storage closets where you can hide everything out of sight.

The hobby will dictate the equipment you need. For example, if you sew, you'll need the machine, an iron, an ironing board, and a big flat surface for cutting. (This could be the floor or a Ping-Pong table.) If you garden, you might want a work area by a sink, and maybe special lighting.

Generally, for any hobby, you need a place to work, a place to store your materials, and a place to show off your successes.

COOKING

WHERE?
The Kitchen Whether you are heating up TV

dinners or concocting something sensational for the salivary glands, it usually happens in the kitchen.

Most kitchens come completely fitted with all major appliances, so your only expense is to buy the dishes, pots and pans, and your bottled Bearnaise or chicken noodle soup. If your kitchen is not fully equipped and you have to buy major appliances, budget for them at the beginning. They will involve a major investment, and one without which you can't eat.

Arranging Kitchen Equipment to Function Efficiently: People who rent their homes usually learn to live with the kitchen equipment as it is. They don't want to get involved with changing pipes or wiring. People who own their own homes may want to build a new kitchen or remodel an old one to create more efficient working conditions.

Positioning Major Appliances: Think of the meals prepared. You might take something out of the refrigerator, wash it at the sink, put it in a pot, and put it on the stove. Since the refrigerator, the sink, and the stove are used in coordination in preparing meals, they should be relatively close together so the cook can save steps. In a small kitchen they should be positioned against the walls in order to leave floor space free for movement.

In a large kitchen, a cooking island or countertop peninsula jutting out from a wall will wrap work areas more closely around the cook. A peninsula might act as a room divider, separating the cooking area from the eating area.

A dishwasher should be between the sink and dish-storage cabinets. Then it is simple to rinse dishes and load the dishwasher, and simple to stand at the dishwasher to unload and put away glasses, dishes, and flatware.

Positioning Work Surfaces: A countertop on either side of the sink allows you to stack dirty dishes on one side and place clean dishes in a dish drain on the other side. A chopping board by the sink will allow you to wash and chop food without moving much.

A countertop by the refrigerator allows you to put down the things you are putting in or taking out. It would be handy to have a cutting

board by the fridge, and your breadbox near that. This way you can whip out the mayonnaise and the leftovers and make a quick sandwich.

A countertop by the stove allows you to set down pots that are in transit between cupboards and the stove, or the stove and the sink. It will also give you a place to put the dishes you are filling with food from the stove.

If your major appliances are waist-high, it is an excellent idea to connect them with countertops of the same height. Then you'll have one smooth all-around work center. Counters can be made of plywood and covered with plastic laminate. Storage cabinets can be built under these countertops. If there is no space between appliances, a conveniently located table or countertop can serve as an extra work surface.

Positioning Storage Spaces—Cupboards and Cabinets: Flatware, dishes, and glasses in everyday use should be stored in an area near the sink or dishwasher so they're easy to put away when washed. Pots and pans should be stored between the sink and the stove because you either move them toward the sink to put water in them, or fill them with food and put them directly on the stove or into the oven.

Often-used canned, boxed, and bottled

The refrigerator, sink, and stove are the three points of the kitchen work triangle. Here the points are conveniently close, connected by a continuous counter that provides generous work surfaces and ample storage below. The tile floor is EASY TO CLEAN. (Photo courtesy of the Tile Council of America.)

food should be stored near the stove, so you can take it out, pop it into a pot and put it on the heat. Mixing bowls should be handy to the refrigerator and to the shelved food so you can stand in one place and mix your magic.

Whenever possible, place storage cupboards and shelves above your appliances; then things will be within easy reach. If you like your equipment out in the open, or if you need to save space, you can hang things on the walls. You can make an artistic arrangement of your wire wisk, garlic press, cheese grater or whatever. A corner or a small wall can be fitted with small shelves for storing spices and sugar, flour, coffee, tea, and other canister commodities.

Rarely used items should not clutter up the cabinets immediately adjacent to your appliances. Put them in out-of-the-way places—on the highest shelves, in a corner cabinet in the kitchen, in a display cabinet in the dining room, in the pantry (if you have one). For a nice decorative effect, you could store things in boxes covered in pretty paper or fabric, or in wicker baskets. You could place these on top of your cabinets interspersed with plants or pottery. You could hang two rows of shelves on the kitchen wall, just below the ceiling, and put your boxes or baskets there.

On an Outdoor Grill Grilling steaks in the backyard is as American as apple pie. You might store the requisite charcoal and lighter near the grill.

Compact Kitchens in Other Rooms You might want to add a small fridge to your office to aid in your after-five relief. You might want to conceal a compact kitchen in the family room or recreation room. If you don't have a regular kitchen, you might buy a hot plate, a plug-in broiler/oven, or an electric frying pan so that you can enjoy your own home cooking.

HOW?
Avoid Accidents Because you can cut yourself with knives, burn yourself with boiling water, poison yourself with rancid meat, the

kitchen must be designed to avoid accidents.

You should have good all-over lighting with no dark areas, and you can have special additional lighting over work countertops. Fluorescent tubes can easily be mounted under cabinets.

Traffic paths must be kept clear so there is no danger of bumping into equipment or knocking things over. Who wants to topple the sauce that the chef has been perfecting for hours?

Spills, when they do occur, should be EASY TO CLEAN up. Counter surfaces might be butcher block, Formica, or ceramic tile. Floors might be vinyl tile or indoor-outdoor carpet. Walls might be covered in washable vinyl-coated paper, or washable paint.

Coddle the Cook Make the cook happy in the kitchen and you may end up with marvel-

One of the problems with cooking is trying to read the recipe without soiling the pages with sticky fingers and without having to bend in half to see it on a waist-high counter. Here is an excellent answer: a cookbook niche built into the over-stove exhaust fan. A nice idea for coddling the cook. (Photo courtesy of the Tile Council of America.)

ous meals. Let the cook arrange things as he/she wishes and choose the colors that he/she likes to live with.

There are two kinds of cooks—innies and outies. Some cooks like everything put away, not a canister in sight. Others like all their equipment right out there, easy to reach—just as the doctor wants the nurse right there with the scalpel.

Some women choose kitchen colors that flatter their complexion. After all, they figure, they might as well look good where they spend most of their time. If the cook is in the kitchen longer than he or she would like, the atmosphere had better be CHEERFUL. Generally, bright colors can raise the spirits, and yellow seems like sunshine.

Does the cook like to be mysterious and work in isolation, or does the cook like to be part of the group and join in conversation even while working? If the cook likes to be sociable, it's a good idea to break down the barriers between cooking and living areas, or organize space for company in the kitchen.

DOING THE LAUNDRY

WHERE? If you live in an apartment building, you might take your laundry out to the Laundromat or to a service, and just occasionally wash a few things out in the bathroom. You will probably still be stuck with doing some occasional ironing, unless you are careful to buy all drip-dry clothes.

You can hide a washer and dryer behind folding doors in almost any room of your home, as long as the plumber can work out the piping. This would be convenient in the kitchen, in an area by the bedrooms, or even in the basement family room. My sister-in-law hides her washer and dryer behind doors in her dining room. The dining table provides a

surface for folding. The most sensible arrangement I've ever heard of is a washer and dryer placed in an anteroom to the upstairs bathroom with the linen closet right beside them. Isn't most laundry accumulated in the bathroom hamper anyway?

HOW? If you have a washer and a dryer, place them so it's easy to transfer clothes from washer to dryer. For example, you won't want the washer door swinging open in your way.

Wherever you do routine activities, the atmosphere should be CHEERFUL! Bright, light colors and punchy patterns can perk up even the drabbest, dullest place. Plants add life and liveliness. (Besides, they do well in a humid atmosphere.) In a laundry room it would be well to put a bright pattern on the walls. After all, the washer and dryer are nothing special to look at.

CLEANING THE HOUSE

WHERE? Unfortunately, you have to clean all over. If you are like most of us who can't afford, or can't find, good help, cleaning turns out to be a do-it-yourself project. It *is* good exercise, but like calisthenics (in my opinion), the quicker it's over the better. You can help yourself by choosing materials and furnishings that are EASY TO CLEAN.

The second "where" is where do you put all the cleaning equipment? You probably want to hide it out of the way in some closet or other. If you have small children, *be sure* that all poisonous things are locked out of reach.

HOW? This is up to you. My college roommate put on music and danced with the broom.

(Design by Robert Caudle, FASID.)

4
HOW DO YOU USE WHAT YOU HAVE?

Most people don't actually start with an empty home or a naked room. They have a fig leaf here, a sofa there. The problem is to integrate old furniture into a new scheme, or to buy new furnishings that will go with the old.

WHAT DO YOU HAVE?

What do you have to work with? Look at every item you have and ask it the following questions: Are you beautiful? Do you have sentimental associations? Are you really useful? If you have negative answers to all the questions, throw the item out, or sell it if you can find a sucker. If it inspired a yes answer to any of the questions, you're going to want to work this item into your design scheme.

What if you have nothing, or almost nothing? If you will eventually move to a larger home, buy furnishings you'll be able to mix with others later. Limit yourself to a few periods or styles, and restrict yourself to a few wood tones and colors. Dual-purpose furniture can work one way now, another way later. For instance, a sofa bed can move from the living room to the den. A Parsons table can be used now for dining, and later for a desk.

If you have very little furniture, and don't want to buy more, make people look at your walls. Wallpaper or wood paneling can make a room feel furnished.

What Do You Have That's Beautiful? You will want to organize your design scheme to enhance your beautiful objects.

Place your beautiful piece in a position of importance. You can make it the focal point of the room by placing it opposite the entrance, or by organizing your major group of furniture around it.

Underplay other things so your beautiful object stands out all the more. For example, if you have a colorful painting, you might underplay the rest of the room by using no-color neutrals. If you have very fine furniture, you will want to avoid dramatic effects on the walls or floor so that you can keep the focus on the furniture. Neutral walls are the proper foil for fine furniture, or for fabrics with bright colors or bold patterns, or for artwork. If, alternatively, you have an especially beautiful wallcovering or floorcovering, you will want to underplay the furnishings with neutral or blend-in colors.

Your beautiful object can be different in style from the rest of the room. Differences draw attention. It might be a traditional piece in a modern room, or a modern piece in a traditional room. Alternatively, your beautiful object may inspire you to select other furnishings and accessories of the same period or style. In this case, your stand-out piece can

What to do with a marvelous old bedstead George Washington might have slept in when it fits only a double-size mattress? The family heirloom can easily be used with super-size bedding. Use extender rails, which need no carpentry or other adjustment. (Photo courtesy of the Simmons Company.)

be different in some more subtle way. It may be larger in size. It may be rounded while other things are straight, or straight while other things are round. It might be bolder in color, or made of different materials.

What Do You Have That Has Sentimental Associations?

Things with sentimental associations make you feel warm inside and happy. And isn't that a feeling you want all through your home? Objects that inspire such feelings can inspire the design of the whole home. You may feel this way about objects from your parents' house, or from your grandparents', about things you picked up on a happy holiday, about gifts from favorite people, about symbols from your past, or equipment for your hobbies or special interests. By all means, use these things in your design scheme. They express your personality, and make your home a much more interesting place.

But what do you do when the sentiment is not yours, but your mother's? When she points to her enormous mirror with gamboling golden cherubs running their fat fannies all around the frame, and says, "I want *you* to have this, dear," what do you do? You could have a stroke, or try tact. You could tell her how touched you are that she would want to share with you something that means so much to her. Then you could explain how beautiful (lie) you think the mirror is, but how difficult it would be to integrate with your furnishings style. Alternatively, you could take the mirror and have fun with it. It *would* give your home a sense of humor.

What Do You Have That's Useful?

Anything that fits your needs can be put to use. It doesn't matter if it's ugly. Your useful and good-looking objects will play an active part in your decorating scheme. You will want them to attract a moderate amount of attention. Your useful and unbeautiful objects can serve their purpose without drawing any attention at all. You can camouflage them by making them blend into the background. They could be the same color as the walls or floor, or they could be an unobtrusive neutral color. If your furnishings are not so hot, you can distract attention from them by doing something dramatic with the walls. Make the walls a bold color or a lively pattern and no one will bother to look at your furnishings.

You can salvage all sorts of furniture. Upholstered pieces may be reupholstered or slip-covered. A rug of the wrong color may be dyed, or cut to fit a room. Desks, tables, and chairs can be refinished or painted.

You can alter the seeming size of a piece. If you have furniture that seems too small, cover it in a bright color, a pattern, or an uneven texture to give it more visual impact. Because it commands attention, it will seem bigger. If you have furniture that seems too large, underplay it and it will seem smaller. Make it neutral, unpatterned, and untextured. Make it match its background and it will seem to disappear. If the background wall has an all-over pattern, the same all-over pattern on the piece will work like jungle camouflage. If you have furniture that is too overstuffed, upholster it in vertical stripes. They make the figure look slimmer.

If you have furniture you can't change, try to enhance it. Old furniture is flattered if the rest of the room is mellow too. Patterned wallpaper in medium soft tones blends with the old without pointing up its frailties. If you have cast-off furniture that is pretty dingy, be sure that the walls and floor are not clear colors. If they are, the furniture will look even grayer and drabber by contrast. If you have furniture that seems too strong in color, you can modify its impact by using the same color in lighter or more neutral versions elsewhere in the room, and mixing in a lot of plain neutrals.

Any pattern you have, and like, can inspire your color scheme.

HOW CAN YOU USE IT?

WOOD FURNITURE The wood tones of your furniture will give a lot of direction to your scheme. Wood furniture has to go with wood floors or wood paneling, if there is any. To create compatibility, you might have to refinish the floors in a similar stain—or refinish the furniture. Avoid too many wood tones in a room. Two is enough.

Wood Suggests Appropriate Colors Wood tones have color. They swear at some other colors, and swing with others. Before you make any final decision about the colors of your room, hold swatches or chips of the colors you're considering next to your woods to see how they look together.

Pine, oak, and teak are slightly orange in color. They combine well with oranges—pumpkin, nutmeg—and with golds, greens, and blues.

Cherry, mahogany, and rosewood have reddish tones. They blend beautifully with reds and greens, as well as with soft blue.

Walnut looks handsome with bright warm colors, like deep pink, orange, rich yellow, and vivid green.

Maple mates well with modified mossy green, warm beige, and soft yellow.

Fruitwoods are flattered by pastel tones of dusty pink and pale blue or green.

Ebony looks extremely rich when combined with pale neutrals like beige and cream.

Contrast is the key to DRAMATIC effects. Dark woods are set off by pale, pastel hues. Bleached and light-colored woods are set off by dark or warm colors. (They also look breezy with cool colors like avocado or turquoise.)

Woods Suggest Appropriate Textures Pine, oak, and hickory suggest INFORMALity and strength. They require coarser textures—those that look or feel a little rough or uneven. For example, tweed is rough; corduroy is uneven. Delicate, smooth fabrics, such as silk, are out of place.

Walnut is middle-of-the-road; it can be FORMAL or INFORMAL. It goes with medium textures—those that are neither especially rough nor smooth. Linen, most cotton prints, leather, and chintz would work well.

Mahogany and rosewood are FORMAL, and suggest elegance. They require delicate, smooth textures that also express elegance and formality. Think of silk, satin, and velvet fabrics, deep-pile rugs, roses, lightweight brass, and other shiny accessories.

Old Wooden Pieces Can Be Redeemed If you think the piece is ugly, paint it the same color as the walls. You'll never notice its size and shape. One adventurous architect I know stacked up a pile of old and unprepossessing furniture and then painted a wild supergraphic all over it and the wall. The furniture seemed to disappear into the design, but there were still all those useful drawers for storage!

Heavy or formal furniture can achieve a light and lively look if painted in white or another light color. Many designers have recycled Victorian furniture this way. Many others have achieved a more modern and casual look by giving their old formal furniture a coat of paint.

Miscellaneous wooden pieces will seem to belong together if they are painted the same color or finished in the same way.

Old painted or wooden pieces can be refinished. To refinish an old painted piece, start with paint remover. Be careful to follow directions because paint remover may be poisonous or caustic or both. Wear rubber gloves and use an old paint brush. When the paint

You can redeem wood furniture you find or inherit and combine it with what you have—if you're careful. Here the chairs are Chippendale; the table and the armchair are inspired by Louis XV. All the pieces can go together because they have curves in common. The chairs are coordinated with similar white upholstery. *(Photo courtesy of Lees Carpets; design by Rivian Marcus.)*

remover has had time to do its thing, scrape off the paint with a scraper or with #3 steel wool. In ornate areas, you might need a toothbrush or a nut pick. In a day or two, repaint in the color of your choice.

To strip a stained piece, use a good bleach—either straight or diluted with one-half water. It is recommended that you do this outside.

To create a satin finish, concoct a mixture of equal parts white vinegar, boiled linseed oil, and turpentine. Let it soak in for ten minutes, then wipe off the excess. Wait twenty-four hours and do it again. You can repeat this procedure daily for as long as you want to get the finish you desire. The secret of success: be sure to let the solution soak in only ten minutes.

UPHOLSTERED FURNITURE Unless you want to reupholster the furniture or slipcover it, you will want to work around the color or pattern of your upholstery.

If you have patterned upholstery, this may be the basis of your color scheme. Search out the lightest or most neutral color in the upholstery pattern. Paint the walls that color. Add white for the ceiling color. The floor could be the same as the walls or slightly darker. The window treatment could be in the same pattern as the upholstery or in a medium-bright hue from the pattern.

Upholstered furniture in a solid color can also be the start of your color scheme. You will want the other furnishings to coordinate with it. See Chapter 19, "Color," for more specifics.

Do you want to change the upholstery you have? Reupholstering is worth doing if your sofa or lounge chair is in good structural condition. Reupholstering is sometimes more costly than buying new. Call in a local upholsterer for an estimate. He will come with fabric samples, one of which will probably fit your scheme. If not, you can usually supply your own fabric. (It is worthwhile to order extra arm caps. These save wear and tear and are easily removed for cleaning.)

Slipcovers make magic. Presto chango. The old toad can turn into a prince. Even good-looking upholstery can put a fresh new face for the summer season—in slipcovers of crisp, cool cotton or chintz. In a matter of minutes your room has a whole new look. Slipcovers are easily made for square-back T-cushion lounge chairs and sofas. Roundback club chairs and chairs with exposed wood on the arms are harder to slipcover.

Miscellaneous upholstered pieces will seem to go together if they are covered in the same pattern or color.

A FLOORCOVERING If you have an Oriental or other outstanding rug, it is a prize piece that commands attention. You don't have any choice but to organize your room around it, and to use its colors as the basis of your scheme. Walls should be muted to avoid an overpowering effect, and furniture should not compete with the rug. Oriental rugs are handsome in combination with both traditional and modern furnishings.

If you have a rug or wall-to-wall carpeting in a bright or lively color, the color must be repeated somewhere else in the room, say on sofa pillows or on a drapery trim. Otherwise, it will look like you just moved into someone else's home.

If you have a neutral rug or wall-to-wall carpeting, you don't have to pay much attention to it. Since it's neutral, it is not commanding attention.

An old rug can be dyed to fit a new scheme. It can be cut to fit a smaller room (edges should be finished with carpet-binding tape). To fit a larger room, you can have a border added.

If you have old carpeting you can't replace, you can layer area rugs on top of it if the room is large.

ART/ACCESSORIES/COLLECTIONS Art or accessories could inspire the design scheme of a room. You might take your color scheme directly from a painting you love—or even an ashtray you love. Alternatively, you might decide to do your room in all neutral colors, so that the colors of your painting or art objects stand out even more in contrast. Generally, if

A charming painting is the inspiration of this room. First, it is placed in the most attention-getting position—over the sofa. Second, the understated background sets it off. The walls are pale yellow, the sofas a darker yellow, and the floor cream. Third, the flowers in the painting are the inspiration for the use of a similar floral pattern on the wing chair and sofa pillows. It's all a happy harmony. (Design by David Barrett; photo by Richard Champion.)

you want to hang art on the walls it is best to make the walls a plain color rather than patterned.

The styles of your treasures can point to the direction of the style of the room. For example, if you collect Early American pewter, it is likely that you would want the room to be INFORMAL, not furnished with fussy formal gilded antiques.

You must plan a place to put your art or accessories. A special painting or a group of art objects can be the center of attention of a room. You can place them so that they are the first thing you see as you enter the room and/or gather your major furnishings around them. Special spotlights can add to the impact.

Objects in a collection should be displayed together to maximize their impact. If you scatter a few things here and there, the effect won't be nearly as dramatic as a comprehensive grouping. Coordinate your collection. You can hang objects on a wall, a screen, or a pegboard. You can put them in a lighted cabinet, on open shelves, on a tabletop, or even in a special display table under glass.

What do you have in your collection? Do the objects have anything in common? Similar objects, or objects chosen with the same theme in mind, have a natural relationship. Put together, they will enhance each other. Diverse accessories that have nothing much in common can be unified if you display them together against the same background. Then, at least, they have the background in common. Put them on the same wall, or the same tabletop, or the same tray, or organize them in a wall unit or cabinet.

Housing a Collection The type of furniture you choose to house your collection depends on the type and size of your collection, your budget, how long you intend to stay in the place, and the style of the room.

Built-in storage/display units—shelves, niches, alcoves—must be constructed during the first stages of decorating. They are permanent and architectural. Built-in units may have glass shelves, be backed with mirrors, and be illuminated from within.

Built-in units should be defined by some architectural feature. They can go from wall to wall, from wall to fireplace, from corner to window, or they may be installed between columns. Built-in units may extend from floor to ceiling.

Built-on shelves may be removed and taken with you when you go. You may place shelves on brackets on the walls or even in the windows.

Free-standing movable units come in all sorts of shapes and sizes and are easily taken with you when you go. They must be chosen to suit the style of the room. Glass or Plexiglas shelves or étagères are neutral. They don't seem to take space, and they don't compete for attention with your art objects.

Tall display cases or bookshelves are handsome flanking a fireplace, a long sofa, or a tall window. Free-standing units usually require some space on either side.

Small accessories may be grouped on tables—glass-topped tables, tables of richly grained wood, skirted tables. If you are on a budget, you can use a painted stepladder to display small objects.

WHAT GOES WITH WHAT YOU HAVE?

What you buy depends on what you already have. The style of the furniture you have might suggest the style of the room. Pieces of the same period go together.

You also might integrate your piece into an ECLECTIC mix. A modern piece can perk up a room that's too traditional. A traditional piece can give dimension to a modern room. How can you make periods mix? Think of a cocktail party where there are a lot of diverse people. After a while they all have martinis in common, and they begin to talk to each other. It's the same with furniture. Diverse pieces can mix together as long as they have something in common. The connecting link can be similar size, shape, formality, wood tone, or color.

1. Pieces of the same period go together.

2. Pieces that are predominantly the same scale go together—small, medium, or large.
3. Furniture that has mostly straight lines seems to go together.
4. Furniture with the same kind of curves goes together.
5. Pieces that are predominantly smooth and FORMAL go together.
6. Pieces that are predominantly rough and INFORMAL go together.
7. Similar woods finished in similar ways go together.
8. Pieces in the same or similar colors go together.

In short, pieces that fit the same descriptive adjectives go together. For instance, if you think "bright and shiny," you may think of steel and glass, mirrors, foil wallpapers, or your crystal collection. All these things are bright and shiny—they go together. If you think "rough," the word may suggest heavy massive shapes, tweed, stone, or pottery—they all go together.

Suites of Furniture versus Unmatched Pieces Suites of furniture are, of course, designed to go together. But often they are boring; they show no sign of your individuality. Combining individual, unmatched pieces is more challenging, but the results are guaranteed to be more interesting.

However, it is normal to choose some things that match. Dining chairs usually match, but the host and hostess chairs may have arms, while the others have none. A few pairs make a balanced room arrangement easier. In the living areas, you might want to pick a pair of sofas, a pair of chairs, or a pair of tables, commodes, or bookcases.

Pieces of the Same Period Go Together Furnishings born of the same sort of heritage go together. Furnishings from one country from one period are related like brothers and sisters. There is enough similarity between them to create a unified feeling. There is also usually enough variety within the style to create the contrasts you need.

However, a word of caution. Unless you are living in a museum, it looks kind of silly to try to reproduce a period room. After all, no matter how vivid your fantasy life, you are not Louis XV or Madame Pompadour. Your room might well be inspired by some historical period, but an attempt at duplication is dubious.

Styles of the same period in different countries are often related like cousins. It is possible to restrict yourself to one period in time and pick pieces from different countries.

Why do pieces of a period go together? Because they are similar in size, shape and inspiration. For example:

During the fifteenth- and sixteenth-century Renaissance, furnishings in Italy, Spain, and England all tended to be large and straight-legged.

In the Baroque period in the seventeenth- and early eighteenth-centuries, the international style was large and curve-legged. This includes Italian styles, French Louis XIV, and English Queen Anne and Chippendale.

Then came the feminine, small, and curve-legged Rococo styles inspired by French Louis XV and copied by Chippendale in England.

In the late eighteenth century, the world was again inspired by the styles of ancient Greece and Rome. Hence was born the small straight-legged Neo-Classic Pompeian style expressed in English Adam, Sheraton, and Hepplewhite and French Louis XVI.

In the early nineteenth century, with the rise of Napoleon, the classic style became heavier and more dramatic. It is expressed in the splay- or flare-legged styles of French Empire, English Regency, and American Duncan Phyfe.

The nineteenth-century Victorian period took inspiration from every era. Generally furniture was heavy in weight and ornament.

The Modern movement brought on an international desire to get back to clean-lined designs and honesty in materials.

Historical styles are basically dark or light in color. When the English were freezing in their castles, they preferred dark woods and dark colors to keep them warm—at least psychologically. When the French were entertaining in their boudoirs, they preferred light woods and pastel colors to stimulate gaiety.

Within each historical period there is a difference between the smooth styles of the city slickers and the rough styles of the country folk. The city slickers traveled, were rich, and had skilled craftsmen and a great variety of raw materials available to them. The fashions they formulated were of expensive materials and richly decorated. Later the country folk would follow the fashions, but they would simplify them. They would make them of less expensive materials in a rougher, sturdier style, and leave out lots of the ornament. The rough did not mix with the smooth.

You Can Make Your Own Marvelous Mix Pieces of a period work together because they have certain consistencies of size, shape, color, or texture. You can mix together furnishings from all sorts of periods and places as long as you keep some general consistencies.

In Chapter 11, "Life-style," and Chapter 12, "Style," you can look up what will be compatible with what you have.

The polished wood of the heirloom chairs and the slick surface of the glass-top table are both smooth and shining, similarly FORMAL in feeling. In a simple, understated modern interior, antique furnishings give a sense of dimension in time, a comforting continuity. (Design by Robert Caudle, FASID.)

5

HOW MUCH MONEY CAN YOU SPEND?

The money you can spend will, of course, determine what styles you can afford to buy. But no matter how little is jingling in your pockets or piled up in your bank account, you have to provide your home with the essentials.

BUY THE FURNISHINGS YOU NEED TO FUNCTION

What you do in your home will determine the furnishings you need. You may be lucky and already have some furnishings that fulfill your requirements.

Buy the Basic Necessities First

Bed or beds
Seating pieces for the living room (say a sofa and two chairs)
Window treatment for privacy and maybe darkness
Lighting
Bed linens and blankets
Bathroom linens
Kitchen utensils
China
Flatware
Some sort of table surface

Air-conditioning/heating units (may be supplied)

What Should You Spend on the Basic Necessities? If your bed makes your back ache, you may have a miserable morning. Your attitude may be rotten by the afternoon, and by the evening you may be exhausted. It simply isn't worth it! Buy a bed that keeps you comfortable. The same goes for seating pieces. *Buy the best you can afford.* Since you're investing in the best, you might select styles that will stand the test of time. Don't go kicky; go classic.

Second, Buy Those Other Items You Need for Functioning Like tables beside beds and chairs. You can start out with make-do designs and replace them with better pieces as you can afford them.

Buy Nonessential Items Last The nonessential pieces that complete your scheme can well wait until you can afford them.

A Buying Plan? You might decide what you want now, and then plan to buy a few major pieces each year. This idea not only gives you the time to save money, but has the added advantage of giving you the time to feel out exactly what you want.

A family with small children would be wise to defer the purchase of delicate or expensive pieces until the children are old enough to be careful of them.

YOU WANT VALUE FOR YOUR MONEY. HOW DO YOU GET IT?

There is a formula for figuring out the *real* cost of anything. It is: the initial purchase price plus the cost of maintenance divided by the days of usefulness. For example, a very expensive piece that will last a lifetime is a better value than a bargain piece that will wear out in a year or two and have to be replaced.

Before You Buy Anything, Decide How Long You Want It to Last   There is no use in spending lots of money on something that will outlive its usefulness to you. For example, the family that rents will not in the long run benefit from an investment in structural changes; the landlord will. Children will outgrow children's furniture. If you move often and don't take your furnishings with you, you will want to buy inexpensive items that you can get rid of readily. For example, wall-to-wall floor coverings are tough to take with you when you move.

If an item will get heavy wear for a long time, it is worth investing in the best quality you can find, because if a cheap item wears out, you will have the expense of replacement. It is also smart to buy a classic or simple style so you won't get tired of it, and so your room won't look dated.

Before You Buy Anything, Decide What Kind of Wear It Will Get, and What It Will Cost to Keep the Item in Good Repair   Wear depends on who does what in your home. Children are an automatic guarantee of heavy wear. If an item will get heavy wear, or medium wear over a long period of time, you will have to pay to keep it looking good. You might choose to spend more initially on an item that resists wear or that requires a less costly method of cleaning. Cleaning can be as simple as throwing slipcovers into the washing machine or as complicated as hiring a team of experts to do an on-location job.

Value Is Also What Works   Any item you buy must fit in with your life-style, with the space you have available, and with the furnishings you already have. *Never buy on impulse.* It can lead to disaster. Take your time. This book should help you realize what you need. The safest course is to buy nothing until you have planned the whole room.

YOUR BUDGET

There are all sorts of ways to skin a cat and to dress a naked room. Good design doesn't depend on the amount of money spent. It depends on appropriateness—appropriateness to your life-style, your space, and your furnishings. It also depends on making the most of your assets.

If you have a next-to-nothing budget, your best asset is color. Color has no price-tag and it can work wonders. A wall graphic, or a powerful poster, bright walls, or a lively upholstery can give the room a pleasing personality. IN-FORMAL furniture styles are the least expensive. Styles are usually simple and natural looking.

If you have a medium budget, it would be worthwhile to buy one super-good piece, and skimp on others. The special piece could dominate the place and give it real character. This would make a much more interesting room than one that was all-over ordinary.

If you have a large budget, you can afford expensive materials and FORMAL styles: butter-soft leathers, rare antiques, name paintings, intricate wood-paneled walls, handwork by master craftsmen, silk brocades. In this case, it would be best to be subtle with color and pattern. You don't want to overpower the quality of the objects.

A fine-quality antique or antique reproduction can last lifetimes. Furnishings made of the best materials and the finest-quality craftsmanship are good investments. With inflation they will be more expensive to purchase in the future. And if built to last, yours will increase in value with old age. The original of this canopied rice bed was made in Charleston in the 18th century. The Baker reproduction of mahogany exactly duplicates the original. (Courtesy of Baker Furniture Co.)

MONEY-SAVING IDEAS

For those who want a decorator look without spending much money, drama is definitely desirable. Color or pattern can create drama without costing much money. A bright color or bold pattern on the walls or on a large upholstered piece can make a strong statement and give a room character. Everything else can be organized to blend in.

Paint is about the biggest boon to a budget. You can paint the walls, the floors, the furniture. Coordinated color can make almost anything go together.

Wallpaper is a big bargain for the money. Pattern on the walls will make a room feel furnished, so you won't have to spend much money elsewhere. Emphasis on the walls will distract people's attention from the furnishings.

If you would rather emphasize the furniture than the walls, relatively inexpensive patterned fabric can cover a large upholstered piece and the windows for plenty of pizzazz.

FURNITURE No matter what your budget, you shouldn't skimp on your bed and most important upholstered pieces. You can cut corners on secondary pieces.

A word of warning: Avoid inexpensive furniture that is pretending to be expensive furniture. To the educated eye, it will just look like a poor substitute. If the piece simulates expensive or exotic woods and pretends it required handcraftsmen to carve it, avoid it. Look instead for clean lines, interesting, unpretentious textures, and zappy colors. The effect of inexpensive design is in its sweep, not in its subtlety.

Inexpensive Pieces There are (bless them), some manufacturers who make nice-looking designs at a reasonable price. Chairs, coffee tables, end tables, étagères, bookshelves, and dining furniture are among their offerings.

Director's chairs (also known as deck chairs and safari chairs) are useful as occasional chairs in a sofa grouping, as dining chairs, as chairs around a card table, or as desk chairs. They are available in foldable or nonfoldable versions. They come with canvas seats and backs in a wide range of colors, or leather seats and backs. The frame is available in a number of colors or wood finishes. Nonfoldable versions are often shown in metal.

Porch furniture can be used inside now, and put on a porch later—when you have a porch. Rattan or wicker pieces can give a room a nice textural variety, and right now they are a hot fashion item.

Many plastic pieces are inexpensive. Clear plastic can mix with anything and look like it takes no space. Brightly colored plastic furniture can add a lively color accent to a room.

Unfinished Wood Furniture Unfinished wood furniture is inexpensive, and you can have fun finishing it. You can paint it, stain it, wrap it, or do something snazzy with the hardware.

You can paint it to blend in with the walls, or to match another color in the room. You might make it part of a sensational supergraphic painted all over it and the wall. There are many ways to play with paint. You can use spray cans, stencil kits, or antiquing kits. Antiquing kits are available at most paint stores. Any amateur can do it, and mistakes may look like marks of age. You may have such fun with paint that you won't want to stop with one piece. You could match cube end tables with a chest or a Parsons table to create a custom "decorator" look.

You can stain and finish your raw wood furniture. To prepare the piece, sand it with a fine sandpaper until it's smooth, then dust off the grit. To stain the piece you'll need oil stain in the color of your choice, and clean rags. Apply the stain in the direction of the wood grain, and wipe up the excess stain with clean rags as you go along. Dry the piece overnight. To protect the piece and give it a foundation for waxing, mix equal parts of shellac and denatured alcohol and stir well. Paint a thin layer of this over the surface with a paintbrush. Let it dry overnight. The next day rub down the surface (in the direction of the woodgrain) with fine steel wool to take off the coarse shine. Wipe off the dust with a clean cloth. The last step is to wax. Use cheesecloth to apply paste wax all over the entire surface. Then wipe lightly with another piece of folded cheesecloth. When the wax becomes hazy, buff the surface along the grain with cheesecloth. Voilà!

You can wrap a piece of unfinished furniture in contact paper, wallpaper or fabric. Contact paper sticks on; wallpaper or fabric can be stapled on. The piece you wrap can match something else in the room—upholstery, walls, or windows.

You could do something special with the hardware. You might paint the knobs that come with the piece, or choose something else that you think will coordinate better with the room.

Second-Hand Furniture They say there's great pickings on New York's Park Avenue on Thursday nights. That's when the rich are supposed to discard what bores them. Actually, a lot of people discard what bores them. Tag sales, garage sales, estate sales (that's for what bores the relatives), auctions—all are super sources. Antique shops in unprepossessing places, second-hand furniture stores, thrift shops, and junk shops have other buried treasures. You can also find suites of furniture in downtown stores that specialize in repossessing unpaid-for furniture (how depressing).

What do you do with it when you've got it? Paint can cover a multitude of sins. If the piece has the wrong proportions, you might cut off its legs, or even add some. If the piece is too ornate for your taste, you might take off its decorations.

Mail-order Catalogs and Discount Distributors Mail-order catalogs often offer inexpensive furniture. Do you know of a shop where you can get designer dresses without the labels? Furniture manufacturers often do the same thing. They get rid of their excess stock by removing their label and letting a mass distributor sell it.

Homemade Furniture Anybody can buy some boards and brackets and hang shelves. And heaven knows what wonders can emerge from a basement workshop. If you're clever

It started with the secretary, found at an inexpensive, out-of-the-way antique shop; a twin bed bought at a department store; and a French chair found on the street with its springs hanging out. The clever, but broke, designer used her ingenuity. She cut down the headboards, found a fabric at one dollar a yard, had her sister quilt it for free, and upholstered the mattresses—all to make a delightful daybed. She had the Louis XV-style chair restrung, and then covered it herself with straight pins and a 59-cents-a-yard mattress ticking. The French cane chair she bought new at a bargain price directly from the manufacturer. The elephant was found at an inexpensive Oriental import store. The Plexiglas table came from a factory outlet, and the rug from a Greek handcrafts shop. She may have worn out her shoes, but she achieved a fine effect on a few sous. (Design by Pamela Ferry; photo by designer.)

with a sewing machine, you can make your own slipcovers and bedspreads.

Home-Assembled Furniture You can assemble all sorts of tables. For a dining table you can get a pedestal base from a restaurant supply store. You can buy an unfinished wood top, finish it, and attach it.

You can transform a two-drawer filing cabinet into an end table by painting it, stenciling it, or covering it with contact paper that coordinates with your room. Store rarely used stuff in it and face the drawers to the wall.

To make a skirted table, you can put a solid circle of plywood on top of anything that will support it. (You can even nail it to an old stool.) Then hang a floor-length cloth over it. The cloth may match your draperies or be a bright-colored felt. If you want, you can add a glass top to protect the fabric.

For a coffee table, you can put an overhanging plate-glass top over almost anything of the right height. If you live near, or are passing by, a construction site, you might pick up a cable spool. They make great little (or big) tables.

Bookcases made of bricks and boards are a standard money-saver. Orange crates and all sorts of other sturdy boxes may be piled up into bookcases, or even used as end tables. One fellow, who moves a lot, painted a carton he got from the grocery store, turned it over, and used it as a coffee table. When he moves, all he has to do is flip his box over and start packing!

To make a desk, use two two-drawer filing cabinets, separate them to create a kneehole, and lay a board, a hollow-core door, or a piece of plywood, possibly covered with Formica, over the top. You can select the parts in coordinating colors or paint the whole thing yourself.

You can make a sofa from a hollow-core plywood door. Just put a mattress on top, bolsters in back, and legs beneath. You can make a twin bed into a sofa, if you have big enough bolsters, or piles of pillows.

To make a headboard, you can have a piece of plywood cut the width of your bed and the height from the floor you want. Wrap it in fabric, stapling it on the back, and attach the board to the wall. (You might want a layer of soft foam cushioning under the fabric.)

For an even more inexpensive headboard, you can staple felt or other fabric to the wall in back of the bed, in whatever shape you want. Edge the fabric with narrow wooden beading or braid trim to give it a finished effect.

FABRICS Sheets can be used instead of the usual fabric or wallpaper. All sorts of big-name designers are doing sheets these days, so the selection is marvelous! Sheets have many advantages. They are relatively inexpensive, they are easily washed, and they are wide—from seventy-two inches (twin) to one hundred eight inches (king). This means that you will have fewer seams when covering a wall, and no seams when you're covering a table or making a shower curtain.

The sheet designer may have a sheet design coordinated with other sheets—say a pattern with a background fabric, a print with a stripe, a print with plaid, or what have you. This saves you the problem of guessing about what goes together.

You can do almost anything with sheets. You can make floor-length draperies or cafe curtains out of them. (You may want to line the draperies to give them more weight.) You can slipcover a chair, drape a table, cover a cush-

ion, upholster the walls, make a lampshade. Some sheet manufacturers will offer you specific suggestions.

ACCESSORIES Accessories can give a finished look even to a skimpily furnished room, and they don't need to cost a lot.

Pictures can be posters or inexpensive prints. An unusual fabric can be framed as a picture, or stapled to the wall with a wooden edging added. Pillows can place a little pow of color here and there. Pottery will jazz up a bookshelf or a tabletop. Nothing can beat plants and flowers for giving life and spirit to a room. Besides, they give off oxygen and make the air fresher.

THE FLOOR Painted floors are the cheapest solution of all. Both wood and concrete may be painted, and you can do it yourself. For example, a playroom floor might be painted bright lacquer red, spattered with black and white.

Resilient floors such as vinyl range in price

This couple had a love of the theater, a one-room apartment, and very little money. Instant DRAMA is achieved by painting the walls a shiny chocolate-brown and hanging a theatrical poster over the sofa. The convertible sofa is colored a neutral (and adaptable) beige. Other furnishings are inexpensive; most a crisp, bright white. (Courtesy of the Simmons Company; design by Douglas Sackfield.)

and can be installed by you. Vinyl-asbestos tiles are the least expensive vinyl. They are hard wearing and good looking.

If you want a soft surface for the floor, you could buy an inexpensive area rug, or cut an old rug to fit the size of the room. Regular wall-to-wall carpeting is usually too expensive, because in addition to the cost of the carpet, you have to pay for underlay and professional installation. However, there are clever ways to get around this problem: You could wait for sales or buy remnants. (Don't buy cheap wall-to-wall carpeting. It usually doesn't wear well.) If you buy a carpet with a foam-rubber backing, you eliminate the expense of an additional underlay. Carpet tiles can simulate wall-to-wall carpet. They come with backing so you need no underlay. You can install them yourself. You can have one color or mix tiles in a pattern.

THE WINDOWS If you want curtains and/or draperies, you will save a lot if you can make your own. Ready-made curtains and draperies are available in most department stores and cost very little, but usually ready-mades come in standard sizes and don't fit every window size and shape.

You can make a fabric look more expensive than it is! An inexpensive fabric will hang like a richer, thicker material if it is lined. A handsome braid trim will make a bargain fabric look like something special. If you want a formal-looking window treatment, don't buy those rich fabrics. They are outrageously expensive, and a rich material used skimpily looks miserable. It is better to buy a cheaper fabric and use it lavishly. Often inexpensive dress materials simulate finer fabrics. When they are lined, they look like the real (rich) thing.

You can make a window shade into something special. You can take a standard one and trim it with braid, or stencil a design on it. You can take a piece of fabric matching something else in the room and have it laminated to a shade.

You can frame a window with screens or

The first essential—a comfortable sleep sofa. After that, imagination. Carpet remnants arranged in a variation of the sofa stripes. A tile counter top picking up the striped theme and doing it in its own direction. Tractor seats for stools. And—why not?—sports equipment for accessories. A LIVELY, inexpensive answer. (Photo courtesy of the Simmons Company, Champion Building Products; design by Michelle Wiser and Carrie Ahrens, interpreted by Michael Love, ASID.)

panels on either side. You might staple a fabric onto the panels.

You can build a plywood frame around the windows—across the top and down the sides. (This structure is known as a "lambrequin.") It could be painted to match the walls or a window shade, or it could be covered with wallpaper or fabric.

GOOD INSULATION WILL SAVE YOU MONEY With rising fuel costs, why throw money out the window? Insulate. Close off the air spaces around the windows with weatherstripping and caulking. Window air-conditioners should be closed and covered from the outside, and all the spaces around them should be sealed.

Window shades can help to keep heat in in the winter and out in the summer. It is reported that they can save up to 8 percent in heating fuel costs and up to 21 percent in air-conditioning costs. Glass storm windows and draperies are also good insulators. Special thermal draperies, lined with foam, are particularly effective.

Don't obstruct radiators with draperies or furniture if you want to get the most for your money.

If you live in a house, it might be worthwhile to insulate the attic. If you're handy, you can do it yourself and then *you* can take credit for reducing your home's heat loss by as much as 25 percent!

PART TWO

YOUR NAKED ROOM

What do you say to a naked room? Ask it questions. Get to know it intimately while it is naked; then you will know how to dress it best.

Take out a sheet of paper for each room in your home. The next chapter will help you analyze each room's assets and liabilities. Note down any suggestions that seem to fit. Make sure to jot down any capitalized words that seem to be a good description of what you need.

Next, decide who will use the room and what will go on in the room. The people and the pursuits will give you a good idea of what the room should be like.

The requirements of the architecture, combined with the requirements of the activities, will lead you a long way down the path to discovering the right decorating decisions for you.

(Design by Sarah B. Jenkins, ASID, W & J Sloane; photo by Ken Heinen.)

6

WHAT IS THIS ROOM LIKE?

The room itself will give you a lot of design direction.

WHERE IS THE ROOM?

The position of the room on your floor plan will help you make a lot of decorating decisions.

It will help you decide *what* should go on in the room. For example, it's most convenient to have the dining area near the kitchen, or to have small children play near to where an adult can keep an eye out. It might be smart to place the den in a quiet area away from the main areas of activity. You might put the baby's bedroom close to a bathroom.

Where Are the Doors and Where Do They Lead? The position of the room on the floor plan and the location of the doors will indicate where people will walk, and how often.

Rooms on the path to the kitchen or other popular rooms will get heavy traffic. The floor-covering had better be DURABLE.

Does the room have a door that opens to the outdoors? If so, you should be concerned about tracked-in dirt. You might choose a flooring that is EASY TO CLEAN, patterned, or similar in color to the earth outside. People and dogs might also be wet when they come in; in that case, your flooring should be WATERPROOF or MOISTURE-RESISTANT.

Where Will People Walk? People will walk through the room from door to door, and also from door to light switch. Wherever people will walk, leave a passable path. All traffic lanes should be as short and direct as possible, and at least thirty inches wide. Lanes should be level, so people don't have to limp along with one foot on the floor, another on a rug. You can use furniture to direct the traffic path of preference. It is also useful (especially in corridors) to light the way.

Will You Want To See the Adjacent Room? Depending on the function of adjacent spaces, do you want a sense of separation and privacy or a sense of connection and communication—or sometimes one and sometimes the other?

Sense of Connection. Rooms that share your vision should look good together. If adjacent rooms are wildly different in style, they will set your eyeballs spinning in shock and give the whole home a jarring, uncomfortable effect.

You can coordinate adjacent rooms by sameness or repetition. To stretch space, the walls, ceilings and/or floors can be continuous.

You might use the same continuous colors, but change textures from room to room. For ex-

In this room the sofa is placed by the fireplace not only to make a comfortable conversational grouping, but to define the traffic path to the sun porch. For a continuous, flowing feeling the peachy colors of the living room are brought out to the sun porch—but mixed with white for a light, fresh feeling. (Design by Cathey Manley, IDS; photo by Stuart Manje.)

ample, you might want your living room to be more FORMAL than the adjacent den. Then in your living room, your upholstery materials would have smooth surfaces, and in your den they might have rough-woven looks.

You might repeat colors, but use them in different areas. For example, a hall can be STIMU-LATING because you don't spend much time there. You could paint the walls orange. In the adjacent living room, which you would want to be RELAXING, you could use orange as an accent color on lamps and throw pillows.

You might vary a color according to the temperature and lighting conditions of each room. For example, if the room is cool, you can mix your basic hue with warm colors. If the room is warm, you can mix your basic hue with cool colors. In a dark or small room, you might make your basic hue lighter. In a bright or huge room, you might make your basic hue darker.

You might repeat a pattern in adjacent rooms. For example, the walls in the dining room might be patterned to give liveliness to all that wood furniture. The living room might feature the same pattern in upholstery and/or draperies.

You might choose compatible, coordinating patterns for adjacent rooms. For instance, you might use "reverse" patterns, say a blue design on a white background in one room and the same design in white on a blue background in the other room.

Sense of Separation. If you want to block the view from one room to another, you can do it by erecting some kind of barrier—you can close a door, hang a curtain, set up a screen, place a tall bookcase (with a finished back) in the way, or use a camouflage of plants and trees. If you want a sense of separation without blocking the flow of air and space, you might erect a partial partition.

If you want a sense of separation without blocking the view, you might change the floor levels from one area to another, or hang clear Plexiglas panels from the ceiling to separate spaces.

Sometimes Connection, Sometimes Separation. Accordion doors, movable panels, draw draperies, doors that open and close, and light movable screens all give you this flexibility.

WHAT SIZE IS THE ROOM?

Just as your clothes look best if they fit you, furnishings look best if they fit the size of the room. Furnishings and patterns should be in the same scale as the room.

SMALL A small room is a limited space. It doesn't need its limitations thrown in its face. It usually needs to be treated with a light touch.

Furnishings should be small-scale or light-looking.

Small rooms are easily overwhelmed. Like the ninety-eight-pound weakling that can't lift the hundred-pound barbells, a small room can't carry strong dramatic effects. It must be soothed and smoothed and treated gently. You will want subtle effects, CALM contrasts.

If the space seems confining, you might strive for SPACIOUS effects.

If you like the COZY feeling of a small space, you might emphasize the room's coziness.

Furnishings should be small-scale or light in impact. Small-scale furnishings suit the size of the space. However, you want to avoid the cluttered look of lots of itty-bitty pieces. Use built-ins wherever feasible. Built-in seating or wall-to-wall bookcases become part of the architecture. They save space and keep the room from looking cluttered. Alternatively, choose one or two bigger pieces in light wood tones or light colors to mix with the small pieces. The big or medium-sized pieces can give grandeur and even a sense of architecture to the room. The large piece might be an armoire, a secretary, or a wall of shelves that can serve for storage. One large storage piece would leave the room far less crowded than several smaller ones. A large piece with small component parts can make a small room seem larger by subtle deception—shelves may be narrower than expected, seats lower, pads thinner. In general, long, low lines seem to stretch a space. Choose long rectangular and oval shapes rather than squares and circles. Also select furnishings with slender, crisp lines. They will look smaller than they are. (An aside: To avoid accidents, a curved coffee table is better in a small space than one with sharp corners.)

Pale and neutral colors are light in impact. Furnishings that are close in color to the walls or floor also have light impact. For example, if you have a piece of furniture that seems too big for the space, color it the same as the walls. It will seem to disappear. Avoid large dark or bright furnishings or pieces that contrast strongly with the walls. They would overwhelm a small room.

See-through furnishings of glass or Plexiglas certainly are light-looking, so are light leggy pieces of bamboo, wicker, or rattan.

The window treatment should be simple and uncluttered so it doesn't overpower the room. Avoid cascades of swags, heavy fabrics, and boldly patterned draw draperies. They will suffocate the room. Shades, blinds and shutters are all appropriate, and so are light open-weave or sheer draperies and curtains.

The focal point should not be overpowering. Something on the wall will save floor space. You might make a mirrored wall, a scenic wallpaper, a mural, or a picture the focal point.

A wall covered with mirror is great for a small room—it will seem to double the size of the space.

The color scheme should have subtle contrasts, not mind-boggling bold ones. You might choose one color and vary it lighter or darker, brighter or duller, and mix it with white (that's called a monochromatic scheme).

Pattern must suit the size of the room. In a small room, you will generally want a small-scale design. Small-scale designs on the walls tend to recede and make the walls look farther away. They also can give a subtle tex-

Sliding doors covered in the same scenic wallpaper as the rest of the room allow this bedroom a sense of separation from its adjacent bath. The scenic wallpaper is as refreshing as a walk in the woods. Its depth of dimension gives spacious feeling to the small room. (Photo courtesy of James Seeman Studios, Inc., Wallcoverings.)

tural effect. If you want a larger-scale design, choose one that is light and airy and has a sense of depth. Otherwise, it will be too aggressive.

A CALM room usually has very little pattern. However, a subtle pattern can be used lavishly in a small room. If the walls, windows, and large furniture are all covered in a subtle design in pale, cool, or neutral colors, the room will seem unified, uncrowded, and interesting.

MEDIUM-SIZED A medium-sized room places few decorating restrictions on you. It's easy to live with; you don't have to compensate for its character. Other factors besides size will probably direct your design.

Generally, medium-sized rooms need *medium-sized* furniture, maybe mixed with something smaller or larger (but not both).

A medium-sized room often looks small when it's empty. To an extent, the more you pack into it, the larger it seems—but don't get carried away!

LARGE A large room is a strong space. The furnishings need to be large-scale and strong just to hold their own. And just as no one can miss a basketball player when he walks into a room, large rooms are dramatic. They can handle DRAMATIC effects—bright, bold colors and strong contrasts.

If the wind is whistling through and your voice echoes, you might want to try to make the place more COZY and WARM.

If you are really turned on by having such a large space, you might emphasize its size by making it seem even more SPACIOUS.

Furnishings should be large-scale or strong in impact. The furnishings have to stand up to the size of the room to look like they belong. Use large or tall pieces, mixed with pieces of medium scale. Avoid furniture of small scale. It will look lost, or make the room look cluttered.

You can choose furnishings in dark woods and bright colors. Pieces in dark or bright col-

ors appear to take up more space than they actually do.

Furniture groupings may be large, and you may have several of them. It is normal to break up a large room into different areas of activity. Area rugs, furniture, or screens can define the areas, or you might change the floor levels with a platform or a sunken area.

A bold window treatment adds the proper balance to a large room. Here is the place for heavy draperies and swag valances. A small, understated treatment would look lost.

The focal point has to stand up to the size of the room—be dominant and DRAMATIC. You could have one red wall, a large painting, or a big bright piece of furniture. If the room is extremely spacious, you may want a secondary focal point—along a smaller wall, in a corner, or in front of a window. It might be a specially lit sculpture or a smaller painting.

The size of pattern should be proportionate to the size of the room and its furnishings. Large rooms need large designs.

WHAT SHAPE IS THE ROOM?

Not all of us have perfect proportions. Neither do rooms. Sometimes we have to be sly and trick the eye. Do you like your room's shape? If you don't, you can change it without lifting a hammer. Bright, warm, or dark colors make things appear nearer. Soft, cool, or pale colors make things appear farther away. Vertical stripes make things seem higher. Horizontal lines make things seem wider. The right dress is cheaper than plastic surgery or structural changes.

Do the halves of the room match? If so, the room will project a FORMAL feeling. It will seem even more formal if there are nice moldings and other delicate architectural detail. If the halves of the room don't match, its organization is looser and more INFORMAL. You can dress it accordingly.

SQUARE/BOXY If the room is square, it can

seem small. If it does, don't cut up the space.

Arrange furniture against the walls. Long, low pieces, such as storage units, bookcases, and TV or hi-fi consoles can carry the eye on a lengthwise path and seem to stretch the room. To reduce angularity, you can also soften the corners. Fill a corner with tall plants. Place a small sofa diagonally across a corner with plants behind.

Color can change the boxy feeling. Paint three walls in a pale color. Paint the fourth wall in a bright color. The pale walls will back off and seem farther away. The bright wall will seem to come closer. With these visual changes, you'll no longer feel that you're sitting in a box. Caution: Be sure to place some heavy-looking furniture on the wall opposite the bright wall to balance the room.

RECTANGULAR　Rectangular rooms whose width is more than half the length are usually the most pleasant.

However, avoid making a rectangular room look like a railroad car. Do not place all furniture so it points in the lengthwise direction.

This elegant room employs many space stretchers. A platform built up under the windows along the end and side walls creates a long horizontal line that seems to push the walls out. One wall is mirrored, doubling the size of the room by illusion. A long banquette is built in along the platform to preserve uncluttered unity. (Courtesy of W & J Sloane.)

This would happen if you placed a sofa along the long wall, flanked it with rectangular end tables, put a rectangular coffee table in front of the sofa, and hung a rectangular picture over the sofa. Your eyes would seem to be whipping down a tunnel. Stop the eye by putting furniture across the short end of the room, at right angles to the long walls. Round end tables, or a round or square coffee table, will also help you in avoiding the tunnel effect.

LONG AND NARROW　To make a long, narrow room seem like it has better proportions, you will want to cut its length, or stretch its width.

You can cut the seeming length of the room by placing furniture at a right angle to the long wall. Low furniture, such as a desk, a sofa, or a pair of chairs, can come out from the wall and serve to separate areas. The area in back of the seating can be used as a passageway, a dining room, or whatever. (Be sure that the back of the seating pieces is turned toward the traffic. Who wants to stare at the parade?) If you have a very long sofa, place it against the long wall, and let the smaller chairs come out at right angles.

High pieces such as a storage wall or high bookcases placed at a right angle to the long walls will seem to divide the space into two rooms. The new room you define may be used as a study area, a sleeping area, a den, a dining room—anything.

You can also cut the length of the room by interrupting the flow of the floor. You could change the floor level by building a platform at the end of the room. Also, if you place a pair of matching rectangular rugs side by side, perpendicular to the large walls of a long room, you will visually cut the room's length. Generally, wide horizontal stripes on the floor can make the room seem shorter.

Wide vertical stripes on the long walls will also seem to shorten the room. The eye will move from one stripe to the next and seem to take tucks in the walls.

Another way to shorten the vista is to attract the eye to the far wall. You could paint the wall in a bright, dark, or warm color, paper it in a pattern, or panel it. You might place a large eye-catching piece of furniture there.

The secret to stretching the width of a room is to create a line that seems to push the walls out. For example, place long low furniture wall-to-wall across the short end of the room. (It might be a sofa with tables on either side.) The row of furniture will create a strong horizontal line which will seem to push the side walls out. Another idea is to put horizontal or diagonal stripes on the floor. Diagonal stripes are even more dynamic than horizontal ones. They seem to force the walls to back up out of the way.

L-SHAPED If the el serves a separate function (dining, sleeping, music corner, study

An effective el treatment, this design shows both separation and coordination. An area rug defines the dining grouping, while the dining chairs feature legs of curves similar to those of the stool in the foreground. The dining chairs would look welcome in the conversational grouping. (Design by Garcia/McMaster.)

area), its decoration should set it apart from the rest of the room without making it distinctly different. Furniture in the two areas should blend.

The floor can provide a change. You might have wall-to-wall carpet in one area, hard tiles in the other. You might add an accent rug to the main area. You might change floor levels. Platforms aren't so hard to build.

Ceiling heights, too, can change to define areas.

You might suggest a separation between the el and the main room with screens, draperies, étagères, or even trees against the side walls at the opening of the el. Alternatively, you might place a divider in the center of the space and leave room for traffic paths around to the sides. For an open, airy look, you can hang Plexiglas panels or see-through fabric panels from a ceiling track.

To close off the space, you might use sliding screens or doors, draw draperies, or opaque panels of fabric. Tall bookcases or storage walls also can provide a visual barrier.

ROUND OR CURVED In a round or curved room or area, round or curved pieces of furniture will give a feeling of harmony.

DOES THE ROOM HAVE A FIREPLACE OR A VIEW, OR DO YOU WISH IT DID?

If you are blessed with a fireplace or a view, you have a natural focal point. You will want to draw attention to this asset and arrange furniture around it. If you can't count a fireplace or a view among your blessings, you can use the tricks of the trade to create a focal point.

How to Draw Attention to a Fireplace Imagine a roaring fire in the dead of win-

To draw attention to the fireplace, designer Donghia arranged furniture around it, a painting over it, and interesting accessories on the mantel. He even placed plants of graduated size to one side. They form a diagonal line that points to what he wants to be the center of attention. (Courtesy of Kroehler Manufacturing Company; design by Angelo Donghia.)

ter, the licking, dancing flames, the radiating warmth, and the appealing aroma. It's irresistible. But what about a fireplace when there is no fire? You have to do something to make it look interesting. Of course, you can decorate the hearth with andirons, a pile of logs, fire tongs, and a bin. In the summer, instead of logs you can arrange greens.

To make the fireplace stand out even more, you can paint it to contrast with the wall behind it. It might be a different color, or the same color in a gloss paint. (Shiny surfaces attract attention.) You might spotlight the entire fireplace wall. Put your most interesting accessories on the mantel and/or hang a picture or mirror above.

A Fireplace Will Influence Your Furniture Arrangement A fireplace is a heavy architectural feature. It needs to be balanced. Something of approximately the same size and mass should be placed to face it. It might be a sofa, an armoire, or a bookcase. Other furnishings should be grouped around the fireplace.

What do you do with the space flanking the fireplace? Bookcases are always a success.

They can be built in, if you don't mind making a permanent investment in your home. If you're on the move, mount shelves on brackets yourself, or buy portable bookcases or cabinets. Small lamp tables may also flank the fireplace. Small bachelor chests, narrow console tables, or even half-moon shelves bracketed to the wall will all hold lamps for reading in adjacent seating.

What if you have a fireplace with openings on both sides of the hearth? There's no wall to put furniture up against. What can you do? You can put a bench or an ottoman in front of the fireplace or to one side. You can place handsome side chairs on each side of the fire, facing into the room with their backs against the chimney breast. This is an old French trick—which provides easily accessible pull-up seating. A good-looking occasional chair can be placed diagonally in front of the fireplace. It would look cozier if it had a backdrop, say a folding screen, or even a tall tree.

The Style of the Fireplace Will Influence the Style of the Room Such a forceful architectural element as a fireplace will give direction to your decorating. The furnishings and the fireplace have to be compatible. Is your fireplace rough or smooth? Traditional or modern?

If you have a rough stone chimney, or a fireplace of brick, rough plaster, or unpolished paneling, your furnishings could be COUNTRY/RUSTIC. They should at least be INFORMAL. To stand up to the strength of the fireplace, furnishings must be sturdy and a bit rough-textured. Little delicate furnishings would look silly in such a room—like seating a big bear in a Louis XVI chair. A big sofa with a pine frame upholstered in tweed or corduroy would look appropriate.

If you have a fireplace of smooth marble, polished wood, or a design that shows delicate detail, you must not treat the room too roughly. It would be like taking a prima donna on a camping trip. Such skin is used to the soft life. The room should be dressed with more FORMALITY.

A traditional fireplace naturally harmonizes

The massive brick semicircular fireplace surely inspired this design scheme. Shapes are predominantly curved, and textures predominantly rough. There's a large leatherette sofa, a wagon- **wheel cocktail table, two scooped-out chairs of wicker, even an antique bedwarmer. Wall-to-wall carpeting softens the scheme. (Photo courtesy of Milliken Carpets.)**

with TRADITIONAL furnishings of the same inspiration. It can harmonize with other periods if it shares something in common—like the same sort of straight lines or the same sort of curves, the same sort of color or wood tone, the same sort of roughness or smoothness. If you want it to match modern furnishings, you'll have to change its facade.

The tried-and-true method of dressing up a traditional fireplace is to center a mirror or painting above it with candelabra or wall lights on either side. Instead of one large painting, you might hang a group arrangement.

A modern fireplace, of course, complements MODERN furnishings. For interesting emphasis it can contrast with a period piece or so, but basically, it needs to have something in common with the rest of the room.

For accessories with a modern fireplace, hang shelves on surrounding walls to display a collection, or to house a bunch of books. Spotlights hidden in the ceiling can set the show asparkling. Small paintings can be hung between the shelves, and plants and small sculptures can add intrigue. An attention-getting piece of art might hang directly over the fireplace.

If You Don't Have a Fireplace, but Wish You Did With the help of a carpenter or builder, you can create a fake fireplace. You can have the feeling without the fire.

If you want a MODERN style, the facade can be composed of a simple, modern shelf and a hearth made from wood, slate, or brick. Once these two elements are attached to, or set into, the wall, add the accessories—andirons, a pile of logs, a bin, and fire tongs. Only don't give anybody matches!

If you're looking for a TRADITIONAL style, you can find period mantels and surrounds in specialty shops, second-hand stores, and junk shops. You can even sometimes snitch them from wrecking outfits. Just attach them to your wall.

You can buy a free-standing stove. Many modern styles are Scandinavian in origin. They have a pot-bellied front, a hood, and a tall chimney. They are available in brilliant colors and in metal. Antique porcelain stoves are charming in traditional rooms.

If You Have a Super View, Draw Attention to It   If out your window you have a gorgeous vista of the countryside, or a scintillating view of the city lights, you will want to play up this asset. Keep your window treatment simple. Leave your windows naked or frame the view with draperies, shutters, or screens to the sides, and perhaps a table underneath. Avoid strong pattern at the windows. Pattern draws attention to itself, and you want to draw attention to the *view.*

To play at being panoramic, you might want to put mirror on the wall opposite the view to reflect and multiply the vista. To add extra special sparkle (especially to a view of city lights), you might want to line the insides of the window casing with mirror.

If you have a window wall next to a private garden, light up the exterior at night. The outside lights will take the glare off your windows.

If You Have a View and Want Privacy Too   You might want a versatile treatment so that at times you can shield yourself from cold drafts, too much sunshine, or a little peeping-Tom-foolery. You might draw side draperies, pull simple shades or blinds, or close shutters. To filter light during the day and block the view at night, you might choose a combination of sheer curtains and draw draperies.

You might consider a two-tiered treatment—particularly useful in bathrooms and bedrooms. Cafe curtains and shutters in two tiers allow you to close the bottom ones while opening the uppers. Roller shades that pull up from the bottom are useful too.

A Good View Will Influence Your Furniture Arrangement   Arrange your furniture so people can see out. Seating can face the view or be at right angles. If the view closes down at night, it's a good idea to place seating at right angles to the window. Then it can face something else of interest, such as a fireplace or a chest with pictures over it.

You might consider raising the floor level with a platform if that would improve your perspective of the view. You might build in a window seat.

A Good View Can Inspire Your Color Scheme   It is an excellent idea to repeat indoors the colors you see outdoors. The repetition will create a most happy harmony.

If You Have an Ugly or Boring View, Conceal it   If you want to let in some light and air, you can fuzz the view with glass curtains or casements. Blinds can be tilted to let in light while obscuring the view. (I'm particularly fond of those skinny-slat blinds.) Roller shades that pull up from the bottom can cover the view at eye level while still leaving an upper opening for air. Glass shelves can be installed in the window casing, and provide a place for plants or glass objects that will shine in the sun. If you want to dramatize the light while concealing the view, a piece of stained glass hung in front of your window would be inspirational.

If you don't care about light and air, you can erect a permanent barrier between indoors and out. A permanently down shade could have an original design on it. It could be a fabric shade matching something else in the room, or it could be part of a screaming graphic across a whole wall. You could block the view by fitting something into the window casing. It might be a charming old wood carving. It might be almost any kind of fabric. A tapestry, a fabric remnant, or even a decorative beach towel could be stapled to a simple wooden frame and then compressed to fit into place. It will leave no nail holes, and you'll have no recriminations from the landlord when you move.

If You Don't Have a View, But Wish You Did A room with a view need not have a window. Scenic wallpapers and murals give a get-away view into the distance without breaking down the walls. They, like windows, can be framed with draperies, if you wish. Scenics and murals are especially appropriate in sparsely furnished rooms such as dining rooms or foyers.

WHAT ARE THE WALLS?

What Are the Walls Made of? Stone, brick, various building blocks, and rough-textured plaster are strong materials. The room must be given an INFORMAL treatment. Brick is flattered by bright autumn colors and rugged color combinations such as brown/black/white, or orange/brown.

If you have wood-paneled walls, you must make sure that the wood tones of furniture do not conflict with the walls. If you live in a contemporary house with plywood walls, you can't do better than to use orange in your color scheme. Bright autumn colors are usually pleasant with paneling. It is possible to paint over wood paneling, but caution: Latex paints cannot be successfully applied over some bare woods.

If walls are covered with old paint or paper, you can work with it. You can strip it or scrape it to make a clean start, or you can cover it up. Alkyd resin paint will usually cover old paint or paper in one coat.

Smooth plaster walls are suitable for painting or papering.

What Condition Are the Walls in? Perfect walls are, of course, no problem. Imperfect, uneven, or cracked surfaces are. You can repair them or disguise them.

There are a number of decorative disguises for imperfect walls. A well-selected paint can camouflage. Choose the color and texture carefully.

The walls were in hopeless condition but costly restoration wasn't worthwhile. The answer is yards and yards of inexpensive fabric gathered on rods at the ceiling line and at the baseboard. Then, for added impact, a tent top. This truly is a Cinderella story. (Design by Warren G. Arnett, FASID, Gus Mestre, ASID; photo by Bob Braun.)

Recommended colors are light blue, light green, flesh color, ivory. Avoid white or lemon yellow; these colors will exaggerate the irregularities of the wall. Avoid glossy paint. It, too, highlights every imperfection in a wall. Textured paint, such as paint with sand in it, can conceal uneven surfaces, but it is a permanent treatment—not easily removed.

Wallpaper is a better camouflage than paint. Fabric-backed wallpaper is especially good. Alternatively, a backing paper applied before wallpaper can smooth out small bumps. Avoid unlined foil wallpapers. They require perfectly smooth walls. A wallpaper with a small all-over pattern is a good choice. It can disguise bumps and blemishes, and it will give an unobtrusive textured effect.

Fabric-covered walls are a heavier-duty camouflage than wallpaper. You can glue or staple the fabric to the walls, or you can hang it between rods attached at the ceiling line and the floor line. If the fabric hangs free from rods, it's easy to take with you when you move.

You can construct walls in front of the walls. You can attach low-cost four-by-eight-foot plasterboard over studs. (Then you might stucco the plasterboard to give it a textured effect.) You can panel the walls with wood to give the room textural and architectural dimensions. You might try plastic-laminate paneling; it comes in all sorts of decorative designs, and it can hide a multitude of sins. You can brick over a wall—just make sure that the floor can support the weight of brick. To minimize weight problems manufacturers have designed special kits of shallow bricks for facing walls.

Unsightly pipes and other non-attractions may be painted the same as the wall so they visually seem to disappear. You may hide them behind screens, draperies, or paneling. If your home is INFORMAL and whimsical, or if this is, after all, only the laundry room, you can paint your pipes a crazy color to draw attention to them for fun. You might even wrap them with hemp rope for a natural and textured effect.

The Size of the Walls　Furniture placed against the wall should be in harmony with the size of the wall. It should look neither crowded or lost. Movable pieces need a little breathing space on either side. Built-ins can go wall-to-wall and look fine, because they become part of the architecture.

A large uninterrupted wall space without windows and doors is a logical place for your largest piece of furniture. You could make this wall into a focal point by doing something interesting with the wall and by gathering other furniture around your major piece. For example, you might hang an interesting painting above a sofa, or a fabric panel matching the bedspread above a bed.

If all the walls are broken up with windows and doors, don't try to squeeze furniture against the small wall spaces. Pull furniture into a cozy grouping out in the middle of the room—either free from the walls or touching one side wall. In this manner the space by the walls will be left free for walking to and from all those doors and windows! You might put your bed out in the middle of the room and back it with your bureau.

Windows and Doors Need To Be Balanced　If the space is cut up by too many doors and windows, or if they are placed in random positions, you will want them to blend into the background. Cover them in the same color or pattern as the walls to minimize their choppy effect.

If doors or windows are equidistant or if they face each other across a room, they balance. You can paint them a different color from the walls and still achieve a harmonious effect.

If you have a nice-looking window or door with nothing equidistant or facing to balance it, you can balance it with furniture. Choose something of similar size. For instance, you can balance a door with a highboy, an étagère, or a bookcase. You can balance a window with a chest with a picture over it.

Special Problem Walls　Where the walls aren't vertical, or are part of a sloping ceiling, it is wise to treat walls and ceiling the same. Diamond-patterned wallcoverings are successful on such walls.

Walls broken up by jogs, alcoves, or niches might create a nifty nook for a special piece of furniture that seems to fit. An alcove, if it is big enough, can even become a focal point. It can be emphasized by a contrasting color, or by a border trim around it.

If the walls are thin and you can hear your neighbors, you will probably want to use sound-absorbing materials. Fabric-covered walls or paneling work well. You might use a thick Rya rug as a wall-hanging, or even carpet your walls. To avoid complaints from your neighbors, it would be wise to put your musical equipment and TV against outside or un-shared walls.

WHAT IS THE WOODWORK?

The term *woodwork* refers to any interior fittings made of wood. Most often it means the doors, window frames, mullions (the divisions between windowpanes), moldings at the ceiling line, and baseboards at the floor line. The term also includes other built-in architectural features made of wood such as mantels, paneling, molding on the walls, chair rails, dadoes, wainscots, pilasters, columns, and built-in cabinets or bookcases.

This large room was blessed with fourteen-foot ceilings and beautiful cornice moldings. To emphasize the moldings the designer painted them to contrast with the walls and ceiling and underlined them with a thin brass band. For continuity the window frames (and vertical blinds) are also white. (Photo courtesy of the Window Shade Manufacturers Association; design by Noel Jeffrey.)

NORMAL If the woodwork is normal, and rather boring, you don't have to pay special attention to it. Generally, it is painted to blend as closely with the wall as possible. It is often painted in a glossy finish, so that fingerprints may be washed off with water.

STUNNING If the woodwork is stunning and the room is large, you can emphasize the woodwork with a color that contrasts with the walls. Contrast in woodwork from wall color is welcome; it breaks up the space and makes it seem more COZY. Be consistent. Paint your doors and windows the same contrasting color in order to give unity to the scheme.

If the room is small, woodwork should still be similar to the walls. A contrasting color risks breaking up the space too much and

making the room look cluttered and confused. You can draw subtle attention to the woodwork by using paint in a gloss or semigloss finish.

If you have beautiful moldings around the windows, hang simple curtains or shades entirely within the window frame so as not to distract from the moldings.

If you wish you had traditional architectural detail, you can buy moldings and other architectural elements. They may be made of wood, plaster, or plastic. For example, to give traditional charm to a plain door, you can add wood moldings bought at any lumber yard. The moldings may be painted in a second color to emphasize them.

You can create architectural effects with wallpaper. You can hang a border trim around the ceiling line. You can place paper on the lower third of the wall and top it with a border or a molding to create the effect of a dado.

If you wish you didn't, you can minimize traditional moldings and door pediments by painting the walls and woodwork the same uniform pale neutral color. (You also could strip the moldings off the walls.)

WHAT ARE THE WINDOWS?

WHAT'S THE EXPOSURE? The exposure will affect which colors look good in your room. Intense direct sunlight because it has so much yellow in it will make colors seem hotter and brighter. To compensate, you might choose cool colors toned down with gray. Dim, indirect light will make colors seem colder and duller. You might choose warm, bright colors to give liveliness to the room.

Northern North light because it is indirect and virtually shadowless has the least effect on the purity of colors. This is why artists sleuth for studios with northern exposures. North light is cool. Cool colors such as blue and green will make the room seem cold. If you live in the tropics, this might be desirable, but if you live anywhere else you might want to choose warm colors such as reds and oranges to offset the natural coolness of the room. These colors would also brighten the room if it seems too dark.

Eastern With an eastern exposure, you get warm but not intense light in the morning, and shade in the afternoon. Your color choice will depend on what time of day you use the room. If you use the room only in the morning, you might want to use cool colors. If you use the room only in the afternoon, you might want to use warm colors because cool colors would appear very cold. If you use the room throughout the day, you might want to mix warm and cool colors, say in a scheme of blue with pink, or green with orange. If the room seems too dark, you will want to choose bright, light colors.

Southern Southern light is warm and bright for most of the day. In this room warm colors would seem hot, and bright colors would seem overpowering. Choose cool colors toned down with gray to absorb and soften the brilliance of the light.

Western With a western exposure you get shade in the morning as the sun rises. In the afternoon you get intense bright light full of red and yellow rays—working up (or rather, down) to the sunset. Warm or bright colors in this room would make it seem like a sauna with no exit. Choose cool blues and greens toned down with gray. If you eat dinner at the time of sunset, don't use this room for a dining room. You'll have to wear sunglasses to supper.

WHAT TYPE OF WINDOWS DO YOU HAVE?

If you'll want to open and close your windows for air, your window treatment can't be in the way! Different types of windows operate in different ways. Some slide, some swing, some simply stay shut.

The sliders include double-hung windows (the most common kind in this country, with two sashes that slide up and down), horizontally sliding windows, and horizontally sliding

patio doors. They don't present any particular problems, except that you need to be able to get to them easily.

The swingers include casement windows (with sash or sashes hinged at the side), awning windows (hinged at the top), hopper windows (hinged at the bottom), and jalousie windows (horizontal slats that pivot like a venetian blind). The swingers often have control cranks. Because the cranks would be in the way, you cannot have window treatments flush to the glass. If the window swings into the room, clear the way. You might hang overdraperies on swinging brackets, or you might have a track that draws draperies to the sides, out of the way.

The closed cases include most clerestories and skylights, picture windows, and window walls (although any type may have parts that open). Obviously, you don't need to get to

The architecture offered no moldings, except the basic baseboard, and French doors that wouldn't be opened. To achieve an elegant TRADITIONAL effect the designer dressed the windows with tieback draperies and a swagged fabric valance and on the adjacent wall hung a wallcovering simulating an Oriental screen. The horizontal division between the two parts of the screen creates a line of architectural interest. (Design by Robert Metzger; photo by Peter Vitale.)

them to open them, but you might want some conveniently rigged treatment so that you can cover them up when you want less light or more privacy.

Bay or Bow Windows Full of romance and old-world charm, the bay or bow window creates an alcove or a little recess in the room. It may be made of one large window or several (usually double-hung). Two or more windows set at angles form a bay; a rounded shape forms a bow. For great cozy comfort, the recess may be fitted with a window seat. The window itself would be at home with almost any style drapery, or fold-back shutters. This window may become the focal point of the room.

Here is the perfect place for putting the furniture you want to emphasize, such as a porcelain stove or an antique chest. A love seat and coffee table, a dining table with chairs, a draped table, or a desk and chair also work well. If furniture is emphasized, the window itself should provide an interesting and attractive backdrop.

French Doors French doors are usually standard-height doors with glass centers, usually hung in pairs. You can hang individual shades over the glass or you can mount shirred sheer curtains on rods attached above and below the glass. If you want overdraperies, hang them on swinging brackets that can move out of the way when you open the doors.

Fan-shaped Windows and Transoms Shirred glass curtains are ideal. The top rod may be curved around the window's arch to shape the shirred curtains into an attractive sunburst.

Dormer Windows In certain homes, the walls upstairs slant in line with the roof, but there are vertical poked-out places for windows. These are dormers. The dormer is often difficult to decorate because there isn't much space around it and you probably won't want to block whatever light there is. Cafe curtains,

simple curtains hung within the frame, roller shades, austrian shades (that rise in scalloped puffs), and roman shades (that rise in accordion folds) would all work.

Picture Window A picture window is a natural focal point. If you have a good view, you can complete the picture by putting a table underneath and two chairs to the sides. Your window treatment should be simple and understated so as not to detract from the view. If the view is no great attraction, make the window treatment itself draw attention. A color contrasting with the walls or an interesting texture would do the job.

Window Wall A window wall differs from a picture window in that it extends from wall to wall and from floor to ceiling. If your knees could see, they'd have a good view here. Sometimes window walls have sliding sections—often called patio doors—so that you can walk right out into the view. In this case you have to be careful not to obstruct passage. Separate shades might be a solution. You might mount draperies so they can all pull to one side, out of the way.

This extended dormer window is dressed with shutters. It's a clean, crisp treatment that doesn't crowd the space and offers total control of the light. To take advantage of the view, a window seat was built in over a radiator. An open grill below allows the heat to escape. (Design by Everett Brown, FASID; photo by Yuichi Idaka.)

Since window walls integrate indoors and out, this might be a clue to composition. You can bring the outdoor colors in. You can also repeat the natural woods you see.

Since the people outdoors can see in just as well as you can see out, you might want to make some provision for privacy, like drawing draperies or pulling blinds at night. At night a window wall can become a spooky big black expanse. Lights can reflect an unpleasant glare. The obvious answer is to cover your windows, but you can also light up the outdoors. Illumination outdoors breaks up your black wall and allows you to continue to see freely.

Window walls also present a problem of balance. When left naked, they are light—so light, in fact, that they disappear. The wall opposite a naked window wall might also be treated lightly—maybe with mirror, to reflect the view. If you dress your window wall in heavy draperies, bright colors, or bold patterns, it will look overweight. The other side of the room will look like it's stuck on the up side of a seesaw. Window walls are successfully dressed in wall-to-wall light casement cloths, or in wall-to-wall vertical blinds.

Ranch (or Hopper) Window Maybe it was designed for a man sitting on a horse to look in through. This is a wide window (or windows), usually less than two feet tall, set high in the wall. It is usually a real problem to decorate because its proportions are often poor in relation to the wall, and it is often too high to relate to the furniture. In old houses, such windows are sometimes called "piano windows." They were designed to have an upright piano under them. In ranch houses these windows often appear in the bedroom—to put the bed under. (A high headboard helps.) The ranch or hopper window is conventionally treated with draperies ending at sill level. If it is treated in the same color or pattern as the wall, its awkward shape will be less obvious.

Clerestory Windows These small, shallow windows let in light from on high. They are a row of windows under high eaves, or under the peak of a split shed roof. Their distinguishing characteristic is that they form a "clear story" over a solid (usually inside) wall and hence over an adjoining roof. Clerestory windows can give you sunshine while allowing you privacy. If the sunshine gets too strong, it is best to get up-from-the-bottom roller shades to fit the windows.

Cathedral Window A cathedral ceiling is a soaring ceiling, often found in today's A-frame homes. A cathedral window is a triangular window on an end gable wall under a cathedral ceiling. It is best dressed simply, if at all.

Skylight or Sloping Studio Window These windows bring in sunshine from the ceiling. If the sunshine is too strong, get professionally installed window shades on tracks.

WHAT SIZE ARE YOUR WINDOWS? The size of the window will indicate how much emphasis it merits. Of course, its actual measurements will tell you how much material you need for draperies and/or curtains, and the exact size for shades, shutters, blinds, or structural treatments.

Large A large window with a good view can be the center of interest in the room. You can frame the view with curtains to the sides and a table underneath.

If you will cover the large window, cover it with something understated—such as a casement cloth or vertical blinds. Bold colors or bright patterns would be too much in such a large expanse.

Medium-sized You might want to make this window look more important. Give it a good frame. Leave shutters open to the sides, or hang draperies out over the wall. A patterned fabric would add to the impact.

Small You will not want to emphasize the puny proportions of this window. Make it match the walls so it doesn't draw attention.

Different Sizes Windows of different sizes in the same room present a problem. You will want to blur their differences. You can make them all blend into the walls by making them the same color or pattern as the walls. For example, you could have roller shades made of a fabric matching the wallpaper.

You can make them look the same by building some kind of structural treatment over them—grilles, latticework, lambrequins. Then you could conceal the differences with shades or curtains. You might even fake sunlight by concealing a fluorescent light behind camouflaging curtains.

You can make them look the same by hanging curtains or draperies cleverly. For example, say you have a large window and a smaller window. The curtains could conceal part of the large window, and be hung out over the wall by the smaller window, so the two windows look the same.

You could hide the problem, if the windows are on the same wall, by hanging a unifying drapery over the whole mess.

Long (Horizontal) Vertical blinds look especially effective at long windows.

Tall, Thin A simple fabric panel, shirred or gathered at the top and set into the window frame, can't miss.

WHERE ARE THE WINDOWS? To achieve a harmonious balance, opposite walls, and the halves of each single wall should be equally weighted with furniture or windows or doors.

Equidistant or Facing Marvelous. If you treat the windows the same, they will balance each other.

Almost (But Not Quite) Equidistant or Facing You can make the windows look like they are in a balanced position. Hang your draperies well out over the wall surface to give the illusion of a window in the proper position.

Window Alone and Unbalanced Balance it with a piece of furniture of similar size, say a chest with a picture over it.

Windows at Odd Intervals You can make them match the walls so their position is not noticeable. In some cases, the simplest solution is to extend draperies from floor to ceiling across an entire wall. It gives a unified effect. However, it does take yards and yards of material.

Corner Windows Two distinct windows may meet at a corner. There they are, exchanging views, while what do you do? Might as well consider them married and treat them as one.

A Window Alone in a Corner Hang a mirror of the same shape as the window on the other

Corner windows take on a special charm when handled as a single unit. A cotton-covered valance turns the corner to unite the two windows architecturally. Then tieback curtains, matching the wallcovering, smooth out the broken-up walls. A ledge built under the windows unifies them further, covers radiators, and creates space for shelves. (Photo courtesy of Breneman, Inc.)

wall of the corner and treat it the same as the window. You'll have double the effect.

DO YOU HAVE AWKWARDLY PLACED RADIATORS AND/OR AIR-CONDITIONERS? The answer is to camouflage and unify.

You might cover up the whole wall with draperies—floor to ceiling, wall to wall. Hang them out in the room far enough so the air-conditioner doesn't make a bulge. (Some fabrics may shrink or stretch in front of heating or cooling vents. Be sure to ask for a fabric that is "dimensionally stable.")

You could choose a lower tier of cafe curtains with tie-back draperies. The tier can cover that air-conditioner, and be pulled aside when you want.

Shutters may be repeated to conceal unsightly radiators below the windowsill. Actually, all sorts of structural treatments can camouflage radiators. You could build a box around your radiator and cover the front with cane, metal mesh, wood slats, or any other airy material that will let the heat out.

Radiators the same color as the wall behind them don't attract attention. Don't worry about them.

WHAT IS THE FLOOR?

If your floor is on or below ground level (say in the basement), you may have a problem with dampness. Certain floorcoverings cannot be used. Absorbent materials are to be avoided. Do not use cork tiles, linoleum, felt-backed vinyls, or wool carpet.

The condition of your floor will indicate how much preliminary work must be done before you can add the floorcovering.

WOOD Your decorating tasks are simplified. You can have the wood floors polished and waxed as a background for an attractive area

rug. Or you can finish them with gloss or satin polyurethane so that you can wash them with water.

You can paint or stencil a wooden floor, but unless you protect it with coats of polyurethane, it will need to be repainted with regularity, say once a year.

You can lay rugs, carpets, vinyl tiles, other resilient floorcoverings over a wooden floor. A new wooden floor can be nailed to a wooden subfloor. You can do almost anything, but *you cannot have masonry work done over a wood floor.* The weight would be more than the wood floor could support. If you would like the look of masonry, you must try a resilient look-alike—a brick-patterned vinyl, for example.

CONCRETE You *can* have masonry work done over a concrete floor. As a matter of fact, masonry work *requires* concrete flooring.

Wood floors can be installed over a concrete base.

Resilient flooring such as vinyl tiles can be laid over concrete. Just make sure the concrete flooring has no damp spots. Damp spots will unglue the adhesive and cause the flooring to pop up. Asphalt tile and vinyl-asbestos tile work well over concrete.

With the proper underlay, carpeting can be applied directly over concrete flooring.

The cheapest thing you can do with a concrete floor is to paint it. If you're feeling inspired like the artist Jackson Pollock, you might splatter it.

WHAT IS THE CEILING?

You'd be amazed at how you can manipulate its sense of height.

TOO LOW There are several devices for making the ceiling seem higher. The tools are color, line, and lighting.

Light or pale colors are airy. They create a

SPACIOUS feeling. Painting the ceiling white or off-white is a safe and sure way to make it seem higher. If your wall color is fairly light, add white and slosh it on the ceiling. Painting the ceiling sky blue is also rather suggestive of space. (Have you ever seen a church ceiling with angels and cherubs ushering the way to sky-blue heaven? That's the magic of sky blue and deep-perspective design.)

Any vertical lines will seem to stretch the height of the ceiling. When a ceiling seems too low, the distance between the floor and the ceiling seems too short. Vertical lines make the eyes go up and down, and make the length seem longer. You can create that vertical line by putting a pattern of vertical lines on the walls. You can have paneling installed on the vertical. You can dress your windows with floor-to-ceiling vertical blinds or straight side draperies; both create a long line that seems to say, "See, this is a big distance." Avoid those horizontal valances over the top of windows, because they cut across the vertical line you are trying to establish. Draperies themselves might be vertical in pattern. Tall folding screens are another vertical presence. You might even paint the upright elements of your bookcases a contrasting color to emphasize the vertical line. Another trick: Low-backed furniture and low-to-the-ground furniture make the distance to the ceiling seem higher.

Indirect light reflecting down from the ceiling gives the illusion of raising the ceiling height. You might have tall lamps casting light directly up at the ceiling, and then reflecting light back down into the room. Cove lighting (bulbs hidden behind a molding attached on the upper wall near the ceiling line) do the same. Cove lighting seems to create the sensation of serenity and openness.

If you're daring, you might cover the ceiling with mirror. That's sure to bring on a high!

TOO HIGH When a ceiling is too high, those vertical walls seem awfully long. It's a long distance up and down. The thing to do is to break up the vertical view by having something cut across it.

You can draw a horizontal line around the walls at the point where you'd like the ceiling to be, and then paint the ceiling color down to that line. It will have the effect of lowering the ceiling.

You can draw a horizontal line a third of the way up the wall and treat the bottom differently from the top. (The bottom will be called a dado.) This treatment will break up the height of a tall wall.

Wallcoverings with horizontal designs or paneling installed horizontally will seem to lower the ceiling.

Wider valances across the window tops will serve to bring down the ceiling. They should be an inconspicuous color so you don't notice their width. Interest along the bottom edge of the valance will attract your attention so you see no higher. You might make valances of plywood and shape the bottom edge in an interesting way, or you might have some border trimming along the bottom edge. You might choose draperies with horizontal stripes.

Other things besides horizontals can interrupt the vertical view. A grand chandelier

To create an intimate effect for convivial dining, the designer deemphasized the height of the ceiling. He kept objects of interest low. He trimmed the bottom of wider-than-usual valances with ruffles. He painted the mirror between the windows and over the mantel with trompe l'œil (fool-the-eye) objects of only a certain height. He lowered a light over the dining table. (Photo courtesy of Celanese House; design by Chuck Winslow, ASID.)

dropped down from the ceiling will catch your eye so you look no higher. Be careful, though, that it doesn't literally catch your eye. Hang it high enough to clear the heads of tall people.

Color can help. Dark colors seem closer than light ones. In order not to defy gravity, ceilings generally should be light, but you can add a little gray to your wall color and paint the ceiling with that to produce a subtly lower look. If you use a color that is very different from your walls, be sure to use the color in noticeable quantity elsewhere in the room. Then the ceiling will seem like it belongs to the room and didn't just fly in from outer space.

Lighting can help. Light coming directly down from the ceiling makes the ceiling seem lower.

If all else fails, of course, you can hang a dropped ceiling. A grid with light from above creates a slick architectural effect. I know a clever woman who painted her ceiling black, then created a lower white grid by stretching string back and forth. A fabric tent creates a soft decorative effect. You can even hang a board on wires from the ceiling and put plants on it. Stained glass or other translucent materials may be installed with a light behind them. They can create a most DRAMATIC effect, especially if the light is on a dimmer.

DIFFERENT HEIGHTS If your ceiling is of different heights, and you want it all to seem the same, paint the higher part slightly darker and the lower part slightly lighter so the two parts will have the effect of being the same.

Of course, you can hang a dropped ceiling. If your dropped ceiling will be a real architectural construction, you might take advantage of the opportunity and incorporate recessed lighting.

You might want to make ceiling heights feel different in adjacent rooms. For example, to make your living room feel especially SPACIOUS, you could paint the walls and ceiling of the adjacent entryway in a very dark color and the walls and ceiling of the living room in a very light color. Then when you walk from the entry into the living room, you will feel as

though you have walked from a small confined space into a great big airy one. A little tricky, but it works! For the same effect, you might use cove lighting in the living room, and a light shining directly down from the ceiling in the entryway.

IRREGULAR A sloping ceiling, or one broken up by oddly angled jogs, seems to have more grace if it is covered with the same material as the walls. Where the walls aren't vertical (such as the sloping ceiling in a Cape Cod house), a diamond pattern works well.

DARK Dark ceilings seem heavy and should be balanced by dark floors and strong furnishings. In this case, you will probably want light-colored walls to give the room some brightness.

WOODEN CEILING OR BEAMS If you have a ceiling or beams in a natural wood finish, you will probably want the woodwork to match.

If you would like wooden beams, but don't have them, you can purchase synthetic look-alikes. They can create a cottage effect without weighing down the ceiling.

UGLY BEAMS Ugly beams will seem to disappear if they are painted in the same light color as the rest of the ceiling. They also might be bleached to a lighter wood color to make them look less heavy.

HOW MANY ELECTRIC OUTLETS DO YOU HAVE?

You have to figure out how to light up your room at night. If you don't have enough electric outlets, you should call the electrician and add more before you begin decorating.

7

GETTING IT TOGETHER

Now's the time to pull the pieces together.

WHO WILL USE THIS ROOM?

The first requirement for any room is that it be comfortable and convenient for the people who live in it.

GENERAL   If this is a GENERAL room, all users must like the scheme. Have a group conference first to decide on styles and colors. If there will be a lot of activity and traffic in the room, the furniture should be sparse. A room used by both sexes should be UNISEX, unless the room is one person's particular hideout.

If people of vastly different sizes share the room, you'll probably need furniture of different sizes to make them comfortable. If a little lady is married to a long-limbed basketball player, she's got a problem. Furniture of approximately the same size goes together. How is she going to combine large and small furniture in one room and make them seem to go together? She's got to underplay the big piece to minimize its size, and emphasize the small piece to make it look bigger. She can underplay the large piece by making it blend into its background. It can be the same color as the walls or floor. She can make it an unnoticeable neutral. She can play up the small piece by covering it in a punchy pattern or color.

SHARED   You might like to divide the territory in a shared room—particularly in a room shared by children. You might actually draw a line down the center of the floor. Alternatively, you can use furniture to separate the space. You could use a free-standing storage unit or a bookcase. I know a clever designer who built a double-decker bed with a difference. He placed the bed in the center of the room. On the lower level, he built wall up one side of the bunk. On the upper bunk, he built wall on the other side. With this clever squared-off S shape, he made two private rooms out of one!

INDIVIDUAL If this is one individual's room, the design should reflect his or her preferences. The person's age, size, sex, interests, and inclinations can give you guidance. (See Chapter 2.)

WHAT WILL GO ON IN THIS ROOM?

What activities will go on in this room? Make a list of them. Then look up each activity in Chapter 3. Write down the furniture required, and any suggestions for furniture arrangement or appropriate atmosphere. (If you want to avoid making a room look cluttered, try to think of furnishings that can work in more than one way. For example, a desk beside a sofa can function as an end table.)

Do you have any furnishings that would meet your needs? If you wish, you might refer to Chapter 4 to see what decorative treatments your furnishings suggest.

What furnishings do you still need to buy? Are they a priority or can they wait? For ideas on how best to budget, see Chapter 5.

WHEN WILL THIS ROOM BE USED?

Time spent determines how dramatic the room can be, and how tough the furnishings should be.

CONSTANT USE A room used constantly should be RELAXING. If the scheme is too dramatic, it will quickly become tiresome. If it is too calm, it will quickly become monotonous.

High-activity areas in constant use require DURABLE furnishings. Examples are the family room, the kitchen, the bathroom, and certainly the children's rooms!

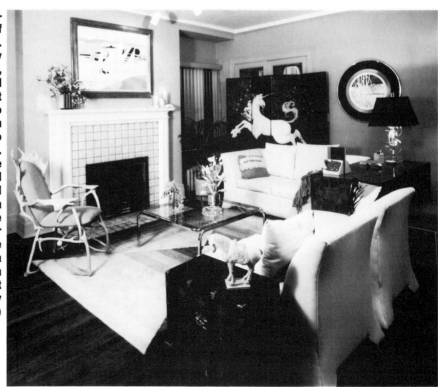

Who uses this room? A just-married couple with a love of life and a distaste for cleaning. What do they do here? They enjoy conversing, reading, doing desk work, and entertaining their friends. What furnishings did they have to work with? His and hers from previous apartments. When do they use the room? All the time. The result? A RELAXING, simple scheme with two upholstered chairs facing the fireplace and a matching sofa to the side, a desk functioning as end table to the sofa, and his horn chair set off alone on the other side of the fireplace. Pattern in a rug, a painting, pillows, and a painted screen add interest and liveliness. (Design by Pearl D. Snyder, ASID.)

PART OF THE DAY   When? Which part of the day? The natural light at that time of day will affect your color choice (see Chapter 6, pages 69–87). If the room is used mostly in the evening, light sunny colors will make it look warm and cheerful in night light. An illuminated outdoor garden would be refreshing.

Rooms that are used only part of the day can be more DRAMATIC than rooms used constantly. You won't stay in the room long enough to get tired of it. For example, a dining room can stand brighter colors and a more stylized scheme than the living room.

A room used part of the day takes less wear and tear than other rooms, so you can pick more delicate furnishings and fabrics. However, it still doesn't hurt to have fabrics soil- or stain-proofed.

OCCASIONALLY FOR SHORT PERIODS

Rooms that you pass through quickly can be DRAMATIC. As a matter of fact, the room must make a quick impression, or it has missed its opportunity. No one stays long enough to see subtleties. Entries, foyers, corridors, and powder rooms can all take a strong statement.

WHAT SHOULD THIS ROOM BE LIKE?

That is truly up to you. But here is a general analysis according to room types. Label each room in your home with the characteristics you want it to have.

THE LIVING ROOM   Who uses it? Everybody. The living room is a GENERAL room, it should be UNISEX.

For what? The main activities of a living room are usually conversation and entertaining, so the atmosphere should be comfortable and RELAXING and should express cheer and hospitality. Comfort means many things. It

Who uses this room? A single parent and his teenage son. Both men prefer casual living and easy cleaning. A commercial artist during the day, the father likes to paint in his leisure hours, and he likes to show off his work. What goes on in this room? The room is used for conversing, eating, and entertaining. When is the room used? It gets constant, hard use. The result? A sturdy modular sofa, a DURABLE wood coffee table, fabrics and flooring that take tough treatment, paintings on display, and an eating arrangement in back of the sofa by the kitchen door. All simple and EASY TO CLEAN. (Design by Jack Shanahan, ASID.)

means choosing furniture that suits the size of the people using it. It means controlling the temperature, noise, and light so they are not offensive. It also means creating an atmosphere that makes people feel at ease. Avoid creating a museum atmosphere. It will make your guests nervous that they will spill, trip, or knock something over, and they'll long for escape. Comfort might also mean some sense of softness and luxury. You might choose soft textures such as carpeting and cushy upholstery.

For how long? Because a living room is used constantly, it shouldn't be too stimulating. It should be relatively RELAXING and easy to live with.

THE ENTRANCE HALL OR FOYER Who uses it? Strangers who ring your doorbell. The entrance hall or foyer should screen the living area of your home from the curious eyes of casual strangers. Friends. The entrance hall should welcome your guests and serve as an introduction to your home. It should give them a foretaste of what they will discover in the rest of your home. The general style of decoration should be related to that of other rooms.

For what? Basically, for coming and going. You need enough room for people to pass through the door or group together to say hi or good-bye. People put their coats on and take them off at the entrance. You'll need a coat closet, and if the weather is wet, a WATERPROOF flooring. Since people like to catch a quick glimpse of themselves as they come in or out, a mirror would be appreciated. They might like to lay down a package or hat for a moment, so some sort of free surface is handy. Since it's easier to put on boots while sitting, you might want a chair. For your own convenience, you might want to store your gloves and scarves in a chest by the coat closet. If the entrance is large or your home is small, you might want to use your entrance for dining, or for an extra sitting space.

For how long? People pass through quickly. The room must have instant impact; it can be STIMULATING.

Who uses these rooms? What does he do here? The room on the right is his foyer, where he welcomes guests and displays plants. The center is his living room, where he reads, relaxes, and entertains. And the room on the left is his kitchen-dining area where he cooks, eats, entertains, and does desk work. When does he use these rooms? The foyer he uses only briefly. The living room he uses constantly, and the kitchen-dining area he uses for regular short periods. The result? The foyer and kitchen have STIMULATING red walls. The living room has CALM white walls with a wooden wainscot. The living room, done in modulated tones of cream, beige, and brown, achieves interest through a variety of textures. Plastic laminates, used all over the home, ease cleaning. (Design by William Ismael, ASID.)

THE DINING ROOM Who uses it? All members of the family, guests. It is a GENERAL room; it has to please everybody.

For what? Basically, for eating. A WARM, STIMULATING atmosphere encourages sociability and digestion. Since food does sometimes slop and spill, you may well want the room to be EASY TO CLEAN.

Since a dining room is used only part of the time for meals, it might be used at other times for other activities. It could act as a library if you store books along the walls. (It's great to have reference books handy to support your point at dinner.) Desk work could be done at the dining table, provided suitable lighting is arranged. You might mount a TV high on the wall, so it doesn't attract undue attention when it is off. If you want to listen to music, you can put a speaker or a violinist in the corner. If the room is large, you might arrange upholstered seating pieces for conversation. A chair or a sofa might convert to a bed, or you can conceal a bed behind curtains or screens.

For how long? If the dining room is used only part of the day, it can be STIMULATING. If a number of people use the dining room for meals every day, the furnishings should be able to stand a certain minimum of hard wear. If the dining room is used rarely, furnishings can be more delicate.

DEN/LIBRARY/STUDY Who uses it? This may be Dad's office at home—his private retreat—or it may be a general room used by the whole family. If the room is mostly a man's, it may be MASCULINE.

For what? Desk work and reading are the main activities of any den. They are quiet pursuits and require a QUIET atmosphere. If space allows, other activities can be delightful in a den. It's a nice place for a quiet conversation, or an intimate evening alone with Beethoven, or a challenging game of chess or backgammon. Dinner for two in front of the fire also has something to say for it.

For how long? The den is usually used for intermittent long periods. The mood should be CALM.

Who uses this room? Clearly a person who adores the sea and sailing. What does he do here? Sleeps, studies, reads, and does desk work—not to mention daydreams. When does he use the room? All the time. The result? Materials are downright DURABLE. The room is CALM in tones of brown, and almost everything is designed to suggest the sea. (Design by Jack Shanahan, ASID.)

GARDEN ROOM/PORCH Who uses it? Everybody.

For what? Basically, for sitting and enjoying the sunshine, plants, and flowers. A garden room should have a sunny INDOOR/OUTDOOR effect. All kinds of activities can occur here—conversation, reading or handwork, eating, drinking, entertaining, games, hobbies (especially gardening).

For how long? The garden room/porch may be a seasonal room used mostly in the summer. If so, you will want to achieve COOL effects. (For use in the winter, you might like to add a rug.) What time of day will you use the room? You may have to control the light so it's not too bright at midday.

THE KITCHEN Who uses it? The cook. The cook should select the scheme and things should be arranged for his or her convenience. Everybody else might use the room for eating, or just for keeping company with the cook.

For what? Preparing food, cooking, and cleaning up are certainly the main activities of the kitchen. The place has to withstand spills, moisture, cooking fumes. It should be EASY TO CLEAN. The kitchen can have a food theme—after all, this is what this room is all about. You might choose a wallpaper with a design of celery stalks or spice jars. You can hang molds or copper pots and pans on the walls, adorn counters with canisters.

If the kitchen is large enough, it's convenient to have an area for eating. It could be a counter, a free-standing table, or a breakfast nook.

For washing and ironing, you might hide a deep sink, a washer, and a dryer behind folding doors. An iron and ironing board might be stashed in the closet. Cleaning equipment—mops and brooms and Mr. Clean—might keep company in the closet. Often the kitchen acts as Mom's office. If you have the space and the inclination, the kitchen might also function as a family room for playing, reading, and watching TV.

For how long? Sometimes the cook is in the kitchen longer than he or she would wish. It's

Who uses this room? A couple who has retired to Florida but comes back to Chicago for the summer. What do they do in this room? Affording a beautiful view of the lake, this sun porch is used for almost everything. When do they use the room? Constantly. The result? Easy-maintenance materials that create a COOL impact. The floor is black-and-white checkerboard vinyl, the upholstered seating and rug are textured white. The straight-back chairs, which repeat the grid of the floor, are black, as is a Parsons table. For flair, round tables are draped in silver, and a painting in hot colors is attached to the ceiling—a wonderful idea for a room without walls. (Design by Marilyn Rose, ASID.)

best to soothe the spirit with a CHEERFUL atmosphere. The room should be stimulating enough to make the cook feel creative, but not so stimulating that energies are exhausted before bringing out the pots. The mood should be RELAXING.

FAMILY ROOM/RECREATION ROOM You might make a spare bedroom, the basement, the garage, or part of the kitchen into a family room.

Who uses it? Every member of the family and their guests might use this room, or it might be the special hangout of the kids.

For what? Basically, a family room is used for active play and for entertainment and hobbies. It is a room where you are more likely to put in the dog than put on the dog. The atmosphere should be rugged and relaxed, DURABLE, EASY TO CLEAN, INFORMAL. It's a place for fun and frivolity—for high good spirits. To encourage a merry mood, make the room STIMULATING. Active play is usually noisy. If you want to quiet the noise down or keep it from traveling to other rooms, you can insulate for sound. Active play requires free floor space, and furniture that isn't easily knocked over or damaged. (Your active play might also include a Ping-Pong table or a pool table.)

For how long? A family room is usually used constantly. It had better be DURABLE.

THE BATHROOM Who uses it? A bathroom can reflect the personality of the person or persons using it. You may want a sophisticated and formal feeling in a guest lavatory, or a joyous young feeling in a child's bath.

For what? Washing and grooming. The bathroom is the place where people take care of their bodily needs. They usually like to do this in private. The activities of the bathroom involve water; therefore, materials should be WATERPROOF/MOISTURE RESISTANT.

Optional activities are myriad. For reading you might provide storage spaces for books and magazines, and maybe even a comfortable chair. For dressing, you might have a small stool or bench, a full-length mirror,

Who uses this room? A young married couple who doesn't take life too seriously. What will they do in this room? Sleep, make love, dress, joke, laugh. When? For how long? Who knows? The result? A fantasy environment complete with carousel horse and tent top. The furnishings are serivceable and inexpensive. (Design by Pearl D. Snyder, ASID.)

closets and drawers for clothes storage, or even a frilly dressing table. You might want a telephone extension in the bathroom. Stereo speakers on the walls. A desk. You might have a cozy couch for napping after the bath. If you have the space and money, you might make your bathroom into a luxurious health and beauty spa with sunlamps, a whirlpool, a sauna, exercise equipment, a massage table, and a masseuse!

For how long? A bathroom that is used constantly should be EASY TO CLEAN.

CORRIDORS AND STAIRCASES Who uses them? Everybody.

For what? People have to use corridors and staircases to get where they are going. Light the way so they can see where they are headed without tripping or falling. Because corridors and staircases connect rooms and floors, their decorative treatment should be coordinated with the rooms they connect.

For how long? People pass through quickly, so the effect can be STIMULATING. (One of my favorite effects is a gallery of pictures or paintings on one wall, lit by a ceiling track light.)

BEDROOMS Who uses them? The design of a bedroom should be entirely dictated by the person or persons who use it. A bedroom is a highly personal place. It is often a person's only retreat from the rest of the world. It should make him or her feel secure, relaxed, reinforced. The person should be surrounded with the things he loves—be it pictures of the grandchildren or of baseball batter Hank Aaron.

For what? A bedroom can be used for many things, but most of all it is a place to be private, to get away from the others. How can you enhance that privacy? Ideally, the bedroom is located at some distance from the living room, so you really can keep the others at a distance. You can close doors. You can soundproof the room so the outside noises don't get in, and the inside noises don't get out. Thick, heavy textures will absorb sound and seem to shut out the world.

Basically a bedroom is used for sleeping and for dressing and grooming. If a bedroom is used exclusively for these purposes, it can be designed to look like a bedroom. The bed can be the focal point. If a bedroom is used just for sleeping, a small space is sufficient. Alternatively, you might prefer the bedroom to be your private living room. In this case, you might like the beds to look more like sofas.

For how long? Children and teens tend to spend a lot of time in their bedrooms. Materials there had better be DURABLE. Adults tend to spend less time in their bedrooms, and they are also more careful. Materials can be more delicate.

PART THREE

TRANSLATING WHAT YOU WANT INTO DECORATIVE IDEAS

What do you want your home or your room to be like? Look up the words that you want to describe your home or room and see how they translate into colors, patterns, styles, and so on.

8

MAINTENANCE

Your happiness in your home might depend to some degree on how much you have to fuss over your furnishings. If you like to fuss, fine. You can select delicate designs that yearn for your tender loving care. If you don't like to fuss, you'll be frustrated if your furnishings ask more from you than you want to give. You would be wise to select EASY TO CLEAN and DURABLE designs.

Besides your own feeling for cleaning, you must consider what will happen to a room during normal use. You'd rather your child play tag outdoors than in your living room, right? There is also the more subtle subversion that can come from tracked-in dirt, from leaving a whiskey glass on a wooden coffee table, from kitchen grease splattering the walls, from spilling on your lap and finding your napkin on the floor. Consider the consequences. Select furnishings that can cope with the problems you might have.

EASY TO CLEAN

The secret to easing cleaning is to choose easy-maintenance materials. Plastic is a star in this respect. Vinyl or vinyl-coated wall-coverings and wall paneling are easy to wet wash. You can even get crayon off them. Window shades can be laminated with patterns coated with washable plastic. Vinyl floors and wood floors covered with polyurethane can be swabbed down with a wet mop. Plastic-laminate surfacing, like Formica, can cover counters, desks, what have you, and make cleaning a cinch. Chairs can be upholstered in fabric-backed plastics, like Naugahyde. (Some of it even looks like leather.) Furniture made all of plastic is easy to wipe clean, and some of it can be left outdoors. Plastic truly is a modern miracle for the harried houseperson.

Glass and ceramic tile are also easily washed. You might want to cover your cocktail table with glass so you won't see all those awful liquor rings after a party. Glass tops can protect the surface of any table. They are great on draped tables. (You don't have to wash the fabric so often.)

Most woods are easily dusted and polished, but they are vulnerable to stains and burns. Never wash untreated wood with water. It warps.

Paint is dust-free. Enamels and glossy paints can be washed. You might want the woodwork around doors and windows to be semi-gloss or gloss paint so you can get the fingerprints off.

As for fabrics, before you put them to use, treat them with a stain-repellent finish such as Scotchgard or Zepel. You can have it done, or do it yourself. Some fabrics can be bought al-

This child's bedroom is a breeze to clean. The bed, bench, and desk are covered in Formica plastic laminate, a cinch to wet wash. The bed is built down to the floor so no dust balls can roll under.

The mattress, quilt, and pillows are covered in easily laundered, colorful cotton. (Photo courtesy of the Formica Corporation; design by Ristomatti Ratia.)

ready treated. Otherwise, choose what's washable. And maybe no-iron. By the way, you can shake dirt off shiny fabrics like chintz.

COLORS Dulled colors can help you hide dirt. You might select a carpet by the entrance that is the same as the color of the earth outdoors. You might conceal your dog's hair by choosing a carpet in a color close to his coat.

PATTERNS Patterns can conceal dirt and spills. For a rug under the dining table, pattern is better than plain. Even tweeds and heathery mixtures camouflage soil.

TEXTURES Smooth is easier to clean than rough. One swipe with the dust rag or mop and you've got it all. Uneven surfaces get little bits of dirt in the crevices and cracks. They can be a nuisance to a housecleaner in a hurry.

STYLES Built-ins are wonderful; they become part of the architecture. No dust balls can roll under or around. The old Shakers had the right idea about cleaning. They built the heavy storage furniture into the walls and left the light furniture out in the open space. Light furniture is easy to shove around when you're sailing through with your mop and pail.

LIGHTING Lighting installed in the ceiling saves dusting.

ACCESSORIES The fewer accessories, the less there is to dust. Pillows might have zip-off washable covers.

WATER-PROOF/MOISTURE RESISTANT

The entrance hall in a wet climate, any bathroom or kitchen, a house by the beach, and all outdoor furniture should be resistant to wetness. Your key to easy maintenance is to choose materials that are nonabsorbent.

If you want a hard floor, use ceramic tile. Marble, slate, and flagstone are hazardous because they are slippery when wet. If you want wood, cover it with a couple of coats of polyurethane to protect it from warping.

If you want the semi-softness of a resilient floor, choose vinyl. Rubber tile is slippery when wet (if it is smooth). Linoleum is sensitive to moisture.

If you want a soft rug or carpet for the floor, choose one made of man-made fiber. Nylon, polyester, and polypropylene olefin (used in indoor/outdoor carpet) are nonabsorbent and resist moisture and mildew. Avoid wool; it absorbs moisture.

For the walls, paint can provide a moisture-resistant sealer. Wall coverings that are vinyl or are coated with vinyl are waterproof, and so are vinyl tiles and plastic laminates. Ceramic tiles are old-reliable. Wood may be sealed to resist water.

Furniture made of plastic or glass can take moisture. Aluminum won't corrode like many metals. Much metal furniture designed for outdoor use has been treated to take the weather. Lacquered fabrics don't absorb like your favorite paper towel. Wetness sits right there, waiting to be wiped away.

For accessories—there's your sponge and rubber duck.

DURABLE

Any area where a child plays had better be durable. Materials must take tough treatment.

Durable treatments for the walls include oil-based paint, which is washable. (Water-based paints are not easily washed.) Plastic and vinyl-coated wallcoverings are immune to soiling. They are colorfast and keep their freshness. Vinyl wallcoverings are even more so. Vinyl tiles and plastic-laminate paneling can take the same tough treatment. Ceramic tile is hard-wearing as well as waterproof. Wood paneling, a favorite for family rooms, is not only durable, it offers insulation.

TEXTURES Textures may be hard or soft, rough or smooth. The point is that they should stand up to wear.

For the floor, resilient treatments are the

Muddy, sandy, rain-soaked feet walk in this back-door entrance. The WATERPROOF, DURABLE quarry-tile floor is ready for them. The family likes to gather in this seating area by the kitchen before meals in order to be sociable (and also in order to check on the cook's progress). A little horseplay is often the way of the day. The furnishings are made of tough stuff—laminated wood, wool, solid wood, and canvas. (Photo courtesy of American Olean Tile Company; design by Benjamin duPont.)

This room, shared by two sisters, is DURABLE and EASY TO CLEAN. The floor is patterned vinyl. The beds are built-in bunks with storage below. The desks are made up of boards over file cabinets. And the pillow chairs would be hard to hurt. The shutters at the window are suitably sturdy. (Photo courtesy of GAF Corporation; design by Abbey Darer, ASID.)

best. They will repel or withstand stains from spilled foods, finger paints, and even dog doo. Vinyl tiles can be highly decorative, and they can take a lot of punishment. Other choices are sheet vinyl, vinyl-asbestos tiles, rubber, and linoleum.

Hard-surface floors are fine. Wood is durable, especially if protected by coats of polyurethane. Quarry tiles can be used for heavy-duty areas inside and outdoors. However, hard tile floors are tiring to the legs and feet if one stands for long periods of time; they are also not a soft surface if someone falls.

Soft-surfaced floors can cushion falls. Children can run their trucks over low tight pile. High shaggy pile is warm and friendly. Tight construction of carpet is essential for good wear, so choose one with dense pile for heavy-traffic areas. Uncut pile (the kind that forms loops) wears far longer than cut-pile carpeting—especially when short and closely packed.

At the windows, fabric treatments should be practical. Practical fabrics include strong linens, burlap, cotton, ticking, chintz. Practical fibers are certainly those that are washable. You might choose one that needs no ironing. Check labels and hang-tags to be sure. Ny-

lons, polyesters, acrylics, and other synthetics are all sold under various trade names. Shutters will last for years, and so will those skinny-slat blinds.

STYLES Furniture should be hard to damage, easy to maintain, and sturdily built. Some durable sturdy styles include EARLY ENGLISH, EARLY AMERICAN, some EARLY COLONIAL, some SPANISH, PENNSYLVANIA DUTCH, and SHAKER. Some plastic furniture takes tough wear. You might not mind if hand-me-downs and early marriage purchases suffer the slings and arrows of outrageous fortune. Most furniture made of laminated woods can take very tough treatment. Bentwood can bounce. Think of the lion tamer with his bentwood chair! Avoid rickety period pieces and styles that seem too formal.

Avoid veneers, finishes, and upholstery materials that are easily damaged or stained. Tabletops must resist stains and perhaps cigarette burns. Some wood surfaces easily ring or stain. You can protect them with a sheet of glass, or you can choose a glass-topped table. Formica and other plastic laminates are highly durable, resistant to staining and other damage. They are scrubbable, and many are brightly colored and highly decorative. (Many serving counters and units come with plastic-laminate tops which keep stains from penetrating.) Some modern manufacturers have developed special finishes that are impervious to cigarette burns. Ceramic-tile surfaces are sturdy and easily washed.

As for furniture upholstery, there isn't much you can't scrub off Naugahyde or other vinyl plastic. Vinyl can look like leather, but it is much much cheaper, and very hard wearing. Olefin fabrics such as Herculon are a good bet for durability. As for other fabrics, heavy, closely woven fabrics last the longest, fabrics such as heavy rayon, wool, nylon, or heavy cotton. Special finishes can protect fabrics against spots and stains. Scotchgard, Zepel, Syl-mer are some labels. The fabrics may be pretreated, or you can spray on the finish yourself. Extra arm covers are a good investment. They are easily removed for cleaning. Always be sure to check out upholstery materials before you buy. The label, the hang-tag, or the salesman should tell you about the material's wearing and maintenance qualities.

LIGHTING Lighting should be out of the way in a room where there's active play. It can be attached to the ceiling or walls, or you can place fat and sturdy lamps on solid tables away from traffic.

ACCESSORIES For accessories, you can use plenty of pillows with zip-off washable covers.

A sun porch should be COOL and light-looking as well as DURABLE and EASY TO CLEAN. The architects provided horizontal movable lattice panels to control sunlight and a wood-slatted ceiling to absorb sound. The designers covered a resilient floor with a flat-weave rug and chose furnishings of light-looking wicker. Printed upholstery provides punch. Plastic ball chairs contribute to the sense of fun. (Design by Short & Ford Architects, Keith Irvine & Thomas Fleming, designers; photo by Horst.)

(Design by Rubén De Saavedra, ASID; photo by Daniel Eifert.)

9

ATMOSPHERE

To achieve physical comfort, you might have to adjust for the temperature, the lighting, or the noise. If you are feeling too hot or too cold, somehow that fact has an unpleasant way of dominating your mind. If a room is too dark, it seems depressing. If it is too bright, it can actually hurt your eyes. And as anyone who has been awakened in the middle of the night by a garbage truck knows, noise can be highly irritating. It not only interrupts sleep at night, it can ruin concentration during the day. If a room is too noisy, this is certainly a condition to be corrected. Alternatively, a room can be so quiet that it gives you the spooks. You will want to liven it up.

WARM EFFECTS

In addition to turning up the thermostat, you can create a warm effect with your decorating. Imagine sitting by a fire with a warm, thick blanket wrapped around you and your feet in a fur rug. That's warmth, right? Now what you can do to make your room feel warm is to suggest all the same things.

COLORS The bright, warm colors of fire: reds, red-oranges, orange-yellows. Browns, including wood tones, are warm too. They are actually just a darker, duller orange. In general, dark colors seem to come closer. What is closer is cozier. What is cozier is warmer.

TEXTURES Soft textures can actually insulate. Just think of getting up in the morning and putting your feet on a cold bare floor as opposed to a warm soft rug. Rugs and carpeting keep the floor from looking or feeling cold. The thicker and shaggier the carpet, the warmer the feeling (and the more informal).

Think of pulling heavy, lined draperies across the windows and sinking into a soft, fully upholstered chair. Fabrics can give a feeling of warmth too. Upholstered furniture and skirted tables give a warmer feeling than furniture exposing bare legs. Draperies around windows and four-poster beds can eliminate drafts. You can even insulate your walls by covering them with fabric (you might put actual fiberglass insulation underneath). The fabrics you choose for the room might be heavy and warm to the touch—like corduroy or velvet, or even tweed.

Wood-paneled walls also offer insulation while their color creates the sensation of warmth.

STYLES Furniture styles can be big, heavy,

elaborate. You might select big furnishings that seem to wrap around you and hug you—keeping the cool drafts from your back. A wing chair is an old favorite, designed for this purpose. In a conversational grouping, you'll want to keep the seats close together so you don't lose the heat of the conversation.

LIGHTING   Incandescent lighting is warm in color. It gives a toasty glow. And, of course, the glow is great with firelight and candlelight.

ACCESSORIES   When, baby, it's cold outside, you want something good to look at inside. In the winter, you can haul out your favorite doo-dads: marble eggs, mineral rocks, silver boxes, varied pieces of china or crystal—anything bright, vivid, or unusual. Remembering the warm textures and colors, you might bring out fur pillows, woolly wall hangings, red candles, warm wood carvings.

To give your room that special human warmth, you might display treasures that project your personality: memorabilia, collections, groups of pictures. You might put out flowers, candy, nuts, or booze to make the room even more inviting.

Walls sheathed in plywood paneling, armless sofas covered in chocolate-brown corduroy, an Indian-inspired rug in tones of red and ocher, a wooden storage system, even generously scaled swivel chairs of light brown wicker—all conspire to give this family room a WARM, friendly feeling. (Photo courtesy of the Simmons Company.)

COOL EFFECTS

Besides buying an air-conditioner or a Casablanca-style fan, there are other ways to achieve a cool effect.

Imagine yourself sweating and sweltering in the heat, feeling all sticky and icky. What would you like to do? You'd probably like to strip off your clothes and jump in the water, and perhaps sit in the water and sip an iced drink. You can make your room feel like you do in that pool.

COLORS   Pale and cool. Start with the color of water. Pale blues and greens. Light colors feel open and airy—even the pale neutrals. Nothing beats white for crisp cool. You might want woodwork in a gray stain. It's cooler than brown.

TEXTURES   Hard and slick. Think of the feel of that glass in your hand. It's smooth and slick and cool. Now think of how nice ceramic tile feels on hot bare feet. Ceramic tile and other masonry work require concrete slab flooring, and it is a permanent investment. (If you're using ceramic tile throughout the house, choose a color that is somewhat neutral—white, gray, beige, or Spanish red.) If you like the look of masonry, but have a wood floor or are going to move soon, choose a vinyl look-alike.

Furniture can be hard and smooth too. Steel and glass, see-through Plexiglas, and even Formica in light or cool colors. You might prefer wood in light colors.

Avoid a lot of fabric. It looks heavy and hot. At the windows, you may want only shades or blinds, or a simple casement. The fabrics you do use should be crisp and snappy, maybe duck or chintz. Plastics and leathers are smooth—but beware, you stick to them when you're hot! Cotton is comfortable.

Rough natural textures such as cane, wicker, rattan, and bamboo have a cool effect.

How refreshing to come back from the beach on a hot August afternoon to this slick, soothing, COOL room. The bare floors feel fine on burning feet. Comfortable seating perched above airy, open supports is positioned perfectly for cocktails at sunset. The swooping simple shape in the background is a room divider that functions for storage. (Design by Carder & Nahon, Architects; photo by designers.)

You could select matchstick or bamboo blinds and put your plants and paraphernalia in rough-woven baskets.

STYLES Furniture should be reduced to the bare minimum, and there should be air and space between the pieces. Furniture should be light-looking, clean-lined, without much detail.

LIGHTING You may want to filter or shade the natural light if the sunshine is too strong. Dim light can seem cool.

ACCESSORIES The best thing to do is to clean out the clutter so that the space looks free and open and uncomplicated. Do use cool green things like plants and flowers. You might have a few accessories that say "summer," like seashells and so on.

CHANGEABLE WITH THE SEASONS

Basically you're going to want warm colors and thick textures in the winter and cool colors and slick textures in the summer. But if you're like most of us, you're not going to want to repaint the room each season. What can you do to change the feeling without much effort?

It would be wise to have your walls and floors in a rather neutral color. You can leave floors bare in the summer and cover them with rugs in the winter. You can change the pictures on your walls—have ones with warm reds and oranges in the winter and ones with cool blues and greens in the summer.

You could hang heavy draperies in the winter and take them down in the summer, leaving only thin white curtains or bamboo shades.

Slipcovers make magic. For summer you can slip on a crisp cool chintz, maybe in a floral pattern.

You might have a reversible bedquilt or seat cushions—one side in a thick warm texture for winter, the other with a cool-looking print for summer.

You can make an effective change simply with accessories. In the winter you can bring out all your colorful little doo-dads. In the summer you can strip the place clean, and add refreshing touches of green.

LIGHTER AND BRIGHTER

Some unused spaces in your home might bounce to life if you could make them lighter and brighter. The basement and attic, for instance.

This Manhattan apartment is made LIGHTER and BRIGHTER with white walls, a white sofa, uncovered windows, and a large mirror reflecting the light and the view. It is clear in this apartment that white is the color that best reflects light. (Design by Irini Sarlis-Morfopoulos.)

COLORS Choose warm colors that have a lot of white in them. Pale colors make the most of what light there is. They reflect it and bounce it back into the room. White reflects all light. Other colors reflect light in proportion to how much white they have in them.

Yellow is the answer to a small dark room. It seems like sunshine. And because it is such a lightweight color, it can be used full-strength without becoming overpowering or making the room seem smaller. In a cold, dark room, light orange will lend a sense of coziness and cheer. Pale reds or pinks create a warm, happy glow that is most flattering to the skin. In a dark room, white, flesh, peach, and yellow are all good color choices for the walls.

TEXTURES Shiny surfaces reflect light too. You might paint your walls in glossy enamel. You might hang mirrors to multiply the light. You might polish your wooden floor or cover it with smooth-surfaced slick tile. For fabrics you might choose polished cottons or chintzes, or if your room is dressy and FORMAL, you can select shimmering silks and satins.

Smooth, slick surfaces create a cool feeling. If you don't want your room to feel too cool, this is another reason for choosing warm sunshine colors.

LIGHTING At the windows it's likely that you won't want to block what natural lighting there is (unless you happen to be a vampire). You can give the illusion of more natural light by placing a fluorescent tube in back of your curtains or shades.

ACCESSORIES For a shimmering effect, put glass objects on a table with a mirror behind.

DARKER OR DIMMER

If the light is too bright, you'll want to absorb some of it to make the room feel comfortable.

COLORS Choose cool colors that have been toned down by the addition of gray. Dark colors absorb light and keep it from reflecting back into the room. Black absorbs all light. Other colors absorb light in proportion to how much gray they have in them. To soften the natural light, add some gray to the color of your walls. Really dark colors on the walls will absorb so much light that your electric bills may go up. (Dark walls will also make the room seem smaller.)

If all that light is also making the room feel too warm, you will want to choose cool colors—blues and greens. Generally cool colors in grayed tones are a good choice for the walls of bright rooms.

TEXTURES Rough or uneven surfaces have the effect of softening bright light. Light will hit an uneven surface at different angles, so the light is broken up and not bounced back into the room.

On the walls, avoid glossy paint and other slick surfaces. If you do choose paint, use a flat, matte finish. If you intend never to change the walls, you can use paint with sand in it. Textured wallcoverings such as grasscloth, or even wallcoverings printed to look like textures, are useful. Think of those Mediterranean villas with their light-absorbing rough plaster or stucco walls. Even an uneven surface in white will help reduce glare. Rough-textured building materials such as building blocks, brick, and shingles are excellent for diffusing light and minimizing its impact.

For the floor, a rug of any kind is better than slick tile. To keep a cool feeling, rough-surfaced sisal is useful. If you want a warm (and informal) feeling, choose a deep carpet. The more uneven or the shaggier the rug, the more light it will absorb. If the floor must be hard, choose an uneven color or texture—something like brick or a mottled mixture. If the surface must be smooth and uniform, make it a dark, cool color.

To achieve a DARKER, DIMMER effect, these walls are covered with matchstick bamboo (maybe made from window shades). The jungle print on the sofa has enough variety to make fading less obvious. The pile of the rug and the nap of the velvet ottoman create subtly uneven textures that also help to absorb excessive light. (Photo courtesy of KayLyn, Inc.; design by Foster Hamilton.)

For fabrics, choose those with uneven surfaces such as tweed, or nubby weaves such as Haitian cotton, or those with nap, such as corduroy or velvet. Again, uneven surfaces absorb and diffuse light. Remember that soft uneven surfaces create a warm feeling. To avoid a sense of sweltering, you might want to choose cool colors.

You will want to choose materials that will not fade or rot in the strong sunshine. Choose colors that will fade in a mellow way. Avoid dark or bright solid colors; choose instead textures or prints that won't make fading so obvious. Line your draperies—it will make them last longer. Natural fibers fade sooner than synthetics, but synthetics rot sooner than natural fibers. (What a choice!) A cotton lining will help preserve any material at the window. Silk draperies should always be lined. This beautiful fiber can't stand up to strong sunlight.

LIGHTING For the windows, you will want to choose a treatment that softens and filters the light. Casement curtains, glass curtains, sheer curtains, open blinds, open shutters, and window shades will all do the job. If you will need to darken the room for sleeping, or for showing home movies, you can close shutters, you can buy special black-out linings for your draperies, or you can buy room-darkening window shades. If you want to reduce the lighting level in the room, choose opaque shades or tightly woven thick fabrics for the windows.

QUIETER

There may be honking horns and swearing on the street outside. There may be stereo freaks next door. There may be kids playing outside. You might well want to insulate yourself from all these sounds. Sleeping, studying, reading, and desk work require quiet.

Also, you or yours might make a lot of noise within the room that you don't want to travel down the hall. Noisy activities such as child's play, games, watching TV, or playing music might require acoustical insulation.

Belgian linen-faced velvet covers the walls and windows and is hung from the bed. Soft seating is fully upholstered. This room would be not only sensuous to the touch, but as QUIET and intimate as a cocoon. (Courtesy of the Belgian Linen Association; design by Richard W. Jones, FASID.)

COLORS Colors don't actually change the noise conditions in a room, but they do have a psychological effect. Dark colors feel quiet like a cave.

TEXTURES Soft. Texture is the key to controlling sound. Soft textures suck up sound. You may want carpeting to cover the floor—and walls. You may want full-width draperies at the windows to muffle outside noises and shut out the outside world. You may want to cover your walls with sound-absorbing fabric. You can even extend fabric to the ceiling and make a tent top. You may choose heavily upholstered furniture or even a draped table to soften sound.

Porous or uneven surfaces break up sound waves instead of bouncing them straight back into the room. That's the secret behind acoustical ceiling materials. Don't paint these ceilings. The paint will clog the pores and ruin the effect. With a carpet, the higher and thicker the pile, the more sound it will absorb. (Incidentally, cut pile absorbs more than looped pile.) If you are putting fabric on the walls, a cotton padding underneath will help to absorb even more sound.

NOISIER

Sometimes noise is a positive. Vigorous activities, play, and parties are stimulated by some noise. Some constant soft sound can block out or blunt sharper, more irritating sounds. Some offices actually pump in what they call "white" sound. It sounds something like the whirring of an air circulation system. To harmonize the sounds in the air, some people play music all the time.

COLORS Light bright colors can make you feel like whooping it up.

TEXTURES Hard, slick surfaces bounce sound around, almost make it echo. Doesn't your voice seem to echo when you enter an empty room? It's because there is nothing soft on the floors, walls, or windows. Hard, smooth walls reflect sound and so do bare windows. Hard wood or masonry floors make sounds reverberate. Vinyl floors are slightly quieter than masonry. (They are a good choice for a

This room is prepared for a party. The hard slick texture of the walls and the cabinetry will help bounce sound around and liven up the atmosphere. The carpeted floor and upholstered seating will absorb some sound so the party doesn't get too raucous. (Note that these art collectors mount their paintings on sliding tracks so they can change exhibits at will.) (Design by Gamal El-Zoghby; photo by Robert Perron.)

playroom or party room because they are easy to clean and available in all sorts of wonderful designs and colors.)

Furniture or accessories of hard metal, marble, or glass will perk up a room full of soft upholstery.

10

SENSE OF SPACE

What size do you want the room to feel? If you have a small room, you may want to make it feel bigger and more SPACIOUS, or you may want to emphasize its small size making it super-COZY.

If you have a large room, you may be so happy to have a large space that you want to do everything in the world to emphasize it, or you may feel the room seems too big, cold and empty and want to make it more intimate and COZY.

It's up to you. The size you want a room to feel depends on whether you feel comforted or confined in small spaces and on whether you feel exhilarated or exposed in large spaces.

The climate and the architecture may also affect your choice. In a hot climate, SPACIOUS rooms seem cooler; in a cold climate, COZY rooms seem warmer. If you have an attractive view you might want to link the indoors with the outdoors. An INDOOR/OUTDOOR effect will stretch your sense of space. If you are a modernist, it's good to remember that most modern architecture strives to create a sense of spaciousness.

COZY

You want the room to be cozy, to wrap around you and comfort you. It needs to seem to come closer. You will want to break up the large expanses of the floor and walls. You can break up the flow of the floor with a patterned flooring or with area rugs. You can break up the stretch of walls by painting the woodwork to contrast with the walls. Wall hangings, pictures, and paintings will also break up the wall space and make the room more intimate and interesting.

COLORS Bright or dark colors on the walls or floor will seem to draw the walls in closer. For example, you might have walls of chocolate brown, red, deep maroon, dark gray, plum, navy blue, deep mustard, or bottle green.

PATTERNS Pattern seems to take up space. Pattern used in large areas—the walls or floor—will make a room seem smaller. Most designs seem to come forward; flat (two-dimensional), bold patterns do so particularly. Large patterns are best used in large rooms. Large rooms can take more pattern than small rooms. Generally, the more pattern in a room, the greater its sense of coziness. (However, too much pattern can make the room look like a gypsy caravan—so stop while you're ahead.)

Soft textures and WARM colors help to make this room COZY and inviting. The area rug is deep. The generous L-shaped sofa is upholstered in camel corduroy. And the wraparound tub chairs are fully upholstered in brown with camel-colored dots. The walls combine warm wood and the camel color. The shutters, which conceal a radiator and an air conditioner, are dark brown. (Design by Michael Love, ASID.)

TEXTURES Soft, uneven textures are really cozy. Think of deep rugs, Grandma's afghan, or your fur throw. Soft carpets and fabrics convey a sense of warmth, intimacy, and privacy. For example, the windows may be treated to full-length draperies to cut out the outside world. Softly upholstered furniture, say in velvet or corduroy, is cozy to cuddle up into. Even a draped table will absorb sound.

Hard textures that are uneven are more cozy than hard textures that are smooth. Compare brick to marble. The variations in light caused by an uneven surface keep it from seeming slick and cold.

STYLES Furniture styles that are large, dark, or heavy seem to take more space than they actually do. Heavily upholstered furniture has more presence and seems cozier and warmer than leggy pieces that the winds can whistle under. You might select styles that seem to wrap around you. High-backed pieces, and even bookcases and screens, can be used to divide a large space into more intimate areas.

Furniture arrangements pulled out into the center of the room make that center the essen-

tial space. The wide area around the center is deemphasized. Large rooms can often handle several different groupings of furniture for conversation or other purposes.

LIGHTING Lighting only in certain areas makes the rest of the room fade out. Pink bulbs can make a place seem warmer and cozier. Light coming directly down from the ceiling makes the ceiling seem lower. You might create a room-softening effect with shadows. Put a light on the floor under a tree or other greenery. The light will come up through the branches and cast dramatic leaf shadows on the walls and ceiling.

ACCESSORIES Accessories in abundance can give a large room intimacy and personality. In addition to your strictly functional furnishings, you can add tables for displaying collections, pedestals for sculpture, plant stands and étagères.

If you have a lot going on in a room, it will seem smaller. That's sometimes a pleasant feeling. Think of the happy discoveries you make in a cluttered, crowded antique shop.

SPACIOUS

If you want to stretch a space, smooth it out. Sameness smooths. For example, if you want two adjacent rooms to seem like one large space, treat the walls and floor the same in both rooms. If you want to make a room seem larger, make the woodwork the same pale color as the walls, the ceiling the same as the walls, slightly lighter, or white, and the floor the same as the walls or slightly darker. Keep contrasts subtle so as not to break up the space.

Remember the magic of mirror. It can create the illusion of a room twice the size. You might hang a mirror on the wall, or mirror the whole wall. Just be sure that the mirror reflects a pleasant view, and beware of reflecting any conversational grouping (it makes people self-conscious).

COLORS Pale neutral or cool colors. Pale colors reflect light and make the place seem airier. Neutral and cool colors recede—they seem farther away than they actually are. You can't beat plain vanilla or white for walls. Other choices are: bone, off-white, champagne, pale ecru, and misty grays, greens, blues, and blue-greens.

PATTERNS In general, avoid patterns. They break up space, and you want to smooth out the space.

Three-dimensional patterns are the exception. They can give you a sense of space and depth where there isn't one. You might have seen scenic mural wallcoverings in dining rooms or entry halls—you know, the horses on the hunt, or the sailboats in the harbor, and like that. These give you a vista without a window.

Some other patterns for the walls can create the illusion of depth: small patterns that look like textures, and patterns with dark receding backgrounds.

And now a trick. I've said that sameness creates a unity that stretches space. Well, if you want to create interest in a small space on a budget, you can cover the walls, the windows, and the large upholstery in the same *subtle* pattern. Make sure it's subtle, or it won't work.

Usually, a spacious room doesn't have pattern on the walls or floor, but only on accessories.

TEXTURES Smooth and shiny. Smooth textures have no surface variety to attract attention; they keep the eye moving on. Whether hard or soft, you will want the floor treatment to be smooth and continuous, wall-to-wall. You may have hard ceramic tile, marble, or wood, or resilient vinyl. Ceramic tile is particularly suitable when the room should be waterproof, the climate is hot, or the home is a Spanish style. If you choose soft carpeting, make sure the surface is even, not shaggy or carved. You could use a room-sized rug, but avoid area rugs. You don't want to break up the flow of the floor.

Shiny textures reflect light and make the room seem more open and airy. Mirror is the most magical. Shiny wallcoverings of silver, gold, and other metals work in the same way as mirrors, reflecting and expanding space. There is also the shiny wet-look of some vinyl wallcoverings. Walls may be painted with glossy paint or lacquer. However, be cautioned—all these treatments must begin with perfectly smooth walls.

STYLES Furniture should blend into the background or be light-looking. Large, bulky pieces should be placed against the walls to free floor space. They should be colored the same as their background. A bureau or book-

This SPACIOUS room is always prepared for a party. To create an open, flowing feeling the designer defined areas with platforms, not walls, and covered everything continuously in carpeting. Large furniture, backed up to platforms or built in, is upholstered in a color similar to the carpeting. Furniture out in open space is light-looking or reflective. (Design by Yvette B. Gervey.)

This house by the lake is integrated with its environment. The large doors and windows bring the outdoors in, but the INDOOR/OUTDOOR effect is furthered by wood-paneled walls and a plain wood floor. Interior furnishings are simple, so attention is drawn to the great outdoors. (Design by Bass, Ferri, Berke & Johnson; photo by James L. McGuire.)

case the same color as the wall or a bed the same color as the floor will fade away and not seem to take much space.

Furniture out in the open space should be light-looking or leggy. Avoid putting full-length upholstery or slipcovers in midroom. They will stop the eye and interrupt the flow of space. Furniture made of see-through materials such as glass or Plexiglas will serve its purpose without seeming to take any space at all! Furniture made from reflective metal or mirror will seem to disappear, even while it is multiplying space by reflection. Furniture of bamboo, wicker, cane, or rattan has an airy, open, earthy look that won't crowd a small space.

Keep furniture to the minimum, and make arrangements light and airy.

The window treatment should be simple. Draperies, curtains, or shades at the windows might match the walls and blend into the background. Casement curtains and sheer curtains create a soft, light look. Blinds, shutters, or shades don't take up floor space within the room. I'm particularly fond of the light-looking skinny-slat horizontal blinds.

LIGHTING Lighting should be evenly distributed throughout the room to waste no space in shadows. Strive to bathe the room in soft all-over lighting. Lighting reflected down from the ceiling is effective, and it tends to raise the ceiling by visual illusion.

ACCESSORIES Accessories should be minimal. You might have one or two dominant pieces to give character to the space without crowding it.

INDOOR/OUTDOOR

If the inside is visually connected with the outside, then the space might seem as big as all outdoors! How do you make the connection?

Through the architecture. Large windows and window walls break down the visual barriers between indoors and out. A continuous flooring going from outdoors in links the two areas in a most attractive way. An outdoor deck might be matched on the inside with a wooden floor. If the outside floor is masonry, the inside floor could be the same—if your base flooring is concrete slab. If not, you'll have to use a resilient look-alike—a vinyl tile posing as flagstone, slate, or whatever—as wood sub-flooring cannot support masonry.

Continuous walls going from outdoors in also hook together inside and outside. For example, you might have a continuous wall in a weathered wood finish. The less distinction that is made between the two areas, the more they will open into each other.

Even without the aid of an architect, you can create an INDOOR/OUTDOOR effect. How? By repeating indoors what you see outdoors. Place a mirror opposite the view. It will repeat the image and double its impact.

If you see green grass all year long, pick a deep-pile carpet in the same green and then the indoor and the outdoor spaces will seem like one continuous lawn. In any case, make the same green the basis of your color scheme.

If you see plants, put more plants indoors. Then the whole area will seem like a continuous garden.

If you see trees, bring in the browns. You might have wood-paneled walls, and neutral nature colors for the floors. You might mix brown with sunshine gold for draperies and upholstery, and then add accents of bright blooming color, like orange.

If you see the sea, bring in the blues and greens. The sea might also be the theme of the room. You could have seascape paintings and a collection of seashells. To warm up the room, you might add accents that are splashes of sunshine—yellow and red-orange.

If you see a city skyline, mirror trim around curtainless windows helps gather up the glitter.

11

LIFE-STYLE

Certainly your home should fit your life-style. Furnishings that fit your life-style will create psychic comfort. To see what I mean, all you have to do is imagine a two-year-old toddler in a room full of precious porcelains. Or imagine yourself entertaining an ambassador and having to offer him a chair that is one foot off the floor. You get the picture.

If you live in a log cabin in the woods, or are sick of the city scene, you might want a COUNTRY/RUSTIC atmosphere.

If children will use this room, if it will be a place of play or other vigorous activities, if your attitude is relaxed and casual, if you don't have unlimited resources, you will probably want your room to be INFORMAL.

If sometimes you want to be relaxed and casual and other times you want to be more reserved and formal, a SEMIFORMAL style would suit your needs.

If children won't have run of this room, and you want this to be a place for quiet and dignified activities, if your personality is reserved and you have a bottomless budget, a FORMAL atmosphere is suitable to you.

Your life-style may change. You may come into an inheritance, and if you have children, they will grow up. How do you see yourself living in five years, ten years, twenty? It is a good idea to plan with your future in mind.

Your home should enhance the life you lead.

COUNTRY/RUSTIC

When is a RUSTIC room appropriate? You might be living in the sticks or in a simple country cottage. Rustic rooms are certainly appropriate to converted barns, ski lodges, and log cabins. This might be a vacation house where you want to relax and get back to basics. COUNTRY/RUSTIC styles are easy-care and can take tough treatment.

You might even be living in the city but be an honest, earthy sort of personality. You might be broke. It's best to be basic on no money, and it's a good investment. Simple, solid things last.

COLORS Bright and clear. No subtle shadings here. Colors are simple and straightforward. Red is red and blue is blue. (Such strong colors look great set off by large areas of white.)

PATTERNS Primitive or naïve. Gingham plaids and polka dots suggest the clean simple style of the country. Bright, flowery peasant motifs are fun too. Our own settlers offer examples. For instance, Pennsylvania Dutch

Rough-plastered walls and wooden beams begin the COUNTRY/RUSTIC feeling. Fabrics make the impact grow. Repeating a ceramic circle on the floor, a round table is covered first with ruffled gingham, second with a bright floral fabric, and third (for easy maintenance) with a glass top. The washable cottons are also on rounded wicker chairs. Bright, colorful, everyday objects such as pots and plates are used as accessories. (Design by Yvette B. Gervey.)

furnishings are best known for their cheerful painted decoration. Hearts and tulips, trees-of-life and peacocks, eagles, deer, and farmyard birds are painted on furniture and family documents. The same symbols are woven, embroidered, or appliquéd on fabrics and adorn pottery, tinware, and toys. Sometimes sayings were added.

The Scottish settlers in the Appalachian mountains painted their furniture with the motifs of the star, rope, barberpole, bellflower, diamond, and scroll. The Dutch colonists in New York, Long Island, and New Jersey painted their chairs black and decorated them with floral designs. The Scandinavian settlers in the Midwest painted their chairs with rococo scrolls and flower motifs like those in Scandinavia.

TEXTURES Rough or bold. The rougher and more unrefined, the more rustic. For example, the walls, floors, or fireplace might be of rough stone or brick. The walls could be covered with barnsiding or be paneled in pine or another unpretentious wood. The walls might be rough-plastered to show trowel marks and then whitewashed. The floors might be wide wooden planks. There might be big wooden beams supporting the ceiling. Furniture could be crudely crafted of solid common woods and simply stained or painted. Chair seats may be woven of rush.

The soft textures might have a handmade look. You could use hooked or braided rugs. Fabrics might have a homespun look like rough, heavy linens, or they might look hand-embroidered or hand-appliquéd. They might be sewn together in patchwork patterns.

STYLES Furniture styles are simple or unrefined. Examples are EARLY AMERICAN, some SPANISH, some FRENCH PROVINCIAL, PENNSYLVANIA DUTCH, and SHAKER. Ornament is not elaborate. There may be cheery painted designs, or crude carving. Wood turnings are common in traditional furniture.

The early settlers in this country and the peasant peoples in Europe furnished their homes with the basics. Since they had no closets, they made many storage pieces. They had large cupboards with closed storage below and open shelves above for pewter and pottery. They had high chests of drawers for clothes, low chests for blankets and the daughter's dowry.

Seating had simple lines. There might be benches by the table, rounded-back Windsor chairs and straight ladder-back chairs and a favored rocker. There might be a big trestle table or a gateleg or other dropleaf table that folds to save space. Babies began life in wooden cradles and worked up to four-poster beds.

Today we have other materials besides rough woods. Wicker, rattan, and bamboo convey an earthy, outdoorsy feeling. Simple plastic pieces in bright colors have a down-to-earth functional feeling. Light metal folding furniture is unpretentious. And hooray, today you can bring more comfort to the country with pillows and padding covered with washable fabric—maybe simple corduroys or cottons.

Window styles should be simple too. Windows might be treated to tied-back sill-length curtains in common fabrics, maybe with a ruffle at the edge. Simple shutters work well too.

ACCESSORIES Accessories are functional. The early Americans decorated their walls with firearms, earthenware, and china. The Pennsylvania Dutch hung up their spoons and kitchen utensils. Everyone hung up pictures of their elder relatives to keep an eye on the children. Samplers with inspiring mottos or morals served the spirit. Copper, tole, brass, pewter, pottery, waxed woods, and wrought iron—all materials crafted by hand—made up the small objects in Colonial homes.

INFORMAL

When is an INFORMAL room appropriate? If the room will be used by children, or for rough vigorous activities, or for long periods of time, it will get heavy wear. Informal furnishings are DURABLE.

If your personal style is casual, easy-going, and friendly, informal furnishings will help you express yourself. Also if your budget has boundaries, it's good to note that informal furnishings cost less than formal ones.

If you were to draw a vertical line down the middle of your home, would the sides match? If not, your home is an informal architectural style; informal furnishings would feel at home in it. Some examples of informal architectural styles are EARLY ENGLISH, EARLY AMERICAN, NORMAN FRENCH, some MEDITERRANEAN, some MODERN, and ranch houses in general.

COLORS Bright with strong contrasts. Strong colors go well with the natural-looking textures of informal furnishings.

PATTERNS Patterns may be linear, drawn from nature, or pictorial. Stripes, plaids, and checks, and other designs that are linear or crisscrossed in design have casual effect.

All-over designs drawn from nature—your total garden variety of designs—create a relaxed effect.

Some pictorial designs are appropriate. For example, you might want sailing ships in a little boy's room or owls in the library.

The size of the design should fit proportionately with the size of the room and its furnishings, but on the whole, small motifs seem more informal.

TEXTURES Uneven or unshiny. Texture is a great determinant of informality. Textures in an informal room tend to be natural and unpolished. They tend to have uneven surfaces, or look like they have uneven surfaces.

Rough architectural materials such as stone, brick, various building blocks, stucco, cork tiles, and rough wood paneling are uneven and blend with informal furnishings.

Consistently, most informal fabrics are uneven or unshiny. Corduroy is the country cousin of velvet. (Its ribs make it uneven.) Velvet can be informal if it's crushed. Dull, heavy fabrics make good upholsteries. Wool is wonderful, especially with EARLY AMERICAN and Danish modern furniture. It has a rich texture and takes color marvelously. Linen can be most informal when rough and heavy, when it seems to have the texture of burlap. Cotton is informal when rough-textured. Herculon olefin is a damage-defying upholstery. Felt always reminds me of pool tables, but it can cover other sorts of things too.

Duck, sailcloth, canvas, and ticking are informal fabrics with a crisp look. Denim conveys a make-yourself-at-home relaxed atmosphere. Chintz is shiny, but its pattern can make it seem informal. Leather and imitations such as Naugahyde are smooth, but in bright, bold colors, they're informal.

Rugs and carpets that are thick and shaggy and loose-looped are certainly uneven and informal. Mottled colorations or tweedy effects

The brick wall and the free-standing fireplace inspired this room's INFORMAL feeling. To stand up to these strong architectural elements, a modern modular-seating system of substantial size was arranged in two groupings on either side of the fireplace. For fun, a pumpkin-shaped ottoman was added. A wallhanging of interesting, uneven textures, a basket for firelogs, and a ceramic candlestick are accessories of suitable strength. (Photo courtesy of Selig Furniture.)

even on smooth surfaces give an informal ambience.

STYLES Informal furniture is often hefty in scaling and substantial-looking. Informal styles include EARLY AMERICAN, EARLY ENGLISH, some SPANISH, and some FRENCH PROVINCIAL. SHAKER furniture is light-looking but still simple enough to be informal. Informal furniture is typically made of solid common woods—pine, oak, ash, maple, birch, pecky cypress—and often has a raw unfinished look that suggests the country.

Long, low furniture creates a horizontal line that is informal and calm. Low furniture could hardly be formal. It's hard to seem stiff with your knees under your chin!

Furniture with curved lines is gracious and relaxing. Bentwood chairs are an informal favorite. They look as right today as they did in Victorian ice-cream parlors.

Furniture arrangements are not always in matching pairs. Matching pairs create a formal balance. To create a casual effect, you won't want too many of them.

Informal window treatments are simple. Sill-length curtains create an informal effect. The curtains might hang straight or be tied back to the sides. Valances might be ruffled or box-pleated. The fabric should be inexpensive and cheerful.

Bamboo shades are quite informal and give a nice textural effect. Roller shades used solo, with no additional draperies, are definitely informal, even if the shade is laminated with a pattern that matches something else in the room.

Shutters have an architectural appearance. They may be stained or painted in some happy hue.

ACCESSORIES Accessories are heavy-looking and a bit earthy. For example, you would use pewter, not silver; brass, bronze, or copper, not gold; glass, not crystal.

SEMIFORMAL

When is a SEMIFORMAL room appropriate? If the activities in this room will sometimes be formal and sometimes be informal, you'll want to be ready for anything. Semiformal furnishings will fit either occasion.

Semiformal furnishings can also be mixed in with informal furnishings or with formal furnishings. They are wonderfully adaptable. They are the middle ground between extremes.

COLORS Colors are neither super-bright, nor super-subtle. If bright, bold colors are informal, and pale, subtle colors are formal, then those colors in the middle are semiformal. Choose colors that are neither bright nor pale. (See Chapter 19: Choose Your Color Scheme.) You might make your scheme of colors of the same value—all equally light, or equally dark. (If you squinted, they would all seem the same shade of gray.) You might choose three colors that are right next to each other on the color wheel. Any three colors that are next to each other on the color wheel have a color in common, so this sort of scheme is called "related" or "harmonious." Colors that share blue are green, blue-green, blue, and blue-violet. Colors that share yellow are green, yellow-green, yellow, and yellow-orange. Colors that share red are red, red-violet, violet, and blue-violet—or, the other direction, red, red-orange, orange, and orange-yellow.

A color scheme of harmonious hues of the same value creates a rich effect, and you don't need to have fabulous furniture or accessories. To avoid confusion, be careful to make one color dominate. Cover two-thirds of your areas with it—for example, the walls *and* floor, or either of those and some large furniture.

PATTERNS Most patterns are semiformal. Except for the most powerful and primitive and the most subtle and sophisticated, the majority of patterns can be considered semiformal.

Patterns of medium size are thought to be semiformal. Large-scale designs tend to be formal; small-scale designs tend to be informal.

Finely detailed designs tend to be formal. Crudely executed designs tend to be informal. Anything in between seems semiformal.

Smooth, shiny backgrounds tend to be for-

mal; rough or dull backgrounds tend to be informal. Anything in between seems semiformal.

The elements of size, drawing, and background can be mixed around to create a semiformal effect. For example, if the drawing and background are fine but the size is small, the effect can be semiformal. Some small French brocades are semiformal. If the drawing is crude, but the size is large and the background is smooth, the effect can be semiformal too. Imagine some large bouquets of flowers on shiny chintz.

Clearly, there is an enormous selection of semiformal patterns. Most cotton prints range from informal to semiformal. Near Eastern Oriental rugs are a timeless example of adaptability.

TEXTURES Textures are neither especially rough nor smooth. The really rough and coarse

This SEMIFORMAL room is ready for anything. Rich chocolate brown is the color of walls, tables, and the background of the upholstery print. Cream is the color of wall-to-wall carpeting, carved in a diagonal pattern to give it dimensional interest, and of Chippendale chairs, painted to seem less formal. Crisp white on the ceiling, the upholstery print (and its "reverse" on the screen), and lamps adds sparkle to the scheme. (Design by Braswell-Willoughby, Inc.)

textures are informal and the super-smooth and lustrous textures are fancy and formal. To achieve a semiformal effect, textures can be modestly uneven or dimensional. They can be simply smooth without being especially lustrous.

Most rooms begin with adaptable semiformal textures. Walls may be smooth plaster; floors may be polished wood or cut-pile carpet in a plain color.

Furnishings made from walnut wood or other woods of medium-smooth graining are semiformal. They can be combined with informal oak or with formal mahogany. Furniture with caning can go anywhere and it can give a room the uneven texture it needs.

Smooth or gently dimensional cottons, linens, and wood are go-anywhere fabrics. So is leather and its vinyl look-alike. Chintz is versatile and snappy.

Rug and carpet surfaces may be smooth or carved in patterns. (Those wild shags *are* informal.)

Grasscloth is a favorite wallcovering. It provides a room with all the uneven texture it needs. The smoother and more refined it is, the more formal. The rougher it is, the more informal.

Woven baskets have a go-anywhere appeal. They too can provide a room with its uneven texture.

STYLES Furniture is medium-sized and neither crude nor elaborate. Semiformal styles include EARLY COLONIAL/QUEEN ANNE, FRENCH PROVINCIAL, GERMAN BIEDEMEIER, and some VICTORIAN. Civilized but sturdy is a good way to describe semiformal furniture. It has unpretentious grace—some refinement of line without being finicky or fancy. It is neither crudely carved nor richly ornamented. It is neither oversized and impressive nor delicate and dainty. Its ornament, if any, is simple. Its texture is medium, like walnut wood, and its size is average. All sorts of simple styles fit into this category. Because it is middle-of-the-road, semiformal furniture is adaptable to almost any environment. You can dress it up or down

depending on the upholstery you choose.

At the windows, almost anything goes. Anything between elaborate silk swags and ruffled gingham curtains can be considered semiformal. Cafe curtains are rather informal, but adaptable. In general, sill-length curtains are more informal than floor-length curtains or draperies. Draperies hanging straight are timeless, and for that matter, so are shutters. Those skinny slat blinds can be semiformal if they are not a bright color. Bamboo shades and woven wood blinds have an uneven texture so they tend to be informal, but if their texture is rather refined, they can pass as semiformal.

FORMAL

When is a FORMAL room appropriate? When durability is not an issue. When the room will not be used by children or careless adults. When the activities of the room are relatively quiet, so there is no danger of knocking things over. When you wish to express a mood of dignity and reserve, or you want a rich, luxurious, elaborate, dressy, delicate, feminine, or sophisticated decorative effect. Your budget must be bounteous.

The architecture of your home might well be symmetrical and formal. It may have classical architectural detailing, including columns, pilasters, niches, or fine wood-paneled walls.

COLORS Soft, pale colors are beautiful with fine furniture. For instance, in the time of Louis XV and Louis XVI, the favored colors were grayed tones of pastel greens, blues, and rose, along with ivory and beige.

Pale and neutral colors have another reason for being in a room with fine furniture. They won't upstage the furniture! In such a room you will want to underplay color in order to keep the focus on furnishings. You especially will want to underplay the background. You might have the walls and wall-to-wall carpeting in the same pale or neutral monotone to create a soft, smooth backdrop for your furnishings.

This living room couldn't be more FORMAL in feeling. Everything is arranged in symmetrical, matched pairs. The furniture is Louis XVI in style. The fabrics are rich. Accessories include gold and crystal sconces and Oriental urns. The background is underplayed, but still rich in detailing. (Design by R. Michael Brown.)

Color contrasts in a formal room are usually somewhat subtle. You might make your whole scheme out of one color. You can vary it lighter or darker, brighter or softer. This sort of scheme is called "monochromatic." You might make your scheme all out of neutrals. For example, the walls and floor might be pale beige; the large upholstery and draperies ivory; the small pieces of furniture brown, and the accessories black. For another example, the walls and floor might be pale gray; the large upholstery and draperies a black-and-white pattern; the small furniture black, and the accessories white. These neutral sorts of schemes are CALM and dignified (and require interesting textures).

For a more lively atmosphere, you can mix a single color with neutrals. For example, the walls and floor might be yellow, the large upholstery and draperies a brown-and-white pattern, the small furniture brown, and the accessories white. For another example, the walls and floor might be white, the large upholstery and draperies red, the small furniture black, and the accessories red and white.

For a richer but still restrained effect, you might choose darker colors that are softened

with gray. For example, colors of the GEORGIAN or Williamsburg era are these muted medium-value colors: gray-blue, soft red, mustard, and brown, plus pearl, cream, and white.

If your room and your furnishings are large, you might well want an even bolder color scheme to stand up to the space. That's what Napoleon wanted. The EMPIRE style was invented for him to attest to his power. The proportions of the furniture are heavy and the colors are bright enough to salute. Bright or dark colors can suggest a richer, more dignified, and more MASCULINE mood. For a regal effect, you could mix gold with emerald green, sapphire blue, or ruby red. The colors of precious metals and gems are certainly rich. Gold is especially attractive in metal, gilt, or silk. Silk in gold shimmers with depth and richness.

In a formal room it is usual to have matched things of the same color facing each other to achieve balance.

PATTERNS Patterns may be large in scale, delicately drawn, crafted by hand, or made of luxurious materials. Most formal patterns are extravagant in some way. Large-size patterns are appropriate for large rooms and large pieces of furniture; the largeness itself suggests a luxury of space.

Beautifully detailed drawing or definition of design shows an extreme of careful craftsmanship. It suggests a luxury of time and attention. Actually, any pattern crafted in any way by hand tends to be more expensive than its machine-made counterpart. This includes hand-tied Oriental rugs, needlepoint, and silk-screened fabrics and wallcoverings.

Luxurious materials—silks and satins, even real wool or mercerized cotton—suggest caring enough to select the very best. Even a subtle stripe on an elegant material can be formal.

Hard-to-get, rare, or antique designs have a luxurious value as well as exotic éclat. An exquisite imported wallpaper from China, France, or England has long been a sure way to express elegance and formality, not to mention the Oriental rugs!

Some types of designs have a classically formal feeling. This is true of damask and brocade fabrics, Aubusson and Savonnerie rugs, most Oriental rugs, most fine-patterned porcelain and china, and the best scenic wallcoverings.

To complement your formal furnishings, choose a pattern of the same sort of shape—a curved design if your furniture is curved, a straight-lined design if your furniture is square or rectangular.

If your furnishings are exquisite, you might not want any pattern at all to distract attention from their delightful details. The outlines of the furniture against the wall, the lines of the draperies, and the books in the bookshelf might provide all the pattern interest you want.

TEXTURES In a formal room, textures are basically smooth and shiny. There should be a variety of hard things and soft things, and there should be some texture that is mildly uneven.

Hard, shiny textures certainly include rich, smooth woods. The floor might be polished parquet. The walls might have rich wood paneling (perhaps painted in a pale, soft color). The furniture should be made of fine polished woods such as rosewood or mahogany. These rich woods suggest elegance and must be used with delicate textures. Walnut is a semiformal wood; it can mix with formal furnishings.

Marble is high on elegance—and expense. You could use a hard marble floor in a foyer or in other areas where you don't spend much time. Hard floors are noisy and tiring to the feet. For more comfort underfoot, you could use a resilient floorcovering that looks like marble. (Most resilient floorcoverings like vinyl are informal. However, a resilient that looks like marble, perhaps with brass dividing lines or inlays, is no slouch for sophistication.)

Hard surfaces can be painted with shiny paint. Walls may be glazed or painted with glossy enamel. Small pieces of furniture may be lacquered to a high shine.

Glass and crystal, foil wallcoverings, and hard, shiny metals catch the light and set it sparkling. Gold and silver, brass, chrome, and steel all contribute a glamorous glitter. You might have a modern steel-and-glass table, or traditional gold-leaf picture frames, a crystal chandelier, a lightweight brass chandelier, or brass drawer pulls.

Fine porcelains and china also have beautiful light-reflective surfaces. They, too, give a formal feeling.

Soft, shiny textures include lustrous silks and satins. Silk is the ultimate in elegance—and expense. Be careful with it at the windows; it soon rots in strong sunlight. Silk draperies should always be lined, and beware of using silk on the sunny south side of the house. Because it looks terrible to use an expensive material skimpily, sometimes it is much smarter to purchase a cheaper fabric and use it lavishly to create the effect you want. Rayon and acetate are synthetics that simulate the look of silk. A good lining will make any drapery fabric look heavier and richer.

Linen seems dressy when it is smooth and shiny, and butter-soft leathers have a look of luxury. Chintz is semiformal, but since it is shiny, it mixes well with a formal room.

Soft, smooth surfaces in general create a luxurious comfort quotient. Imagine deep pile rugs, generous upholstered pieces, fabric on the walls. These soft surfaces also absorb sound and give a feeling of privileged privacy. Flat rich rugs like Orientals, needlepoint, and flat furs are less warm and comforting, but they are still extremely formal.

The uneven texture in a formal room must be restrained, rather refined. It might be furniture with caning. It might be a fabric with nap like velvet, or a fabric with a gentle texture, say the slubs of silk. It might be the textured effect created by a fabric with a pattern in the weave—a one-color brocade or damask, for example. It might be a flocked wallcovering. It might be a rug with its pile carved to different heights.

STYLE Formal furniture is a marriage of ele-

FORMAL furnishings can work well even in a small space. Here matching French cane-back chairs with blue velvet cushions are pulled up to a tiny table that, surprisingly, can serve for an elegant, intimate dinner. The blue of the cushions is inspired by the porcelain dinner dishes. (Design by Andrew F. Tauber; photo by Billy Cunningham.)

gant materials and fine craftsmanship. This fact is as true for today's modern styles as it was for Napoleon. Today it might involve hand-polishing stainless steel; then it might have involved making brass slippers for the feet at the end of table legs, but it's really all the same—it's the best.

Formal furniture styles include GEORGIAN, AMERICAN FEDERAL, FRENCH LOUIS XV AND XVI, AMERICAN GREEK REVIVAL/FRENCH EMPIRE/ENGLISH REGENCY.

Throughout history, formal furniture has changed in size and shape, but it all has quality in common. Having quality in common makes FORMAL furniture go together, but having size and perhaps shape in common too makes it go together even better.

Today elegant modern furniture is made in all sizes and shapes. It can stand alone or blend with traditional styles of similar size and shape. Today, too, many of the larger-scaled traditional styles are being reproduced in smaller size—not only so they can fit in our homes but so they can blend with our other smaller-scale furnishings.

Furniture arrangements are symmetrical. Pairs, matching pieces, or repeated pieces placed opposite each other make for a symmetrical arrangement. Symmetry and formality go together like identical twins. For example, you might have matching chairs opposite each other on either side of a fireplace, opposite the fireplace a sofa, and on either end of the sofa, matching tables. Do stick a singleton in somewhere for relief.

Formal window treatments tend to be elaborate. Traditionally, formal window treatments are topped with fabric swags or fabric-covered valances. Draperies reach the floor or more. They might be tied back with elaborate fringes. There might be a glass curtain underneath.

Such elaborate window treatments require large rooms. They would be overpowering in a small room. So what do we do today when we are living in smaller spaces? We can modify the flourishes and flounces. Simplify. We might make the draperies similar in color to the walls so they blend with the background.

If we want an airy, delicate effect, we can hang pretty, puffy austrian shades. If we want a stark modern effect, or simply an architectural ambience, we can hang vertical blinds. Shutters are timeless. They've long been part of the window's wardrobe.

ACCESSORIES Accessories from the Orient are suitable for most formal traditional rooms. Crystal, silver, and porcelain accessories will give any room a FORMAL feeling.

Mirrors also create something of a formal feeling by repeating what they reflect—they make matched pairs and symmetry. Mirrors give a glisten. They are an exciting backdrop for a table or console holding crystal or glass, flowers, or other decorative accessories.

(Design by Rubén De Saavedra, ASID; photo by Daniel Eifert.)

12

STYLE

What do you like? MODERN, ECLECTIC, or TRADITIONAL? If traditional, whose tradition do you like? How can you choose?

Personal preference is the most important factor in the choice of style. Look through this chapter. What styles strike a responsive chord in you? You might want to choose furnishings that express your family's ethnic heritage. For example, if your background is English, you might want an English Georgian piece or two.

You might choose to reflect the influences of the area you live in. For example, New Orleans has had a French influence; you might want some French furniture. In Arizona, you might want some American Indian artifacts.

Since there should be some compatibility between the architecture of your home and the furnishings you put in it, that could be a clue to the selection of styles. Matching furnishings styles to the style of architecture is always harmonious (but not necessary).

The amount of space you have will affect what styles will work for you. Many believe that modern styles permit you a greater sense of space with less true space. (That's partly because we modern people are living in smaller spaces than our ancestors.)

What will go with the furnishings you have and intend to use? Furnishings of the same period or style are, of course, compatible, but contrasts can be refreshing, and exciting!

Of course, your life-style will help direct your selection. Some styles are more formal than others.

MODERN

Why choose modern? Because you want to be a person of your time. Because you are earthy. Because you like light and air and openness and materials that are what they are. Because you believe that "less is more," and can even be liberating. Because you are looking forward to the future.

What characterizes a modern interior? A modern interior is SPACIOUS, structural, simple, and straightforward.

Spacious. Since we seem to be living in less space, modern architects strive to achieve a spacious effect. They've broken down the walls and the barriers between indoors and out. Floor plans are open, allowing light and air to flow through the interior. Partial partitions may define areas, but light and air can still go up, under, or over. Large windows and continuous wall or floor treatments going from indoors out link limited interiors to expansive exteriors.

Modern interior design, too, strives to stretch space. Continuous carpeting or masonry in a neutral color may cover the floors of the whole home. All walls may be painted the same to contribute to the flowing feeling. Window treatments tend to be simple to let in the maximum amount of light and air. Mirror might cover a wall to make the most of the light and double the sense of space. Furniture arrangements blend in or are airy and open so as not to crowd the space. To further the architectural link between indoors and out, the color scheme is often inspired by the view.

Structural. The actual inspiration for modern furnishings is modern architecture. The old-style furnishings just didn't look right in the new buildings. New furnishings were designed in materials and shapes that complemented the architecture. The exterior and the interior were thought of as one total unit. For example, light-looking "floating furniture" of steel and glass was created to complement soaring steel-and-glass skyscrapers.

In a modern interior, the room itself is an integral part of the design. It is not something to be covered up and embellished. Walls are often in architectural materials—concrete blocks, brick, rough plaster, or wood. Furnishings might repeat the materials of the architecture, as with those steel-and-glass tables for the skyscrapers. Furnishings might repeat the shapes of the architecture—for ex-

ample, a round table in a rounded cove or a rounded window, or a rectangular seating arrangement in a rectangular room. Furnishings, indeed, might be an extension of the architecture; for example, a sunken floor or a raised platform might create a special conversational area. Storage cabinets might be built in along the walls. Lighting may be incorporated into the ceiling. Even the window treatment might seem structural—floor-to-ceiling vertical blinds, for instance.

Simple. You've heard the slogan "Less is more." To eliminate clutter and confusion (and to minimize maintenance), modernists strive for the elemental. They analyze what needs to be done in a space (the functions) and try to find the most basic form that fits. Hence, another modern slogan: "Form follows function." For example, to accommodate conversation, a traditional grouping of seating might be a collection of independent pieces, each seeming to ask for attention. A modern grouping might provide just as many seats, but in one big simple shape. It might be a big blocky square made up of modular units or a carpeted platform.

Straightforward. The modern movement was

MODERN furniture was designed to complement modern architecture. The steel and glass of skyscrapers are repeated in a light-looking desk. The bed, bookshelf, and nightstands are organized into one simple architectural shape. To stretch space, the walls and floor are one continuous pale color, and the skinny blinds on the windows do nothing to obstruct the view. (Design by Michael Love, ASID; photo by Jaime Ardiles-Arce.)

born partly out of disgust with the excessive ornamentation of the previous period. The modernists wanted to get back to the basics, back to honesty in materials as well as to simplicity of structure. The natural textures of materials take the place of ornamentation in the modern interior. The interplay is interesting. Warm wood versus the cool glamour of stainless steel. The soft slubs of a woven fabric versus the roughness of a woven wicker basket. Everything is what it is.

COLORS To stretch space, the colors of the interior might echo the colors of the view out the windows. To emphasize the natural textures of things, fabrics and furnishings are often left in their natural state. For example, wool fabrics may vary in color from black to off-white. Who has ever seen a purple sheep? Emphasis on the natural has led to the popularity of earthtone colors, especially the off-whites, beiges, and browns.

Pale colors are popular for walls and floors, especially pale neutrals and blues and greens, because they back away and make a room or a home seem larger.

Often a rather neutral interior is punctuated by a bright splash of color. The modern movement is into bold strokes. An INFORMAL or STIMULATING room can use a lot of bright, bold color.

PATTERNS Modern rooms usually emphasize textural variety rather than pattern, but often they are sparked with bold geometrical or primitive patterns. Many modern pattern designs are inspired by modern paintings. They may be clean, simple geometrics or abstracted natural forms.

TEXTURES A variety of textures is important in a modern interior—the rough versus the smooth. This interplay emphasizes the true nature of materials. You might have rough woven baskets, bamboo or matchstick blinds, rough sisal matting or cork tiles for the floor, fabrics with nubby natural weaves, grasscloth, brick,

MODERN molded plastic chairs don't have a leg to stand on. Plastics technology has allowed new freedom of form, new sculptural shapes. This EASY TO CLEAN eating area has a ceramic tile floor and a table surfaced in plastic laminate. The MODERN mood is completed with track lighting, vertical blinds, and a bold graphic on the wall. (Design by Richard W. Jones, FASID; photo by Harry Hartman.)

or barnsiding on the walls. Those are some rough and uneven textures. For the smooth, you could have chrome or stainless steel, glass, mirror, marble, clear acrylic or other plastic furniture, leather upholstery, lacquered walls, ceilings, or furniture, silver foil, shiny silver blinds at the windows.

STYLES One of the great contributions of the modern movement is modular furniture. You can take it and rearrange it wherever you go. You aren't stuck with furnishings that fit your last house but won't adjust to your new one. Today there are many modular seating systems and storage systems that are good-looking and good investments.

Modern technology has allowed us to create furnishings in exciting sculptural shapes. Plastic has presented possibilities never known before. Now we have all sorts of marvelous seating shapes in molded polyurethane (often upholstered in stretch fabric). Hard plastic furnishings often have pleasantly flowing forms, and color is intrinsic to the material—it can't chip or scrape off. Transparent acrylic is another exciting modern material. The edges catch the light and seem to glow.

As mentioned before, a lot of modern furnishings are built in or otherwise integrated with the architecture. Platforms and conversation pits are popular.

To coordinate with the simple shapes and honest materials of modern furnishings, you could use traditional COUNTRY/RUSTIC pieces that also have honest materials and simple shapes—Shaker furnishings are an example.

LIGHTING In a modern room, lighting is often incorporated into the ceiling or walls. It clears out the clutter of having lots of lamps. Lighting may be recessed into the ceiling or walls at the time of construction, or, like track lighting, it may be attached after.

Modern lamps are one of the delights of the day. Many are actually illuminated sculptures. There is a wonderful array of exciting forms and shapes, running from trim and tailored to fluid and free-form. Steel and plastics are popular materials.

ACCESSORIES Plants, plants, and more plants. The modernist is getting back to the nature of things, and bringing nature indoors as well.

As mentioned before, useful or decorative handcrafts are chosen as a nice contrast to mass-manufactured furniture.

Modern graphics and art are important.

ECLECTIC

Why choose eclectic? Because you want to reflect both today and yesterday. Because you want the freedom of not committing yourself to any particular period. Because you want to surround yourself with the things you love, whether old or new. Because you like the spacious feeling of modern, and the time-worn textures of the old. Because an eclectic mix is unpredictable and more interesting. Because it allows you to express yourself.

What characterizes eclectic? Eclectic is a mix of the old and the new. Because pieces don't come from the same time frame, they need something else in common in order to establish a relationship. They could share compatible colors, or the same wood tones. They could be the same sort of size, or the same sort of shape—straight-lined or curved. They could both be formal or informal, i.e., smooth or rough. The more they have in common, the more similar they seem and the more they blend together. However, contrast is part of the kick of an eclectic interior. The less they have in common, the more they set each other off. For example, a sleek metal glass-topped coffee table could really set off a favorite antique. It is important to pick your contrasts carefully. Too many contrasts create chaos.

To tie together the old and the new, it may be useful to give some parts of the interior a "timeless" treatment. For the floor, masonry, wood, and smooth-surfaced carpeting are ageless. For the walls, paint is the safest bet. At the windows, shutters defy time; draperies hanging straight are ageless. Sheer curtains and casements are pretty timeless too. Simple shades—including roman shades, which fold up in pleats—are adaptable. Furniture with clean, simple lines will never seem dated, and it will go with anything. A Lawson sofa is an example. For lighting, architectural lighting incorporated into the ceiling or walls doesn't make a decorative statement, so you don't have to worry about it. As for lamps, ginger jars go with anything. Plain cotton, linen, silk,

The bed is mid-19th century. The table and chair are French. The cabinet is Early American. What makes it all work? Most furnishings have curves in common. The background is given a timeless treatment. A modern fabric updates the traditional treatment of bed and window. And being the most distinctly different in style, the modern painting draws attention. (Design by Richard W. Jones, FASID.)

and velvet are forever fabrics.

What can help blend the old and the new? Color and pattern. Traditional patterns recolored in a present-day palette are good mixers. Stripes go with anything. Uniformity of color makes miracles. Traditional French chairs can be painted white and upholstered in bright or pastel leather. Then their light color and slick-surfaced seats will help them mix with modern. Any characteristics in common help the old blend with the new. (See "What Goes With What You Have?" in Chapter 4.) As an example, country-made INFORMAL furniture of the last century mixes marvelously with modern. Both share simple lines and unadorned surfaces.

What do you want to emphasize? The thing you want to emphasize can make the most dramatically different statement of style. Accessories alone could be your point of contrast. You could have a totally traditional room zipped up by avant-garde accents, or a modern room toned down by traditional accessories—beautiful books, old urns, or inkwells. One terrific eclectic room I saw recently had all traditional furniture counterpointed by exciting modern sculptural lighting.

IF THE ROOM SEEMS TOO TRADITIONAL You will want to simplify the room and bring in contemporary colors and modern materials.

Simplify. Lighten up the window treatment. You might bring the room up to date simply by removing the valances. You could replace heavy silks or velvets with fresh, crisp cottons, or airy casement cloth. If the views or the windows themselves are beautiful, you might replace the curtains with simple blinds or shutters.

Clear away the clutter on tabletops. Sometimes even the smallest ashtrays and cigarette boxes can make a room seem old-fashioned. Replace the small old pieces with one beautiful big piece of contemporary sculpture.

Clear out that forest of lamps. You might want to mount architectural fixtures on the ceilings or walls, use contemporary fixtures, or simplify the shades of your old lamps. Get off-white paper shades, either opaque or translucent.

A furniture rearrangement could make the room seem less stiff and formal. Break up those matching pairs of things and the room will seem more informal and relaxed.

Now you can dress up some old things and give them a fresher feeling. Look for fabrics with traditional designs in contemporary colors. You could use the fabric for draperies and/or upholstery. Traditional chairs might be painted in white lacquer or upholstered in slick patent leather.

And bring on the new! Replace a traditional piece or two with something made of modern materials—slick steel and glass or plastic. Traditional side chairs could be replaced by modern ones. A traditional butler's tray coffee table could by replaced by a Parsons table in clear red or yellow lacquer, or a steel-and-glass coffee table, or a coffee table in clear or bronze translucent plastic. Accessories alone can give a modern upbeat feeling to a traditional room. Choose modern graphics, paintings, sculpture. Most galleries will let you try them at home before you buy.

IF THE ROOM SEEMS TOO MODERN You will want to add an antique or two to make the mood more mellow. Simple designs blend best with modern, but you might want to create a more dramatic and daring contrast by choosing an elaborate old piece of furniture.

You might want an Oriental rug for the floor. Oriental rugs blend beautifully with modern furnishings, plus you'll have all the romance and allure of the East.

For fabrics, traditional designs in modern colorations can tone down a too-modern room. These designs bring together the best of both worlds.

Accessories alone can bring in an old-world flavor. Old books and Oriental objects are beautiful blenders. An old painting in an ornate gilded frame can set off sleek chrome-and-glass and leather furniture. Because of

the dramatic contrast, the painting would make a perfect focal point.

TRADITIONAL

Why choose traditional? Because you like to feel a sense of continuity with the past. Because you feel comfortable in a home like the one you grew up in. (And maybe you've got your mother's furniture.) Because you like to invest in antiques. Because you want to choose things that have stood the test of time and haven't gone out of style. Because you want to reflect your family's heritage. Because your home is a traditional style. Because there is a lot of traditional furniture in the stores.

What characterizes traditional? Each traditional style reflects its own place and times. There are seven major factors that shape a style:

1. The climate. To cool the temperature, Spanish homes were designed to be open to the outside, and floors were covered with slick tile. To keep out the cold, Early American homes were built with tiny windows.
2. The history of the region and the heritage of the people. Invasions and migrations have affected the styles all over the world. English styles have had influence in New England, Spanish in New Mexico.
3. Travel and communications. In the eighteenth century, seamen traveled to China. The treasures they brought back—the beautiful silks and china—became important features in the wealthier homes.
4. The state of the economy, or how much money there was to spend. The early Americans made do with very little. In the eighteenth century, England enjoyed great wealth. Georgian styles reflected luxury and elegance.
5. Beliefs and life-style. Early Americans were so religious they thought luxury a sin, so they made themselves uncomfortable with straight, cushionless chairs. Conversely, Frenchmen of the Louis XV era relished their time rollicking in boudoirs.
6. The available raw materials. Early Americans cut down pine trees to make their furniture. In Queen Anne's time there was a wealth of walnut.

What tradition appeals to you? Do you identify with any particular period or style? Each traditional style reflects its own place and time. **EARLY AMERICAN** interiors were stark and simple. Furnishings were handcrafted from local materials.

VICTORIAN interiors were opulent, displaying the exuberance of new wealth and the capacity of newly invented machines to make repeat patterns. (Photos courtesy of The Metropolitan Museum of Art.)

7. The skills of craftsmen. English artisans of the eighteenth century reached a high point in history. The peasant peoples throughout history have made cruder variations of popular city styles. (And we won't mention the bookcase of boards I nailed together in the basement.)

To choose a certain traditional style, it is best if you identify in some way with the circumstances of its creation. If you relate in some personal way to a style of the past, that relation will breathe life and energy into the furnishings built for another time. It will also express you in a way that shows depth and dimension throughout time. It will be a mutually flattering match.

In my opinion it seems phony to try to reproduce an authentic period room in every detail. This is your home, not a museum. I believe a traditional style can inspire and direct the design of your home, but it's okay to incorporate electric lights and other conveniences of modern living. By the way, your whole home should have some harmony of style. Generally, you should not make radical changes in style from room to room.

If you are buying traditional styles, you will want to shop for quality. Age isn't everything. Just because something is old doesn't mean it's valuable, useful, or even beautiful. Will it function? Can it serve for storage or seating? If

it won't serve much purpose, can you afford the space for it? Is its size compatible with the room? Most old furnishings were meant for rooms bigger than those that most of us live in today. Many reproductions are scaled down to smaller sizes for smaller spaces.

Is the piece true to its period? To judge whether a piece is true to its period, you have to know the seven criteria that shaped the initial creation of the style. The public library has many books, and many museums reproduce the rooms of the past. Study them and you will develop an eye for authenticity. Also the following review will give you guidance. When you know what the real item should look like, you can appreciate not only the antique, but the authentic reproduction.

Early English

Why choose Early English? It is DURABLE, strong, MASCULINE, and INFORMAL. It can take heavy wear and careless treatment. The style is especially suitable for half-timbered houses, or other brick or stone houses inspired by Tudor, Elizabethan, or Jacobean models.

What characterizes Early English? The lifestyle was boisterous and undainty. Think of Henry VIII chewing his mutton chop, with the

The architecture, with its heavy wooden beams and diamond-shaped leaded windowpanes, suggests EARLY ENGLISH styling. The furnishings follow through. The desk/cabinet unit repeats the diamond-shaped panes. The furniture, made of hardwood, is large, heavy, and rectangular. The chairs are Jacobean—with upholstered seats and backs nailed to rectangular frames. The drapery is a tree-of-life design, true to the time. (Photo courtesy of Hickory Manufacturing Company.)

grease all running down-oh. Furniture was built of solid oak to take tough treatment. It was built more for service than for comfort. The style was inspired by a fusion of Gothic and Italian Renaissance forms.

COLORS The golden color of oak characterizes an Early English interior.

PATTERNS East Indian hand-painted cotton was imported into England at this time. Most designs were variations on the "tree of life"—a design featuring a central flowering tree. Tapestry wall hangings provided pattern and so did wood carving with Gothic and strapwork designs.

TEXTURES Textures were mostly hard. Flagstone or slate covered the floor on the first floor. Upstairs floors were made from random-width oak planks.

In half-timbered houses, the timbers that formed part of the structure became a design feature of the interior walls. In brick or stone houses of the Tudor period, the upper walls were covered with rough-finished plaster. The lower walls were covered with a wainscot of oak panels with Gothic decoration. In the Jacobean period, the interior walls combined small wood panels with Italian-style pilasters, columns, and entablatures.

Initially ceilings exposed heavy beams. Later in the period, the rough beams were covered with a flat plaster ceiling, which was often decorated.

A stone fireplace was an essential feature of the room. The windows were leaded glass, and houses usually had a prominent bay window. Furniture was made of hard wood, and accessories included hard metal armor.

For some sense of softness—and to block the drafts—tapestries were hung on the walls, and four-poster beds had velvet hangings. There were some Turkish rugs on the floor.

STYLES Furniture was heavy, large, and rectangular. Case and cabinet furniture had the same sort of decorated panels as the wall wainscots. Furniture ornament consisted of simple inlay, crude low relief, strapwork carving, and split-spindle decoration—which was a short turned piece of wood, split into two parts and applied to a surface. There were also caricature carvings of humans.

Principal pieces were: chests, cupboards, wardrobes, desk-boxes, dressers for tableware, settles, chairs, stools, tables, beds and cradles.

Representative pieces include:

The turned chair—a heavy chair with a triangular wooden seat, and all supports made of short, thick turnings

Wainscot chair—a rectangular seat with turned or column legs, arms slightly shaped, and a high wood back

Jacobean chairs—upholstered seats and backs nailed to a rectangular frame

Large oak refectory tables—some of the extension type

Dropleaf and gateleg tables

Huge four-poster beds enriched with bulbous
ornament

LIGHTING   Fixtures were of wrought iron or
brass.

ACCESSORIES   Accessories were few in
these austere interiors. They included armor
and trophies of the chase. Eating imple-
ments—silver, pewter, and heavy earthenware
for platters and cups. Tapestries were used for
warmth, color, and room dividing. Turkish rugs
came back on English ships. And Chinese
pottery, porcelains, and paintings came with
the tea trade.

Early American

Why choose Early American? It is DURABLE,
COUNTRY/RUSTIC, or INFORMAL. It expresses
America's earliest heritage, is space-saving,

**An adaptation of all-American EARLY AMERICAN, this
room gives us a sense of persons in our past. A
portrait of an ancestor hangs over the fireplace.
A sampler, a rag rug, and a patchwork quilt look
lovingly handmade. The Windsor chairs, apothecary
chest, wardrobe, four-poster bed, and dower chest
are simple pine designs similar to those that served
earlier generations. (Photo courtesy of Sugar Hill
Furniture; design by Shirley Regendahl.)**

and relatively inexpensive (at least in reproduction).

The person/persons using the room can be
careless adults or children or they might just
prefer styles that are simple and straightforward. The activities can be rough and vigorous, such as those in a family room. The
region you live in might be one of the original
thirteen colonies, or you might just live in the
country. The architecture of your home could
be an Early American style, a Cape Cod cottage, a farm house, or an unpretentious house
or apartment. Your space might be limited.
That old Yankee ingenuity came up with many
multipurpose designs. Your budget can be
modest. Early American reproductions run in
the low to medium price range.

What characterizes Early American? Early
Americans came from the European countryside to a cold climate where they built
themselves small spaces and functional
furnishings of local materials and settled
down to a modest life of religious conviction
and self-reliance. Their furnishings are therefore cruder and simpler variations of earlier
European styles, clean-lined (and sometimes
uncomfortable) because of an antipathy to luxury, and often multifunctional in order to save
space. The settlers did indulge in color to
brighten their drab days. They made bright
red, blue, and green dyes out of plant juices. If
you want to see a restoration of an Early American community, visit Old Sturbridge Village in
Massachusetts.

COLORS   Originally colors were strong and
clear greens, reds, and blues. Time has since
softened them to soft greens, golds, pump-
kins, nutmegs. Colors should be chosen for
their compatibility with the piney wood tones.
Caution: Be careful when you buy reproductions. Avoid pieces with orange-colored varnish, instead of a mellow soft brown. That
orange will limit your color scheme.

PATTERNS   Prints of the period include
paisley and crewel designs, oriental prints,

and checks and plaids. Wallpaper styles of the period include designs with stripes and pomegranates. Handmade hooked or braided rugs put pattern on the floor. The ladies worked on patchwork quilts and on patterns in needlepoint and embroidery.

TEXTURES   Textures are mellow. There is nothing very sharp and shiny. Wood is important. Floors were usually wide or random width pine planks. Often three walls were plastered and one wall was paneled, maybe with random planking painted in silvery blue, gray, or pale red. Sometimes the lower part of the wall (dado) was paneled. A chair rail—a protective molding about thirty inches above the floor—would finish the paneling, and above that the wall would be painted. Some Early American rooms have all walls paneled in knotty pine. Furniture is wood—made of pine, hickory, maple, oak, cherry, and ash. There might be wooden shutters at the windows.

Fabrics look homespun, rough, and simple. For example, curtains at the window might be rough and heavy linen.

STYLES   Styles were simple and sturdy, and furnishings were sparse. Furniture might be brightly painted or decorated with wood turnings or crude carving.

Because there weren't any closets, an Early American interior features furnishings for storage: hutches, wardrobes complete with drawers and cabinets, corner cupboards, dower chests.

Tables would often fold up to save space. Styles include the gateleg, the dropleaf, the butterfly table, and a flip-top chair table. Trestle tables were often used too.

Chairs include the ubiquitous rocking chair, the Windsor chair and love seat, ladder-back and slat-back chairs, rush-seated chairs, and that flip-top table/chair. Loose cushions might add comfort. About the only authentic upholstered piece was the wing chair.

Beds began with wooden cradles, worked up to trundle beds and the four-poster.

Curtains at the window sometimes were softened with ruffles and with valances of ruffles or box pleats.

LIGHTING   Firelight and candlelight are major. Brass candlesticks are appropriate to the era. Appropriate lamps have a rustic look and are usually made from wrought iron, tole, copper, or pewter.

ACCESSORIES   Think of all those ladies sewing patchwork quilts at sewing bees, and sewing samplers by the fire. Copper, pewter, and other metal accessories are appropriate. Most accessories were actually useful objects. Metal warming pans made beds toasty.

The paneled chimney breast, the random-width floorboards, and the deep-set windows are clues to COLONIAL styling. Following the feeling, the highboy, the wing chair, the cellarette, the oval table, and the Queen Anne dining chairs are all reproductions of authentic early 18th-century designs by American craftsmen. The wing chair features a crewel pattern typical of the period. (Photo courtesy of Hickory Furniture Company.)

Firearms, earthenware, and china were in regular use. Maps were instructive, and portraits of family members kept everybody honoring their elders.

Early Colonial/ William and Mary/ Queen Anne

Why choose Early Colonial? It is dressier and more refined than Early American, but not so formal and sophisticated as Georgian. Because it is neither crude nor elaborate, this SEMIFORMAL style can fit into many interiors. Upholstery might dress it up or down. These styles are especially at home in American Colonial and Georgian interiors, and those with plain surfaces mix with modern. Solid construction makes these pieces DURABLE.

What characterizes Early Colonial? Like Early American, Early Colonial furniture was simple, utilitarian, and patterned after models in the European homeland. William of Orange ascended to the English throne in 1689, bringing with him a combination Dutch-English style which came to be known as William and Mary, after the king and his queen.

American colonial pieces modeled after William and Mary styles were characterized by straight and sturdy solid wood construction, slatted backs on chairs, elaborate stretchers on highboys, lowboys, and tables, scrolled legs, and carved feet. Woods were pine, oak, maple, walnut, and birch, and they were usually left unfinished except for staining and waxing.

Queen Anne succeeded William and Mary on the English throne, and her influence, too, began to be felt in styles across the sea. Queen Anne pieces are characterized by walnut wood; as a matter of fact, Queen Anne's reign (1702–1714) is known to decorators as the "Age of Walnut." The Queen Anne period brought with it the comfort and grace that was to come into full flower in the later Georgian era.

Queen Anne pieces are characterized by plain surfaces without molding or paneling and by a lack of underbracing. Legs are the curved cabriole ending in the club foot, the paw, or the claw and ball. There is some veneering and lacquer work, and sometimes cockleshell (scallop shell) ornamental carving. The wood was almost always walnut, but pine, ash, oak, and lime were also used.

Representative pieces include: the wing chair, the splat-back chair, the corner chair, the *first* easy chair, the love seat, highboys and lowboys, a chest-on-chest, secretaries, a high poster bed with a canopy, and a dropleaf table.

Georgian

Why choose Georgian? It is FORMAL, graceful, gracious, comfortable, and sturdy. It is derived from English inspiration. It is high-to-medium in price. It is at home with English Georgian architecture, eighteenth-century American Colonial architecture, and modern houses of the Colonial type.

What characterizes Georgian? The Georgian era (1714–1810) is known as the "Golden Age of Design." Spanning the reigns of George I, George II, and George III in England, the period sparkled with excitement. Trade with the Orient awakened interest in all things Chinese. Archaeological excavations of ancient Roman cities kindled interest in classical culture. Travel to France and Italy inspired simulation of continental styles. Exquisitely gifted English craftsmen interpreted all these influences in inspired designs that still mark a high point in history. Thomas Chippendale, George Hepplewhite, the two Adam brothers, and Thomas Sheraton made furniture that was copied in America and Europe. Wedgwood and Spode created graceful pottery and china. Noted silversmiths produced fine designs in silver. Reynolds and Gainsborough painted portraits. Truly, English Georgian interiors were the ultimate in gracious, graceful living.

In America, greater wealth and sophis-

By the 18th century America had grown out of her awkward infancy. Greater wealth and sophistication demanded more refinement in design. The pieces of the period have become classic because they express elegance without artifice, formality without stiffness. Reproductions of the period, typically of mahogany, enjoy perennial popularity. (Photo courtesy of Drexel Heritage Furnishings, Inc.)

tication brought greater elegance. American colonists wanted the same quality and craftsmanship as was found in European designs. Fine furniture-makers appeared. John Hancock, John Goddard, Moses Dodge, and Gilbert Ash were some of the most outstanding. Their basic models originated in England, but they adapted designs to American tastes. Until the Revolution, the major influence was Chippendale. The restored town of Williamsburg, Virginia, exemplifies this era. After the Revolution, in the Federal era, the Adam brothers were the greatest influence on American design.

Today American and English Georgian pieces are still the most sought-after of antiques, and there are many reproductions of Georgian styles on the American market.

COLORS Colors of the Georgian era are rich and restrained. They are neither light nor dark and they are muted with gray to make them soft. In America, colors of this era are often referred to as "Williamsburg" colors. They include gray-blue, mustard, muted red, warm brown, as well as pearl, cream, and white.

PATTERNS Wallpapers from China, France, and England included both scenic designs and all-over patterns. The very wealthy had Oriental carpets (or "Turkey carpets") for their floors. Many fine fabrics had delicate designs.

TEXTURES Smooth and shiny FORMAL furnishings. The walls were often finished with fine wood paneling with trim based on classical architectural forms. Some walls had plain painted plaster between the wooden dado (on the lower part of the wall) and the cornice molding at the ceiling.

Typically the furniture was made of mahogany or satinwood, polished to a high luster.

Windows were treated with elaborate draperies (usually made of imported textiles), hung with valances, swags, and jabots with elaborate fringes and tiebacks.

Decorative fabrics include velvets, damasks, taffetas and other silks, and upholstery of leather or haircloth.

STYLES *Chippendale.* Thomas Chippendale was the dictator of style in the early and

This is a Chippendale chair—actually a fine reproduction. The 18th-century original with its richly carved splat back comes from an historic private house. Although basically consistent in size, Chippendale's dining chairs show ornament inspired from all over space and time. (Photo courtesy of Baker Furniture Company.)

middle Georgian period. Inspired by French Rococo, Gothic, and Chinese motifs, Chippendale fashioned furniture that encouraged imitators on both sides of the ocean. His chairs are often used for dining and as occasional chairs.

The Chippendale pieces inspired by the French Rococo styles of Louis XV are characterized by the curved cabriole leg and carved motifs such as rocks, shells, foliage, ribbons, birds, and scrolls. In his pieces of Gothic inspiration, Chippendale revived the Gothic arch, clustered columns, and medieval tracery. In the styles now known as "Chinese Chippendale," the artist adapted Chinese motifs, including pagodas, key-fret bands, and lacquerwork, and used straight legs.

Hepplewhite. George Hepplewhite was a great influence in the late Georgian era. Basically inspired by classical motifs, he was the leader of a trend toward more delicacy of line and proportion. Hepplewhite has several innovations to his credit. He popularized the use of satinwood after 1765. He started decorating furniture with painted motifs. He helped to launch japanned furniture—pieces covered with lacquerwork and high-relief designs. And he invented the sideboard.

Some Hepplewhite chair backs were shaped as shields and ovals and decorated with designs of "Prince of Wales" feathers. Legs were straight or tapered, and often slender with fluting or reeding (vertical grooves).

The Adam Brothers. Robert and James Adam were the most forceful tastemakers of the late Georgian era. They were architects. They began by designing the building, then they would design everything down to the spoon on the table. The Adam brothers made total environments. They were inspired by the ancient artifacts being dug up in Italy. Adam styles are slender and light in feeling and small in scale. Shapes are circular, oval, hexagonal, and octagonal. Legs are square and tapered, or round and fluted. Motifs are classical: urns, plaques, medallions, scrolls, wreaths, festoons, fans. Furniture might be decorated by painting, inlay, or veneering.

Sheraton. Thomas Sheraton was the last great English designer of the eighteenth century. His furniture was known for its subtle grace and originality. Sheraton had a mechanical mind and developed a lot of multifunctional furniture: tables that turned into desks, tables that became library steps, a combination bureau/bookcase, and desks with secret compartments. Dining-room furniture was his specialty, but he also made very small-scale pieces suitable for bedrooms. His chair back—square with the straight top broken by a raised section—is popular, and frequently copied today. Sheraton was the first to use porcelain plaques as furniture decoration. His style was classical, borrowed from the Adam brothers and Louis XVI.

Eighteenth-century Colonial. American furniture was inspired by Queen Anne, Chippendale, Hepplewhite, and Sheraton. The woods commonly used were mahogany, cherry, gum, and curly maple.

Characteristic furniture legs were the carved cabriole leg with a claw-and-ball foot in high relief and the straight, square leg with fluting and reeding on the outer side. Characteristic carvings were scrolls, shells, pierced-back splats, and strapwork. Under the Hepplewhite influence, design motifs included "Prince of Wales" feathers, medallions, wheat, and festoons. Oriental lacquer and japan finishes became popular.

Representative pieces include the wing chair and the Martha Washington chair. For storage there were highboys, chest-on-chests, breakfront secretaries, and linen presses. Tables included tilt-top tables and two- or three-part dining tables. Desk styles included the kneehole, the tambour, and the blockfront. And then there was the American field bed.

LIGHTING Lamp bases, wall sconces, and candelabra were made of Wedgwood and Spode pottery, Chinese porcelains, crystal, silver, tole, bronze, and glass.

English eighteenth-century lamps were often Greek urns and other classical designs influenced by Robert Adam or Chinese-inspired designs. American Colonial lamps were elegant, reflecting a French influence as well as the English.

ACCESSORIES It was the rage to collect china—china imported from the Orient, as well as from fine European manufacturers, such as Spode and Wedgwood. Other important accessories include Chinese lacquered pieces, tall clocks and wall and mantel clocks, Delft tiles around the fireplace opening, pictures—portraits, landscapes, and sporting subjects—busts and statues in marble or bronze, mirrors, Stiegel and Sandwich glass, and last but not least, fine silver.

American Federal

Why choose American Federal? It is FORMAL, generally light in scale. It is an outgrowth of English and American Georgian styles. It is classic in inspiration, and expressive of America's new nationalism.

What characterizes American Federal? The winning of the Revolution inspired new furniture designs, those that proclaimed patriotism and the birth of the Republic. The symbols of the eagle, trumpet, and thunderbolt expressed nascent nationalism, while the classical motifs of the acanthus leaf, the saber, the cornucopia, the lyre, and the rosette associated the new United States with the great states of ancient Greece and Rome. Classical influence was also high on the European continent at the time. Napoleon was busy associating himself with the ancient Emperors of Rome, while the English were fascinated with the archaeological diggings and the discoveries at Pompeii.

Examples of American Federal architecture are Thomas Jefferson's Monticello and University of Virginia, and the Boston State House by Charles Bulfinch.

COLORS Colors become lighter and brighter than in the Georgian era.

This is a Duncan Phyfe dining room (circa 1810). The architectural influence of Adam is discernible in the ornamentation of the fireplace and the mirror above. It is delicate, symmetrical, and classical. The chairs are distinctly Phyfe FEDERAL. They are characterized by curved X shapes on both base and back. The weight of the windows and the server between them suggests the oncoming influence of the French EMPIRE style. (Photo courtesy of The Metropolitan Museum of Art.)

PATTERNS Classical themes and Oriental designs, delicate in scale.

TEXTURES Fine and FORMAL.

STYLES English Adam styles greatly affected interior architecture. Classic columns and niches in formal symmetry were often part of the wall treatment. These were restrained and refined in style in order to harmonize with the delicate proportions of Sheraton and Hepplewhite furniture. There was less wood paneling than in the Georgian era. Wood paneling was often kept to the fireplace wall, and to dados and cornice moldings. The other walls were of plaster and covered with paint, imported silk textiles, or scenic wallpapers from China, England, or France.

Duncan Phyfe was the most influential furniture designer of the Federal period. His furniture was extremely original, yet an evolution of the English Sheraton and Hepplewhite styles. He typically worked in mahogany, but sometimes used rosewood or cherry. His furniture is characterized by curves. Lyre-shaped bases are typical. Chair legs are concavely curved and may be reeded and fluted. Decorative motifs are classical and patriotic. Representative pieces include: chairs with lyre backs or X-shaped backs, sectional or extension dining tables, sofa tables with dropleaf ends, tambour tables, a butler's desk, and a Sheraton-type desk.

ACCESSORIES Accessories of the era include tall clocks, shelf clocks, architecturally framed mirrors. Trade with the Far East brought products from China, Japan, and India: furniture, silk, glass paintings, fine porcelains, Canton china, hand-painted wallpapers, embroideries.

French Louis XV and Louis XVI

Why choose French Louis XV or Louis XVI? They are both small-scale, lightweight FORMAL styles. The difference between them is that Louis XV (1723–1774) is curved and has natural motifs, and Louis XVI (1774–1789) is straight-lined with classical motifs. They both

The warmth and intimacy of this bedroom is fostered by French Louis XV bergère armchairs and an upholstered bench. The undulating curves seem soothing and sensuous while the delicacy of the designs inspires a sense of elegance and luxury. The style conveys the same message now as it did in the 18th century. (Photo courtesy of Caldwell's Interiors, Syosset, L.I.; design by Mayo-DeLucci.)

have a delicate, elegant effect that seems FEMININE in its appeal. An occasional piece of Louis XV or XVI can add interest and beauty to furnishings of basically sturdier style. Because they are small in scale, these styles are suitable for a small space—but only if your budget is bountiful. This is the high-priced spread. Your home might have a French architectural influence. You might live in Louisiana or another area where French settlers have had an impact, or you just might be a city sophisticate.

What characterizes Louis XV? This was an era of entertaining in boudoirs. It was a big change from the grand-scale gaudy show that Louis XIV managed at the Palace of Versailles. Furniture became small in scale, colors became soft, and sensuous curves took over the shape of everything. Madame de Pompadour, Louis XV's mistress, was setting the styles.

The style she fostered became known as Rococo, named after the rocks and shells that were its favorite decorative motifs. New furniture was designed for the new life-style of the time. The chaise longue appeared for the first time, along with the bergère (a comfortable armchair with enclosed arms) and duchess chair. The toilette table and the tea table were

also invented; these too made the boudoir more relaxing and inviting.

What characterizes Louis XVI? The florid forms of Louis XV underwent a classic cleanup. Marie Antoinette, queen of Louis XVI, had had a classical education. She liked the looks of things Greek and Roman. She had a fondness for simple, straight lines. Her mood was enhanced by the moment. This was the time that archaeological excavations in Italy were turning up the towns of the ancient Roman Empire.

Louis XVI furnishings adopted classic motifs, straightened their lines and legs, but kept all the grace and delicacy of the earlier era.

COLORS Favorite colors of both periods were grayed tones of pastel greens, blues, and rose, along with ivory and beige. Wood was light-toned or painted pastel.

PATTERNS To coordinate with the small size of the furnishings, patterns were also small in scale. In the Louis XV era, patterns were curved and asymmetrical, and the design motifs were taken from nature. In the Louis XVI period, the patterns were straight-lined and balanced, and the design motifs were inspired by classical themes.

TEXTURES Textures in both periods were smooth and luxurious. Walls were paneled with delicately carved wood, often decorated with painting, fabric, or wallpaper inserts. There were luxurious French Aubusson or Savonnerie rugs on the floor. Windows featured draperies with swag valances. Furniture was made from fine woods—satinwood, fruit-woods, and ebony. In addition to printed cottons, fabrics included many fine silk weaves: brocades, damasks, taffetas, satins, and moirés. Soft textures provided a sense of intimacy; shiny textures, an air of elegance.

STYLES *Louis XV.* The curved style of Louis

XV is characterized by the cabriole leg and the scroll foot. Chairs have short, flaring arms, and ornately carved broad backs. "Bombé" chests were designed with convex fronts. Furniture was decorated with rococo and shell motifs in unbalanced arrangements. Decoration included carving, inlay, marquetry, painting, gilding, and metal mounts.

Louis XVI. The straight-lined style of Louis XVI is characterized by balanced arrangements of classical motifs: acanthus leaves, bows, rosettes, oval plaques, staffs entwined with laurel leaves, lyres, urns, flaming torches. Decoration included gilt mounts and marquetry.

Representative pieces include the couch or daybed, the cabriolet chair with hollowed-out back, the bergère chair, and an oval-backed chair. There was a half-round commode, a gaming table, a flat-topped desk, and the semainier—a chest with seven drawers, one for each day of the week. A special display cabinet mounted on a small table was called a vitrine.

LIGHTING Lamps were made of elegant materials—usually crystal, silver, or porcelain. They were designed first with Rococo embellishments, and then with classic themes.

ACCESSORIES Aubusson tapestries, needlepoint, and tooled leather added extra softness. Ormolu clocks, and porcelains and fine ceramics from St. Cloud, Sèvres, and Dresden gave lovely light reflections. And busts, statues, and small objects expressed each era—first Rococo romanticism, and then Roman and Pompeian classicism.

French Provincial

Why choose French Provincial? You may like French furniture, but not want the most opulent effects.

What characterizes French Provincial? French people outside the court needed furniture too. Since styles were set at court, people looked there for inspiration. They copied the courtly styles with various degrees of elaborateness and success. City copies were the sleekest and most sophisticated and had the most ornament. Bourgeois styles were a bit more modest. Country styles were still more rustic and rough. French Provincial is the general name given to all the regional copies of courtly furniture during the reigns of Louis XIII, Louis XIV, Louis XV, and Louis XVI. (Louis XV was particularly popular.)

French Provincial is especially admired because it retains all the grace of line of the courtly furniture, while cleaning out all that opulent ornament. Most of the reproductions in this country are of bourgeois/city styles rather than the peasant variations. They are SEMIFORMAL and versatile, looking at home in interiors that range from informal to formal. Prices are a bit on the high side.

COLORS Colors can be delicate blues, greens, and roses.

Country French furnishings have grace of line sans fussy formality. They are SEMIFORMAL and adaptable. The pieces pictured here have the curved lines and flower-and-shell ornament derived from Louis XV court styles, but the styling is simpler. Upholstery frames are painted white, and the asymmetrical flowered fabric is bold with an upbeat fun feeling. (Photo courtesy of Baker Furniture Company.)

PATTERNS Printed cotton toile fabrics are of the period and perfect. They are two-color scenic repeat designs, showing young girls in the country and little settings like that. Checked patterns are appropriate. If furniture is curved, you might choose patterns with curved lines. If furniture is straight in line, you might choose a similar sort of pattern design. You might repeat the decorative motifs of the furnishings in floorcoverings or fabrics.

TEXTURES The textures you choose depend on the formality of the furniture. The most sophisticated styles are at home with silks and such. Rough pieces with rush seats look at home with earthier fabrics.

STYLES *Country Provincial.* Country craftsmen dispensed with inlays, gilt, and painted decorations. They made their furniture of whatever woods were at hand—chiefly oak, chestnut, beech, elm, and cherry. They would leave the wood unfinished or rub it down with wax to bring out its graining. Chair seats would be woven of rush. Furnishings of a typical country cottage were limited, basic. There were straw-bottom chairs. (The capuchin chair with turned frame, open back, and rush seat was a favorite.) There was a rectangular table, perhaps flanked by long, low benches. Storage occurred in cupboards. Tall cupboards were popular, with closed storage on the bottom and open shelves above to display pottery. Chests and wardrobes contained clothes. Four-poster beds took care of the sleeping shift.

City Provincial. City provincial furniture was simpler than its court counterpart, but more refined than its country cousin. It, too, eschewed elaborate ornamentation, and left its common woods in the natural state. But it comforted itself in upholstery. Chairs and sofas were upholstered on seats, backs, and arms or arm pads. Tables and chests, although they retained something of a rustic character, showed a greater delicacy of line.

To complement city provincial furniture,

floors could be covered in an elegant floral carpet in pastel tones reflecting the period. Cotton toile fabrics, embroidery, silk, and other printed cottons are also appropriate.

American Greek Revival/ French Empire/ English Regency

Why choose these styles? They are inspired by the ancient cultures of Egypt, Greece, and Rome, but unlike the delicate interpretation of Louis XVI, these styles are distinctly MASCULINE in mood. Proportions are large and heavy, colors are bold and assertive. Since materials are expensive and/or exotic, these furnishings convey an elegant FORMAL feeling. And because they are so bold and strong, the mood they make is STIMULATING/DRAMATIC.

What characterizes American Greek Revival? After the Revolution, Washington and Jefferson expressed the idea that the new republic should be represented by the architectural forms of democratic Greece and republican Rome. It took a while for the idea to catch on, but it did. Other things helped. The Greek War of Independence (1821–27) caught the American imagination. At the same time, France and England were using classical themes. French Empire and English Regency were the latest fashions to follow. Besides all that, the country was expanding, and houses had to be built. A "Temple" style of architecture, with a pedimented portico inspired by the Parthenon, had been used for public buildings; why not for homes? With no reason why not, the style was adapted to residential architecture. Southern plantation homes are an example. Greek columns were used inside and out. Detail expressed classic motifs: the fret, acanthus leaf, and honeysuckle.

What characterizes French Empire? Napoleon spent a lot of time trying to aggrandize himself. He conquered countries. He also

The American GREEK REVIVAL style was inspired by French Empire and English Regency. This early 19th-century American parlor features a French-style Récamier sofa on one wall. Named after Madame Récamier, who is seen lounging on one in a famous painting by David, the sofa has a much higher head than foot. Heavy proportions, dark woods, bright colors, and shiny textures characterize most furnishings of this era. (Photo courtesy of The Metropolitan Museum of Art.)

dominated the decorative arts. He wanted to surround himself with all the grandeur and pomp of Caesar and Alexander. He commanded the noted designers Percier and Fontaine to create it. They created furnishings of imperial impressiveness. Proportions were heavy. Lines were strong and straight. Materials were masculine, with large expanses of highly polished wood and intensely assertive bright upholstery. Decoration symbolized Napoleon's power and military might. The initial "N", surmounted by a laurel wreath and an imperial eagle, decorated furniture, plates, and glasses. A bee was another symbol for the Emperor. Military themes from Greece and Rome associated Napoleon with ancient power plays. Motifs from his Egyptian campaign— sphinxes, pyramids, obelisks, and lotuses— spread his success. Winged figures gave a mythological momentum to the man. If Percier and Fontaine lived today, they would do well in public relations!

What characterizes English Regency? English Regency furniture was named after the Prince Regent, who later became George IV. Like French Empire, it was inspired by Greek, Roman, and Egyptian styles. Its lines were

rather heavy and MASCULINE. From a rather simple beginning, English Regency furnishings wound up wild. The Prince, you see, had a taste for the exotic. Furnishings began to be extravagantly ornamented with carvings of animals. A pleasure palace was designed for the Prince by John Nash. For theatrical effects, the Royal Pavilion at Brighton couldn't be outdone by Hollywood. Bright lacquer glows from walls and ceilings, reflected and intensified by entire walls of mirror. Against this background, you'll see a sphinx, all bright and brassy, or Chinese dragons cavorting. Ornamental monkeys climb the furniture. Bells ring. It's like a fantasy land of exotic adventure. The Oriental, the exotic, and extravagant expressions of the classical past all mix in this manic mansion. It's a bit much, but it sure is a show!

COLORS Bright and powerful. Walls of an Empire room were often painted in intense color, and walls of Regency rooms were often bright lacquer. Dark "Pompeian red" and rich colors taken from the Orient—golds, greens and pinks—are characteristic.

PATTERNS Motifs came from Egypt, Greece and Rome, and the Orient. The classic lotus, acanthus and laurel leaf, honeysuckle, lyre and urn were joined by sphinxes, lion's heads, and winged figures.

TEXTURES There were a lot of shiny textures. Polish, lacquer, metals, and gold leaf did the dazzling. Empire pieces were made of polished red mahogany, sometimes ebony. Regency pieces were made of mahogany, pearwood stained black to look like mahogany, black japanned beechwood, lacquered bamboo, and other exotic woods. Furniture was boldly decorated with bronze and brass ormolu mounts. Window valances, too, were made of pressed brass.

STYLES Proportions were heavy. *Greek Revival* furniture was an American version of French Empire and English Regency. It was heavy in proportions, curved in form, and decorated with metal ornaments. Chair and table

BIEDERMEIER is an Austrian or German interpretation of French Empire. The unmatching sleigh-shaped beds are fashioned of richly figured woods and decorated with gold-and-black enamel ornaments suggesting Napoleon's Egyptian adventures. The chest with its symmetrical metal mountings alludes to power and prestige, but its diminutive size makes it cozy. (Photo courtesy of Lees Carpets; design by Seymour Louis Kaiser, ASID.)

legs were often capped with plain or ornamental cast-metal feet.

Representative pieces of the *Empire* period are chairs of Greek outline and Roman decorative detail, folding furniture (good for taking to war), the Récamier sofa, the gondola bed, the daybed, a desk with raised drawers on top, heavy chests, display cabinets (also called vitrines), and small tables with tambour fronts.

Representative pieces of the *English Regency* period are the sleigh bed, the revolving bookcase, stools with animal heads and lion's paws, the curule armchair, the high-standing writing desk and the Davenport writing desk, nests of tables, extension tables, card tables, and a round pedestal table.

German Biedermeier

Why choose German Biedermeier? Biedermeier reproductions are used in the U.S. because they are quaint, can get along with a lot of other styles, and they are not outrageous in price.

What characterizes German Biedermeier? Biedermeier is the name of a style of furniture produced in Austria and Germany during the first half of the nineteenth century. It is based on the Napoleonic Empire style, but the name "Biedermeier" was taken from a cartoon character—the Archie Bunker of his day. He was a self-satisfied and stout country gentleman with opinions on everything, and the strongest ones on subjects he knew nothing about.

The Biedermeier style is generally heavy and clumsy, but appealing anyway. Some pieces succeed at being relatively graceful. The style also incorporates pieces of peasant inspiration—with crude shapes, painted patterns, and naïve carving.

Victorian

Why choose Victorian? For fun is the best reason. You might find the romance of the era appealing. The furniture is fairly sturdy and it is

A **VICTORIAN** love seat, passed through generations of the family, faces the fireplace. Its cover was worn, so the designer chose a new fabric that reproduces an authentic design of the Victorian era. To give the room a calming unity (unlike the Victorian era) he covered the walls and two slipper chairs in the same pattern. Now the daughter delights in her inheritance. (Design by Everett Brown, FASID; photo by Henry S. Fullerton III.)

SEMIFORMAL in style—that is to say, it can mix with formal or informal furnishings. You might choose it to express the place where you live. The Mississippi River valley and San Francisco, for instance, have a heavy Victorian influence. Your house might be Victorian in style. Or not. A few Victorian pieces make a nice contrast in a clean-lined modern room. You might have some Victorian furnishings, or think you can beg, borrow, or steal some.

What characterizes Victorian? In England, Queen Victoria wasn't much interested in the decorative arts, and the artisans of the time seemed spent. The inspiration and inventiveness of the Georgian era had been supreme. There was nothing to do for an encore. However, the people demanded novelty. Artisans gave them novelty—willy-nilly. It was like an international food bazaar. Take a taste of Greek, Turkish, Gothic, Venetian, Florentine, Egyptian, or a little Louis XV. Mix them up if you like, for a new taste sensation. Occasionally something special would pop up out of the stew.

Popular woods were black walnut, mahogany, ebony, and rosewood. They were often carved with fruit, flowers, leaves, and nosegays. Gilded pressed-metal ornaments and mother-of-pearl inlays were used occasionally. Papier mâché furniture made its appearance for the first time.

During the Victorian time, English chintzes came into a great flowering. Themes were from the garden, meadow, brook, and field; shapes were natural, and colors bright and happy.

In America, except for the unhappy dislocations caused by the Civil War, 1840–1880 was an age of affluence and expansion, of exuberance and enthusiasm, of naïveté and sweet sentimentality. The industrial revolution was making millionaires, while Victorian morality prompted some ladies to knit stockings to cover the piano's naked legs—and some men to seek solace in their fraternal orders. In retrospect, the age was wonderful for its whimsy and dauntless vitality.

The newly rich wanted the best there was in the world—all of it, all at once. They had a lot of cultural catching up to do, and they were hungry consumers. They stole styles from everywhere in the world.

The entrance into the machine age caused dislocations. People were trying to make by machine what had been made by hand, and they usually did a bad job of it. Some sensitive artistic types rejected the idea of the machine altogether. The most forward-looking began to conceive designs that could best be made by machine—a thought that eventually led to the modern movement. Machine-made reproductions of Gothic, French Empire, and Louis XV styles were often clumsy and awkward. But the invention of the coiled metal spring led to the introduction of the first all-upholstered furniture. Heavily fringed multicushioned sofas—circular, face-to-face, and back-to-back—are now intimately associated with Victoriana. Machines made wallpaper and carpet, too, resulting in the smaller-scale repeat patterns that moved all over Victorian walls and floors.

John Henry Belter was the master craftsman of the time. Perfect for the era, his furniture was fanciful but durable. It was based vaguely on Louis XV forms, and elaborately ornamented with fruit, flowers, and foliage. He should also be credited with industrial invention. He was one of the first to steam and press laminated veneers in order to create continuous curved wooden forms.

The first development of photography, daguerreotypes, decorated Victorian walls. Daguerreotype cases with covers represent the first use of plastics in this country.

Art historians criticize the Victorian era for a lack of artistic integrity, saying what is perfectly true—that Victorians were more interested in industry than in art. However, stripped of its excesses, Victorian styles are appealing.

COLORS Colors were strong and heavy. For example, red and green and black were favorites. For use today, it is recommended that you lighten the colors.

PATTERNS There were too many. In the era, there was often a confusing array of conflicting patterns—on walls, windows, floor, and upholstery. Victorian styles look more appealing these days against plain-colored carpets and walls.

TEXTURES Textures were heavy, plush. For example, the windows had the works: heavy draperies with swags, valances, jabots, and heavy fringes—and sheer lace curtains underneath. You can lighten the load today by giving a less elaborate treatment to your windows.

STYLES Curved. Most furniture forms were modeled on Louis XV Rococo. Furniture was reproduced with more or less success based on Gothic, French Empire, and Egyptian styles. Furniture frames ranged from the simple and serpentine, to those with elaborate carving and piercing. Upholstery was often button-tufted.

Newly invented all-upholstered seating was covered in heavy red or green plush or black horsehair, and trimmed with tassels and fringes.

Wicker furniture was popular for summer houses.

Other Victorian furnishings include: the hassock and ottoman, the Turkish divan, nests of tables, tables with mother-of-pearl inlay, and papier mâché furniture.

Furniture placement was cluttered. (You can clean it out.) You might use a few Victorian curved forms to contrast with other clean-lined designs.

LIGHTING Lighting was provided by gas lights. A glass chandelier was often centered in the ceiling. Glass fixtures were often etched or painted.

ACCESSORIES Lots of them. Antimacassars (little doilies) were put on the backs of chairs so that men's hair grease wouldn't ruin the upholstery. Whatnot shelves held bric-a-brac. Shell and bead curtains hung between rooms. There were blackamoor statues and small statues portraying sentimental or historical subjects, in bronze or putty-colored composition material. There were charcoal portraits and silhouettes cut out of paper by itinerant artists. There were needlework mottoes and sentimental steel engravings. Daguerreotype cases were decorated with historical, patriotic, and sentimental themes, fraternal or political emblems, and Christmas, Easter, and Valentine designs. There might be Currier and Ives colored lithographs—but not in the parlor. And to add a little life to the floor, there might be a bear-, lion- or tiger-skin rug, complete with head and snarling teeth.

Spanish

Why choose Spanish? Spanish styles are DURABLE, strong, heavy, MASCULINE, colorful, and often relatively inexpensive. Spanish settlers have had an influence on Florida, California, and the Southwest. Spanish styles look great

Heavy beams, stucco walls, and tile floors bespeak SPANISH. The heavy, rectangular furnishings do too. To soften all the hard textures, there is a squared sofa upholstered in a rich, wool stripe and a small rug in a dynamic design. In a Spanish interior bright colors contrast with dark woods, rich textiles contrast with slick tiles and give warmth to spare-room arrangements. (Photo courtesy of the Simmons Company.)

with Spanish architecture, and they can often add a colorful note to rooms of other styles.

What characterizes Spanish? Spanish settlers in this country brought with them the styles of the Renaissance. They came to a climate as warm as their home, so they readily adapted their native architecture to the new land. To create a sense of coolness, furniture was sparse, the interior was open to an outside patio, and floors were covered in cool, slick tiles. To convey their sense of power and presence, their furniture was strong, heavy, and dark, and their colors were bright and bold. Leather, wrought iron, and nailhead trim contributed to the masculine mood. These people came to conquer.

COLORS Bold contrast of bright versus dark. Dark woods contrast with intense colors

in tile, plaster ornament, painted woodwork, or wool textiles.

PATTERNS Strong geometrics and scrollwork patterns, reminiscent of the iron grillwork of Spanish architecture, are typical.

TEXTURES There is great textural variety—smooth tiles versus heavy wood and rich wools. Floors are usually hard. Typically, all the floors, including the patio, are paved with brick, stone, or tile. (The tile might be a replica of a regional pattern.)

Walls are usually hard and sometimes rough. They might be plain smooth plaster or rough plaster, showing trowel marks. They might be ceramic tile or brick.

Wood is dark, usually oak. The woodwork is typically limited to the doors and ceilings. The ceiling is usually beamed. Heavy wooden interior shutters are at the windows.

To soften all these hard textures, there might be a colorful throw rug on the floor, ornamental leather on the walls or furniture, rich wool textiles, or red velvet.

STYLES Many Spanish furnishings available today are reproductions of Spanish Renaissance styles. They are heavy in proportion (sometimes to an extreme). The dark woods are deeply carved. Sometimes styles incorporate wrought iron and/or nailhead trim. Some surfaces may be covered with red velvet or painted.

Representative pieces include a type of ladder-back chair with the topmost rung enlarged and elaborately carved, a strong rectangular trestle table, squarish, open-backed chairs upholstered in leather, and a portable writing cabinet (called a vargueño). The vargueño is a big box (often in walnut) with handles on each end, which sits on a separate support. The front is hinged closed with strong, complicated metal locks. Inside, there are many cubbyholes and compartments, each elaborately decorated.

For RUSTIC interiors there is a primitive type of Spanish Colonial furniture available that features crudely carved wood and chairs with rush seats. Rustic Mexican chairs and china cabinets are also available.

LIGHTING You might have a wrought-iron chandelier, or pierced tinware light fixtures.

ACCESSORIES Leatherwork, ironwork, and ceramics—including heavy earthenware pottery—are features of a Spanish interior. Today we are importing a lot of decorative tin, including tinware mirrors, and a lot of exuberant paper flowers from Mexico. (American and Mexican Indian accessories mix well with Spanish styles.)

This is a PENNSYLVANIA DUTCH chest dating from about 1780. It is made of yellow pine and poplar and painted with unusually elaborate decorations. There are the typical tulips, but also endearing unicorns and galloping horsemen overlooked by birds. This COUNTRY/RUSTIC style is most CHEERFUL. (Photo courtesy of The Metropolitan Museum of Art, Rogers Fund, 1923.)

Pennsylvania Dutch

Why choose Pennsylvania Dutch? You might live in Pennsylvania and want to project part of that state's heritage. You might live in the country. Pennsylvania Dutch is a COUNTRY/RUS-TIC style. You might want something DURABLE. You might want a CHEERFUL piece or two; with its painted decoration, Pennsylvania Dutch furnishings create a happy mood.

What characterizes Pennsylvania Dutch? The Pennsylvania Dutch are religious fanatics with a sense of humor. They are actually Swiss and German Mennonites who settled in eastern Pennsylvania after William Penn offered them religious freedom and land. To keep their customs, they kept to themselves. They were "Deutsch" or German, but their English neighbors called them "Dutch" because it was easier.

The Pennsylvania Dutch are still keeping to themselves. They reject all forms of modernity—including both bathrooms and electricity. They have peculiar and plain customs, but they are not sour and dour.

Their furnishings are best known for their cheerful painted decoration. Hearts and tulips, trees-of-life and peacocks, eagles, deer, and farmyard birds are painted with bright, happy abandon on furniture and family documents. The same symbols are woven, embroidered, or appliquéd on fabrics, and adorn pottery, tinware, and toys. Sometimes sayings are added.

The furnishings themselves are simple, functional country styles. Large cupboards feature closed storage below and open shelves above for pewter and pottery. Chests and wardrobes contain clothes. Table types include sawbuck tables, long oak refectory tables, dough tables, tables with low stretchers, and round-topped, splay-legged tables. Chairs include many of the Windsor type, bannister-back, splat-back, and solid-panel back. There is also a European peasant chair with raked legs and a solid shaped back. Spice boxes and work boxes complete the ensemble. The furniture is durable and well made. Woods are pine, cherry, oak, or walnut.

Pennsylvania Dutch houses and barns generally resemble Colonial types. Some are made of stone; wooden ones are often painted red. Hex signs on the exterior protect the home from witches.

On the inside, a big living room/kitchen features a fireplace with an enormous log mantel. Walls are plastered and whitewashed and feature folk pictures. Kitchen and dining utensils of iron, copper, and wood also hang on the walls.

Fabrics are made from home-grown flax. The linen is usually embroidered with needlework or adorned with appliqués.

Shaker

Why choose Shaker furnishings? Because they are beautiful in their simplicity. This COUNTRY/RUSTIC or INFORMAL style is transcendent in its purity. The pieces are unornamented, light in scale, delicate in proportion, and graceful in shape. However, for all their refinement, Shaker furnishings were built to be functional. They are solid and DURABLE designs. Shaker furniture looks right in informal Colonial interiors; it also blends beautifully with modern.

What characterizes Shaker furnishings? The Shakers, a communal religious sect applied clean thinking to everything around them, which resulted in some very fine furniture. Eschewing excesses, they reduced furniture to its purest, most functional form. And having a religious commitment to quality of craftsmanship, they produced technically perfect pieces. Although Shaker furniture is sensible and sturdy, its lines are refined and graceful. It is much admired by modernists, who also believe that the form of an object should be strictly determined by its function.

Clean thinking extended to the arrangement of the Shaker home. Large cupboards, chests, and drawers, designed for specific storage purposes, were built in. Free-standing pieces were light and easily moved, all for ease of

The SHAKERS produced some of the most forthright furniture in America at the end of the 18th century and beginning of the 19th. They were religiously opposed to ornamentation and shoddy workmanship. Their designs are pure in concept and execution, as this exhibition of Shaker furnishings indicates. The Shakers also liked rooms that were EASY TO CLEAN, so they hung chairs from pegboards. (Photo courtesy of the Milwaukee Art Center Collection; photo by P. Richard Eells.)

cleaning. This concept, too, has been followed by the modern movement.

Shaker furniture was made of local woods, including pine, cherry, and maple. It was lightly stained or given a thin wash of red, yellow, or blue color. Chairs resembled Early American ladder-back or Windsor types. Dining tables were large for communal eating. Beds had low headboards and footboards and were typically painted green. Other furnishings include swivel chairs, benches, stools, blanket chests, sewing cabinets, slant-top desks, washstands, chests, and highboys.

(Design by Juan Montoya; photo by Bill Rothschild.)

13

SEX

You can play it up; you can play it down. You can even play around.

GENERAL/UNISEX

A room shared by both a man and a woman should be neither masculine nor feminine, unless it is one person's particular hideout.

COLORS Good general colors are white, pale blue, green, yellow, gold, and, of course, the neutrals. Stay away from the too feminine pale pinks and lilacs. Colors of medium value—neither especially pale, nor especially dark—are unisex.

PATTERNS Geometric patterns will please almost anybody if they are not too bold or dark in color. Men like flowers too—if they're not too fussy and frilly.

TEXTURES Strike a middle ground. Rough, coarse textures seem masculine, and delicate frills and laces seem feminine.

STYLES Choose furnishings of medium size. Delicate spindly chairs make men feel uncomfortable, and gargantuan pieces could make a little lady feel overwhelmed.

MASCULINE

What is the stereotype of the he-man? Large, rough, earthy, willing to wrestle a bearcat, direct and to-the-point in conversation. (This reminds me of all the Westerns of my childhood.) A man's room can be done in the same bold strokes. Contrasts can be strong—men are generally thought to like conflicts more than women.

You might select a theme that expresses adventure and exploration, courage or conquest. Animal-skin rugs—zebra, bear, lion—might suggest a conquering hero in the jungle. All sorts of sports themes suggest rivalry and victory or mastery over nature. What are his hobbies? You can bring them home to him. Nautical motifs will bring home the sea. Horses might arouse visions of the Wild West for Sonny and of the track for Dad. Best of all, consult the man in question. His preferences and opinions should be respected in *his* room.

COLORS Dark or bright. Down-to-earth neutrals or rich characterful colors—deep dark ones, or bright socko ones like red. Some good rugged color combinations are: black/brown/white, orange/brown, and rust/brown/olive. White, black, and red are strong and successful together.

Even though we all still love John Wayne movies, we're getting away from the old sexual stereotypes. It's better to be individual. The individual who uses this room likes a sense of strength. He's got it in a boldly scaled contemporary canopy bed of olive ash burl and in four compatible geometric designs that have strong contrasts between dark and light. (Photo courtesy of Thayer Coggin, Inc.; design by Milo Baughman.)

PATTERNS Geometrics: plaid in dark colors, strong stripes, checks, and other geometrics. Menswear fabrics can be used for upholstery. Paisleys in strong colors and splashy abstract-expressionist patterns are sensual but still safely masculine.

TEXTURES Earthy. Wood tones are wonderful. You might want wood-paneled walls, wooden shutters, or woven wood blinds in addition to wooden furniture. Brick, stone, and rough-textured plaster have a natural look too.

As for upholstery, leather and suede are as good as pipe tobacco for conveying a masculine mood. Heavy-wear vinyl can pose as leather. Wools and tweeds are good; men have been dressing in them for years. Soft corduroy or velvet in a dark color would add a little sensuousness to the masculine muscle.

Fabrics that are nubby or bumpy—burlap, heavy linen, and textured casement cloths in addition to rough wools and tweeds—give an earthy atmosphere. So do shaggy rugs. Some wallpapers are printed on grounds that have a rough burlaplike texture.

STYLES Whether ornate or simple, the furniture should convey a feeling of strength and solidity.

In the TRADITIONAL category, you could select large-scale English GEORGIAN, ENGLISH REGENCY, or FRENCH EMPIRE for a FORMAL feeling. For a SEMIFORMAL effect—GERMAN BIEDERMEIER, or SPANISH styles, including those with wrought iron and nailheads. For an INFORMAL feeling, most RUSTIC styles are heavy enough to be considered masculine. EARLY ENGLISH is a good example.

Masculine MODERN styles include straight-lined designs in natural wood, big bulky upholstery, and large commanding storage pieces. In general, choose furniture with tailored lines.

For a tailored look at the windows, you could select shutters, draperies hanging straight, vertical blinds, or skinny-slat horizontal blinds. Roman shades—which fold up in neat accordion pleats—have a clean, crisp look.

LIGHTING Fixtures can be arranged so that there are bold contrasts between light and shadow. That will create a strong, dramatic effect.

ACCESSORIES He will probably want to frame his awards, citations, and diplomas and display his bowling trophies. You also may want to reflect his mettle—with brass, pewter, or wrought-iron accessories.

FEMININE

Although it is often untrue, women are thought to be light and delicate, soft, and sweet. These characteristics can convey a feminine feeling in a room. Women are also thought to be mediators, peacemakers. It follows that their rooms should have soft contrasts, not big, brazen, bold ones.

COLORS Pale or soft. Pale pastels are light and delicate. Pink and lilac are particularly feminine in feeling. It is a good idea to choose colors that are flattering to the complexion of the lady of the room. Ask her to look in her closet and tell you which colors she feels best in.

PATTERNS Curved designs with natural themes, flower prints. Women have traditionally been thought of as being curvy and intuitive. Therefore, feminine designs are curvy and often inspired by nature. However, geometrical designs, if they are in pastel colors, can be considered feminine.

TEXTURES Soft and smooth. For example, you might want smooth wall-to-wall carpeting. If a young person is using the room and you want a durable vinyl floor, you might add some soft, fluffy scatter rugs.

Fabrics can be sheer, lightweight or delicate-looking, like lacy casement-cloth or sheer curtains, batiste, voile, piqué, silklike nylon and polyester. When fabrics are heavier, like velvet, they will still achieve a light look if they are pale in color.

The light-looking curved furniture is inspired by French LOUIS XV. The unifying pattern on furniture, walls, windows, and ceiling is delicate in design and natural in subject. The fluffy fur rug is soft and sensual, and the mirror and lacquered desk are shiny and glamorous. It all adds up to what you would call a FEMININE room. (Design by Everett Brown, FASID; photo by Yuichi Idaka.)

If you do want an uneven texture, make it a subtle one—like the slubs of silk. Some wallpaper patterns are printed on grounds that look like raw silk.

STYLES Lightweight and/or curved. Most TRADITIONAL furniture styles of this description are based on FRENCH LOUIS XV. Small-scale, straight-lined pieces are also appropriate for feminine FORMAL rooms. These styles include LOUIS XVI, and some GEORGIAN—Adam, Sheraton, and Hepplewhite. For a more INFORMAL feeling, VICTORIAN styles and curved wicker designs are fun. All kinds of furniture can be made to look feminine if painted or upholstered in pastel colors.

The drama of the angular architecture is respected but softened in this FEMININE bedroom. The wall in back of the bed is softened with a shirred fabric in a light-looking plaid that repeats the diagonal line of the roof. Draperies hanging straight emphasize the verticality of the window, but the free-flowing leaf design eases its angularity. A carpet contributes comfort, and wicker furnishings light-hearted unevenness. (Photo courtesy of Champion Building Products.)

You might want curves at the windows too. Curtains can be finished with ruffles instead of hems. You could have tie-back draperies or puffy, fluffy austrian shades.

LIGHTING There should be an even distribution of light, creating soft shadows instead of stark contrasts between light and dark. Soft shadows have something of a feminine allure.

ACCESSORIES Crystal, gold, diamonds—whatever pleases her. If all else fails, you can waft perfume around the room.

SEXY

Where appropriate? It's up to your discretion.

COLORS You might want to choose a scheme of warm colors. Dim light combined with warm colors flatters the complexion and creates a friendly, relaxed atmosphere.

TEXTURES Thick, shaggy, soft, pleasant to the touch. This is the most important factor. Thick, soft textures not only appeal to the senses, they create a feeling of warmth, and because they absorb sound, they create a feeling of privacy.

For the floor, you might want a deep pile carpet or fur rugs.

Walls can be soft too. You might cover them with carpet or with fabric. You might select a wallcovering that is flocked or has a corduroylike texture.

Heavy draperies at the windows might be pulled to cut out the outside world and to create a cozy, private place. (Of course, a romantic view, if it is private, is good too.)

Furniture might be heavily upholstered in fabrics soft to the touch. Satin and velvet are sensuous textures, and so are suede and butter-soft leather.

In addition to the soft textures, you need

With light under the platform, the bed looks like it's floating on air. The soft, quilted bedcover, the carpeted floor, and the dark walls lend a warm, intimate atmosphere. The mirror at the head of the bed and the dramatically directed lighting add excitement. For more mood making, stereo speakers are built into the walls on either side of the bed. (Design by Juan Montoya; photo by Bill Rothschild.)

some shine to sharpen the excitement. Mirrors and metal will add glitter and glamour.

STYLES Furniture should be generous in size to be accommodating. It might be big, soft, and voluptuous, and rounded in shape.

LIGHTING Dim or luminous lighting contributes a mysterious allure. Firelight or candlelight are often enough. If you need other lights, put them on a dimmer switch. Light should be a warm color—choose pink bulbs. Warm light will give your skin a good glow.

ACCESSORIES To top it off, choose other things that appeal to the senses. Fur feels good. You might want fur pillows or throws. A well-stocked bar often helps people to unwind and become more responsive to their senses. Music can move moods and free the spirit from the ordinary and everyday. Lovely smells can arouse the senses—be it after-shave, perfume, or the aroma of dinner cooking.

(Design by Braswell-Willoughby, Inc.; photo by Yuichi Idaka.)

14

MOOD

The mood you select for a room depends most on what would enhance its activities. In a room where you sleep or study the mood should be CALM. In a room where you have parties the mood can be STIMULATING. In a room where you do everything, such as a studio, the mood should be RELAXING.

The mood also depends on how much time you spend in the room. The shorter the time spent, the more DRAMATIC the room can be. You won't stay there long enough to get tired of it.

In general, large rooms can take DRAMATIC effects. Small rooms usually can't. Flamboyant personalities love dramatic effects, conservative types don't.

CALM/PEACEFUL

You want to relax. You want relief from all the noise and nonsense you've had to suffer all day. Peace and Quiet. Oh, why is it so hard to come by? Refer to Chapter 9 to see what you can do to create quiet. Read on to see how you can tune out trauma. What is your idea of rest and release? Sitting by a deserted beach at dusk? Staring out to infinity at the horizon? Feeling comforted in the quiet of the soft subtle light? You can recreate the mood in your room. Minimize movement. Let everything be soft and subtle. Let the eye slide from one thing to another without noting much difference between objects. Let it blend into one harmonious unity.

COLORS To create calm, avoid strong contrasts. You might choose a monochromatic scheme, using variations of just one color, or you might choose a scheme of two colors that are similar to each other. The cool colors, the blues and greens, are calming—unlike the reds and oranges, which stir things up. Darker, grayer colors are calming too. When we feel a sense of serenity at dusk, it is because everything is washed in gray light. A touch of gray can calm down almost any color. Most of us like to sleep in the dark; it follows that dark colors are restful.

PATTERNS As we said, pattern is lively. If you want your room to be super-calm, you should avoid pattern altogether. However, you could choose a subtle pattern—one with closely blended colors with maybe a textured effect or subtle stripes. Alternatively, you could limit pattern by using it only on accessories.

TEXTURES Soft, smooth textures suggest

serenity. A carpet-covered floor is not only soft to the touch, it absorbs sound. Fabric or carpet on the walls can make a room into a soundless sanctuary.

STYLES Furniture in straight-lined styles seems calmer than curved-lined styles. Long low units—like bookcases or chests—create a restful horizontal line, a line like the horizon, or like you asleep. Furniture that blends into the background helps to minimize jarring contrasts. It can be built in, or be the same color as the walls.

LIGHTING Lighting is a major mood-maker. Evenly distributed, soft, subtle light suggests openness and serenity. There are no jarring contrasts, and nothing is saying, "Look at me!

This bedroom would make anybody feel pampered and PEACEFUL. The draperies around the bed lend a look of luxury as well as a soothing (and sound-absorbing) softness. Color contrasts are subtle—the bed blends with the walls. To temper the tempo, the only pattern is in accessories. The lighting is soft and warm. Everything to smooth and soothe the nerves. (Photo courtesy of the Simmons Company.)

Look at me!" General light reflected down from the ceiling creates this effect. Dim lighting is relaxing and mysterious and creates a feeling of intimacy.

ACCESSORIES Accessories might inspire rest and reflection. You might choose a Buddha or a painting of the sea.

STIMULATING/ DRAMATIC/LIVELY

You want a happy, jolly, cheerful room. How do you achieve it? Imagine yourself giving a cocktail party. You've planned for weeks, and now, finally, you have all those drinks, hors d'oeuvres, and nice people in the next room. You have all the ingredients for fun, *but you've got to get the party moving!* You need someone to tell a funny story, or to appear in a dramatic outfit, or to do something outrageous or silly. It's the same with a room; you've got to create some excitement. What creates excitement?

COLORS Bright warm colors like red, orange, and yellow energize like sunshine. Clinical studies have even shown that they make people feel excited and impulsive. Strongly contrasting colors are dramatic. Opposite colors like red and green, blue and orange, or purple and yellow are so different they make each other more intense.

PATTERNS Bold pattern is exciting. Think of some smashing supergraphic. Patterns that have strong contrasts within the design are attention-getters. For example, imagine how strong a red-and-black design would be. Patterns that contain curved lines are especially stimulating. Circles or swirls stir things up. In general, the more pattern, the more lively the room.

TEXTURES Hard and uneven textures are

Want a DRAMATIC room? Do something unexpected. These New Guinean sculptures surprise and excite. Exotic objects in general arouse adventurous imaginings. Make your statement emphatic. The sculptures are lit from ceiling track lights. Make contrasts stark and strong. Here there are strong contrasts between dark and light colors and nubby and slick textures. (Photo courtesy of W & J Sloane; design by Albert Etienne Pensis.)

lively. Hard ones are lively because they reflect sound and bounce it around. For example, in a party room you might want a hardwood floor. The noise may add to the sense of excitement. Also, hard floors are easier for dancing.

Brick walls, stone walls, nubby fabrics, shaggy rugs all have uneven textures. Because they absorb light unevenly, they have variations of light and shadow. This variety attracts interest and causes the room to be more stimulating.

STYLES Anything that expresses an extreme is dramatic. For a RUSTIC effect, you might choose furniture made of raw logs, or for a FORMAL effect you could select late ENGLISH REGENCY furniture complete with its sphinxes and Chinese dragons.

In short, let loose. I covered the entrance corridor of my apartment in silver paper—walls and ceiling. With the reflections of the blue carpet on the walls, people feel like they are walking into a fishbowl, but they love it.

LIGHTING Lighting can create drama, as you know from your days on stage. The person under the spotlight is *it*. You can dramatize your furnishings or plants or pictures by spotlighting them. (One of my favorite ideas for an entrance or a corridor is to have a gallery of pictures spotlighted from the ceiling.) You can even spotlight your draperies by rigging up a fluorescent tube under the valance. Put a light wherever you want to create emphasis or excitement.

Strong differences in light and shade also give a theatrical sense of excitement, but make sure the differences aren't so stark that they hurt your eyes.

Bright light can create a brisk or buoyant atmosphere.

ACCESSORIES You might prefer to make your dramatic statement with accessories. Primitive sculpture from New Guinea, for example, is sure to start conversation. Anything extraordinary, or exotic, will give a room extra vitality—the excitement of the unexpected. You might even salvage a beguiling gargoyle from an old wrecked building.

RELAXING

In most rooms you want neither to dance nor to fall asleep. You simply want to feel alive and alert. In these rooms you should create a moderate amount of contrast. How? Think of the extremes. The no-contrast room has quiet, cool colors that all blend into each other, no pattern, and no texture—nothing much to attract the eye. The hyperactivity room bowls you over with strong, warm colors, patterns, curved lines and lumpy, bumpy textures. A relaxing room is more moderate.

COLORS Colors may be medium-value (neither extremely light nor dark). Colors may contrast a medium amount. You might choose brighter cool colors, or duller warm colors.

PATTERNS Simple linear patterns are your

This is a RELAXING room. The ceiling is wood; the floors are a similarly colored terra-cotta tile. The walls and furniture are white. The large areas are certainly simple and calm. The pierced screen and the rug create an interesting contrast. One is a pattern of light on dark, the other of dark on light. Subtle interest is added with patterned pillows and a painting. A red mirror is a bright accent. (Design by Everett Brown, FASID; photo by Yuichi Idaka.)

best bet. The pattern should contain a medium amount of contrast. A simple rule of thumb—if the room seems too dull or drab, add pattern, if too stimulating, remove pattern.

TEXTURES Textures may be smooth or gently uneven. For example, you might choose a subtly uneven grasscloth for a wallcovering.

STYLES Straight-lined furniture is more calming than curved. You would choose mostly straight-lined furniture, and add something curved for contrast.

You can orchestrate color, pattern, and texture to achieve the effect you're after. For example, if you want a moderate room on the calm side, you might choose deeper-toned cool colors, no pattern, and some uneven textures. If you want a moderate medium room, you might choose pale or neutral colors, simple linear patterns, and smooth textures. If you want a moderate effect on the stimulating side, you might choose brighter colors, linear patterns, and some uneven textures.

A room that is used constantly should be relaxing. Here is a sample scheme for a studio apartment: Carpet the floor in a refreshing and restful blue or green. Paint the walls white or a lighter shade of the carpet color. Dress the windows with simple draperies in a pattern that combines the colors of the floor and of the walls. Upholster the largest piece of furniture in the same pattern as the draperies. Color the smaller furniture in wood tones or in a brighter shade of the carpet color. Accessories could be black, white, or a brighter shade of the carpet color. Baskets can provide the punch of an interesting textured surface.

CHEERFUL

A room where you do the laundry, the ironing, or other uninspiring activities should be cheerful.

COLORS Light warm colors are particularly

Who could be down in the dumps with this ebullient pattern on the walls? Having the same pattern quilted on a love seat drawn up to the table makes the CHEERFUL feeling even more cozy. Upholstering the interior of an antique armoire in a dotty design is fun. Covering the lower part of the wall and the rush-backed chair seats to match makes the upbeat atmosphere complete. (Design by Yvette B. Gervey.)

cheerful. Yellow is as cheerful as sunshine. It adds brightness to a room without appearing to shrink its size. Orange is upbeat, and light red is a happy hue.

PATTERNS A particularly pleasing pattern can do a lot to brighten your mood. Pattern on the walls is a particularly good idea when your furnishings aren't interesting (who could wax ecstatic over a washer and dryer?).

TEXTURES Snappy textures have a bright and energetic effect. Glazed chintz is crisp—besides that, dirt shakes off it. Molded plastic furniture also has a slick, fresh feeling. Wicker and other light-looking textures that suggest the garden give sunny suggestions.

Plants and flowers add a festive feeling to this simple setting. A sense of sunshine and space can make one feel like king of the castle. This MODERN room was designed to take advantage of the view and the light. A built-in banquette provides plenty of seating in one big simple U shape. The vertical blinds control the light without obstructing the view. (Design by Yvette B. Gervey.)

STYLES Most COUNTRY/RUSTIC styles are cheerful. For example, many PENNSYLVANIA DUTCH pieces have charming and lively painted decoration.

ACCESSORIES How about a happy surprise? A bright bird in a cage in the dining room? Some wacky accessory that tickles and delights you? Plants and flowers make people happy—and they add oxygen to the air.

PART FOUR

DECIDING YOUR DESIGN

By now you probably have more decorative ideas than you know what to do with. How are you going to make sense of it all? How are you going to make choices? How are you going to organize the room so it isn't a hodgepodge? So it seems to have professional polish? Keep reading. This part of the book will tell you how to work the parts of the room together into a harmonious whole.

15

GIVE YOUR ROOM AN IDENTITY

Just like people, rooms with a definite identity are more fun to be with. They elicit a reaction from you, make you feel alive.

The greatest difference, I believe, between designer rooms and other rooms is that designers decide what identity a room should have and then go with it without waffling around. The rest of us might know what we want, but there are so many friends and relatives giving us *their* opinions that we lose heart and confidence. We compromise the room's identity and it ends up ordinary.

Not necessary. How would you describe a person? Tall? Short? Medium-sized? Curvy? Angular? Hard? Soft? Rough and rugged? Delicate and refined? White? Black? Blonde? Brunette? Gray-haired? The point is that every person has a definite size, shape, texture, and color. These characteristics are part of the person's identity. A room, too, should have a definite size, shape, texture, and color. These characteristics are part of its identity.

Isn't it true of all the interesting people you know that each has his or her own special point of view? That point of view may be formed by the person's background, business, or special interests, but whatever it is, it will come out in conversation because of what the person emphasizes. A room, too, should have a point of view. It should show the good judg-

ment to emphasize its assets and underplay its liabilities.

Isn't it true that a well-balanced person is the best company for long or consistent periods of time? Some seeming sense of sanity helps even out the highs and lows of everyday living. A room that will be a comfort to you, too, should seem well-balanced. It can be consoling when the rest of the world out there seems to be falling apart.

The beautiful thing about designing a room is that you can give it the identity you wish for it. It isn't always so easy with people.

CHOOSE A DOMINANT SIZE

You will want to choose furnishings that go with the room. Select a size that fits. Large rooms are best dressed with large furnishings, small rooms with small.

You will want to choose furnishings that go together. Furnishings that are similar in size go together. Large furnishings go together, medium-size furnishings go together; small furnishings go together.

What size will fit your room? Small, medium, or large? Choose one. Go ahead, really do

What suits a large room? Large furnishings. Two massive sofas in tufted brown leather and two large built-in banquettes on either side of the fireplace provide a great deal of seating space without compromising the room with clutter. The eighteen-foot-high ceiling provides wonderful walls for showing super-sized modern canvases. (Design by Lila Schneider; photo by John Veltri.)

choose one. Making choices will simplify your design problems.

Say you selected "medium-size." You will want your room to project a medium-size feeling. Now say you have a piece of furniture that is large. You can make that piece seem more medium-size by making it light or neutral in color and not letting it contrast too much with its background. Say you have another piece that is small. You can make it seem more medium-size by giving it a bright color, a pattern, an interesting texture, or making it contrast considerably with its background. See, you can make adjustments for size, while still allowing the room to project a "medium-size" feeling.

One or two pieces may actually seem smaller or larger than the norm, but there *has to be* a norm.

Pieces that are built into the architecture don't count, because they become part of the architecture.

CHOOSE A DOMINANT SHAPE

After choosing size, the second step in giving

your room an identity is to choose a shape. Furnishings should be predominantly curved or predominantly straight-lined. Which one will you want to choose?

What shapes are in the architecture? Furnishings that repeat the shape of the room or repeat the shape of outstanding architectural features create a sense of harmony. For example, if your room is square or rectangular, you might repeat the shape of the room with straight-sided modular seating arranged in a square or rectangular shape. If you have arched windows or doorways, you might like to repeat the curves of the architecture in round tables, in chairs with curved legs, or in a camelback sofa. If you have a rounded bow window, a love seat of a rounded shape or a round table would look pretty in the window.

What mood are you after in this room? Because straight lines and angular shapes are inspired by mathematics, they are considered to be intellectual and classic rather than emotional and romantic. They convey a sense of order and create a mood on the CALM side. Curved shapes are inspired by nature. (No, you've never seen a square flower.) Curves are considered to be emotional and romantic. They inspire a mood on the STIMULATING side.

Actually, every room needs some of both

sorts of shapes. A room with too many straight-lined, angular shapes looks stiff. A room with too many curves looks frantic. However, to have an identity, a room must have *more* of one shape than the other.

Which shape do you want to dominate? Straight-sided shapes or curved shapes? Choose one. Go ahead. Plunge. Choose one. For better or worse, a room with an identity is better.

If you chose straight-lined shapes, you will want a predominance of furnishings that are square or rectangular. You could also choose striped patterns and hang draperies straight to the sides of the windows.

If you chose curved shapes, you will want mostly furnishings that are circular, oval, kidney-shaped, or have curved legs or backs. Patterns with curved designs, swags and softly tied-back curtains or draperies, and plants of all kinds contribute other curved lines.

CHOOSE A DOMINANT TEXTURE

To coordinate furnishings with your room, it is best that both be of the same type of texture. For example, a room with brick walls, rough paneling, or a strong stone chimney is rough or INFORMAL. Coordinating furnishings can be big, sturdy, and made of the less expensive woods. Tweeds, burlap, fabrics with nap, shaggy rugs, and pottery would feel at home in this room. All are unsmooth and unshiny.

If you live in an eighteenth-century Georgian home with highly polished paneling of an expensive wood, and you're always ducking crystal chandeliers, your furnishings should be suave and smooth to fit in with this elegant ambience. Think FORMAL, smooth, and shiny. Formal antiques, highly polished woods of mahogany or rosewood, silks, satins, silver, mirrors, and foil wallpapers would suit the scene.

If your home is neither especially rough and informal nor smooth and formal, you can choose medium textures that are SEMIFORMAL and mix with anything. Walnut wood, cut-pile carpets, cotton, leather, linen, and chintz all fall into this category. (These could also dress up an informal room or dress down a formal room.)

Texture is the greatest determinant of formality. For example, you wouldn't wear a burlap bag to a fancy dance, or silk shoes on a walk in the woods. Choose the texture that fits the formality of your home and your life-style: rough/dull/INFORMAL or medium/SEMIFORMAL, or smooth/shiny/FORMAL.

The architecture presented rough plaster walls, heavy wooden beams, and built-in cabinets. The shapes were straight and the textures uneven and INFORMAL. In this dining area the occupants wanted a sociable STIMULATING mood, so the designer chose to counter the architecture with a predominance of curved shapes. Following through with the informal feeling, textures are uneven and unshiny. (Photo courtesy of Lees Carpets; design by Barbara Adler.)

CHOOSE A DOMINANT COLOR

Because equal amounts of different colors are boring or confusing, there should be more of one color in the room than any other. Because the walls and floor are the largest areas in any room, any color that covers them both will definitely be the dominant color of the room. Any color that covers one of them (either the walls or floor) and large furniture and/or the windows would also be the dominant color of the room. Often—especially in rental buildings—people choose to leave walls white and floors in pale polished wood. These then would be your dominant colors—but because they are neutral you can ignore them. In your furnishings, you still should have more of one color than any other in order to give your place personality.

Colors have three characteristics: hue, value, and tone. Hue describes the family of color—whether warm, cool, or neutral. Value describes the lightness or darkness of the color. And tone describes the brightness, softness, or dullness of a color. What color do you want to characterize your room? Choose its three qualities.

Choose Its Hue

WARM—warm colors are reds, oranges, orange-yellows, and reddish purples. Choose warm if you want the room to be WARM, STIMULATING, or COZY. (Brunettes often prefer warm colors.)

COOL—cool colors are blues, greens, green-yellows, and bluish purples. Choose cool when you want the room to be COOL and RELAXING or CALM and SPACIOUS. (Blondes and gray-haired people often prefer cool colors.)

NEUTRAL—Neutrals include white, black, gray, brown, and beige. You can achieve a CALM, earthy feeling with brown, a light SPACIOUS feeling with white, and DRAMA and sophistication with black.

Choose Its Value

DARK—Dark colors approach the color of black. Choose dark when you want the room to be DARKER OR DIMMER, QUIETER, more COZY, more CALM, or more MASCULINE.

MEDIUM—Medium colors are neither dark nor light. Choose medium colors when you don't want to change the natural lighting conditions, when you don't want to change the seeming size of the room, and when you don't want the room to feel particularly masculine or particularly feminine. (Medium colors are UNISEX.)

LIGHT—Light colors are pale and approach the color of white. Choose light colors when you want the room to be LIGHTER AND BRIGHTER, you want the room to feel SPACIOUS, or you want the room to feel FEMININE. (Pale colors blend with FORMAL, smooth textures such as marble and polished paneling.)

Choose Its Tone

BRIGHT—Bright colors are pure, without any gray in them. Choose bright colors when you want the room to be STIMULATING/DRAMATIC or if you want the room to feel COZY. Intense colors advance. When they cover large areas, such as walls or floors, they make a room seem smaller. Yellow is the exception. Because it is such a lightweight hue, even the brightest yellow doesn't seem to shrink the size of the room. Babies and young people love bright color. Bright color is CHEERFUL and usually INFORMAL. It blends with rough textures—stone, brick, barnsiding. On the walls or floor, it can distract attention from mediocre furnishings. (Bright colors used together usually must be balanced by white or other neutrals to avoid seeming gaudy.)

SOFT—Soft colors have a bit of gray in them to tone down their impact. Colors that cover large areas are usually toned down to some extent. Light, neutralized colors are most often used for walls (all those off-whites). Slightly darker, neutralized colors are most often used for floors. (The addition of gray helps the colors conceal dirt.) Soft colors are RELAXING—easy to live with; they don't bludgeon you with brightness. Most adults prefer these more muted colors. Soft neutralized colors are also the best foil for fine furniture.

A predominance of one color helps give a room character. The dominant color here is white. It covers the walls and the large three-piece bed platform. This light neutral color makes the room feel SPACIOUS and LIGHTER and BRIGHTER. (Happily the bed platform is covered in Formica so it is EASY TO CLEAN.) (Photo courtesy of the Formica Corporation; design by Ristomatti Ratia; photo by Elyse Lewin.)

DULL—Dull colors have a considerable amount of gray in them. Choose very grayed neutralized colors when you want the room to be CALM and very easy to live with, or when the natural light is excessively bright and you want to make the room DARKER.

Color is a wonderful way to convey the character you want your room to have. For example, you might want the dominant color of your living room to be neutral, light, and soft. This would make it feel comfortable, CALM, and SPACIOUS. You might want the dominant color of your dark-haired son's room to be warm, medium, and bright to give him a flattering LIVELY and CHEERFUL atmosphere.

GIVE YOUR ROOM A POINT OF VIEW: EMPHASIZE ITS MOST IMPORTANT ASSET

Look your room over. What does it have going for it? Does it have a fireplace, a view, an interesting alcove, handsome windows, a long wall? Do you have a particularly stunning piece of furniture, a sensational painting, or a gorgeous rug? Look it all over and figure out what you think is the room's very best feature. You are going to want to organize and arrange your room so that anyone walking in will—zingo—see your best asset.

The size of the asset you choose must suit the size of the room. A large room requires a large, commanding focal point. It may even have a second, less commanding focal point along a smaller wall, in a corner, or in front of a window. A small room needs a smaller focal point, and it can't tolerate more than one. Unless your room is gigantic, the focal point is usually against the wall.

How Can You Emphasize Your Best Asset, or Focal Point?   You can place it on the wall opposite the entrance so it is the first thing people see as they enter the room. You can arrange your furniture around it, so it is obviously the center of attention. You can make it more important by arranging secondary attractions around it, such as pictures. You can make it different from its background in color, pattern, or texture. You can emphasize it with special lighting. Spotlights can emphasize whole areas. Pinpoint spotlights can focus on specific objects, like paintings. Lighting within a cabinet can illuminate the treasures within. Lighting behind cornices and valances can emphasize windows and draperies.

What Is the Room's Best Asset?   Don't despair if you don't have one. You can create one.

A fireplace or a view. See Chapter 6. If you don't have a fireplace but wish you did, you can make or buy a fake one. A chest with a painting over it could substitute for a fireplace as the center of a conversational grouping. You could create a view by buying a scenic wallpaper or painting a mural.

Most modern apartment buildings are distinctly lacking in architectural assets. Without a fireplace or a view, you might choose to emphasize artwork or a large piece of furniture such as a wall unit or an antique armoire. Once you have arranged your furniture around a center of interest, your room will seem sensible. (Design by Diane Spenser; photo by Bill Helms.)

A large piece of furniture. One large piece of furniture can be your focal point. It can face the entrance to the room, or be centered on your longest wall. It might be an armoire, a secretary, a wall of shelves, a piano, a sofa with pictures over it, or a large bed. To emphasize a bed, you might cover the wall in back of it with the same pattern as the bedspread.

A painting. Place it in a position of importance, like over your fireplace, or over your sofa, or over a cabinet on the wall opposite your sofa. The wall behind the painting should be plain, so that the pattern of the painting stands out. The colors of the painting might well inspire your color scheme. Pinpoint spotlights can illuminate the painting surface.

An area rug. Place seating on either side of it, a see-through coffee table on it, and pictures on the wall. If the rug is patterned, you will probably want the areas around it to be plain. Such a patterned rug should be the inspiration of your color scheme.

One wall. One wall can be treated to make it into a focal point. It might be paneled or patterned or painted in a bright color. It might be mirrored. It might be hung with interesting objects, a powerful painting, or a marvelous mirror. You might choose to emphasize an interesting alcove or niche rather than a whole wall.

A good-looking window. If you have a good-looking window that faces a boring view, you might emphasize the window treatment and divert attention from the view. You might choose an attention-getting pattern (if the window isn't too large). You might have elaborate valances and draperies. Underneath, there could be camouflaging curtains, blinds, or shades. A fluorescent light installed up under the valance or cornice could shine down to give further emphasis to the window treatment.

An ordinary window. You can make an ordinary window look like something special. You can frame it to give it added importance. Treatments extending out to the sides of the window seem to give it greater dimension. These include shutters, grilles, latticework, or lambrequins placed to the sides of the window, and draperies that extend out from the window over the wall. A long narrow table underneath the window would unify the composition.

A standard window can be made to look like three. A structural frame can be constructed to house three window shades, even though there's only one real window—located in the center.

UNDERPLAY ITS LIABILITIES Look your room over again. What are its failings? You're going to want to smooth them out so nobody notices.

Color has great power to unify and camouflage. Ugly pipes or radiators painted the same as the wall will seem to disappear. Choppy walls will seem smooth if walls, doors, and windows are all the same color. Awkward windows colored the same as the walls will attain a smooth grace. Floors colored the same or slightly darker than the walls will flow smoothly into the background. Furniture colored the same as the walls will seem to dis-

This room had a problem. On the left there was a door opening onto a terrace, on the right, an ordinary window with a radiator beneath. How to make a harmony of it all? The designer chose dark blue skinny-slat blinds. For the door they go down to the floor. For the window they go down a bit behind the radiator. Then to make the unequal seem equal, the designer painted the radiator to match the blinds. (Photo courtesy of Levolor Lorentzen, Inc.; design by Nickolas Frank.)

appear and thereby seem to make the room larger. Furniture all in the same color or closely blended colors will not draw attention away from an interesting background.

Pattern used continuously over unlike objects will blend them together.

You can conceal unwanted and unused doorways by blocking them with tall furniture, or hiding them behind screens or wall-hangings.

If you have a wall that you wish weren't there, mirror it and it will seem to disappear into thin air.

If your furniture is nothing special, you can underplay it by directing attention to the walls.

Attractive people, and rooms, make the least of their faults.

GIVE YOUR ROOM A BALANCED PERSONALITY

If all the ballast on a ship slid to one side, the ship would sink. If all the furniture were at one end of a room, the room would seem weird and off-balance. Interest and furniture need to be evenly distributed around the room to keep it on an even keel. Generally, opposite walls and the halves of each wall should have equal attraction.

Think of it as a seesaw. Draw an imaginary line through the center of the room. Think of the walls at the ends as people. Do the walls seem to be of equal weight? Draw a second imaginary line through the center of the room between the other two walls. Do those sides seem equal?

Opposite or equally placed architectural features balance each other. Where architectural features are alone you can balance them with furnishings of similar size. For example, opposite a fireplace, you might place a sofa. Opposite a doorway, you might place a high-boy or a tall bookcase. To balance a window you might use a chest with a picture over it. The more similar in size and shape the fur-

nishings are to the architectural feature, the better the balance.

Of course, walls painted all the same color balance each other. If they are not painted all the same, make the opposite ones match. If you are painting only one wall different from the rest, put some heavy-looking furniture on the wall opposite to balance the room.

If facing furniture is identical, it balances, but it creates a rather formal feeling. If you want a more casual effect, you can create an informal balance with unlike objects.

If facing windows and furniture are in the same color or pattern, they balance. This is often why a sofa or bed is dressed in the same pattern as the draperies on the wall opposite.

Large pieces of furniture can be balanced by smaller pieces of furniture if you're clever.

A rough stone fireplace going all the way up to a cathedral ceiling comes on like a heavyweight. It needs something massive to balance it. Such rough stones also suggest an INFORMAL feeling, so one would want an informal asymmetrical arrangement. The designer found his answer in a massive modular seating system. He arranged a large L to face the fireplace, and a small L to the side of the fireplace. (Photo courtesy of Champion Building Products.)

You can make the large object seem smaller by underplaying it—making it the same color or pattern as its background, or making it neutral, unpatterned, untextured. You can make the smaller object seem larger by emphasizing it—making it contrast with its background, or making it bright, patterned, or textured. You might keep the large object dimly lit, and brightly light the smaller object.

You could balance one large object by a group of smaller ones. Another trick of positioning is to move the heavier object closer to the center of the seesaw and the lighter object farther away. This works as well for making arrangements on the mantel as it does for arranging your furniture.

Tall things can be balanced by shorter things if the short thing suggests height. You might upholster the short thing in a vertical stripe.

Bright accent colors should be evenly distributed around the room so they can equalize each other. If they are all lumped together, they will put the room off balance.

Respecting gravity will also help a room keep its balance. For this reason, it is normal to make the ceilings lighter in color than the walls. They may be white, or if the walls are a light color, the ceilings may be painted the wall color with white added. It is also normal to make the floor a darker or duller color than the walls; it may be the wall color with gray added.

If the ceiling is painted a lighter version of the wall color, and the floor is covered in a darker or duller version of the wall color, the ceiling, walls, and floor will create a unified one-color effect.

Of course, you may have other problems. If you have dark ceilings, the floors should be dark too in order to balance the ceilings. (Then you might want light walls to brighten up the place.) If you have light floors, you'll probably want light ceilings too, just so your sense of gravity doesn't go topsy-turvy.

It's best to respect gravity when arranging furniture. Generally, the lower things are in the room, the heavier they can be. The higher they are in the room, the lighter they should be. Always be sure that the base of something seems heavier than whatever is above it. For example, don't put large lamps on small tables. If something heavy sits on something small, you'll have the nervous feeling that the heavy object will fall over or the small object will be crushed. That's natural. Top-heavy arrangements defy gravity. Even objects hung on the walls seem to need support from beneath. That is why it is customary to put a chest or shelf beneath a mirror or a painting.

(Photo courtesy of Celanese Corporation; design by D. Coleridge.)

16

ARRANGE FURNITURE

Once you have established your room's best asset and made it into a focal point, arranging furniture seems simple. You simply arrange the furnishings for the major activity of the room around the focal point. Furnishings can face the focal point across the room, or be grouped around it. After that, secondary furnishings just seem to fall into place.

But let's take it from the top. What are the practical considerations that will help you determine your furniture arrangements? Any arrangement should make your activities comfortable and convenient (see Chapter 3). It should be harmonious with the architecture of the room (see Chapter 6). And it should make your furniture look its best (see Chapter 4).

DIRECT TRAFFIC

Consider where people will walk. From door to door, from door to light switch, from chair to window or TV. You will want to keep traffic paths clear of furniture. There also must be room to move around or in and out of furniture groupings, so plan to clear a way.

You can actually direct traffic by your furniture placement. The fronts and sides of sofas and chairs seem to invite you in to take a seat. Their backs seem to exclude you and encourage you to walk around. It is therefore a good idea to face the backs of chairs and sofas to the traffic.

The entrance to a room should be inviting. If the back of a sofa must face the entrance to a room, place a long narrow table behind the sofa and arrange cheerful accessories on it. That will make the room seem welcoming. If chair backs must face the entrance make the chairs light-looking or see-through so they don't seem forbidding.

SAVE EFFORT— PUT IT ON PAPER

To save shoving furniture around the room, it's easier to be playful on paper. Then you can experiment to your heart's content without breaking your back.

Buy some graph paper. Measure your room. Draw the outlines of your room on the graph paper. A scale of one-quarter of an inch to the foot is usually used. Locate doors, windows, closets, electrical outlets, overhead lights, and light switches on the plan.

With a conspicuous crayon, draw lines where people will walk—from door to door, from door to light switch, etc. You don't want to plunk furniture in the path.

Measure the furniture you have and intend to use in the room. In the same scale as your room outline, draw the length and width of your furniture on graph paper. Label and cut out the pieces of paper and start moving them around on your plan. In this manner, you can find out what will fit where, and you will establish the size of the furniture you need to buy.

To save time you might want to trace the outlines of your room on this grid. One square equals one foot. Be sure to locate doors on the grid and leave room for them to open and close. Draw lines where people will walk, so you'll be sure not to put anything in the way.

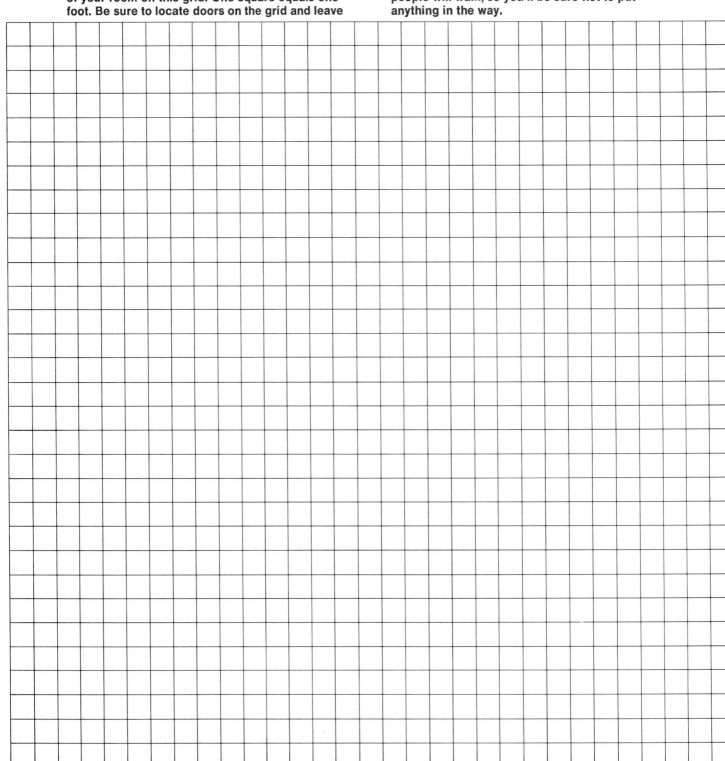

These are the outlines of the length and width of most typical home furnishings. The furniture is drawn in the same scale as the grid opposite (¼ inch = 1 foot). By tracing the shapes of furniture similar to your own and cutting them out, you can arrange and rearrange your furniture without breaking your back. Making a floor plan will also help you avoid buying furniture that won't fit.

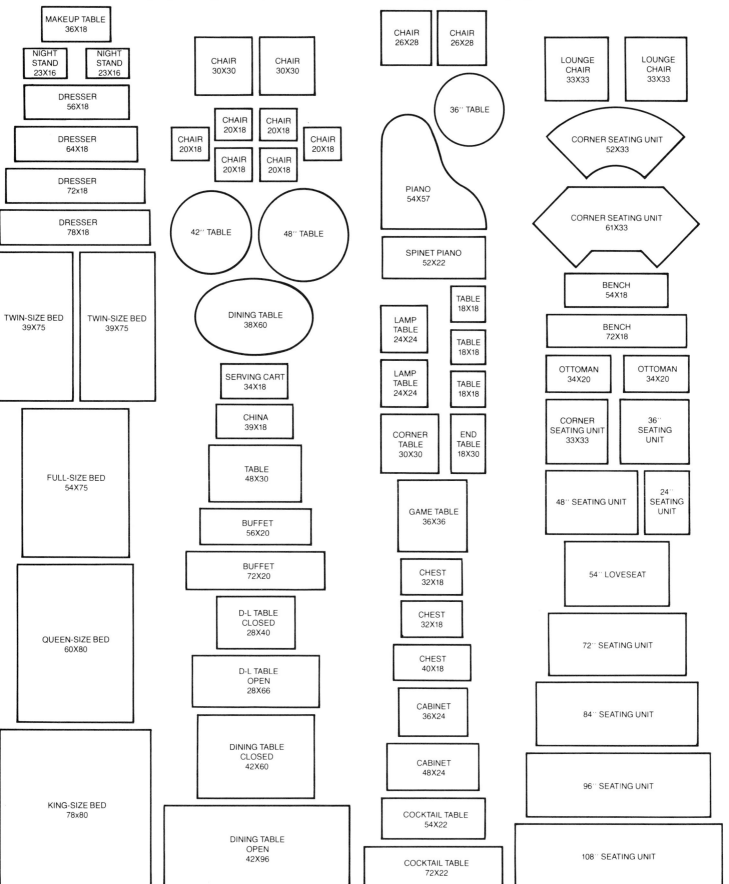

MAKEUP TABLE 36X18

NIGHT STAND 23X16

NIGHT STAND 23X16

DRESSER 56X18

DRESSER 64X18

DRESSER 72x18

DRESSER 78X18

TWIN-SIZE BED 39X75

TWIN-SIZE BED 39X75

FULL-SIZE BED 54X75

QUEEN-SIZE BED 60X80

KING-SIZE BED 78x80

CHAIR 30X30

CHAIR 30X30

CHAIR 20X18

CHAIR 20X18

CHAIR 20X18

CHAIR 20X18

CHAIR 20X18

CHAIR 20X18

42" TABLE

48" TABLE

DINING TABLE 38X60

SERVING CART 34X18

CHINA 39X18

TABLE 48X30

BUFFET 56X20

BUFFET 72X20

D-L TABLE CLOSED 28X40

D-L TABLE OPEN 28X66

DINING TABLE CLOSED 42X60

DINING TABLE OPEN 42X96

CHAIR 26X28

CHAIR 26X28

36" TABLE

PIANO 54X57

SPINET PIANO 52X22

LAMP TABLE 24X24

LAMP TABLE 24X24

CORNER TABLE 30X30

TABLE 18X18

TABLE 18X18

TABLE 18X18

END TABLE 18X30

GAME TABLE 36X36

CHEST 32X18

CHEST 32X18

CHEST 40X18

CABINET 36X24

CABINET 48X24

COCKTAIL TABLE 54X22

COCKTAIL TABLE 72X22

LOUNGE CHAIR 33X33

LOUNGE CHAIR 33X33

CORNER SEATING UNIT 52X33

CORNER SEATING UNIT 61X33

BENCH 54X18

BENCH 72X18

OTTOMAN 34X20

OTTOMAN 34X20

CORNER SEATING UNIT 33X33

36" SEATING UNIT

48" SEATING UNIT

24" SEATING UNIT

54" LOVESEAT

72" SEATING UNIT

84" SEATING UNIT

96" SEATING UNIT

108" SEATING UNIT

PLACE LARGE PIECES OF FURNITURE FIRST

The major piece for the major activity of the room must be considered first—the sofa in the living room, the bed in the bedroom, the desk in the den. This piece can face the focal point, be grouped around the focal point, or *be* the focal point if the area around it is given extra attention.

Large pieces should be evenly distributed around the room so as not to put the room off balance. Large pieces can balance strong architectural features. Again, a sofa can balance a fireplace, a high piece can balance a doorway, and a chest and mirror can balance a window.

Large pieces may need breathing space. Often it is best to center your largest piece against a wall so it has a little breathing space on either side. Even if you are not relating it to a wall, don't crowd your largest piece.

Traditional thinking dictates that large pieces be placed parallel to the walls to echo the lines of the room. For example, in a square or rectangular room, the large piece would also be of a straight-lined square or rectangular shape and it would be placed lengthwise against the wall, with its short end against the wall, or out in the middle of the room parallel to the walls. In a curved room or area, the large piece should be curved and be placed parallel to the wall. For example, think of a kidney-shaped desk or a curved sofa against a curved wall or in a bow window.

Now that more and more of us are living in rooms that are nothing more than boring boxes, many designers have decided to ignore the architecture and place large furniture on the diagonal. They think the lines of the room don't bear repeating. For example, instead of having a sofa facing the fireplace, or at right angles to it, the sofa might be placed to the side of the fireplace in a position diago-

The first piece to place in the living room is usually the sofa. Here it faces the fireplace, but away from the wall, so that traffic can pass in back. Small rectangular chests fit against the arms to act as end tables. An oval coffee table is chosen to soften the straight shapes. A comfortable curved-back lounge chair is drawn up for conversation. (Photo courtesy of Hickory Furniture Company.)

nal to the walls. Then, to achieve balance, a second sofa might be placed to face the first. To balance the fireplace, a bookcase or a dramatic wallhanging might be placed on the wall opposite the fireplace.

PLACE PIECES SERVING THE MAJOR PIECE

The arrangement must make your activity comfortable and convenient. It must flatter your furniture. The pieces should be compatible in size. Don't put some small thing right by a great big thing. Put it next to something of more moderate size so it doesn't look so puny. For example, if you own a big, bulky modern sofa and a delicate Louis XVI occasional chair, don't put the occasional chair next to the sofa. It will look overwhelmed. Place the chair across the room next to a piece of furniture of more moderate size. Then the relationship of sizes will be graceful.

Pieces opposite each other should be of equal mass. If that is impossible, the smaller piece should be more eye-catching than the larger piece. If, for instance, you have a big wing chair and a commodious table on one side of the fireplace and a lightweight occasional chair on the other, you have a problem. You can solve it by upholstering the wing chair in a neutral color, and making the occasional chair bright. If a sofa faces the two chairs you can put bright pillows on the end of the sofa closest to the occasional chair. In this way you can balance weight with color.

In grouping smaller pieces with your large piece, you can keep the edges of the smaller pieces parallel to the lines of the large piece or you can turn the smaller pieces at some other angle. For example, in a conversational grouping it has a relaxing and welcoming effect to turn small upholstered chairs in toward the sofa, or in around a fireplace or a table.

There should be a pleasant variety of straight lines and curved lines. If your major pieces are straight-lined, you might want to add something curved to the arrangement. For instance, if you have a rectangular sofa and coffee table, you might choose round end tables to soften the effect of all those straight lines. Or there might be a curved chair or rocker across the room. If your major pieces are curved, the addition of a straight-lined piece or picture will contribute some sense of order and repose.

Mix up wooden pieces with upholstered pieces. Too many upholstered pieces together can make you feel overstuffed. Too many "leggy" pieces together can make you feel that your room is on the run. There should be a pleasant variety of soft surfaces, such as upholstery, pile rugs, or draped tables, and hard surfaces, such as warm wood, shiny steel and glass, or bright lacquer.

Give your arrangement the acid eye test.

How does it look? If two pieces seem to detract from each other, place them in different parts of the room so they are not seen simultaneously. Then each might show off to advantage.

PLACE SUPPLEMENTAL PIECES FOR MINOR ACTIVITIES

These should be placed according to the convenience of the activity, what suits the architecture, and what suits the piece.

Are you wondering what to do with a long wall? A table with mirrors or pictures above can fill the space or become the focal point. A long table (say fifty-four inches) can be placed in a corner with a reading chair and ottoman to its side, and another reading chair at its end. A stereo cabinet under a gallery of paintings could fill the wall.

Other empty walls might be filled by a freestanding étagère with a chair, a Parsons table with a bench, or a chest with two side chairs.

Are you wondering what to do with a window? A desk can be placed directly under a window or perpendicular to it. This way you can take advantage of the natural daylight and have something to gaze at while you are gathering your thoughts.

A low bench, a table, a chest, or display shelf under a window can give the window added importance. A buffet under a window in a dining room would be a natural focal point. Think of the sunshine on your silver. Chairs look fine with their backs to a window, but watch that your fabric doesn't fade. A sofa will work with its back to a window if the proportions of the sofa and the window seem coordinated.

Are you wondering what to do with a corner? Three types of things work in corners: curved things, things that fit, things that soften.

Curved pieces can be placed diagonally in corners. They ease the angle of the corner.

A bedroom is a room for the bed, but usually we wish there were space for other furnishings as well. A desk is often desired. This room had an awkward half window flowing into a sliding glass door. To take the best advantage of the natural light and to unify the awkward architecture, the designer placed a white Parsons table against the window wall. It continues the lines of the vertical blinds. (Photo courtesy of Stauffer Chemical Company; design by Peg Walker.)

You might try a chair with a rounded back, accompanied by a round table, or a curved sofa. A round or an octagonal table could hold a collection of accessories to give interest to the corner. If skirted, it could brighten the corner with a pretty touch of color. If you're a musician, you can place your grand piano grandly in the angle of the room.

Things that fit in the corner include old-fashioned corner cupboards. These provide storage while adding architectural interest. Cornered shelf and desk units are useful in studies and in children's rooms. A square or rectangular table may be placed in a corner with chairs or beds against the adjacent walls. This might be a great place for a curio cabinet or shelves holding a collection, or for a sectional sofa that fits. Using corners is one great way to save space.

Things that soften the angularity of the corner include those most popular plants and trees. (Especially useful if the corner is by a window.) Tall vases with long-stemmed flowers or branches can look dramatic, and so can sculpture on a pedestal. Folding screens are another favorite. Besides, you can conceal clutter behind them. A mirrored screen will expand the sense of space without making you look at yourself straight in the face. (The folds of the screen break up the angles of reflection.) Straight-lined furnishings may be placed diagonally in front of corners that have been softened by screens or plants. Another way to soften the impact of an angle is to cover the walls in the same pattern as the furniture in front. The pattern will camouflage the corner.

Place your furniture where it looks best. For example, dark pieces of furniture may seem to

10%
20%
30%
40%
50%
60%
70%
80%
90%
100%

VALUE SCALE

Colors can be straight from the tube and bright, or they can be lightened with white or darkened with gray. Any hue can have infinite variations from light-light, almost white, to dark-dark, almost black.

This scale shows the variations between white and black. The central dot in each square is consistently the same middle value —which just goes to show that we all perceive things in relation to their background. The same dot looks dark against a light background and light against a dark background. On the middle-value square the dot almost seems to disappear. The less the contrast in values, the more things blend together. The greater the contrast in values, the more things stand out.

Most color schemes have some variations in value to create interest. See Chapter 19, the color chapter.

When choosing the color value for the largest areas in your room—the walls and floor—keep the following effects in mind:

Light, pale colors reflect sunlight and lamplight, seem SPACIOUS and airy. Light, pale colors blend nicely with FORMAL, smooth textures; think of marble and mirror. Because of their delicacy, pale colors can convey a FEMININE feeling.

Dark colors absorb light; they can make a room seem DARKER/DIMMER. Dark colors seem to come closer, so they can make a large room seem more COZY. Dark colors are also CALM, like a cave. Because of their weight, dark colors can convey a MASCULINE mood.

Colors that are medium in value don't change the seeming size of a space or alter its lighting conditions or convey any sexual stereotypes.

COLOR WHEEL

All the colors in the rainbow are made out of red, yellow, and blue. It's just a matter of how you mix them. In equal amounts red and yellow make orange, yellow and blue make green, and blue and red make purple. You can create thousands of other hues simply by altering the proportions of the mix. For example, more red than yellow makes red/ orange or russet. More yellow than blue makes yellow/green or citron. More blue than red makes blue/purple or plum. On it goes ad infinitum.

If you mix red, yellow, and blue all together equally, you'll get gray. All three colors together cancel each other out. If you mix together equal amounts of colors opposite each other on the color wheel, you will also

get gray. For example, red is opposite green, a combination of yellow and blue. Opposites add up to equal amounts of red, yellow, and blue.

It follows that if you want to make a color softer or duller, you can add a little bit of its opposite to make it grayer and tone it down. To make a color lighter you of course add white. The brightest colors have no white, gray, or opposite added. They are straight and socko.

A one-hue or monochromatic scheme is composed of one hue in variations. The variations may include the bright straight hue, the hue lightened with white, the hue darkened with gray or its opposite. The hue may be mixed with neutrals, which don't count as colors.

A related scheme, sometimes called analogous, is usually composed of three hues sitting next to each other on the color wheel. Any three hues sitting next to each other share a mother color, be it red, yellow, or blue; that's why they're called "related." In a related scheme usually one hue is lightened with white, another hue is darkened with gray or its opposite, and the third hue is bright and pure.

A complementary scheme is a scheme composed of colors that are opposite on the color wheel. Because opposite colors contrast so strongly, they are often toned down with a tinge of each other's hue or lightened with white.

A triad scheme is composed of three colors that would form a triangle if you drew lines between them on the color wheel. This sort of scheme, too, offers strong contrasts. You might well want to tone down some colors with gray or their opposites.

For more complete information on color scheming, please turn to Chapter 19.

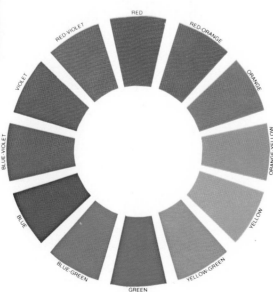

RED
RED-VIOLET
RED-ORANGE
VIOLET
ORANGE
BLUE-VIOLET
ORANGE-YELLOW
BLUE
YELLOW
BLUE-GREEN
YELLOW-GREEN
GREEN

A

ONE-HUE/MONOCHROMATIC SCHEMES

This is a one-hue scheme that you can't call calm. Red is aggressive, but in this bedroom/boudoir, it is simply seductive. Having a low budget and a daring spirit, the designer here recycled second-hand furniture, but gave it glamor and Deco-like drama by covering it in *color*—red satin that blends with the walls. (Design by Cecil Evans, Jr., ASID.)

This light monochromatic scheme in yellow suits the delicacy of the FORMAL French furniture. The floor is an expanse of pale yellow. The walls, windows, and large furniture are covered in the same two-tone pattern of yellow with white. Brighter yellow accents the inside of the draperies dramatizing the bed, plus the tabletop and the pillow on the chair. (Design by Robert Metzger; photo by Peter Vitale.)

This MODERN apartment has a SPACIOUS feeling. The walls are pale and creamy. The carpeted floor and the upholstered seating are slightly darker, creamy colors. It all blends together for a flowing feeling. Accessories provide contrasting color accents. (Design by Diane Spenser; photo by Bill Helms.)

Believe it or not, the painting was selected last. The designer knew a hard-edged modern piece was wanted, so he selected soft peach tones to set it off. Pastel peach covers walls and floor. The upholstered sofa is peach in a darker value. Ashtrays in brilliant blue provide an opposite color contrast. (Design by Rubén De Saavedra; photo by Daniel Eifert.)

B

Bright blue mixed with white makes a snappy scheme in this EASY TO CLEAN kitchen. The clean contrast between the strong bright blue lines and the expanses of white makes a graphic statement that takes this kitchen out of the ordinary. Softening the straight lines, the resilient floorcovering features circular designs blending both blue and white. The dining chairs and table are compatibly neutral. (Photo courtesy of GAF Corporation.)

Subtle contrasts can create a rather FORMAL effect. This delicious dining room is perceived in peach. For emphasis, the architectural moldings are painted in a lighter value than the walls. Continuing the convivial color, peach patterned with white lines covers the dining chairs, and its tones are an element in a large Oriental rug that warms the floor. (Design by Sandra Merriman; photo by Michael A. Peñalba.)

A neutral monochromatic scheme needn't be dull. You can use something besides color to create excitement. Here lighting provides definite drama. Light tubes under the ledge of the seating shine down on the brass base and launch a floating feeling. A snake-shaped pattern in the rug also cuts the conventional. (Design by Robert Metzger; photo by Fritz Taggart.)

RELATED SCHEMES

Blue, green, and yellow are related. Here the dominant color is pale blue. It covers the walls and window treatment. A brighter blue is also used for an ottoman. The secondary color is citron or yellow/green. This color covers the floor. Yellow colors the small areas—a chair and the focal-point display shelf over the fireplace. The pale colors give a soft-light look to a bedroom. (Design by Mario Buatta.)

Again a related scheme of blue, yellow, and green, but here it is darker and more dramatic. The dominant color, covering the walls, is dark green. The secondary color is the blue-green-white-and-yellow pattern on the sofa and windows. Bright yellow in a small chair adds impact. The white floor and dado, plus the white tulips in the rug, lighten the load of the heavy colors and make the room feel fresh. (Design by Mario Buatta.)

Red, orange, and yellow are related hues too. Here a peachy orange is the dominant hue. It covers walls and most upholstered pieces. The secondary hue is yellow. It occurs in patterns on the floor and at the windows. Red, in orangey tones, makes a small

but significant statement in an Oriental chest. Black accents sharpen the scheme. (Design by Albert Etienne Pensis, W & J Sloane.)

D

This soothing related scheme incorporates blue, yellow, and green in pale values. Pale blue is the dominant color, covering the walls and two upholstered pieces. The secondary color is yellow, covering the floor, bed, and love seat. Note that the yellows change in value—the palest is on the floor, the bed is a bit darker, and the love seat is bright. Green is only an accent—found in the leaves of the flowers on the wall. (Photo courtesy of Baker Furniture Company.)

Bright red walls make for a STIMULATING scheme no matter what else you do. Upholstery with a light yellow background creates a strong contrast with the walls, but lightens the look of the room. The middle member, orange, is scattered over the upholstery pattern. Because this connecting link is rather underplayed, the allover effect is only distantly related. The two major colors do not have a hue in common. (Photo courtesy of Baker Furniture Company.)

COMPLEMENTARY SCHEMES

Red and green are opposites on the color wheel; therefore, they are complementary colors. You'll notice that the red of the seating system has a bluish cast, making it more compatible with green. The green is a bluish green, not a yellowish green, which helps it to establish rapport with the seating. Opposites attract as long as they share something in common. The dark rich colors of this room are brightened with walls of white. (Design by Lila Schneider Designs, Inc.; photo by John Veltri.)

Inventiveness can be inexpensive. This ingenious designer built a room around an orange umbrella! To set the stage for drama, he wanted complementary colors. Instead of using orange's opposite, true blue, he used blue's next-door neighbors on the color wheel. The walls are plum and the accessories slate. The effect? Electric! (Design by Andrew Tauber; photo by Billy Cunningham.)

Red, yellow, and blue are the triad hues here too. Blue takes over the dominant position by dressing the dramatic bed, the wall behind the bed, and two side chairs. Bright yellow sheeting looks so inviting, you want to jump right in. Red accents the scheme by outlining the bed draperies and the fabric wall and underlining the windows with flowering plants. (Design by William Turner; photo by Jaime Ardiles-Arce.)

This is a triad color scheme of orange, green, and purple. Covering the resilient flooring and the painted and patterned parts of the wall, orange is obviously the dominating color. The chair cushions, plenty of plants, and an abundance of green accessories make green into the secondary color. Purple is used only as a small accent—actually in iris. (Photo courtesy of Armstrong Cork Company.)

Slate is the color between green and blue. Mulberry is the color between red and purple. Completing the triangle is a color between yellow and orange. This is a dramatic triad scheme—enough to excite, invite, and warm an enormous room. A wild, wonderful, printed velvet upholstery in slate and mulberry covers a generous modular seating system. Black lacquered chairs upholstered in peach square off the L. All colors play on fantasy panels painted on the walls. (Design by Albert Etienne Pensis, W & J Sloane.)

G

WHAT EFFECT DO YOU WANT?

COOL effects are achieved with blues and greens and textures that are slick or cool to the touch. Furnishings should be light-looking and as few as possible. This room has TRADITIONAL ambience and elegance, but still a bright, fresh feeling. An exquisite Chinese screen inspired the scheme. The paint on the walls and the fabric on the daybed were chosen to tone with the screen. (Design by Andrew Tauber; photo by Billy Cunningham.)

This room is as COOL as a gin and tonic. Slick, shimmery surfaces look like ice in a frosted glass. A Venetian wall mirror, a mirrored screen, a glass-and-Lucite dining table all reflect refreshment. White walls, étagères, and chairs keep the look light. A blue rug and blue accessories allude to the water and its cooling ease. (Design by Robert Metzger; photo by Peter Vitale.)

Want to feel WARM? Use the colors of fire—reds, oranges, and yellows. Use them in dark values too. Brown is just a darkened orange. Dark colors come in closer and make you feel cozy and comforted. Soft, thick textures—velvet upholsteries, woolly rugs —seem snug. Patterns in warm colors also seem to stir up some heat. Wouldn't you like to tuck into this room on a cold winter's day? (Design by Garcia/McMaster Interiors.)

Even a large room can become cozy. The uneven texture of the brick wall and the warm wood floors and ceiling helped here. Picking up tones of the brick and wood, walls are painted bright orange. Bright color seems to draw the walls in closer. The expanse of the floor is broken up by placing a piano at a right angle to the wall. A rug further defines an area. An upholstered chair in a generous size, a warm color, and a soft texture also contributes cozy comfort. (Design by Alan Buchsbaum, Design Coalition; photo by Norman McGrath.)

A light-colored wall-to-wall floorcovering helps make this room seem SPACIOUS. The diagonal line of the design seems to push the walls farther away. Large upholstered pieces placed against the walls are colored similarly to the walls so that they will fade into the background and seem to take less space. The rounded tub chairs by the window are colored the same as the background of the carpet for the same reason. Another chair is light-looking wicker and chrome. The simple blinds at the windows keep the aspect airy. (Design by Michael Love, ASID; photo by Jaime Ardiles-Arce.)

WHAT EFFECT DO YOU WANT?

Red walls in one room, red accessories in another create coherence in adjacent spaces. Red is really the only color in the area. Everything else is a neutral orchestration of cream, taupe, and brown. The other-directed drama of the red allows an ECLECTIC mix of underplayed furniture. (Design by Rubén De Saavedra; photo by Daniel Eifert.)

This room achieves a SEMIFORMAL feeling. The exuberance of the bright, striped rug and the colorful pile of pillows is tamed by the other more delicately drawn patterns in the room. The refined lines of the chairs usually express formality, but the rounded-back armchairs are made to relax in a coat of white paint. (Design by Braswell-Willoughby, Inc.)

Orange-and-red exhaust pipes dominate this black-and-white kitchen. Bright color can add an uplifting excitement to a frankly functional room. The kitchen is organized for maximum efficiency. Most counters are covered in easy-on-the-eye almond off-white Formica. Four corner columns and the central island are covered in black laminate in order to simulate the appearance of an Oriental cooking hut with its central firepot. (Photo courtesy of the Formica Corporation; design by Charles Morris Mount.)

A modern painting and a contemporary coffee table can update a room with traditional or timeless furnishings. Coordinating colors allow many mixtures of style. The rug in this room might be Victorian, but because it has the same peach-and-rose tones as the walls and painting, it plays its part in the room's integrated identity. (Design by Mario Buatta.)

Pink, pale, fancy, FORMAL, and FEMININE are the words to describe this room. One-hue schemes allow the emphasis to be placed elsewhere. Here the fine French furnishings and wall paneling, both with gilded ornamentation, attract our attention. The pink hue too inspires a warm, convivial atmosphere for dining. (Design by Leona Kahn, ASID.)

The furniture is fine. The lustrous dining table is 18th-century Irish. The chairs are antique English. To enhance the furniture the colors are pale and neutral. A luxurious Fortuny fabric in a gentle pattern covers the walls and swags the draped windows. The chandelier is Waterford crystal, and the place settings silver. The fine finishes, the lustrous surfaces—everything bespeaks FORMALITY and an elegant ambience. (Photo courtesy of Dallas-Ft. Worth Home/Garden; design by Jaye Skaggs, ASID.)

This CALM room combines styles traditional and modern in a way that arouses no conflict or contention. The room is like taking mixed fruits and pouring cream all over them. Mirrored panels on the walls reflect and multiply the creamy color. The modern coffee table and the upholstery fabrics blend right in. The dark Oriental rug anchors the room, and bright colors pop up in flowers. (Design by Sandra Merriman; photo by Michael A. Peñalba.)

PATTERN—HOW MUCH DO YOU WANT?

Many patterns make a LIVELY mood, especially when their colors are bright and bold. An Oriental chest in bright red lacquer with gold ornamentation picks up colors in the rug and establishes the bright CHEERFUL quality of the scheme. Draperies repeat the red with gold decorations. In yellow lacquer, the walls and chairs make the room sunny. Chairs covered in yellow-and-red plaid unite the scheme. (Photo courtesy of Baker Furniture Company.)

This little girl's room achieves an instant FEMININE feeling with wallpaper of a flowing floral pattern. The pink-and-green wallpaper inspired Grandma to make a coordinating afghan. To further emphasize it as the focal point, the bed is upholstered in a pink-and-white stripe. Other furnishings are underplayed, allowing the little girl's mixed bag of favorite furnishings to work together. (Design by Everett Brown, FASID; photo by Yuichi Idaka.)

Since pattern takes up space, its lavish use usually makes a room seem smaller or cozier. However, this is an exception. An unaggressive pattern in cool colors used lavishly can make a room seem more SPACIOUS. Here the sofa blends into the walls and doesn't seem to take much space at all. The matching draperies unite the bookcase with the walls, making everything seem smooth and flowing. Note also that the furniture out in open space is light-looking. (Photo courtesy of the Simmons Company and Greeff.)

L

The designer here made a dining area out of an entrance hall. To pull it off, he needed to achieve a SPACIOUS effect. He mirrored the walls, built in a banquette, and chose a see-through dining table. For liveliness he put a punchy color on the chairs. To give the banquette a moderate amount of interest, and to break up its expanse, he covered it in a simple black-and-white pattern. (Design by Braswell-Willoughby, Inc.)

A gorgeous Kerman carpet establishes the pattern interest in this room. To set off the carpet, the furniture arranged around it is plain in color, but rich in texture. It is raw tussah silk. Walls and windows are plain too, providing a simple open, airy background that sets off the richness of the rug and upholstery. Accessories are chosen in patterns that enhance the rug. They are in Oriental motifs and carpet colors. (Photo courtesy of KayLyn, Inc.)

If you choose some strong design, don't compete with it. This child's room features a bold graphic (UNISEX) design on the walls. The only other design is a simple striped bedcover that repeats, in smaller scale, the stripes on the walls. With attention drawn to the walls, the room feels furnished even though the furnishings are simple and minimal to allow the most space for romping around. (Design by Carol Levy, L. S. K. Designs; photo by Michael Datoli.)

M

HOW DO YOU MIX PATTERNS TOGETHER?

The designer here took inspiration from the outdoors. Soft earth-brown and sky-blue and light-white are combined in the room's major pattern. Earth-brown is repeated on a console, a basket, and a charming wooden sculpture. Sky-blue and white are combined in a flat-woven area rug, a nubbly woven fabric on the desk chair, and in miscellaneous accessories. Walls and floors are washed in white, spreading the sunshine indoors. (Design by Michael Love, ASID; photo by Feliciano Studio.)

This serene dining room has patterned wallpaper, a patterned rug, and patterned accessories—all handled with delicious delicacy. The wallcovering is a shimmery, reflective foil. Its design is flowing, pale, and delicately drawn. The floorcovering too is pale and light-looking with a broken, open trellislike design. Patterned accessories take their colors from the wall-covering, but acting as accents, they are in brighter intensities. (Design by Mario Buatta; photo by Richard Champion.)

The Oriental rug is certainly the most dynamic design in this room. Other patterns—used on the draperies, the bookcase lining, and on benches—are noncompetitive. The draperies and the bookcase lining mix one carpet color with white. The benches are upholstered in small stripes of carpet colors. Playfulness comes with lining the draperies in a different small-scale design and using a larger version of this same design on the back of the bookcase. (Design by R. Michael Brown; photo by Henry Fullerton III.)

N

The climate is hot so the colors are COOL. An Oriental screen in deep blues sets the scene and provides the focal point. Its diagonal lines inspired the selection of a dual-diagonal chevron stripe in crisp blue and white for the sofa and chair. An area rug repeats the same colors in a simple stripe. The lamp base repeats the blue and white, but in a floral motif. The consistency of color coordinates. (Design by Robert Metzger; photo by Peter Vitale.)

The chair pattern is the start of this scheme, with its yellow, two blues, and white. The yellow is expressed in an expanse on the sofa. The table drapery separates the blues and white in a patterned patchwork. The rug unites it all. Wavy lines frame flame shapes that look something similar to the blue motif in the pattern, except here they combine blue with yellow's hotter neighbor, orange. (Design by Robert Metzger; photo by Peter Vitale.)

To emphasize a patterned painting, put it in a place of prominence and don't compete with it. Here the walls are plain and textured. The rug is the same color as the background of the painting. Upholstery picks up the off-white, pink, and cream of the ladies' dresses. Other patterns are limited to one chair and accessories. The chair emphasizes the painting by repeating its colors in a flame-stitch design. (Photo ocurtesy of Roxbury Carpet.)

O

This simple COUNTRY setting achieves its charm with reverse patterns. The wallcovering has a white design on a background of green. The curtains, ruffled table cover, and seat cushions are the reverse—a green design on a background of white. Reverse patterns are a simple key to coordination. (Reverse patterns also work well in adjacent rooms.) (Photo courtesy of GTR Wallcovering.)

P

disappear in windowless corners. A bright piece might seem gaudy if placed in a picture window. Also, side chairs are meant to be at the side of the room against a wall. They are too light to hold their own in a conversational grouping with sofas and large upholstered pieces, but they are light enough to be moved into the group when there are extra guests.

Low pieces look good in front of windows or fireplaces, or placed in central groupings. Tall display shelves or bookshelves look handsome flanking a long sofa, a tall window, or a fireplace. A rectangular desk might look nice at right angles to a wall or window.

CREATE HIGH–LOW INTEREST

If everything in the room is the same height, it will seem as though a large horizontal band is trying to wrap you up in the room. I suppose it's more pleasant than a hug from an octopus, but it's still not great. Break up that horizontal line with something taller. You could put a tall secretary or breakfront against the wall. You could add a high-backed chair—a wing chair or a rocker—to your collection of seating. You could place pictures over the sofa, at a position higher than the lamps on either side. Any of these additions will give the eye something to look up to, and will improve the view.

MODEL ROOMS OR MAGAZINES CAN BE AN INSPIRATION

When you see an arrangement you like a lot, think of how you might adapt it to your room.

Does it accommodate the same activities you will need to accommodate in your room? If so,

fine. If not, maybe you can substitute a piece of the same size and shape that will function for your needs.

Compare the traffic patterns in this room with your own. Will this necessitate any adjustments?

Compare the size of this room with your own. If your room is smaller, you might duplicate the arrangement with furniture of smaller scale, or you might leave out some of the secondary furnishings. If your room is larger, you might duplicate the arrangement with furniture of larger scale, or you might add supplementary arrangements—such as a desk or game table, or a small table and a pair of chairs. (Your floor plan and furniture cut-outs can help you adjust for the room size.)

Is your room the same shape? If not, you might have to make some adjustments to flatter the shape of your room (see Chapter 6).

Are the room's architectural features the same as yours? Would the location of your doors, windows, or fireplace necessitate substitutions or some kind of rearrangement? Remember you must balance your own architectural features. If the model room has a fireplace and you don't, you might substitute a cabinet or a secretary for the fireplace to create a focal point.

Do you have furniture of your own that you'd like to substitute? Imagine what you have that could create an effect of the same size as what you see in the room. Instead of a sideboard, you could substitute a smaller chest and a pair of side chairs. Instead of a tall secretary, you could substitute a chest with a mirror or painting over it. Instead of a cocktail table, you can substitute a campaign chest that will store things. Instead of a refectory table behind a sofa or against the wall, you can substitute a Parsons table, a desk, or a dropleaf table.

You can also substitute furniture that is higher or lower, but of about the same width. (Those substitutions might help you balance your architecture.) Instead of a china cabinet, use a buffet. (This could fit under your window.) Instead of a table or chest and a lamp, you can have a floor lamp and a bookcase or étagère. Instead of a chest or desk, you can

The first piece placed in this room was the dining table, then the chairs. A high hutch fits between the doors with a nice little breathing space on either side. A console table is the right height for under the windows. High-low interest is achieved by a display of china on a plate rail above the doors and windows, in the hutch, and on the tables, and by a compatible garden seat on the floor. (Design by Everett Brown, FASID; photo by Henry S. Fullerton III.)

have an armoire. (This might balance a doorway.)

WORDS OF CAUTION

Some things it's better to know in advance.

Be sure to leave enough operating space to open drawers and doors. You need a minimum of two feet of free space in front of doors, chests, and cupboards—even your oven. I know a poor fellow who could never open his broiler because a water pipe was in the way.

That's what you might call poor planning!

Do not obstruct what people want to see. If you have a good view, don't cover it up. If you have a mural or a scenic wallpaper, don't obstruct the scene with a tall piece of furniture. You'll ruin the impact of the wallcovering.

Do not crowd the room with furniture. A spare look is elegant. An overabundance of furniture looks cluttered and confusing, not to mention unharmonious. If you seem to need too much furniture to accommodate all your activities, look for dual-purpose furniture. In general, it's best to use only as many pieces as are needed.

Take your time. The more you live with a

room, the more you know what you need in it, and the less likely you are to make a mistake. Take the time to get to know your room and your needs. It will save you money in the long run. It is wise to complete your total room plan before you buy anything. Finish reading this book before you spend a cent!

Another early warning—before you buy anything, make sure you can get it into your home. I have an unhappy friend who ordered a beautiful seven-foot sofa that's sitting in a warehouse because there's no way she can get it into her apartment. It doesn't fit in the elevator and the building owners won't allow her to hoist. In general, it's wise to avoid buying overscaled furniture. Today's housing usually can't accommodate it. (Regular king-sized beds, triple dressers, and enormous sofas are a real problem to place.) Sectional or modular seating and storage can accommodate the same large demands, but they have the added advantage of being easily moved and rearranged. For sleeping luxury, there are king-sized beds called dual beds that are easy to move, but the queen-sized bed is the reigning favorite.

(Photo courtesy of Fibers Division/Allied Chemical Corporation; design by Allen Scruggs, ASID.)

17

WHAT DO YOU NEED? AND WHAT CAN YOU DO WITH WHAT YOU HAVE?

Once you have made a tentative furniture arrangement, you will have a pretty good idea of what you need.

MAKE A SHOPPING LIST

On your shopping list, describe the pieces you need to buy. (Clutch this list in your hand when you later go to the store. It will keep you from making terrible errors.) Include all the following information:

ITEM What do you need to help you function comfortably and conveniently? A table? A chair? A bed?

SIZE What size should it be? It must suit the size of the person using it and the size of the room. It should be a size that coordinates with the other furniture and fits the space available for it. It may have to be large enough to bal-

ance a certain architectural feature or the facing furniture. When possible, write down the measurements required—or at least the range of measurements that will work.

SHAPE Do you want it to be straight-lined or curved? If you want the piece to blend in easily, it can be the same as your dominant shape. If you need variety, you can choose the other shape.

TEXTURE/MATERIAL What should it be made of? You can look at what you have and know what you need. If you have too much wood, you should add an upholstered piece or some steel and glass—or you could lessen the forest feeling by painting some of the wood a pretty color. If you have too much upholstery, add some pieces with legs. If the room seems too severe, soften it with a draped table. Too soft? Add something hard—like a lacquer or a metal piece. A half-and-half mixture of wooden and upholstered pieces works in most rooms.

The material must be able to take the wear it will get. Children and other active or careless people, and areas of high activity or constant use require DURABLE materials. Entrance halls, bathrooms, and kitchens might require WATERPROOF materials. Seldom-used rooms frequented by gentle people for gentle living can have more delicate materials.

The piece may be similar to other furnishings if you want it to blend in harmoniously, or it can be of a different complementary material, color, or wood tone if you want it to stand out.

DECIDE WHAT FURNITURE YOU WILL EMPHASIZE AND WHAT YOU WILL UNDERPLAY

Look at every piece of furniture on your floor plan—both the real and the to-be-bought

The designer of this room wanted a CALM, SPACIOUS atmosphere. He underplayed the background with white walls and vertical blinds and flat gray wall-to-wall carpeting. He chose to emphasize the foreground furnishings—but subtly—to keep the

CALM. The modular seating system, tables, piano, and planter are black. To achieve interest, curves contrast with the dominant straight shapes, and shiny textures contrast with the flat. (Design by Ron Oates; photo by Marty Umans.)

pieces. What visual impact does this piece need to have to achieve balance in the room? If the piece is smaller than what it is balancing, it should have a strong impact in order to achieve equilibrium. If the piece is larger than what it is balancing, it should have an underplayed impact in order to achieve equilibrium. If it is just the right size, it can contrast a moderate amount with its background.

Label each piece on your floor plan in one of these ways: Strong Emphasis/Contrast, Medium Emphasis/Contrast, or Underplay/No Contrast.

Color, pattern, and texture are your tools to emphasize or underplay. The more similar anything is to its background, the more easily it fades into oblivion. The easiest way to underplay anything is to make it the same as its background.

The more an object stands out from its background, the more eye-catching emphasis it will have. It can be bright or bold in color if the background is pale or neutral; it can be patterned if the background is plain; it can have an uneven texture if the background is smooth—or the reverse of any of these.

Which sort of emphasis you choose depends on what would do the most for the room. We'll get to that later.

CHOOSE TO EMPHASIZE THE FOREGROUND OR THE BACKGROUND

Now back up a bit. Look the whole room over.

Even though certain furnishings will be relatively emphasized or underplayed in order to achieve balance, furnishings are only part of a bigger picture. They have to take their place in the context of the room. Are your furnishings and accessories really interesting? If so, you will want to draw attention to them and soft-pedal the background walls and floor.

Are your furnishings sparse or uninteresting? Then you can draw attention away from them by doing something dramatic on the walls or floor.

Do you have a beautiful floorcovering or wallcovering? Then certainly you will want to draw attention to it by making the furnishings rather neutral and unobtrusive.

Is the budget your bugaboo? A good wallpaper is much less expensive than fine furnishings. It's a boon to the budget to emphasize the walls and underplay the furniture.

Are you troubled by the room's sense of space? If you want it more COZY, you could use bright colors or bold patterns on the walls or floor. If you want it more SPACIOUS, deep-perspective scenics or other deep-perspective patterns on the wall will break open the space. Alternatively, a subtle wallcovering pattern, matching windows, and large furniture will unify the room and make it seem uncrowded.

Which is best for you—to emphasize the foreground (the furniture and accessories) or to emphasize the background (the walls and floor)? Play one up and the other down. Every aspect of the room can't be screaming and yelling for your attention. It would make you feel like a person with a box of cookies caught in a playground full of starving, swarming children. Some attentions you could live without.

(Photo courtesy of Selig Furniture; design by Elroy Edson, ASID.)

18

ORCHESTRATING COLOR, PATTERN, AND TEXTURE

Color, pattern, and texture are the tools you use to emphasize and underplay. First of all, let's set out your master plan of what you want to emphasize and underplay in this room.

MASTER PLAN FOR THE ROOM

Dominant Size:

Dominant Shape:

Dominant Texture:

Dominant Color:

Most Important Asset/Focal Point:

Liabilities to Underplay:

Emphasizing Foreground/Underplaying
 Background
or
Emphasizing Background/Underplaying
 Foreground

Bring together your floor plan with its tentative furniture arrangement, your shopping list for furnishings, and, if you have them, swatches of any colors, patterns, or textures that you have and intend to use. You will have labeled each furnishing on your floor plan with the relative emphasis it should have (see Chapter 17). If you have decided to emphasize the background, you will want to tone down the contrasts among the furnishings. Don't give any piece of furniture more than a medium emphasis (you might want to change the labels on your floor plan).

Now, fill in whatever blanks you can in the chart on page 194.

		Underplay or Emphasize?	Material: Durable or Delicate?	Color or Wood Tone?	Patterned or Plain?	Texture: Rough or Smooth? Hard or Soft?
BACKGROUND / LARGEST AREAS	Floors:					
	Walls:					
	Woodwork:					
	Ceiling:					
FOREGROUND / MEDIUM AREAS	Windows:					
	Large Furniture:					
SMALL AREAS	Small Furniture:					
ACCENT AREAS	Accessories:					

HOW WILL YOU DISTRIBUTE COLOR, PATTERN, AND TEXTURE IN YOUR ROOM?

Distribute color, pattern, and texture according to what you want to emphasize and what you want to underplay.

For Strong Emphasis

Contrasts: Bold
Colors: Warm, advancing hues
Dark shades
Bright, pure color
Pattern: Large-scale
Bold contrasts
Texture: Very uneven, or very shiny

For Medium Emphasis

Contrasts: Medium
Colors: Warm colors that are lightened or dulled
Cool colors that are darkish or brightish
Medium values that are neither light nor dark
Slightly dulled or grayed color
Pattern: Medium-scale
Medium contrasts
Texture: Neither particularly rough nor particularly smooth

To Underplay

Contrasts: None
Colors: Cool, receding hues
Light tints
Dull, neutralized, grayed colors
Pattern: No pattern, or light-impact pattern—small-scale with subtle contrasts
Texture: Smooth, dull

How Much Emphasis Do You Want? Your focal point should be the most dramatic attention-getter in the room. Your emphasized area should not compete with it.

Large rooms or rooms that you want to be STIMULATING can take strong emphasis. Small rooms or rooms that you want to be CALM should have medium emphasis. Rooms where you spend a good deal of time should be CALM.

The more dramatic the emphasis, the less of it you need. The more subtle an emphasis, the more of it you can stand.

What Kind of Emphasis Should You Choose? It depends on what would be most effective in enhancing your assets and in perking up the room. Does the room seem to be too much one way or another? You can correct the condition with a contrast.

In this room the designers are emphasizing the foreground. The walls and floor are underplayed. They are plain, neutral, and smooth. The medium areas—the large furniture and the windows—are emphasized with moderate pattern. The small furniture is emphasized with rough texture. And the accessories are emphasized with bright color. (Photo courtesy of Celanese Corpration; design by Abbey Darer and Bobbi Stuart.)

A brilliant color accent is handsome among muted colors. If you don't have any beautiful old woods with a rich patina, or other interesting textures, you can give the room all the interest it needs with strong color contrasts.

If everything is plain, you can choose to emphasize with pattern. If you are emphasizing with pattern, don't compete with it. Keep other areas plain and unpatterned. Other elements may vary in texture—to add variety without detracting. The pattern may be repeated in different parts of the room—say on walls and on an upholstered piece, or on windows and on an upholstered piece.

If the room seems to have too much pattern, choose some plain surfaces.

If all the textures in the room seem dull or flat matte, choose something shiny—say a lacquered coffee table or steel and glass or brass. If your color scheme is neutral and you want a rich and subtle effect, emphasize textural variety. You might have glossy lacquered walls, a thick rug, nubby upholstery, and bunches of baskets. This is a MODERN favorite.

If you have little contrast in color, texture, or shape, you can put more light on the thing you want to emphasize. Or you can create shadows in a lighted area in order to avoid monotony.

THE ROLE OF COLOR IN THE COMPOSITION

Color can be the most exciting aspect of decorating. And the beauty of it all is that one color costs no more than another! Color has marvelous powers. It can improve the size, shape, and features of your room. It can enhance the objects you like and hide the ones that you don't.

There are two secrets to a successful color scheme:

Use Colors in Distinctly Different Quantities There should be more of one color than

any other. This dominant color could cover the walls and floor, or the walls and some furniture, or the floor and some large furniture, or the floor and the window treatment.

There should be a second color used in a medium quantity—maybe covering the large furniture and the window treatment.

There should be a third color used in a small quantity—maybe on the small furniture and/or accessories.

Vary the Intensity of the Colors Used Any color scheme usually combines a light-impact neutral color, a medium-impact brightish color, and a heavy-impact socko color.

If you want to emphasize the foreground—your furniture or accessories—make the large areas of walls and floor the most neutral, the medium-sized areas of large furniture and windows medium-bright, and the small furnishings or accessories socko.

If you want to emphasize the background—the walls or floor—put your socko color here and make your furnishings neutral and your accessories medium-bright.

If you observe these two rules you can mix together almost any colors.

THE ROLE OF PATTERN IN THE COMPOSITION

Every room should have some pattern in it. It gives sparkle, surprise, and interest to a room. The pattern can be a wild supergraphic on the wall or just a painting and maybe a few pillows. What you choose depends on the mood you want to create, the size of the room, and on the furnishings you have. A pattern, by the way, can be the inspiration of your color scheme.

Pattern Is Lively The bolder the pattern, or the more pattern you have, the livelier and more STIMULATING your room will be. The more subtle the pattern, or the fewer the patterns

Every room needs some pattern. Where you put it depends on what you've got. This designer collects Oriental rugs, so he placed his pattern on the floor. So as not to compete with the rugs, the simple furnishings are plain or textured. The patterned painting is noncompetitive because it is seen against plain walls. (Photo courtesy of *Interior Design* magazine; design by Thomas Boccia; photo by Jaime Ardiles-Arce.)

you have, the CALMER your room will be.

Pattern Seems to Take Up Space Because pattern takes up space, in a large room you can use bold pattern, or several patterns. You should use subtle patterns or few patterns in a small room so it doesn't seem crowded.

Pattern Gives Emphasis Patterned areas are more interesting than plain areas. But too many different patterned areas pull your attention every which way and make a room seem exhausting. Patterned areas must be balanced by plain areas.

Sometimes plain areas attract attention: In a room with pattern on the walls, windows, and large furniture, a plain piece would stand out and attract attention because it is different.

A Good Formula If you add up all the surface areas in the room, it is usual to have one-fourth of them patterned. For example, just walls, or just floors, or if the walls and floors are plain, the draperies and two-thirds of the upholstery fabrics may be patterned.

PATTERNS VARY IN EMPHASIS Pattern has different impact, depending on the size of the design, its colors, and the amount of contrast in it.

Heavy-Impact Patterns Give Socko Emphasis

Size:	Large-scale
Colors:	Warm, advancing hues
	Dark shades
	Bright, pure color
Contrasts:	Bold

A heavy-impact pattern will rivet your attention. Because it is so commanding, it is best used in a limited area to make a focal point. Too much of it would be overwhelming. To compensate for its strength, it is best to underplay the rest of the room. There shouldn't be more than one bold pattern in a single room.

Medium-Impact Patterns Give a Medium Amount of Emphasis

Size:	Medium-scale
Colors:	Warm colors that are lightened or dulled
	Cool colors that are darkish or brightish

Medium values that are neither light nor dark
Slightly dulled or grayed color
Contrasts: Medium

A medium-impact pattern may be used generously—on walls, windows, furniture, if you wish. It provides interest without being overpowering. It can be combined with light-impact patterns.

Light-Impact Patterns Tend to Stay in the Background

Size: Small-scale
Colors: Cool, receding hues
Light tints
Neutralized, grayed color
Contrasts: Small, or subtle contrasts

Light-impact patterns won't attract much attention. They are only slightly more interesting than plain surfaces. Many of them give a textured appearance. Subtle stripes and one-color, tone-on-tone designs fall into this unobtrusive class.

Light-impact patterns should be plain enough to serve as good background. Beware of too-small designs. Sometimes at a distance they just look faded or dirty.

Light-impact designs may be combined with medium-impact designs and heavy-impact designs.

THE ROLE OF TEXTURE IN THE COMPOSITION

Texture is generally a more subtle tool of emphasis than either color or pattern. If you have created interest through color contrasts or pattern, you don't have to worry much about texture. If, however, your color contrasts are minimal and you aren't using much pattern, texture is the tool you'll use to make your room interesting. (Many modernists choose this approach.) You will want many contrasts between rough and smooth and between hard and soft.

Textures affect the lighting conditions of a room. Rough or uneven textures absorb light; smooth, shiny textures reflect light and seem to increase it.

There are a few things that everyone should know about the role of texture in the composition: *You cannot combine coarse,* INFORMAL *textures with fine* FORMAL *textures, and there should be some uneven texture in every room.* Okay, so you don't combine burlap and brick with polished mahogany and silks and satins.

It's no problem giving an INFORMAL room an uneven texture. Most INFORMAL things are uneven. Think of loose pile rugs, walls of rough plaster, brick, stone, barnsiding, wallcoverings of cork, textured fabrics—tweed, burlap, corduroy, even rush seats on chairs. In an INFORMAL room, you will create contrast by using some smooth things—slate, wood, vinyl, Formica, glass.

In a SEMIFORMAL room, the uneven texture should be more modified. The more uneven textures there are in a room, or the rougher the uneven textures are, the more INFORMAL the

The rug is a heavy-impact design of bright colors and bold contrasts. Two light-impact patterns work with it. The bed and window seat are covered with a simple windowpane print. The walls are covered with a pattern that suggests jungle grasses. Both are green and cream and unassertive. They seem like other cooling, uneven textures—along with the Haitian cotton, bamboo, and baskets. (Design by Albert Etienne Pensis, W & J Sloane.)

room will seem. The more smooth textures there are in a room, or the smoother the uneven textures are, the more FORMAL the room will seem. You could use a grasscloth wallcovering, a carpet or rug with an uneven or carved pile, fabrics with gentle textures like linen or woven wool. At the windows you might have woven wood or bamboo blinds. Furniture might have caning or woven wicker. Accessories could be bunches of baskets. You could even choose a flat wallcovering or fabric printed to look like a texture.

What about a FORMAL room, where everything is supposed to be smooth and shiny? How do you fit an uneven texture in here? It should be subtle. It might look like the slubs of silk. You could choose fabrics that are silk, or that look like silk. You could choose a wallcovering printed on a background that looks like the slubs of silk. You could choose a fabric with nap like velvet, or a flocked wallcovering. You could choose other fabrics that seem to have a gentle texture—like one-color moirés, brocades, and damasks. Your furniture might feature caning. Your floorcovering might be a luxurious deep pile rug, or a rug with the pile carved to different heights.

Now the next rule: *You should combine hard textures and soft ones.* If everything in a room is soft and squishy, you might feel as though you were being suffocated by a giant marshmallow. If everything in a room is hard and slick, it will seem clinically cold, and as if you were just being wheeled out of the operating room. Clearly there's a compromise.

Emphasis should be on hard textures if: You want the room to seem SPACIOUS and COOL. You want the room to seem LIGHTER (hard surfaces reflect light). You are not worried about noise (hard surfaces reflect sound and thus make a room seem noisier).

Emphasis should be on soft textures if: You want to be able to rumble around naked without hurting yourself. You want an atmosphere of comfort and sensual pleasure (SEXY). You want the room to seem WARM and COZY. You want to absorb light and make the room DARKER. You want to absorb sound and make the room QUIETER.

The person who lives here prefers a casual, INFORMAL life-style, so the dominant texture of the room is uneven. The walls are paneled in pecky cypress, and the floor is covered with a nubby rug. In contrast to all this unevenness, furniture is framed in smooth shiny chrome and upholstered in soft cotton velvet. Then just to be sure the point is made, the room is accented with uneven wicker. (Photo courtesy of James David.)

For variety in a room with hard textures, add something soft—a tapestry wall hanging, an area rug, or a textured wallpaper. In a room with soft textures, add something hard and shiny—a mirror or a steel-and-glass table or étagère. Something slick will add a lot of sparkle and life to the room. You don't need much contrast, just something for spice.

EMPHASIZING THE FOREGROUND

WITH STRONG COLOR Colors can get stronger as areas get smaller.

Largest Areas: Walls and floor generally should be cool, pale, or neutral.

Medium Areas: Windows and large pieces of furniture (sofa, bed, etc.) generally should contrast a moderate amount with the walls and floor.

Small Areas: Small pieces of furniture (ottomans, benches, etc.) can be stronger color and have more contrast with walls and floor.

Accent Areas: Accessories (lamps, ashtrays, picture frames and mats, sofa pillows, etc.) can be a strong, commanding color or pure black or white.

Usually the large furniture and the windows contrast a moderate amount with the walls and floor. If you decide to have the windows match the walls, that's fine—if you create interest elsewhere in the room.

In order to contrast a moderate amount with the background, the large furniture might be a brighter or a darker version of the wall or floor color. It might be covered in a pattern that incorporates the background color. It might be colored in a different hue that has a tinge of the background color in it. For instance, with yellow walls, a sofa might be colored a yellowish-orange.

Often the large furniture and the window treatment match. If the sofa or bed is on one side of the room, and the windows on the other, this matching treatment will help to balance the room.

If you are looking for an especially FORMAL or CALM effect, you may want large furniture and windows to contrast more subtly with the walls and floor. Walls and floor may be pale, cool, or neutral, and large furnishings and windows only slightly less so. This subtle setting would be a good foil for interesting accessories or for a variety of textures from, say, glossy walls to nubby upholstery to baskets in accessories. The point is that you haven't achieved interest through color contrast in the large and medium areas of the room, so you have to achieve interest through texture, pattern, or interesting accents.

Avoid coloring big pieces in commanding colors that contrast dramatically with the background; they will seem to elbow everything else out of the room! If you do have a big bold piece you can do nothing about, mix in some neutrals or moderate colors to temper the contrast. For example, if you have a big dark blue sofa, integrate it into the room by choosing a carpet in a compatible lighter blue. The sameness of hue integrates the two.

If you want to emphasize a medium-sized piece or make it the focal point of the room, make it contrast more than moderately with the background. It will be sure to attract attention.

Small pieces of furniture should be bright to give bounce to the room. A stand-out warm, dark, or bright color will also give a small piece the clout to balance a more neutral piece of larger size.

As for your punchy accessories, make sure they are evenly distributed around the room to give the room all-around interest.

WITH PATTERN ON THE WINDOWS AND/OR LARGE FURNITURE

If the walls and floor are plain, it is usual to have these medium-sized areas patterned to lend liveliness to the room.

Patterned drapery and/or upholstery can be a relatively inexpensive way of giving a room distinctive pattern. (Of course, it depends on the price of the fabric—whether you use sheets or rare silks.) You could paint or stencil wooden pieces.

Another advantage is that this is a CHANGEABLE solution. For example, you could change the bedspread and curtains in a child's room to suit his advancing ages and stages. You could change the draperies and slipcovers in your living room to suit the seasons.

Patterned areas should balance each other. They might face each other across the room. You might have facing windows, facing sofas, a sofa facing a window, or either facing a large patterned painting.

Pattern on the Windows Medium-sized windows are best for pattern in contrast to plain walls. You will not want to put pattern on windows of awkward size or shape unless the pattern matches the walls.

At a window where there's bright light, mixtures and patterns will show their inevitable fading in a more mellow way than plain solids.

Be aware that when a fabric hangs in folds, some design details may be lost. Also, if the pattern is large, it's best to pleat congruently with the pattern to avoid a very messy-looking

This large room featured white walls, a terra-cotta tile floor, a vaulted ceiling, and enormous arched windows. The large space could take a big dose of drama. The designer selected a *mille-fleurs* (a thousand flowers) pattern in bright, contrasting colors, draped it at the windows, and upholstered it on a large sofa. Now the room has wonderful warmth and gaiety. (Design by Everett Brown, FASID; photo by Yuichi Idaka.)

result. It's a good idea to line all printed and highly colored draperies. Otherwise, the windows will look awful from the outside of the house.

A very bold drapery pattern will necessitate plain furniture as well as a plain floor.

It is usual to paint the walls the same color as the background of the pattern. (Floors can be a few shades darker.)

Pattern on Large Furniture   The size of the pattern must be compatible with the size of the piece. Large pieces of furniture in large rooms can handle large patterns. Medium-sized furniture can handle medium-sized patterns. Small furniture looks best in small patterns.

Pattern can enhance the proportions of furniture. If the piece is too small, pattern will give it the power to stand up to and balance a larger, more neutral plain piece. If the piece is too large, an all-over pattern will work like jungle camouflage and make you less aware of its actual proportions. If a piece is too short or too overstuffed, vertical stripes will make it look taller and slimmer. If a piece is too tall or too skinny, horizontal stripes will make it look shorter and fatter.

Generally it is best to put curved-line designs on curved furniture and straight-lined designs on straight-lined furniture, but stripes work with anything.

If you want, you could choose a pattern from the same style or period as the piece of furniture. Generally the formality of the furniture determines the formality of the pattern, but you could choose to draw attention to the piece by making a surprising contrast. For example, wouldn't it be fun to upholster a rather formal wing chair in a plaid—especially if you wanted the room to have a relaxed, INFORMAL feeling?

With large patterned furniture, walls are often painted the most neutral color from the print and small furniture is often a bright color from the print.

With patterned furniture, accessories are often plain. Patterned accessories must be carefully coordinated or they will create an unpleasing conflict.

WITH PATTERN ON THE SMALL FURNITURE AND/OR ACCESSORIES   If the only pattern in the room is in these small areas, the room will project a CALM mood.

It is important that these patterns be evenly distributed around the room. You could have matching pattern on accessories, drapery trims, and pillows, or similar patterns on small chairs and a painting.

Leaving your pattern interest to accessories and small furniture is the expensive way to achieve design interest. Paintings are more expensive than wallpaper.

WITH UNEVEN TEXTURES You could have woven wood or bamboo blinds at the windows, or casement-cloth curtains or draperies of a nubby or uneven fabric. You could have furnishings of cane, wicker, rattan, or bamboo. Or nubby upholstery. You could have bunches of baskets.

WITH VERY SHINY TEXTURES A piece you want to emphasize might have a lacquer finish. It might be mirrored. It might be shiny steel or chrome, brass or gold. All such shiny surfaces attract attention.

EMPHASIZING THE BACKGROUND

WITH STRONG COLOR A strong color on the walls or floor will create a STIMULAT-ING/DRAMATIC effect, and make the room seem more COZY and WARM. In general, the floor is a less overwhelming place for drama than the walls.

Largest Areas:	Walls or floor could be in a warm, dark, or bright color. If the walls are strong, the floors should be rather neutral. If the floor is strong, the walls should be rather neutral.
Medium Areas:	Windows and large pieces of furniture (sofa, bed, etc.) might match the strong color, be a lighter or a duller version, be a compatible neutral, or be a mix of the strong color with a neutral.
Small Areas:	Small pieces of furniture (ottomans, benches, etc.) are usually a neutral or dulled color. They might be the strong background color mixed with a neutral.
Accent Areas:	Accessories (lamps, ashtrays, sofa pillows, etc.) might be a repeat of the strong background color, or a pure neutral—such as black or white.

Caution, if you have decided on a strong wall color. Light bounces from wall to wall; therefore the color of one wall reflects on the others, and the color of the others reflects back on it. For this reason, colors on walls build up intensity—much more than you would ever suspect from looking at a paint sample. To achieve the effect you want, choose a color that is a bit lighter or duller than what you think you want. When you look at a paint sample you are looking only at an inch or so of color, not several square yards. A paint sample may be valid and accurate for choosing accents, but tends to mislead on large areas.

Also, don't go by the color of wet paint. It changes when it dries. Wait until a patch dries to see if you like it.

With strongly colored walls, what do you do with the rest of the room? Furniture often works out best if it is neutral or a variation of the wall color. Pure neutrals are good mixers. Imagine how strong and stunning white furniture would be against dark green walls, maybe with shiny black accents in lamps and accessories. Imagine how smart black and white would look against red.

If the walls are in a warm hue, the furniture could be a lighter and/or duller version of the same hue. You might want accessories in cool colors to temper the temperature.

If the walls are in dark shades, the furniture could be the same color in a lighter version. Generally, you will want to use some light, bright colors or textures in the room to avoid a dull or depressing effect.

If the walls are bright, furniture could be the wall color dulled with gray. You will definitely want to tone down the effect by using some dulled or neutral colors in the room. For neutrals, choose whites (which look smashing with bright colors), blacks, beiges, or browns.

If the room is smallish, it's a good idea to have large furniture match the walls. You have enough excitement without large-scale contrasts.

Caution: Avoid covering large furnishings in hot, dark, or bright colors of a different hue. The place would take off like a gypsy caravan—unless you mixed in a lot of neutrals.

With a strongly colored floor, what do you do with the rest of the room? It is important to repeat the floor color somewhere else in the room so it doesn't look like you just moved into someone else's home. You might put the floor color on drapery trim or just on pillows on the sofa.

If the floor covering is patterned, it might be the inspiration of your color scheme.

Generally, the same principles apply as with strongly colored walls. Furniture that is neutral or a softer version of the strong color is a good bet. Large furniture matching the floor will be harmonious, and its size will be minimized.

The rest of your color scheme might be composed of the strong color mixed with neutrals—whites, blacks, or browns. Walls can be white. Windows can be white mixed with the color. Large furniture might be the same color as the floor or a mixture of white with the floor color. Small furniture can be black or white. Accessories can be black or white or a brilliant version of the floor color.

When the floor is emphasized, the walls should be muted to avoid an overpowering effect.

WITH MODERATE COLOR Instead of emphasizing the background with strong, socko colors, you can do it with more moderate colors. If heavy-impact socko colors are warm, dark, or bright, medium-impact colors are not so hot, dark, or bright. For a moderate effect, warm reds and oranges can be lightened with white or dulled with gray. Actually, to achieve a medium impact, any dark color can be lightened with white and any bright color can be dulled with gray.

If light-impact un-attention-getting colors are cool, pale, and dull, you know you can transform them into medium-impact colors by

In this room the background is emphasized with strong color. The wall-to-wall carpet is STIMULATING orange and so is the focal point wall. Other walls are painted dark green. The furniture blends in because, being yellow, it is light and it shares a hue with all walls. The simple modular furnishings would adapt easily to a calmer mood. (Photo courtesy of Selig Manufacturing Co., Inc.; design by Elroy Edson, ASID.)

making them darker or brighter. For example, darkish and brightish blues and greens are medium-impact colors.

Largest Areas: Walls and floor can both be in a medium-impact color, or one may be neutral.

Medium Areas: Windows and large furniture may be the same as the background color, a compatible neutral, or a different medium-impact hue.

Small Areas: Small pieces of furniture may be neutral, or the background color mixed with neutrals.

Accent Areas: Accessories can be a stronger version of background color, or pure neutrals.

When you have walls and/or floor in a medium-impact color that is neither light nor dark, bright nor dull, you could make your large furnishings and windows paler or duller to CALM down the scheme.

Alternatively, for a rich and interesting effect, you could color your large furnishings and windows in a medium-impact color of another hue. Both colors should have the same amount of gray in them so that if you squinted at them in twilight or in dim light they would both seem the same shade of gray. The gray softens the color contrast and creates a subtle but rich effect. In a room like this, you won't need much in the way of accessories.

If you chose strongly colored furnishings, the whole effect would be STIMULATING and exciting. This would not be a room where you would want to spend long periods of time.

WITH PATTERN ON THE WALLS Except for the most unobtrusive, light-impact designs, pattern on the wall puts emphasis on the background.

If your furniture is poor, patterned walls will divert attention from it. If your furniture is sparse, patterned walls will make the room feel furnished. (This is why patterned walls are often found in dining rooms and halls.)

Patterned walls don't need paintings or other accessories. Buying wallpaper is a lot cheaper than purchasing paintings. Actually wallpaper is the cheapest way to achieve pattern interest—even if the wallpaper is expensive. It saves spending money elsewhere. You can wallpaper one wall or four.

You can wallpaper one wall to make a focal point. You might even wallpaper a panel behind a sofa or bed to give it additional impact as a focal point. The pattern may be the same as the bedspread or the sofa upholstery. (Then to balance the room, the same pattern may be repeated on the wall opposite, either as a wall-covering or as draperies.)

Patterned walls give a small room interest without taking space. For example, it's an answer for a foyer that has no room for furniture.

Patterned walls are the answer in a room where the furniture is sparse or uninteresting. This bathroom is given a splash-proof dash with bathtub walls in dynamic diagonal designs of WATERPROOF ceramic tiles. The bathtub itself is set into a surround of tiles matching the background of the pattern. Mirrored closet doors double the DRAMATIC impact. (Photo courtesy of American Olean Tile Co.; design by Leslie John Koerser.)

You Won't Want Patterned Walls in Some Cases If you have beautiful paintings and pictures, you won't want patterned walls to compete with them. Paintings and pictures look awful against most patterned walls. Walls of subtle stripes are about the only acceptable exception.

If you have a strong pattern on the floor, or on the furniture or windows, you will want to underplay the walls. The only acceptable pattern for the walls would be a subtle textured effect.

What Can You Do with the Rest of the Room, if the Walls are Patterned? The easy answer is to have everything else plain.

If you want to camouflage the size and shape of the windows and/or the size and shape of a large piece of furniture, you can cover them in the same pattern as the walls. This will unify the room and make it seem more SPACIOUS. But be careful that the pattern is soft and subtle. If it is too bold, you'll be overwhelmed.

For a CALM effect, the large furniture and/or the windows might be in the same color as the background of the pattern. For a little livelier effect, they both might be in a second medium-impact color picked from the pattern.

You might cover the large furniture and/or the windows in a secondary pattern related to the walls.

The small furniture should create a contrast. It might be plain in a bright color from the pattern, or it might be in a pattern that makes a complimentary contrast with the walls.

The accessories are usually plain, in a bright color from the pattern, or a sharp neutral like black or white. Patterned walls in flat-appearing designs can stand accessories that have a one-color effect, things like mirrors or simple wall sconces. You might have patterned pillows on plain furniture. The pillows should pick up the colors of the walls. You could trim a plain window treatment in a pattern compatible with the walls.

WITH PATTERN ON THE FLOOR A

This room begins with a medium-impact pattern on the walls. The scale is small, but the contrasts are relatively strong. The floor and furniture are plain. Patterned pillows help blend the sofa with the wall. The ottoman opposite contributes balance. The screens to the sides of the sofa playfully alternate panels with a reverse pattern, which—amusingly—looks a lot like the iris. (Courtesy of Stauffer Chemical Co.; design by Peter Bradley/ Jack Macurdy; photo by Ernest Silva.)

strongly patterned floor is less overwhelming than strongly patterned walls because the area is smaller and the floor doesn't face your eyeballs when you're standing.

Caution: Some patterns just shouldn't be used on the floor. They pop up at you and make you feel like the floor is uneven or wobbly, and that you might fall over or get seasick. Look at a large piece of the flooring and see what you think.

Avoid floorcoverings that lose an important amount of their impact when parts of the design are obscured by furniture.

To protect your investment, choose a pattern you'll love living with for a long time. Avoid extremes. Outlandish bold designs in bright colors soon become tiresome. Vague patterns in drab colors soon become boring. Patterned carpeting can be costly, but if well made it will last a long time. (For example, Orientals are forever.) Masonry is expensive but lasts forever. Patterned resilients such as vinyl are relatively inexpensive and DURABLE.

You Won't Want Patterned Floors in Some Cases If you have strongly patterned walls, you would want a plain floor. Patterned floors are usually best with plain walls.

If you have patterned draperies or upholstery, it's safer to stick to a plain floor.

If you want to emphasize the furniture or accessories, you'll want the floor to flow smoothly into the background.

If the room is small, a pattern on the floor would shrink the space.

What Can You Do With the Rest of the Room, if the Floor Is Patterned? It depends on how powerful the pattern is. A heavy-impact pattern on the floor requires everything else to be plain or textured. A medium-impact pattern on the floor can tolerate a smaller-scaled pattern of similar colors on some furniture. The stripe always works. (Oriental rugs seem to get along particularly well with other patterns.)

Generally with a patterned floor, walls are plain. Furniture is noncompetitive and compatible in color and shape. Accessories may be patterned because they are usually seen against the plain walls or furniture.

WITH STRONGLY TEXTURED WALLS If the natural light in the room is too strong or bright, textured walls are your answer. They will absorb light and make the room comfortably DARKER OR DIMMER.

Again, think of those Mediterranean villas with their light-absorbing rough plaster or stucco walls. Rough-textured building materials such as concrete block, brick, and shingles are appropriate. For a dressier look, you could use a grasscloth wallcovering, or even other wallcoverings printed to look like textures. These have a nice, natural, earthy feel to them.

If the walls are strongly textured, any accessories hanging on them must be suitably strong in character—brightly colored or heavy in weight.

WITH VERY SHINY WALLS Very shiny walls will reflect and multiply the light and make a room seem LIGHTER AND BRIGHTER. Be warned, however, that most shiny wall treatments require perfect walls as a beginning.

In this room the background is emphasized. The walls and beams have a strong wood texture. The tile floor is patterned under the dining table. (This inset of patterned vinyl defines the dining area, adds liveliness, conceals spills, and is EASY TO CLEAN.) Following the INFORMAL feeling of the rustic wood walls, furnishings are simple, traditional COUNTRY styles. Accessories are bright and bold. (Photo courtesy of Champion Building Products.)

Lacquer, glossy paint, metallic wallcoverings, and mirror are the most outstanding shiny treatments.

If a shiny surface is combined with a warm, dark, or bright color, its impact is all the more DRAMATIC. Actually, in order to avoid being depressing, dark colors on the walls *should* be shiny.

TO UNDERPLAY, CREATE SAMENESS

Remember, if the foreground is emphasized, the background must be underplayed. If the background is emphasized, the foreground must be underplayed.

If things are the same, they blend together. There is no attention-getting contrast between them. The eye flows smoothly over them. If the object or area is the same size, shape, texture, or color as your dominant choice, it will fit in with the majority and not attract undue attention.

It can be otherwise un-attention-getting. To underplay areas or objects, you can make things all one color, or closely blended colors. You can make them neutral. Neutral colors like white, beige, gray, and cinnamon brown don't take part in the battle to be noticed. You can make them unpatterned. Plain surfaces don't draw attention to themselves, unless most of the rest of the room is patterned. Light-impact patterns with subtle contrasts are only slightly more attention-getting than plain surfaces. You can make them untextured. The eye slides easily over smooth surfaces. Smooth surfaces don't draw special attention except in rooms full of uneven textures. Subtle textures aren't particularly riveting either.

CONSIDER THE WOODWORK In order to avoid unwelcome interruptions that would chop up the space, it is usual to paint the woodwork as much like the walls as possible. It can match painted walls (or be the same color in a washable semigloss). It can match the foreground or the background of a wallpaper (preferably the color that is most like the floorcovering). It can be stained to match a wood-paneled wall or a wood ceiling.

When would you want the woodwork to contrast with the walls? When the room is very large and you want to break up the vast expanse of the walls. When you have particularly handsome architectural features that are placed in a position of balance—for example, facing doors, or windows side by side. When the woodwork of the room is stunning and you want to emphasize it. (One room I've admired had ceiling moldings painted in soft pastels matching the colors of the accent pillows on the sofa. The rest of the room was mostly white.) Color contrast can also emphasize a piece of woodwork you want to make into a focal point—for example, a fireplace mantel. (In this case, paint windows and doors to match to give unity to the scheme.)

If you want the woodwork to contrast, what color should it be? It can be an off-white neutral, compatible with your wall color. (It is best to choose a semi-gloss paint that can be easily washed.) It could be a natural wood finish. Soft brown is usual; a gray stain is more unusual and gives a COOL effect. For accents on cabinets or bookcases, you can use a bright contrasting color that goes with other parts of the room.

(Design by Sarah B. Jenkins, ASID, W & J Sloane; photo by Ken Heinen.)

19

CHOOSE YOUR COLOR SCHEME

First, the easy way.

THE QUICK AND EASY WAY OF DEVELOPING A COLOR SCHEME

Find some sort of patterned thing that contains the colors and the kind of motifs you'd like to use in the room. This patterned object can be anything. If it is an object that you will actually use in the room, so much the better. It might be a patterned rug or carpet or resilient flooring. It might be a wallpaper. It might be a drapery or upholstery material. It might be a painting. It might be a vase, an ashtray, a dinner dish, any piece of china or ceramic. It might even be the view out the window.

If you don't have a patterned object containing the colors you'd like to use in the room, it would make your life a lot easier if you hunted one up. Nearly every room requires some kind of pattern in it somewhere. It is the tie that binds the colors of the room together. It is much, much easier to begin with this pattern than to find one later.

Choose Three Colors from this Pattern to Use as Your Color Scheme You should choose a light-impact color. This might be the palest or the dullest color in the pattern. Second, you should choose a medium-impact color—one that is neither too strong, nor too subtle. Third, you should pick a bright bold color.

How to Spread Color in a Scheme Emphasizing the Foreground The colors will gain strength as the areas get smaller. Color the background areas of the walls and floor in the light-impact color. The color should be subdued. If you want a light, airy scheme, pick the palest color from your pattern. If this light color seems too bright, you might dull it a bit with gray before you put it on your walls or floors. (A slightly darker color is suitable for the floors anyway.) If you want a darker or duller scheme, select the darkest or dullest color from the pattern to use on your walls or floors. If that color also seems too bright, soften it with gray.

The window treatment and the large furniture should be in the second, medium-impact color. If this color has a tinge of the wall or floor color in it, the two are bound to be harmonious.

The small pieces of furniture—should be in the third, the bright color, picked from your pattern.

The accessories—the accent area—should be bright and eye-catching. They might be in a fourth or fifth color picked from the pattern. They can be a bright bold version of the subdued color on the walls or floor. They might be black or white or another bold neutral. Just make sure that their overall area is small, and that these punchy pieces are evenly distributed around the room.

How to Spread Color in a Scheme Emphasizing the Background Here the bright color might be placed on the walls or floor. If the color seems too much you might lighten it with white or dull it with gray.

The most neutral or pale color might be the color of the large furniture and the window treatment. And the medium-value color might be the color of small pieces of furniture or of accessories.

The pattern that is inspiring your scheme may be a wallcovering or a floorcovering. If the walls are patterned, you can make the floor neutral, and if the floors are patterned, you can make the walls neutral.

The large furniture and windows can be neutral or a medium-impact color. Accessories can be in the strong bright color. The pattern will keep the emphasis on the background.

TYPES OF COLOR SCHEMES

The kind of color scheme you select depends on the mood you want to create and on the attractiveness of the furnishings you have. Subtle color contrasts tend to make a room feel FORMAL, CALM, SPACIOUS, or FEMININE. Bold color contrasts tend to make a room feel INFORMAL, STIMULATING, COZY, or MASCULINE.

FOR A CALM MOOD   If you have very attrac-

tive furnishings, you could do the whole room in variations of one hue. Because contrasts are minimal, the room is CALM, and it can set off your fabulous artworks or glamorous, glittering friends. The variations are as follows:

The One-Hue or Monochromatic Scheme

Basic Color: Whichever you choose

Largest Areas
{ Walls: A lighter or more neutral version of the basic color
Floor: Darker or more neutral than the wall

Medium Areas
{ Windows: Brighter than wall (perhaps a pattern, mixing the basic color with neutrals)
Large Furniture: Brighter than wall (maybe the same as windows)

Small Areas
{ Small Furniture: Brighter than large furniture (perhaps a pattern, mixing the basic color with neutrals)

Accents
{ Accessories: Super-bright (no gray in it at all) Black and white are also good—they're pure

With a monochromatic scheme, you are varying one color by making it paler or darker, brighter or duller, or mixing it with neutrals. Because there isn't much contrast in color, you must make the room interesting in other ways. You'll need a variety of textures, or a surprising accent color. As an example of textural variety, you might have smooth, glossy walls, thick, soft carpet, nubby upholstery, and baskets as accessories. If you want a perky accent color, choose the color that's opposite your basic hue. For example, if you are doing a room all in blues, choose orange accessories. Orange and blue are opposites; so are red and green, yellow and purple. (To avoid a startling surprise, you might want to choose a toned-down version of this opposite hue.)

Special Note: A neutral one-color scheme is CHANGEABLE. You can change the color of the accessories, and change the entire mood of the room. This kind of scheme is a safe bet for

In this city apartment, the designer wanted a CALM retreat from the outside hubbub. He chose a neutral one-color scheme, a symphony of soft grays. The lightest color faces the window wall to maximize the light. A darker gray is chosen for serviceable **upholstery. Textures in the room vary from the smooth glass breaker to the twill upholstery to the rough rattan drum tables. Pink lilies add an appealing accent. (Design by Stedila Design.)**

people who aren't sure of their color preferences, and want to experiment with accents.

Examples of Monochromatic Schemes

Basic color: Green

| Largest Areas | { | Walls: Pale lime |
| | | Floor: Less pale lime |

| Medium Areas | { | Windows: Stronger green (maybe a print with white) |
| | | Large Furniture: Stronger green (maybe a print with white) |

| Small Areas | Small Furniture: Dark fir green |

| Accents | Accessories: White, lemon, blue, or rose, plus black in small quantities |

Basic color: Green

| Largest Areas | { | Walls: Pale green |
| | | Floor: Less pale green |

| Medium Areas | { | Windows: Deep green |
| | | Large Furniture: Deep green |

| Small Areas | Small Furniture: White-and-deep-green print |

| Accents | Accessories: White |

Basic color: Yellow

| Largest Areas | { | Walls: Pale gold |
| | | Floor: Pale gold |

| Medium Areas | { | Windows: Bright yellow |
| | | Large Furniture: Bright yellow |

| Small Areas | Small Furniture: yellow-and-white pattern |

| Accents | Accessories: Black |

FOR A RELAXING MOOD If you want a relaxing mood, and your accessories aren't fabulous, choose a scheme of related colors. A related scheme gives a room interest through variety of color. You don't have to spend money on outstanding accessories, and you don't have to worry too much about pattern or texture.

A related scheme consists of three colors that have the same hue in them. For example, if you like yellow, you can start with that and choose other colors that have yellow in them. You could have a scheme of yellow, orange-yellow, and orange or a scheme of yellow, yellow-green, and green.

If you like blue, you could have a scheme of blue, blue-green, and green, or of blue, bluish-purple, and purple.

If you like red, you could have a scheme of red, reddish-orange, and orange, or red, reddish-purple, and purple.

Alternatively, instead of using three separate hues, you might choose two hues and vary one of them lighter or brighter. For example, you might have pale blue walls and floors, kelly green large furniture, and dark blue small furniture.

Caution: To give your room a clear character, it is especially important with a related scheme that one hue be in the majority. It is a good idea to cover your walls and floor in the same hue. Walls and floors might be exactly the same, or the walls might be a lighter version and the floors a darker version of the same hue.

Examples of Related Schemes

Dominant Color: Pale blue—cool but lively

Largest Areas {Walls: Pale blue / Floor: Pale blue

Medium Areas {Windows: Kelly green / Large Furniture: Kelly green

Small Areas — Small Furniture: Dark blue

Accents — Accessories: White

Dominant Color: Lavender—cool and calmish

Largest Areas {Walls: Light lavender / Floor: Darker lavender

This **RELAXING** room is basically blue. Soft powder blue is the color of the carpet and the background of the inexpensive sheeting that covers walls, windows, dust ruffle, and table. Blue's next-door-neighbor on the color wheel, green, creates a friendly contrast within the printed pattern. Because green has blue in it, these colors have a kinship. They are called *related.* (Photo courtesy of Fibers Division/Allied Chemical Corporation; design by Virginia Frankel, ASID.)

Medium Areas {Windows: Blue / Large Furniture: Blue

Small Areas — Small Furniture: White

Accents — Accessories: White

Dominant Color: Yellow—bright and warm

Largest Areas {Walls: Yellow / Floor: Yellow

Medium Areas {Windows: Sharp orange pattern / Large Furniture: Sharp orange pattern

Small Areas — Small Furniture: Sharp orange

Accents — Accessories: Russet

FOR A STIMULATING MOOD If you want a stimulating mood, and you want to take the emphasis off your furnishings, choose a scheme of strong color contrasts.

Strong color contrasts create a LIVELY, vibrant mood. Such schemes are so attention-getting that you and your guests may not notice anything else.

There are three ways to achieve such a scheme:

1. You could do a *related* scheme (described above) in hot, bright, or dark colors of strong impact.
2. You could do a *complementary* scheme, combining two colors that are opposite on the color wheel. Opposites are: blue and orange, red and green, purple and yellow.
3. You could do a *triad* scheme, combining three colors that are equidistant on the color wheel. For example, you could devise a scheme of red, yellow, and blue, or a scheme of orange, green, and purple.

The Complementary Scheme (of Opposite Colors) Opposite pairs are blue/orange, red/green, and yellow/purple. As you can see, a complementary scheme combines both WARM and COOL colors. (It might be a good choice for a room with an eastern exposure. That gets warm light in the morning and cool light in the afternoon.)

Complementary colors are DRAMATIC together. They are so different that they serve to intensify each other. To avoid an overpowering effect, you can do any of the following:

1. Make one color cover both the large areas of walls and floor and the medium areas of large furniture and windows. Use the other color for small furnishings and accents. In any case, be sure to give one color more area than the other. If you make the mistake of giving these two opposites equal space, you're in for a fight. The competition will set your nerves on edge.
2. Tone down both colors with gray. Since they will then have the gray in common, the opposite colors will seem to go together more easily.
3. Choose opposites that have a tinge of the same color in them. For example, combine a bluish red with a bluish green *or* a yellowish red with a yellowish green. (A bluish red won't look so good with a yellowish green.) If opposite colors have a tinge of the same color in them, the similarity will help them establish a meaningful relationship.
4. Make one color distinctly lighter or darker than the other so that the two colors don't compete on the same level. It is important to be true to the natural weight of colors. For example, yellow should always be lighter than purple. (There is no more repulsive scheme than the combination of mustard and lavender.)
5. Relate the opposite colors to a print that has both colors.
6. Use almost-opposites, instead of exact opposites. For example, instead of using blue with orange, you could use blue with yellow, or blue with red. Since these colors have a closer relationship, they are more compatible.

Strong contrasts make a STIMULATING mood. Here there is the drama of light against dark. The dark color dominates. It is the color of the walls and the background of the large upholstery. The light color is secondary. It covers the floor and the details of the printed design. Dark colors on the walls make a room seem like an enveloping envelope—an envelope you'd rather join than lick. (Photo courtesy of Baker, Knapp & Tubbs; design by Watson & Boaler, Inc., Chicago.)

Examples of Complementary Schemes

Opposite Colors: Red and green, red dominant

Largest Areas { Walls: Pale pink
Floor: Pale pink

Medium Areas { Windows: Deep rose
Large Furniture: Deep rose

Small Areas   Small Furniture: Mossy green

Accents   Accessories: Mossy green

Opposite Colors: Green and red, green dominant

Largest Areas { Walls: Icy green tint
Floor: Icy green

White furniture against dark walls creates a STIMULATING and sophisticated scheme. Here the fully upholstered seating has an especially luxurious look, reminiscent of the luxury ocean liners of the thirties. Mirrors and shiny surfaces, like tinkling cocktail glasses, add uplifting excitement. (Photo courtesy of Selig Manufacturing Co., Inc.; design by Elroy Edson, ASID.)

Medium Areas {Windows: Rose draperies
Large Furniture: Rose sofa

Small Areas   Small Furniture: Rose and white pattern

Accents   Accessories: Deep green

Opposite Colors: Green and red, green dominant
Largest Areas {Walls: White
Floor: Green

Medium Areas {Windows: Green
Large Furniture: Print of red flowers with green leaves

Small Areas   Small Furniture: Red

Accents   Accessories: White

The Triad Scheme (of Three Equidistant Colors)   Distance on the color wheel creates the contrasts that have a strong and striking impact. Equidistant triads are: red/yellow/blue, orange/green/purple, red-purple/yellow-orange/blue-green, blue-purple/red-orange/yellow-green.

Again, there is danger of an overpowering effect. To avoid an overdose of color contrast, you can do any of the following:

1. Use one color in the large areas of walls and floor and the medium areas of large furniture and windows. Use the second color on the small furnishings and the third color on accents.
2. Tone down all colors with gray.
3. Relate colors to a print that has all the colors in it.
4. Mix the triad with a large dose of a neutral color.

Examples of Triad Schemes

Triad: Yellow, Red, Blue, Yellow Dominant
Largest Areas {Walls: Yellow
Floor: Yellow & Red Mixture

Medium Areas {Windows: Red
Large Furniture: Red/Yellow/Blue Pattern

Small Areas   Small Furniture: Blue

Accents   Accessories: Blue & Red

Triad: Yellow, Red, Blue, Neutral White Dominant
Largest Areas {Walls: White
Floor: White

Medium Areas {Windows: White
Large Furniture: Red/Yellow/Blue Print
(Closet Doors: Red/Yellow/Blue)

Small Areas	Small Furniture: Red
Accents	Accessories: White

ASSEMBLING SAMPLES

When you have formulated your final color scheme, it's time to go gathering samples. Get swatches or samples of any of the materials you intend to use in the room: paint, paper, flooring, fabrics. Fool around with them and see how they blend with each other and the woods in the room.

A Few Words of Caution You have to take extra care to be sure that the sample is indeed the same color as what you will buy. Unfortunately, it ain't necessarily so. The sample may have been sitting in a window and faded. Dye lots are different from fabric to fabric and from floorcovering to floorcovering. If you can, try to get a sample from the actual dye lot that you will later buy from. (And by the way, when you buy, buy all at once. If you have to buy a second installment later, the dye lot may not match your original.)

Different kinds of light will affect your colors. Look at your colors in the actual room where they will be used. Look at them at all times of day, on bright days, on dull days, and at night with the sort of artificial light you'll be using.

Texture also affects color. Smooth, slick textures bounce light right off them. As a result, they might look lighter in color than they really are. Thick and uneven textures absorb a bit of light. As a result, they might look darker in color than they really are. Different fibers (wool vs. cotton vs. nylon vs. acrylic) also absorb and reflect light in different ways. Again, try all samples in day and night light on location.

20

CHOOSING PATTERNS

A pattern can be the key to your color scheme. The artist who designed the pattern picked colors that coordinate, so matching these colors is a sure way to a safe scheme. See the preceding chapter on color for actual information on composing your scheme.

The major pattern you choose should be compatible with your choices for dominant size, shape, texture, and color. For example, if your dominant size is medium, your major pattern should also be medium in scale. If your dominant shape is curved, choose a compatible curved-line design. You might choose a floral, or something else with a natural theme. If your dominant shape is straight-lined, you might choose a disciplined, mathematical, straight-lined design. If your dominant texture is rough and INFORMAL, you might choose bold plaids, checks, or bouncy polka dots. If your dominant texture is smooth and FORMAL, you might choose an exquisite embroidery. The dominant color of your room should have a major place in the pattern; it might be its background color.

What style are your furnishings? Heavy furnishings can take dark or bold patterns. Delicate furnishings belong with delicate, light-looking patterns. You might look up your style in Chapter 12. Every important decorative style has particular patterns associated with it.

HOW DO YOU MIX PATTERNS TOGETHER?

There shouldn't be more than one bold pattern in a single room. Generally there shouldn't be more than three patterns in any one room. Too many patterns can make a room seem chaotic and crowded. The more patterns you use, the more subtle each should be in order to get along with the others. You can't have everything vying for your immediate attention. It would drive you crazy.

If You Do Use a Bold Pattern Somewhere: A small splash of a socko pattern might be enough. You could use it on one wall to make a focal point. If the pattern isn't overwhelming, you can use it lavishly—on walls, windows, furniture if you like—just don't compete with it. Generally, other things should match the pattern, be solid plain colors, or be unobtrusive in design. Subtle stripes, one-color tone-on-tone designs, and textured effects fall into this unobtrusive class.

If You Want to Use Several Patterns: Your major pattern should be consistent with the character of the room. It should be the same relative size as the room and its furnishings. It should have the same sort of lines or shapes as the majority of your furnishings—curved lines if most of your furnishings are curved; straight lines if most of your furnishings are straight-sided. The material the pattern is on can be rough and uneven if your room is INFORMAL, medium if the room is SEMIFORMAL, or smooth and shiny if the room is FORMAL. The pattern should have your dominant color in it. As a matter of fact, it can tie together all the colors of your scheme.

Dramatic plants dominate this room and make it seem like an indoor garden. Continuing the theme, the major pattern in the room, covering the sofa and the love seat (seen), is green with blooms on branches. The design, like the trees, is curved but angular. The secondary pattern, a versatile Oriental rug, makes beguiling birds of curved shapes out of straight lines. A smaller third pattern on a pillow gives a compatibly angular interpretation of potted tulips. (Design by Velma Sanford Interiors.)

Your secondary pattern should be smaller in size than your major pattern. It could be the same type of design as your major pattern or a versatile geometric. (Stripes go with anything. Checks, plaids, and even polka dots are good mixers in INFORMAL rooms.) It should use some of the same colors as your major pattern. It might include either your dominant color or the second most important color in your scheme. Generally, the secondary pattern should have fewer colors than the major pattern.

The third pattern should be smaller in scale than your secondary pattern. This is appropriate because your third pattern should be used in small areas—on small furniture or on accessories. The third pattern can be the same type of design as your major pattern, a compatible geometric, or a textured effect. The color of your third pattern can contrast with your major and secondary patterns. Since it will be used in small areas, it will act as a color accent.

Get Swatches   After you have made your selection of patterns, get swatches of them to try out in the room. Let them live together a bit to test out their compatibility. If they do get along well together, you can make an investment in their permanent relationship.

A Heartening Note   Many wallcovering and fabric manufacturers create patterns to go together. They save you a lot of shopping and searching. For example, one design might be a large-scale motif on a patterned background. A second selection might simply be the patterned background design. A third design might be the original large-scale motif rendered in a small scale. Also there's usually a full range of solids done in each of the component colors. (Sometimes these manufacturers even make coordinating carpets.)

THE GOOD MIXERS

STRIPES   Stripes go with absolutely everything. They mix with florals, with geometrics,

A bold graphic painting defines the pattern play in this party room. All patterns reinterpret parts of the painting. A little circular, geometric, daisylike design covers tabletops. A diagonal stripe on the underskirt of the central service table draws the eye right up to the floral centerpiece. A large-scale splashy floral on the other underskirts adds an undercurrent of excitement. (Design by R. Michael Brown; photo by Henry Fullerton III.)

check of the right size. It must fit the size of the room or the piece of furniture it's on.

PLAIDS Plaids are INFORMAL. In bold colors they are MASCULINE; in pastel colors they are FEMININE.

Plaids are particularly useful in tying together a color scheme because they do it so clearly. Each color has its own line and seems strongly defined. One color may seem stronger than the others; or it may be used in a wider stripe. If this is the case, consider the direction of that stripe. If it goes horizontally, it will make whatever it's on seem wider and lower. If it goes vertically, it will make whatever it's on seem taller and slimmer.

Plaids, because they contain contrasts within them, are by their very nature attention-getting. Reserve them for pieces or areas you want to emphasize.

with damasks, with any style of furniture. They are timeless.

Stripes have special powers. Think of the lines of the stripes as arrows and you will understand their powers. The eye will follow the direction of the stripe.

Vertical stripes on the walls push up toward the ceiling and make the ceiling seem higher. Vertical stripes on furniture tend to make the furniture look taller and slimmer.

Horizontal stripes on the wall draw the eye on a lengthwise path. They can make a room seem wider or longer and the ceiling seem lower. (Avoid horizontal stripes for your walls with draperies. The combination doesn't look good.) Horizontal stripes on furniture make the furniture seem wider and lower.

Subtle stripes are a good choice for pattern in a small room. They are not overbearing. Subtle vertical stripes on the wall do not compete with pictures or paintings.

CHECKS You must be careful to choose a

TEXTURED EFFECTS One-color, tone-on-tone designs have subtle variety. They are interesting but unobtrusive. Tweedlike mixtures also have subtle variety. They are appropriate in INFORMAL rooms. Small all-over patterns used in large areas lose their design detail when viewed at a distance. They end up creating a textured effect. However, beware of designs that are too small. Sometimes at a distance they just look dirty.

Textures themselves often have pattern. Think of the pattern of wood grains, or of the arrangement of bricks. This interest should be accounted for in your scheme.

REVERSE PATTERNS Reverse patterns are the same design printed with the colors reversed. For example, one pattern might have a blue design on a white background and the other a white design on a blue background. Reverse patterns provide unity and diversity. They are particularly effective in adjacent rooms.

21
CHOOSING THE LIGHTING

The obvious first purpose of lighting is so you can see. Second, lighting has fantastic powers to manipulate mood. Third, it can direct drama.

Before you do anything, go count your electric outlets. Are your living-room end tables and bedroom night tables convenient to outlets? Is your desk? If you need more outlets, call an electrician to install them. (Be sure to ask him for an estimate of costs before you let him begin work.) Such electrical work should be done at the beginning—before you do anything about walls or floors. If you decide you want built-in lighting, this work should, of course, be done before anything else.

LIGHTING MUST PROVIDE COMFORT OF VISION

Light is essential for seeing what you're doing, and what you're doing will determine how much light you'll need to see. If you're chopping celery with a big sharp knife, you want to see well enough to miss your fingernails. If you're snuggling on the sofa with your favorite friend, a little shadow might add to your alluring mystery. It's all in what you're doing.

Tasks—reading, studying, paying your bills, sewing, typing your first novel—all these things require strong direct lighting. The light should shine directly down on your work surface, be it a desk, a table, or your lap. (But it shouldn't reflect off your work into your eyes.)

If you're just moseying around, talking to a friend or a friendly relative, listening to music, or whatever, you don't need such strong light. But you do need to see well enough not to bump into things. The room would need soft general illumination.

Light shouldn't hurt your eyes. Think of a bare lightbulb dangling down in a dark room. The effect is eerie and unnerving. The contrast between light and shadow is too sharp. Very sharp contrasts between light and shadow are unpleasant and hurtful to the eyes. The answer is to light the room softly all over and add stronger lights where you want them. The contrast then will be between bright and not-so-bright, a livable and attractive contrast. Most rooms have soft general lighting, plus strategically placed direct lighting for tasks or for emphasizing special objects.

LIGHTING CAN PROVIDE FLEXIBILITY OF MOOD

Many rooms today are multifunctional. At a certain time of the day, you may want to work. At another you may want to sit back and turn on to Beethoven. Light can change the mood of a room so completely that you hardly realize that the furniture is the same.

How do you get this flexibility? Through dimmer switches, various light sources, and/or flexible fixtures.

A beautiful old tapestry is set off in a metal-edged fabric frame and highlighted with a picture light. Focusing light on a special object will give it added importance (as well as better visibility). Lighting also reflects back into the room to give soft, general illumination. A few specific lights like this one can give a mellow mood to a room. (Photo courtesy of *Interior Design* magazine; design by Thomas Boccia; photo by Jaime Ardiles-Arce.)

If you substitute a dimmer switch for an ordinary electric switch, you will have an instant mood-maker. You can turn the light up to the brightest intensity or down to the softest lowest-level light. You could have your boss over to work, or your sweetheart over to play.

You could have different lights you use at different times. You could have an overhead light that reflects from the ceiling and illuminates the whole room, plus direct lamp lighting for work times. You could have floor spotlights shining up through the leaves of your indoor trees and plants when you want a little delicate drama. You could play your records and spotlight your paintings, and float away in your artistic ambience.

If you choose flexible fixtures, you might point a light at your book when you want to read, and turn it to reflect light off the wall when you want a quiet conversation. For different levels of lighting, you could use three-way bulbs in your lamps.

DIRECT LIGHT CAN EMPHASIZE YOUR ASSETS

Just as the star is spotlighted on stage, you can spotlight the star attractions of your room. This is a DRAMATIC way to emphasize your assets. The size of the spotlight you choose depends on the size of the object or area you want to illuminate. You could choose a spotlight that casts a wide light to illuminate a fireplace wall, or a whole alcove or niche. You could choose a pinpoint spotlight to illuminate just the small surface of a painting.

Spotlights come in all kinds of fixtures. They can be recessed in the ceiling or walls, or mounted on the ceiling or walls. They can be inconspicuous fixtures on the floor, or attached to furniture or pictures. They can be hidden under valances. They can even be installed within cabinets to shine down on your collection of treasures and set them sparkling.

As well as emphasizing your assets, this

direct light will reflect back into the room and help to illuminate the room in general.

If a room has little contrast in colors, textures, and shapes, the contrast achieved by highlighting assets is particularly desirable.

LIGHT HAS COLOR THAT MUST BE INTEGRATED INTO THE COLOR SCHEME

Lighting and the color scheme are intimately intermingled. They act on each other. You can't see color without light. And light has colors of its own which it projects onto what you see.

Warm light can make warm colors seem hot, and cool colors seem pleasant. Warm light casts a pink, orange, or yellow glow over everything. It comes from southern or western exposures and from light carrying warm reflections—say of a brick terrace outdoors. At night it comes from firelight, candlelight, and all incandescent bulbs (especially pink ones), and some special "warm" fluorescent bulbs.

Cool light can take the heat off warm colors, but make cool colors seem frigid. Cool light comes from northern or eastern exposures and from light carrying cool reflections—say of grass or trees outdoors. At night it comes from most fluorescent bulbs.

Bright light illuminates colors and sets them sparkling. Bright colors placed in bright light might seem overpowering. Colors softened with gray will absorb some light. Very dark or very dull colors absorb an enormous amount of light. You will need a lot of electric fixtures at night.

Dim light has gray shadows within it. It casts gray color over everything. It can make things seem soft and mellow or drab and dull. Dark colors quickly go gray in dim light. Pale colors have enough white in them to survive the gray

shadows. Dim light flatters warm colors, creates a COZY atmosphere. Dim light with cool colors makes a room seem as lifeless, as stone cold, as a morgue.

Decorative Fixtures Can Act as Accents in Your Color Scheme Lamps or mounted fixtures can act like other accessories (such as throw pillows, picture frames, ashtrays) to give a perky punch to your color scheme. These accent areas are usually the brightest or boldest color or colors in the room. Pure black or white are also effective.

CHOOSING THE TYPE OF FIXTURE

Lighting must suit your budget and complement your furnishing style. TRADITIONALLY, rooms have been lit with a combination of decorative mounted fixtures and movable lamps. But the MODERN trend is toward no visible fixtures—use of built-in and inconspicuous fixtures. Actually, invisible fixtures are at home in any interior.

Built-in lighting is integrated into the architecture—built into the ceiling or walls. This involves an investment in the home and construction work. It is therefore permanent and expensive. It has an uncluttered, clean, MODERN effect.

Inconspicuous or *hidden lighting* also contributes atmospheric effects without making a decorative statement of its own. It may be permanent or portable, inexpensive or dear.

Mounted lighting is visibly attached to the ceiling or walls. It does make a decorative statement, so it must fit the formality and style of the room. Prices range from the most expensive crystal chandelier to the cheapest little tin sconce. These fixtures may or may not be dismounted when you move.

Lamps require no installation. You just plug them in. And you can unplug them and take them with you when you go. Lamps are changeable. If you move often, it's best to invest in movable fixtures. Lamps are available in styles to suit any interior.

Many rooms are illuminated with a combination of different lighting types, some providing indirect general illumination, and others providing direct light for close work or accent light for emphasizing special areas.

BUILT-IN LIGHTING Built-in lighting suits rooms of any formality, any style. It is easy to maintain since it is out of the way and requires no dusting. Built-in lighting includes recessed lighting, luminous ceilings, and cove lighting.

Recessed lighting refers to lights that are wholly or partially recessed into the ceiling or the walls. Recessed lighting can be used for general illumination and accent lighting.

For general illumination, the bulbs are covered with materials that diffuse and generalize the light. The covering material might be diffusing glass or egg-crate louvers, and might be contained within the fixture or installed separately in large panels under the bulbs.

Recessed lighting is ideal for low-ceilinged rooms, because it distributes light evenly and casts few shadows, thus making the place seem more SPACIOUS. It is good for general illumination in bathrooms, family rooms, kitchens, and halls.

For direct accent lighting, incandescent floodlights, spotlights, or pinpoint spotlights can be installed in the ceiling. They can be put in strategic positions to illuminate what you want to emphasize—the dining table, a nook or alcove, a fireplace, even a particular picture on a wall. Such fixtures come in a variety of sizes and shapes. They may be round, square, or rectangular metal boxes covered with glass. You might like to put them on a dimmer switch.

Luminous ceilings (or walls) are entirely illuminated. They are usually made of panels of translucent plastic materials with fluorescent lights behind them. To control the intensity of the light, special dimmer devices can be employed. Luminous ceilings are good for general illumination in bathrooms, family rooms, kitchens, and halls. They will make low ceil-

Lighting is recessed to be flush with the slatted ceiling. The effect is clean, uncluttered, architectural. The light bulbs are covered with materials that diffuse and generalize the light so that the room is washed in evenly distributed light. Recessed lighting is particularly comfortable in a kitchen. It gives good general light and is no trouble to maintain. (Photo courtesy of Champion Building Products.)

ings seem higher. Ceilings with colorful custom-designed patterns might be used to create an especially DRAMATIC effect.

Cove lighting. A cove is a more or less L-shaped shield that is placed along the upper wall, at least twelve inches down from the ceiling. Fluorescent tubes are placed within the shield. Since the shield blocks the light from going down or to the side, it is directed up and out. It shines on the upper wall and ceiling, reflecting indirect light back into the room. It can emphasize a high ceiling, and give the room a soft, serene, and SPACIOUS feeling. To provide adequate lighting and some interesting contrast, you will have to add some direct lighting to the room.

The cove covering is usually made of wood, metal, or plaster and is painted the same as the walls. The inside of the cove should always be painted white for reflective purposes.

There are variations of cove lighting. Instead of an L-shaped shield, you might have an I-shaped shield placed out from the wall, parallel to it, with the fluorescent tube between. Because the shield is open at the top and bottom, the light would go up and down, washing both the walls and ceiling. The down light might emphasize the walls, or draperies, or whatever else is underneath. Another alternative is an L-shaped shield that is closed at the top. In this case all the light would go down the wall. The light would emphasize the wall, while reflecting indirect illumination back into the room.

HIDDEN OR INCONSPICUOUS LIGHT-ING

Hidden or inconspicuous lighting suits rooms of any formality, any style, because you don't notice the fixtures. It is used mostly for direct accent lighting. However, some of the lighting might reflect back into the room to give soft, indirect, general illumination.

Fixtures on the floor. Inconspicuous cans on the floor might contain incandescent floodlights or spotlights. They might shine up on draperies, walls, or plants to give them special attention. The bulb should have a covering lens or grid to protect the eyes from glare.

Fixtures attached to furniture or pictures. Small, specially designed spotlights can be fitted onto picture frames. Pinpoint spotlights can be tailored to the exact size of your canvas. Other larger spotlights and floodlights may be attached to furniture or be put in other strategic positions where they can illuminate your special objects or areas. Think of the clip-on spotlights that photographers use. Some floodlights and spotlights come with adjustable swivel brackets. Some have special shutters that control the spread of the light. In all cases, make sure that the light is positioned to avoid glare.

Cornice and valance lighting—similar to cove lighting—is used to accent windows and drapery, and to provide indirect general illumination. It is lighting put behind a horizontal covering (cornice or valance) above a window. Lighting shines down on the windows or draperies, emphasizing them. Light also shines up to the ceiling, casting indirect general lighting back into the room. This highly DRAMATIC treatment works well in both MODERN and TRADITIONAL rooms. Because of their convenient linear form, fluorescent bulbs are usually used.

Lighting in back of window treatments or fabric walls. Fluorescent tubes in back of window treatments or fabric walls can simulate sunlight, emphasize the window or wall, and give the room soft general illumination.

Soffit lighting is lighting (often a fluorescent tube) mounted on the underside of an architectural element. Mounted on the underside of an arch or a lintel over a doorway, it could emphasize a particularly handsome doorway or illuminate a traffic path.

Furniture lighting. If you want to highlight a special collection, incandescent or fluorescent lighting can be attached to the framework of cabinets or cupboards, directed toward the back of the shelving to illuminate the objects or accessories within. This DRAMATIC accent also gives the room soft general illumination.

Lighting under cabinets, over work surfaces can give you good direct light. Linear fluorescent tubes are especially appropriate for this job. You can purchase a ready-made, plug-in unit that will not involve the expense of an electrician and that you can take with you when you move. If the work surface is in the

Cabinets in back of the modular seating pieces have light bulbs hidden within them. The cabinet tops are covered with a light-diffusing material. The result? Inconspicuous lighting that seems to set the room afloat. It's almost like swimming in an illuminated pool at night. The effect is soft and sybaritic (and see-worthy). (Design by Richard W. Jones, FASID; photo by Harry Hartman.)

kitchen, make sure you choose a fluorescent tube of a color that flatters food.

MOUNTED LIGHTING Mounted lighting is attached to the ceiling or walls. Because it has a decorative impact, it must suit the style and formality of the room. Ceiling-mounted fixtures are of three types: track lighting, close-up fixtures, and hanging fixtures. Wall-mounted fixtures include wall lamps and sconces.

Track lighting consists of covered incandescent spotlights or floodlights on a track mounted on the ceiling. The lights may be moved along the track to be aimed at whatever you wish. They can emphasize and accent areas or specific objects. Although track lighting is a rather modern phenomenon, it can work well in a room of any style, if it is kept inconspicuous (say painted the same color as the ceiling). It has many of the advantages of built-in direct lighting, but with more flexibility and less expense. (If you use much track lighting, you might want to plan to put it on a little-used electric circuit to avoid blowing a fuse.)

Close-up fixtures that hug the ceiling generally reflect light against the ceiling and diffuse downlight to provide soft indirect illumination. These are widely used utilitarian fixtures. They are especially appropriate for rooms with low ceilings. The style of the fixture must suit the room. For example, you might choose a crystal-beaded basket for a dressy TRADITIONAL room.

Hanging fixtures are used most often over dining tables. They are also often found in foyers, halls, and stairwells.

Some provide indirect, general illumination by casting all of their light against the ceiling.

Some provide just direct downlight. They are good illumination for a work surface. They have a sharp beam that produces definite shadow patterns. They can have a gruesome effect, unless combined with soft general illumination.

Some hanging fixtures provide both general and direct lighting.

Some hanging fixtures are more decorative than functional. For example, fixtures with exposed incandescent bulbs give sparkle and accent, but not much illumination.

How high should you hang hanging fixtures? The height is determined by comfort, convenience, and composition. If the fixture provides just direct downlight, it should be hung on or below the line of vision. If the fixture has bright exposed bulbs, it should be hung above the line of vision. If you want to hang a fixture at the line of vision, the lighting must be dim. If people will walk under the fixture, it must clear their heads (and not by knocking sense into them). A fixture over a table must be close enough to the table to seem to relate to it. Thirty to thirty-six inches above the tabletop is average. The higher the ceiling and the larger the fixture, the greater the distance from the table. If you want to lower the seeming height of a too-high ceiling, you can hang a chandelier to stop the eye on its trip upward.

Choosing a hanging fixture of the right decorative impact. The materials of the fixture and its design must suit the formality and style of the room. The bulbs should be appropriate too. In crystal chandeliers, use clear, low-wattage incandescent bulbs. In wood or metal chandeliers, use frosted or coated incandescent bulbs. Hanging fixtures might provide an interesting bright color accent in your color scheme, or be of a material that provides a textural contrast. The fixture has decorative impact when it is not illuminated as well as when it is. Consider how it appears against a light wall in the daylight, and against a dark wall when it is illuminated at night.

Wall lamps. The advantage of wall lamps is that they don't clutter up tabletops or take up floor space. They are appropriate to use where space is at a premium. You might use them by a bed to save space on the bedtable. They are also appropriate in rooms where vigorous activities occur, since they can't be knocked over like floor or table lamps. Lamps attached high on the walls are safe and accident-proof.

Sconces are decorative, but they don't provide much light. They are used TRADITIONALLY in dining rooms to give dim general illumination (a complement to candles). They are also often used in halls. Sconces may be placed so

Lights mounted on the ceiling project egg-shaped patterns onto a wall to create an unusual focal point in this all-white room. The occupant, a Middle Eastern executive, wanted a look of luxury and architectural purity. He got it all-white. Interest is achieved by a variety of textures—soft carpeting, upholstery, and floor pillows versus light-reflective glass, mirror, and glossy ceiling. The designers focused further on light reflection as the actual excitement. (Photo courtesy of S. M. Hexter Company; design by Forbes-Ergas Design Associates, Inc.)

that they are similarly distributed on opposite walls, or they may be placed on either side of a picture, a mirror, a highboy, a secretary, or what have you. Sconces with candles on either side of a mirror are romantic in a foyer.

Both sconces and wall lamps are available in styles that provide only indirect light reflected from the walls.

MOVABLE LIGHTING OR LAMPS Lamps sit on tables or stand on the floor. They must suit the decor. They are easily moved; you just plug them in. Most lamps are used primarily for direct task or accent lighting. Many also cast light against the walls and ceiling for indirect general illumination. Some lamps are designed primarily for indirect illumination.

Lamps for indirect general illumination. Lamps with shades that are open on the top cast some light up against the walls and ceiling. The average room requires four such lamps for adequate general illumination (depending on whether other forms of lighting are used.) If only lamps are used, the lamps should have 100-watt bulbs. Low-wattage lamps should be supplemented by other lighting.

Modern, Italian lighting designs give added interest to this architecturally conceived bedroom. The furnishings are all simple, straight shapes. The lamps provide the contrast of curves—and some surprising ones. We have a glowing, swirling shape, an illuminated snake, and a front-flap light reminiscent of the headgear on medieval armor. (Photo courtesy of Fibers Division/ Allied Chemical Corporation; design by Edmund Motyka, ASID.)

Vase and urn lights cast all light up against the ceiling for indirect illumination. The tops of such fixtures should be above eye level to avoid glare. Their strong incandescent bulbs should be totally concealed.

Lamps for direct task lighting. The lamp must be of the proper height and be placed correctly so that it illuminates the work surface or your lap. When you sit down, you should not be able to see the lightbulb.

Table lamps generally should be at your eye level when seated. To have the bottom of the shade thirty-eight to forty-two inches from the floor is about average. (To ascertain the actual height of a table lamp, add the height of the table to the height of the lamp.) For a desk light, the bottom of the shade might be sixteen inches from the tabletop.

Floor lamps are generally placed beside or behind chairs. The height from the floor to the bottom of the shade should be about forty-seven to forty-nine inches.

Lamps for direct accent lighting. Smaller lights are good for dramatizing paintings, plants, or even for grazing a textured wall. Special low-voltage lamps are small. They are easily concealed and they produce quite a beam of light for their size. You might want them on dimmer controls to soften their blaze.

Choosing lamps for style. A movable lamp is a decorative object as well as a source of light. You must consider how it will work with the rest of your design scheme.

It should be consistent in size. If you have a large sofa with a large end table, you need a large lamp. A small one would look silly. If you have a precious little desk and need a light on it, choose a small one. Otherwise, it will look like it will topple over. Floor lamps, too, need to look like they belong with what they stand by. It is important that the lamp shade be consistent in size with the base so that the two together look like one unit.

Lamps function as accessories, accent areas, in your design scheme. If you don't like the lamp, or your scheme is already strong, you might choose a lamp that blends into the background. Otherwise, you might use the lamp to present a perky contrast in your scheme. It might be the boldest color in your scheme, or absolute black or white. If the textures in the room are thick and soft, you might choose a bright brassy lamp. Or if textures are smooth, you might choose a lamp of woven wicker. Because accessories are so small in the over-all scheme of things, bold contrasts here are welcome, not overpowering. Also, since lamps can be made of almost anything, you might find an object that fits the theme of your room and wire it for lighting.

Choosing lamps to go together in a room. Lamps may not be in pairs, but they should be related in size and material. All the lampshades in a room should stop at the same height so your eyes don't have to jump all around the room. It is desirable, too, that all shades in the room be of the same color and material.

Choosing lampshades. The size and shape of the lampshade has to suit the size and shape of the lamp base. First measure the height of your lamp base and lampshade holder. Second, measure the diameter of the largest portion of your lamp base. This will affect the top and bottom diameter of the shade you should have. Take these measurements with you to your lampshade store.

The bottom of the lampshade should meet the top of the lamp. Think of a lampshade as you think of a person's head. A neck is between a person's body and his head. Don't place the lampshade down so low that the top

(or neck) of the lamp doesn't show; also don't sit the lampshade up so high that it seems detached.

What materials should you choose for your lampshades? Translucent shades allow light to shine through them, giving an overall glow of illumination. Opaque shades don't permit light to shine through them. They cast concentrated light down and up.

White or neutral shades are usually best to choose, unless you want to use the lampshade as a color accent in your design scheme. The shade could coordinate with fabric used elsewhere in the room. It could either match or cleverly contrast with its base. If there is trim at the edge of the shade, keep it simple.

Don't be too taken with novelty fads. Lampshades are expensive enough for you to want them to last without looking as dated as an old lady in a miniskirt. Remove the cellophane wrapper when you get the lampshade home. Otherwise, dust will collect between the shade and the wrapper, eventually discoloring the shade.

22

CHOOSING ACCESSORIES

Placing accessories is your last task in decorating your room, and it is often the most fun. Accessories make magic. Suddenly your room comes to life! It has personality and pizzazz, a finished finesse.

But diverse accessories can't just be scattered here and there, helter-skelter. They need to be coordinated with the room, with the furniture, with each other.

WHAT ACCESSORIES DO YOU NEED?

You must choose the accessories you need to function—like lamps, ashtrays, desk sets, wastebaskets, mirrors, clocks, pillows to tuck behind your back, boxes to collect clutter. Make a list of what you need.

Other accessories may be chosen simply for decorative purposes, although in a small room you might not want anything but functional accessories.

WHAT ACCESSORIES DO YOU HAVE?

The person using the room might have some special treasures, or some sort of collection relating to his or her hobbies or interests. These things will give the room individuality and interest, as well as make the person feel at home.

The activity of the room might provide the decorative theme and the accessories. For example, you can have a food theme in the kitchen and hang up your garlic press and wire whisk. You could have a body-beautiful theme in the bathroom—with lovely smelly soaps and perfumes. You could have an athletic theme for the family room, and hang up Sonny's hockey sticks.

The regional characteristics of the place where you live might be reflected in the accessories. For example, if you live in New Mexico you might have Indian artifacts. If you live in Nantucket, you might have pictures of old whaling ships. You might hang a harpoon in your game room.

The accessories you have may have inspired your design scheme in the beginning. A painting you love or another favorite object might have inspired your color scheme. The period or style of a collection or of a certain treasure might have inspired the style of your room. An especially stunning object or group of objects might be your focal point. A collection might have inspired you to buy a piece of furniture to accommodate it—bookshelves for books, an étagère for art objects, a pedestal for a piece of sculpture, a cabinet for a collection.

If in the middle of planning your room, you find you have accessories you definitely want to use, you must coordinate their colors, textures, sizes, and style with the room you are designing.

If at the end you don't have any accessories, you must look the room over to see what it needs.

THE ROLE OF ACCESSORIES IN THE DECORATIVE SCHEME

Accessories Can Help You Emphasize Your Focal Point As you know, the focal point has to be the most interesting, attention-getting point in the room. Accessories can help you draw attention to it. What is your focal point?

The fireplace. If you have no mantelpiece, you can still hang a picture or a wall sculpture of suitable size over the fireplace. If you have a mantelpiece, make sure that the objects you put on it are particularly lovely, because they will attract a lot of attention there. The objects must be large enough to be seen across the room. Nobody likes to strain their eyes to see what's of interest.

How will you arrange things on the mantel? Usually a symmetrical arrangement is best. Place something large in the center, like a large picture or a mirror. If you want, you can place a clock or a bowl of beautiful flowers under this. Place something tall and matching at the ends, like candlesticks, sconces, or vases. If there's room, you might place something medium-sized between the middle and the ends, like plants or beautiful plates or a clock and a statue of similar size. An asymmetrical arrangement is appropriate for an INFORMAL room, but it is harder to balance. Remember that large neutral objects can be balanced by smaller bright or patterned objects. (See Chapter 15.)

In the fireplace you can have a fire, pretty birch logs, interesting andirons, a screen, a statue, a big plant. Somebody even told me about a summer home that had an illuminated aquarium installed in the fireplace.

Around the fireplace you can have interesting fireside accessories—pokers, brushes, and such. An INFORMAL room might have a copper pot full of logs. You could frame the fireplace with bookcases.

A large piece of furniture. You can put interesting accessories in it, on it, beside it, or over it.

You could make a focal point of floor-to-ceiling shelves filled with books or accessories. The shelves can be either free-standing or built into the wall. Books with colorful covers can be interspersed with interesting objects and pretty plants. Paintings may even be hung between the shelves.

Sets of shelves can also frame other attractions. They may fill the wall on either side of a sofa or an upright piano.

A painting. If your focal point is a painting or other outstanding accessory, be sure to put it where it attracts attention. Direct light shining on the painting will give it additional impact.

An area rug. Hang pictures in the area. They won't compete with the rug, but they will help the area gain additional impact.

One wall. If you want to make one wall into a focal point, you could do it by painting the wall a bright color, wallpapering it with a pattern,

Here the focal-point fireplace is emphasized by a large wall sculpture and growling lions heating up the hearth. Two horses of the right height lead the eye from the top of the chaise to a painted wall design to the top of the window treatment, contributing to a smooth flow of high-low interest. The horses also help to balance the tall trees at the other window. Accessories in this room are large in scale to suit its size. (Design by Albert Etienne Pensis, W & J Sloane; photo by Bill Rothschild.)

or hanging interesting accessories on it. A large artwork or a grouping of smaller artworks can give the wall the requisite interest.

An alcove or niche. You can put your favorite accessories in it (maybe just a stunning sculpture) and give the area special direct lighting. For extra sparkle, you might line the niche with mirror. A larger alcove might feature a favored object of greater size.

Accessories Can Help You Give Your Room a Balanced Personality As you know, opposite walls and the halves of each wall should have equal visual attraction. Look your room over. Does it seem a little off balance? The right accessory can balance the scales.

You can balance with something of similar size. A window or doorway can be balanced by a similarly sized chest with a picture or mirror over it. A wall grouping of artworks can balance heavy furniture on the other side of the room. Large plants or sculpture can balance furniture.

You can balance by repeating a pattern. A skirted table can match the patterned fabric of drapery or upholstery on the other side of the room. Patterned pillows matching the draperies across the room can liven up a plain bed or sofa.

You can balance by repeating color. For example, bright accessories evenly distributed around the room will balance each other.

Bright colors and bold patterns and textures are attention-getting. They have heavy visual impact. They can balance more neutral things of larger size. For example, you can put bright pillows on a lightweight chair to balance a more heavyweight chair.

Accessories Can Help You Emphasize the Foreground or the Background Accessories are part of the foreground. If you decided to emphasize the foreground furniture and/or accessories, you will underplay the background walls and floors. If you decide (in Chapter 17) to emphasize the background, you will underplay the accessories.

Emphasizing the Foreground. If your accessories are particularly interesting, you will want to set them off by underplaying their background. For example, paintings, pictures, or wall arrangements of artworks are best on plain—not patterned—walls.

Actually, an underplayed background can give you great flexibility. If your furnishings are rather basic and neutral too, your focal point and accessories can convey the whole character of the room. This is a good arrangement if you want the room to be CHANGEABLE.

If your walls and floor are underplayed, you *need* to give some excitement to your scheme through accessories. Here's where you will put bright colors, punchy patterns, and bold textures. Decorators often use this sort of scheme. Accessories are bright and bold; furniture is a little less so; floors are rather neutral, and walls are very neutral. The smaller the area, the bolder its treatment. (This is a rather safe scheme for a beginner, too.) Also, don't forget the impact of accent lighting. Shining direct light at any accessory will give it emphasis and impact. If you don't have many other contrasts, lighting alone can make the difference.

Emphasizing the Background. If the walls or floor are bold and dramatic, you don't want to get wild with accessories. The place will seem like a funhouse. Neutral or simple accessories can calm down the scheme. For example, you can hang a plain mirror on a patterned wall. Also, if you have accessories you hate, like lamps lifted from your mother, you might want to color them the same as their background so they seem to disappear.

Accessories Can Help You Orchestrate Colors, Patterns, and Textures Accessories, because of their relatively small size, are the accents in your decorative scheme. They usually perk up the room with a lively contrast. Because these contrasting areas are so small, they don't compromise the identity, or dominant character, of the room; they just give that character some interesting extra dimensions. Like a person who can laugh at himself, accessories of a contradictory character give good humor and balance to a room.

Be sure that your accessories are evenly distributed around the room. If they are massed together, they will lose their value as accents and begin to take on a heavier impact.

What kind of contrast do you want to choose? It depends on what would be most effective in enhancing the room (see Chapter 18).

Emphasize or Underplay? If the room is rel-

atively calm, the accent should be bright and bold. If the room is wild, the accents should be quiet and understated.

Color. If colors are muted, a brilliant accent will set them off. If colors are bright, choose a neutral.

Patterned or Plain? A patterned accessory can relieve too many plain surfaces, and vice versa.

Texture. A shiny texture can accent dull ones. A soft one can set off hard ones, and vice versa.

Shape. If your room is full of straight lines, choose a curved accessory. If your room is full of curves, choose something to straighten it out.

ARRANGING ACCESSORIES

What areas need more liveliness? A wall, a corner, a shelf, a tabletop? What should you choose for where?

Compatibility of Size The size or scale of an accessory should relate to the size or scale of its background. Large accessories need large backgrounds. Because they need space to set them off, they usually should be displayed alone. For example, a large painting would need a large wall. A large sculpture would need free floor space around it.

Small or medium-sized accessories can be displayed against small or medium-sized backgrounds, or they can be grouped together to create a larger overall impact suitable for a larger space. For example, if you have a large table, you could put one large accessory on it or group three or five smaller accessories on it. (Groupings of three or five somehow seem to be more pleasing than groupings of two or four.) If you have a large wall, you could hang one large artwork or a group of smaller ones.

Small or medium-sized accessories gain importance when grouped. For instance, small pictures may be mounted together and put in the same frame. A group of small accessories

There was a large empty white wall. The handsome but hard-edged architecture needed something to give it a warmer, more friendly feeling. Amazingly the designer found an enormous African exotic object in warm wood with a primitive painted pattern. The object enhances the architecture, and the architecture enhances the object. (Design by Richard W. Jones, FASID; photo by Harry Hartman.)

on a tabletop can have a tray put behind them to give them a common background and more importance. When grouping smaller accessories, be careful not to crowd them. You will still want to see each individual piece.

Accessories hung on the wall must be compatible in size with the furniture below and they should seem to be supported by what is beneath. The piece of furniture below should never seem more delicate and fragile than the wall arrangement. It would be like putting the circus fat lady on the shoulders of the thin man—a crushing effect. Besides being lighter-looking, it is pleasant if the wall arrangement is a different size or shape than the furniture below. A wall arrangement that is taller and narrower than the furniture is particularly agreeable.

Compatibility of Color The accessory and its background should be compatible in color. Bright colors are set off by a white background. Imagine brightly colored pottery against a white wall. Light colors are set off by black. Have you ever seen a diamond on black velvet? A black lacquered chest or shelf can be just as effective in displaying light-colored objects. The color of the background might be a light or neutral color taken from the object itself.

Backgrounds that have no color will not compete in any way with your accessories. Hence the popularity of glass and Plexiglas shelves and pedestals. The transparent support disappears visually and allows you to focus complete attention on the object. Objects seem to float in air. Another advantage of these shelves is that light can go through them. Light attached to the top of a cabinet with glass or Plexiglas shelves can penetrate to illuminate the objects even on the bottom shelf.

Compatibility of Pattern Versus Plain Patterned accessories are best seen against a plain background. Pattern on pattern is less strong in impact than pattern on plain. A plain accessory can stand a patterned background, but the pattern is more likely to attract attention than the accessory.

Compatibility of Texture If the walls are very rough in texture, accessories hung on them should be heavy-looking or bright. The rough with the rough and the smooth with the smooth. For example, fine porcelain and china look lovely against a background of silk or velvet.

If your accessory is shiny, it looks best against a shiny background. Silver, pewter, and copper look rich against polished wood. Glass and crystal objects gain luminous dimension if placed against a background of glass, mirror, steel, or chrome. You get sparkle aplenty from the multiple reflections. In a dark corner, you might put a glass-topped table against the wall, hang a mirror above it, put glass and crystal objects on the table, then cast direct accent lighting on it. What shimmering excitement!

ARRANGING GROUPS OF ACCESSORIES The pieces in the arrangement should go together. They might share a theme—a subject matter or a style. The colors and the textures of the pieces should not clash. For instance, you might mat and frame all your pictures alike. This would allow you great freedom of arrangement—an especially good idea if you move often and want your art objects to be changeable and rearrangeable. However, various frames and mats can add another element of interest to an arrangement.

Various art objects *can* go together harmoniously if you pay attention to balance. Remember that large sizes, bright or dark colors, and rough textures are heavyweights. Small sizes, pale colors, smooth textures are lightweights. So you can balance a large pale thing with a small bright thing, and so forth.

How Can You Hang a Wall Arrangement? The arrangement should seem orderly. The outside outlines of the grouping might repeat the lines of the room. Since most rooms are rectangular or square, this means that the grouping might be rectangular or square. The components might be lined up to form straight lines across the bottom, across the top, and on the sides.

The wall arrangement and the furniture beneath should seem like a unit; they should be rather close together. You can hang your wall arrangement six to twelve inches above the furniture. In any case, the distance between the two should always be less than the height of either piece.

You can make a trial grouping of your wall arrangement on the floor. Then you can change and rearrange to your heart's content without poking holes in your walls.

Decorators have devised a couple of ingen-

This wall arrangement of art includes pictures of many sizes, shapes, and subjects. Balance is achieved by juxtaposing smaller, brighter objects with larger, duller objects. The rectangular arrangement is lined up on the sides and hung six to twelve inches above the furniture. Note that the lampshade is incorporated as an element of the arrangement. (Photo courtesy of Celanese Corp.)

ious solutions for transferring your artistry to the walls. Cut out a piece of paper the size of each art object in your wall arrangement. Tape the paper to the wall to see how you like it. Alternatively, you can place a large sheet of brown paper on the floor. Arrange your art objects on top of the piece of paper. When you arrive at the arrangement you like, outline the art objects on the paper and mark the points where picture hooks will be needed. Then tack the whole large sheet of brown paper to the wall. Nail in the picture hooks at the points marked, then tear off the paper. All that remains is to hang your art objects.

A FEW WORDS ON DIFFERENT TYPES OF ACCESSORIES

Wherever you want an interesting accent, you can find an accessory to provide it. You can put trim on draperies or shades, place pillows on upholstery, hang things on walls, arrange objects on tabletops, fill out corners with plants or sculptures. But here are some added helpful hints.

PICTURES The term "picture" can include almost anything—oil paintings, watercolors, pastels, etchings, prints, lithographs, photographs, posters, a framed piece of fabric or wallpaper. In addition to hanging pictures on the walls, you can put them on easels, or put them on tabletops and lean them against the wall.

MIRRORS A large part of the beauty of a mirror is the image that it reflects. It is a good idea to place a mirror opposite a stunning view, or opposite a wall of artworks. If a mirror is hung over a table, it will reflect the backs of the objects on that table. This is a good way to enhance your favorite objects or a bowl of flowers. Mirror on an end wall will open up the vista and expand the sense of space. One warning, however: Beware of reflecting a conversational grouping. It might make people self-conscious.

BOOKS Filled bookshelves provide warmth and interest and are appropriate to almost any room in the home. Average-size books require shelves that are only about eight inches deep. Outsize volumes require deeper shelves. Since the height of books varies so widely, it is a good idea to install adjustable shelves. It is smart to install more shelves than you need initially so that you don't feel crowded for space later. In the meantime, you can fill the empty spaces with plants or decorative objects.

Bookcases look good in architecturally defined areas—say between the fireplace and the wall, or between the corner and the window. Wall-hung open-ended shelves are more free-form. You can make an artistic arrangement of them with shelves of different lengths. Books should be accessible to the people who want to read them. (A friend of mine told me that during his early adolescence, his parents were careful to leave an anatomy/sex book on a lower shelf.) The lighting should be strong enough to allow you to read the book titles. If you want to give the bookshelf special emphasis, the wall behind it can be covered with an interesting color or pattern.

PLANTS Growing plants need to be put in a position where they will get sufficient light. They can be hung from the ceiling in baskets. They can sit on windowsills, tables, shelves, stepladders, library steps, pedestals, and glass shelves mounted within the window frame, not to mention independent planters. If natural light isn't sufficient, you can use artificial light. Under electric lights, large plants can give interest to a dull corner or fill out an empty space. They are effective room dividers. Plants can even enhance your fireplace if lights are concealed in the chimney.

To arrange a large grouping of plants on the floor, always begin with the largest plant first. This can be the center or the end of the arrangement. Again your objective is to achieve balance. You can do this by intermingling plants of different heights, shapes, colors, and textures. It is pleasant to finish off the bottom of the arrangement with low-flowering plants, maybe in clay pots.

Containers are important. You should select those that blend with the decorative character of your room. Woven baskets will provide the room with an uneven texture.

Lighting plants is very effective. Inexpensive spotlights can be placed on the floor among the plants, or under trees. Light can shine up through the leaves and cast dramatic shadows on the walls and ceiling.

FLOWERS Flowers are an important color accent in a room. Put them where you want a perky pick-up. The flowers may be the accent color of your color scheme. They may pick up other colors in your scheme, or add a complementary note of seasonal freshness and gaiety.

The size of the container should suit the size of the flowers. The color of the container should be harmonious with the flowers and with the room. For fun, you might use an unusual container. You can use old teapots, mugs, an old wooden box fitted with a metal liner—actually anything that can contain water without leaking.

The size of the arrangement should suit the size of the place where it is put. Small, cute arrangements for small places. You can put a teacup full of tiny posies on an end table. Large dramatic arrangements go in large empty areas. You can put a tall vase of long-stemmed flowers or branches in a corner. Keep dinner-table arrangements low; nothing is worse than feeling you have to cut down the jungle brush in order to see the person opposite you at dinner.

Flowers and the budget. Unless you are blessed with a blooming garden out your back door, cut flowers are expensive. Plastic flowers are cheap—and they look it. Avoid them. Silk flowers and other fabric flowers seem wildly expensive, but they are beautiful and they don't wilt. They provide a look of ongoing elegance. Dried flowers are particularly nice in the fall. They last and last, and you never have to water them. They can be made into dramatic arrangements that you can enjoy for years.

Plants love the humidity in bathrooms. Actually the temperature and humidity in a greenhouse often seem similar to the bathroom after the shower has been running. Be careful to place plants where they'll get enough light. Here mirrors multiply the natural light to the plants' delight. (Design by Rubén De Saavedra, ASID; photo by Daniel Eifert.)

SCULPTURE Sculpture must be placed so that it may be seen easily. Since sculpture is three-dimensional, it is nice if you can walk around it, to examine it from all sides. You can put it on a pedestal. Choose a pedestal made of a material that flatters the material of the sculpture. Glass or Plexiglas will seem to disappear. Rich woods are handsome against shiny metals. A pedestal painted in a neutral color will not attract undue attention.

The sculpture may be isolated in an open area of the room. It may stand in front of long windows where it will be emphasized by the daylight. It may dominate a corner. The sculpture may fit in some architecturally defined area. Even the Greeks put sculpture in wall niches.

Small sculptures may be placed on shelves or étagères, even on a coffee table. Again, glass or Plexiglas shelves or table surfaces will seem to set your sculpture afloat. Do not crowd small sculptures. It is best if each can be seen alone so you can enjoy its lines and detail without confusion.

Direct accent lighting can dramatize sculpture at night. A concealed spotlight can make the magic.

GROUPS OF PHOTOGRAPHS Go ahead and frame your family and friends. You can gather the group together on a skirted table in your bedroom. Sure, it's personal and sentimental, but what's life all about, anyway? Just make sure that all the frames go together.

PILLOWS Pillows not only prop up your back, they are an important accent area in your design scheme. They can offer a contrast in color, pattern, or texture. They can also help balance the room by repeating the color or pattern found on the other side of the room.

PART FIVE

SHOPPING FOR

In this part of the book you can look up the items you are thinking of buying in order to find more specific information about them. The information you find will either reinforce your decisions or make you aware of considerations you might not have thought of before. If you want to change your mind, you can read the pros and cons of all the other choices before making your final decisions.

There are several rules for getting the most for your money:

KNOW WHAT YOU NEED   Make a total room plan so that you know everything you will want eventually. Take your floor plan and swatches with you. It's easy to get confused about colors and sizes in a store. Your floor plan and swatches of wallcoverings, flooring, drapery fabrics, or whatever you have, will keep you on the right track.

Put all the specifications you know on your shopping list. If you can find pictures of what you want in magazines, tear them out and keep them with you. Knowing what you need will keep you from making a drastic impulsive mistake.

KNOW WHAT YOU NEED FIRST   Your first furniture needs will be beds and comfortable seating for the living room. These items should have top priority on your shopping list. Your comfort depends on them; buy the best you can afford. With other furniture, you can make do until you have the money.

YOUR DESIGN

KNOW HOW LONG YOU WANT THE ITEM TO LAST, AND CONSIDER WHAT KIND OF WEAR IT WILL GET If you want an item to last a lifetime, it's a good idea to pay for quality. It will save you money in the long run. Choose a classic style that will not seem dated in a short while. You can change the mood of the room by replacing inexpensive accessories. If an item will not get heavy wear, you need not buy the best construction. You can just buy something that looks good.

SHOP AND STUDY BEFORE YOU BUY Before you spend a cent, study your alternatives. Get a feel for prices, quality, and the services of the store, so you know what you're getting for the money.

For every item on your shopping list, do some comparative shopping. Then you will get a realistic idea of how much such an item will cost. Learn the price range for the item. When comparing similar pieces, find out why one costs more than another. You will learn a great deal about how to judge quality.

If you don't want to take the time to compare similar merchandise in different stores, choose a store you can trust. Choose a service-oriented store that is interested in keeping you as a customer for a lifetime. Stores interested in a one-shot sale won't care if you're dissatisfied.

Read labels and hangtags. See what they say about construction and care and maintenance. If you can't find the label, ask to see the catalog description of the item.

Test for comfort and construction. Sit in chairs, lie on bedding, put your elbows on tables. Poke and peek around to see if the item seems to be made solidly. Ask questions. Don't be intimidated by fast-talking salesmen. After all, you're in control. It's your money.

23

BUYING FURNITURE

Furniture takes a major slice of anybody's decorating budget.

BUYING FOR STYLE

MODERN The price of modern furniture relates to the price of materials and the quality of construction. There are many good-looking inexpensive modern designs on the market.

TRADITIONAL If you are buying traditional furniture, the best way to protect yourself from error is to study the traditional style of your preference. Learn the characteristic qualities of that style—the materials or woods used, the characteristic sizes and shapes. Seek out your style in period rooms in museums or other restorations. If you know what the best examples of that style look like, it's good insurance against the liability of a fast-talking salesman.

Antiques or Reproductions? Good antiques are expensive and hard to find. But unlike used cars, their value keeps going up. Fine quality antiques are a good investment.

An antique in bad condition is no bargain. What use is it if it falls apart? Make sure it is serviceable enough to suit your purpose.

You *can* buy bargain antiques. Antiques are usually thought of as the province of the privileged, but you can buy bargain antiques if you look for the less-sought-after styles in out-of-the-way places like country or roadside shops. You could furnish your whole home in antiques as reasonably as you could furnish it in modern. (You might want to replace worn upholstery with new reproduction fabrics.)

Why buy reproductions? They are easier to find, and often less costly than antiques. However, a reproduction made with the same time-honored techniques as the original can be costly indeed. Qualified craftsmen are hard to find these days, and hand-craftsmanship costs. The result is fine furniture that will increase in value.

Many reproductions, today, are made by different methods than the originals. Traditional hand-carved styles took a lot of time and quality craftsmanship. Imagine the skill it took to carve even a little decorative rosette. Today such ornament is often poured plastic made in molds and then attached to the furniture. The effect is somewhat the same, but the price is a lot lower. Purists prefer plastic to look like plastic and not pose as wood, but if you want inexpensive traditional furniture, these plastic look-alikes are okay.

You might check through the classy magazines and note the names of the manufacturers of the fine reproduction furniture used in the room settings. For nothing, or for a few dollars, you might even send away for their brochures.

Reproductions can be easier to live with than the original antique. Many reproductions are scaled down to suit the size of the smaller spaces we're living in today. Many reproductions are simplified in design—which may also make them more attractive to live with in today's smaller spaces. And it's likely that a newly produced piece of furniture is sturdier than one that's been kicking around for years.

BUYING FOR FUNCTION

If a piece doesn't suit your needs, forget it—it's not a good buy, no matter what the price. Basic furniture falls into four functional categories: seating, sleeping, surfaces, storage. It's important to take care of your sleeping and seating functions first. You can punt awhile with the rest.

SEATING When buying seating, ask yourself, "How comfortable does it need to be?" For reading, relaxing, and conversation you'll need lounge seating. Who will use this seat, and for how long at a stretch? The seating should suit the person or persons who will use it regularly. Lounge seating includes sofas and lounge chairs. They may be all upholstered, or partly upholstered. Sofas come in a wide variety of sizes and styles, including sofa beds. Lounge chairs can be purchased in pairs, if you like. Some lounge chairs are designed to convert into beds. Sofas and lounge chairs are normally thirty to thirty-five inches in depth (an important measurement for your floor plan). The height of the seat is usually fifteen to seventeen inches, but the height of the

total piece varies. A total height of twenty-eight inches is about average.

For the occasional guest, you need lightweight movable chairs. Styles include deck chairs, French oval-backed armchairs, bamboo chairs with pad seats—actually anything you can lift easily. You might bring over the dining chairs, or the chairs from around the card table, or have light movable side chairs against the walls waiting for such occasions. If the guests are young and supple, you might pull over backless benches, poufs, stools, or beanbag chairs.

For seating at a dining table or desk, it is usual to choose a straight-backed chair. Sit on the chair. Is it comfortable enough for a short stretch? Dining chairs are normally sixteen to eighteen inches high. Check for clearance. You need a minimum of seven inches between the chair seat and the table apron. Do the arms get in the way? Arms should not be so high that you can't pull the chair up to the table. Feel under the bottom edge of the chair seat. If it's rough, someone will snag her stockings and pout all the way home.

Chairs may be all upholstered, partly upholstered with a wooden or metal frame, all-wood, wood with a cane or rush seat, metal with wood and cane, or all plastic, rattan, wicker, or bamboo.

SLEEPING Please see the shopping suggestions under "Sleeping" in Chapter 3.

SURFACES Surfaces include anything you can put things down on—all tables, desks, tops of bureaus, chests, sideboards, the kitchen counter—you name it.

When Selecting a Surface, Think of What Will Be Put Down on It Hot plates and cigarettes can burn. Moisture can warp wood and liquor can stain surfaces.

Fine woods need to be protected. You will probably want protective pads or hot plates for your dining table and buffet.

Glass tops are impervious to moisture and easily cleaned. Glass tops over wood can protect the wood, but make sure that moisture doesn't gather between the wood and the glass.

Special finishes can make wood more DURABLE. Acrylics, resins, and other additives can seal the wood and protect it from water and other hazards. A "distressed" finish is designed to make new furniture look old and beat-up from the beginning. The furniture is beaten with chains to give it gouges and marks that look like the ravages of time. Obviously, new gouges and marks would not be noticed. (A distressed finish may also be simulated with paint. Is that a black spot or a worm hole?)

Formica and other plastic-laminate surfaces are DURABLE and scrubbable, and they resist staining. In bright colors they are used for counters in the kitchen. Posing as wood, they can top off storage furniture. This makes the furniture especially durable and serviceable (but it's not in the category of fine furniture).

Ceramic tile is sturdy and WATERPROOF.

Marble must be treated so that it doesn't absorb moisture and stains.

Butcherblock is used for surfaces you will cut on. It has a nice earthy appeal even though it shows knife marks and is hard to keep clean.

When Selecting a Surface, Consider What Purpose It Will Serve   The surface must be large enough to accommodate everything you want to put on it. Surfaces that will hold lamps should be sturdy and well-supported.

Surfaces you sit at—desks, card tables, dining tables, work counters—have to be comfortable for you. Dining tables, card tables, and desks are normally twenty-eight to thirty inches high. If you're shopping for an extension table, make sure the leaves match the rest of the table. Make sure the color and textures are the same. If the table has an apron, so should the leaves. Make sure the table will support the extra leaves adequately.

Surfaces that serve seating should be coordinated with the seating. End tables or side tables should be about the height of the arms of the seating. Two inches higher or lower doesn't matter, but the table should never be much lower than the arm. Side tables usually aren't as long or deep as the seating beside them.

Front tables or coffee tables should be about the same height as the seat cushions. Normally there should be about fifteen inches of clear space all around the coffee table so people can move around. Where space is limited, or where there are children, avoid styles with sharp corners.

A skirted table could give a room a little punch of pattern or color.

STORAGE   Storage pieces include chests of drawers, bureaus, dressers, armoires, sideboards, credenzas, cupboards—any piece of furniture where you store stuff. Storage pieces are often called "case goods" because they are just boxes (or cases) with drawers or doors.

Make sure the piece is big enough to contain all you want to store but small enough to get through the door.

Make sure the parts operate easily. Check the drawers. See that they slide easily. Check the doors. Make sure they fit right, open easily, and stay shut; they probably should have catches in more than one place. Push down gently on an open door. The hinges should be strong enough to take the pressure.

The construction is your clue to quality. The parts or panels of the piece should not jiggle or rattle. If drawers are finished on the inside, this is a sign of fine furniture. See how the fronts and backs of drawers are attached to the sides. Dovetail and tongue-and-groove constructions indicate quality.

Check the hardware. Metal is thin on inexpensive furniture, heavy on fine furniture. Make sure the metal is well secured.

If the piece will be placed away from the wall, as a room divider, make sure it has a finished back.

WOOD FURNITURE

Wood, like a diamond, is forever. Wood has natural variations that are part of its beauty. Variations do *not* necessarily mean that the wood is of poor quality; the wood is just doing what comes naturally. For maintenance, just dust and polish. Wood is vulnerable to stains and burns. Wetness will warp it unless it has been sealed.

HOW DETAILED IS THE DESIGN? This is tricky business. You have to be careful. Elaborate designs are often thought to look expensive, but elaborate applied ornament is used to conceal poor wood and poor craftsmanship. You think you're getting a bargain; but you may be getting a bummer.

Detail and applied design should never conceal the basic shape and structure of the piece. Often applied design strengthens the structure. Look to see what it's up to.

It's hard to fake quality on a piece of simple structure. You can really see the quality of the wood and the craftsmanship of the connections. Simplicity is often the best buy; it stands the test of time.

What are the details made of? Hand-carved wood is expensive. Plastic parts are certainly less expensive.

HOW IS IT MADE? The way a piece of furniture is made is a great clue to quality.

Solid Wood or Veneers? Veneers are *not* a cheap substitute for solid wood. Solid woods are used mostly for INFORMAL, inexpensive furniture. Veneers are used in expensive furniture. The less expensive woods (pine, oak, ash, maple, birch, pecky cypress) are the ones used in solid wood construction. The expensive and exotic woods (such as English walnut and rosewood) are the ones used in veneer construction. The "veneer" is a very thin layer of wood applied over the surface of a piece of furniture to give it a beautiful and decorative finish. The veneers might cover the top and the front of the piece and be laid in a way to take the utmost advantage of the beauty of the wood grain. Sometimes veneers of contrasting woods are "inlaid" in patterns.

Furniture legs are usually made of solid wood.

Laminated Wood Laminated woods are woods laid in layers like a Dagwood sandwich. Laminated wood constructions are used for skis; they are downright DURABLE. They tend to be INFORMAL and not so expensive. A lot of Danish modern designs are made in light laminated woods.

Plastics Posing as Woods Plastic laminates, because of their durability, are often used to cover tabletops. This is never done in expensive furniture, but it is a practical idea for inexpensive furniture that needs to take tough wear. Check the finish where the lamination meets the wood. Make sure the finish doesn't flake.

Look at the Joints Where pieces of wood are joined together, they may take special stress. Look to make sure the joint is strong and well supported. This is especially important in furniture that will have to take tough wear. Look to make sure the joining is smooth. Run your hand over it. Remember that wood expands and contracts with the weather, so the joints may leave a little leeway.

Look at the Legs Do they look strong enough to support what they are holding up? Legs should be securely fastened. Curved legs are somewhat less sturdy than straight legs. A stretcher (a horizontal piece of wood) connecting the legs gives added strength and support.

HOW IS IT FINISHED? The finish is a large factor in the price of a piece of furniture. If it has been finished by hand with days and days of tender treatment, you will have to pay for that craftsmanship. But your piece of furniture may one day be a valuable antique (you should live so long!).

Give the finish the acid eye test. Do all the parts of the piece of furniture seem to blend together in color and graining? Are there streaks and drips? Deposits in the crevices? Pieces of hair? Lumps?

Finger the finish. Does it feel smooth and attractive, or bumpy like an orange peel? Does the finish come off in your hands? Scratch the finish lightly with your fingernail on the edge. The finish should not flake off.

If you combine different wood tones in one room, make sure they are compatible. Woods can be stained, bleached, or painted. Paint can conceal woods of poor quality.

UPHOLSTERY

Upholstery is soft. It conveys a sense of comfort and warmth, and it absorbs sound. Upholstery all the way to the floor provides a nice contrast in a room full of leggy furniture.

An upholstered piece of furniture has to be comfortable to the person or persons using it. The only way to tell is to have them sit in it!

Because reupholstering is expensive, it is best to buy upholstered pieces in materials that have good endurance. And because reupholstering isn't even worth doing if the piece isn't structurally sound, it's a good investment to buy the best upholstered piece you can afford. For this major piece, you might want to choose a simple style that can adapt to changes in the room as the years go by.

It is difficult to judge the construction of upholstered furniture because you can't tear a sofa or chair apart to see how it is made. It is especially important with upholstered furniture to trust the name of the manufacturer and the reputation of the store.

You can look at the outside of the piece to see how well it has been tailored. That can give you a clue to quality. Are the seams straight? Avoid "wavy" welting—it should be

straight. Do patterns match? A design found in the center of one cushion should be found in the center of all the others. Lines that are meant to meet should meet. Matching a plaid pattern is particulary tricky. Are the details done nicely? For example, buttons should be well secured. They should be hand-sewn *through* the filling.

All Upholstered or Partly Upholstered? Furniture upholstered to the floor has more presence and seems bigger, warmer, and cozier than furniture showing its legs. All-upholstered furniture is often called "overstuffed." The term doesn't mean that the furniture is too fat; it just means that it is completely covered in upholstery.

Furniture showing its legs and frame seems lighter and cooler than all-upholstered furniture. Partly upholstered furniture is often called "exposed-frame" furniture because you can see the structural frame.

Separate Cushions or Tight Back or Seat? Separate-cushion construction is more costly; it take more material. If cushions are reversible and the same size and shape, you can interchange them to distribute wear. The "deck" or "platform" under the cushions should be of a tightly woven, color-coordinated fabric.

Tight backs or seats are less costly, but more difficult to clean.

The Upholstery Material There is an enormous variety of materials to choose from. Be sure that the type of material you choose and its color (and pattern if any) are harmonious with your overall scheme. And be sure to check out its wear and maintenance characteristics.

Fabrics used for upholstery should be closely woven. This makes them last longer. It is wise to treat upholstery fabrics against staining and soiling. They may be treated at the factory, or you can spray on Scotchgard at home. Some feel it is worthwhile to order extra armcaps to protect arms from wear and tear. These are easily removed for cleaning.

Leather is expensive, but it is beautiful and long-lasting if kept supple. It feels and smells wonderful and can suit almost any room. The only problem with leather is that you stick to it when you are hot. Suede is beautiful, but perishable. It cannot take tough treatment.

Vinyl. Naugahyde and other vinyl-coated fabrics are the choice for heavy-duty installations—in places where there are pets, children, or people who put their feet on the furniture. Vinyl is highly DURABLE, easily washed, and long-lasting. It looks like leather, but it is much much cheaper. The disadvantage, like leather, is that you can stick to it when you are hot.

Would You Want to Use Slipcovers? If your upholstered piece is structurally sound, but the upholstery is shot, you can cover it up rather than go through the expense of reupholstering. Slipcovers are easily made for square-back T-cushion lounge chairs and sofas. Round-back club chairs and chairs with exposed wood on the arms are harder to slipcover.

Slipcovers can give your room a whole new look in a matter or minutes. It's quick-change artistry. Slipcovers give you the versatility to change with the seasons. You might have upholstery in a warm color for the winter, and then pop on slipcovers in a cool color for the summer. Floral fabrics introduce an especially summery feeling.

On the other hand, if your upholstered piece will get heavy constant wear (say in a family room), you might prefer to reupholster to retain a neat look. Slipcovers can slip.

The Material of the Cushioning The material of the cushioning may be super soft or extra firm. What makes you comfortable? The material of the cushioning not only has control of comfort, it determines the price, the look of the seating, and its life span. To find out what cushioning is used, look at that label that says "Do Not Remove Under Penalty of Law." With such an attention-getting title, that's a label you shouldn't miss.

Down or feathers are expensive. They create a big, soft bulky look, but they don't bounce back after being sat on. You have to keep puffing the pillows up. People with allergies might have a problem with feathers or down.

Foam is used extensively in medium- to high-priced furniture. Foam fillings are made in different densities, allowing different degrees of softness or firmness. Firm foam fillings have a lot of bounce per ounce. They can offer comfort without being bulky. They are often used in streamlined furniture designs. Very soft foam may have the same big bulky look as feathers and down. Foam fillings bounce back after being sat on, leaving your seating looking neat and tidy. Foam rubber (latex) is not resistant to mildew and will deteriorate over a period of time. Polyurethane foam resists all moisture and mildew.

Kapok and Sisal are not used very often, and then, generally in poorer quality furniture.

Hair is not used very often either, but occasionally in some moderate- to higher-priced furniture. It bounces back. Unfortunately, it absorbs moisture and might have an unpleasant odor. People with allergies might have a problem with it.

Fiberfill is usually wrapped around the cushioning to provide an extra sense of softness. It is the layer between the cushioning and the outer upholstery. The fiberfill should be mildew-resistant and mothproof. Fiberfill made of polyester, polyester and down, or polyester and foam is used in medium- to high-priced furniture. Fiberfill made of cotton is used in less expensive furniture.

If you want a really squishy, downy effect, you could choose down and feathers, or you could choose less expensive foam wrapped with polyester-and-down fiberfill. If you want simple, soft seating you could choose foam wrapped in polyester fiberfill. And if you want plain, firm seating, you could choose latex foam rubber or polyurethane.

The Construction of the Upholstery Today a lot of upholstered furniture is made from molded polyurethane foam of different densities. Some of these pieces have a structure underneath of hardwood or rigid plastic.

If you are buying a conventional TRADITIONAL piece, you might want to know how it is made. The best traditional furniture is made with a frame of kiln-dried hardwood. (This would be noted on the label.) The frame is joined with dowels and reinforced with block corners. Then the base webbing is put on as a support for the springs. Webbing is usually made of strips of four-inch-wide, closely woven fabric, interlaced so there are only small gaps. Then springs are tied carefully in place. In furniture with coil springs, a quality piece of furniture has at least nine springs per seat—a dozen is luxurious. Then comes another layer of webbing to help compress the springs. Over that comes burlap, then fiberfill—perhaps several layers of increasing fineness: excelsior, horsehair, cotton (now probably polyester), perhaps with a layer of cloth separating the coarsest layer from the next. Muslin is placed on top of the fiberfill, then the upholstery fabric. The last finishing step after the finish fabric is tacked to the bottom of the frame is to cover those edges and the bottom webbing with black cambric.

METAL FURNITURE

Hard metals can provide a nice contrast to soft upholstery, carpets, and drapery. Shiny metals, like jewelry, can add a touch of glamour and sparkle. If they are highly reflective, or if they are combined with glass, they can make a room seem more SPACIOUS. Actually, metal and glass tables are useful in almost any interior.

Silver-Colored Metals Silver-colored metals seem especially COOL and MODERN. Continuous tubular steel framed furniture is distinctly modern. Until 1925, furniture was mostly made of wood. Then, as the story goes, Marcel Breuer was inspired by the handlebars on his bicycle and invented the first continuous tubular steel frame for furniture. Gleaming metal may be used in sculptural shapes, as in Mies van der Rohe's famous Barcelona chair, and in pedestal supports for tables and chairs.

Steel is subject to high polish. Steel that is alloyed with 10 to 20 percent chromium is called stainless steel. Stainless steel with a high content of nickel will retain its polish and resist corrosion.

Chrome is a plating of an alloy of chromium.

Aluminum is a lightweight, strong metal, and it won't rust. It is often used for INFORMAL outdoor folding furniture.

Tinplate (tin coating rolled steel) is a soft silver-colored metal used only for accessories. In Mexico pierced tinplate is used decoratively for lamps and mirror frames, among other things.

Silver, of course, is so valuable that it is used mostly for luxurious accessories.

Gold-Colored Metals Gold-colored metals seem WARM. TRADITIONAL furniture was often ornamented with brass or gold. Sometimes the metal is worked to look like bamboo. Brass and glass coffee tables blend well with TRADITIONAL rooms. Brass or bronze may also be used in MODERN rooms where a warmer feeling is desired.

Brass has a bright, yellowish appearance. It is susceptible to high polish. Since it tarnishes easily, it is often protected by a coat of shellac. Unfortunately, however, the shellac won't completely prevent the brass from changing color. Brass needs to be polished often to keep its shine.

Bronze obtains its surface finish by being dipped in baths of acids. These finishes are only light veneers which may disappear if the object is handled frequently or exposed to the weather.

Copper is a soft orange colored metal. It will tarnish, but water won't make it rust. For this reason, it is often used to line planters. Copper is too soft a metal to be used as a structural frame for furniture.

Gold is, of course, the ultimate metal, but it is unsuitable for structure.

Wrought Iron Heavy black wrought iron was used in SPANISH interiors. Black wrought-iron accessories are also appropriate to EARLY AMERICAN interiors. Wrought iron can have a lacy look. It is often used to make casual or porch furniture. It may be painted. Wrought iron shouldn't be left in the rain.

Is the Metal Cast or Welded? Many metals may be bent or cast into their shapes. With this kind of furniture, run your hand over it to check for smooth surfaces. Other metal furniture may have its parts welded together. Check the joinings to see if they are strong and smooth. Avoid metal furniture that has screws and bolts. These joints will eventually wear away and become unsteady.

The thickness of the metal is a major consideration, too. The piece shouldn't sound tinny when tapped. The structure should seem hefty; it shouldn't wobble, although it might well be designed to be springy (like a Breuer chair).

PLASTIC FURNITURE

Plastics that look like plastics are distinctly MODERN. Plastics technology has allowed furniture new freedom of form. Plastic can be molded or cast in a wonderful array of flowing forms and sculptural shapes. This is true of both hard furniture (rigid plastic) and soft furniture (upholstered furniture made of polyurethane foam). The Italians have been leaders in developing these designs.

Colors and textures are unlimited. Plastics can be clear like glass, translucent like stained glass, or opaque. Plastics in pure colors can be a punchy part of a color scheme. Textures can be almost anything—from smooth and slick to snakeskin.

For ECLECTIC excitement, add a classic plastic piece to your collection of antiques and

reproductions. It will perk up the place.

If you're looking for a TRADITIONAL effect at a bargain price, you can find furnishings with plastic parts molded to look like wood. These parts are usually made of polystyrene or polyester. Check the hangtag. You don't want to be paying for hand-carved wood if you're not getting it.

Plastic Laminates Used for Surfacing Plastic laminate is used as a surfacing material to cover furniture. It is highly DURABLE, resistant to soil and stains, and it is EASY TO CLEAN. It may cover entire pieces of furniture or just the tabletops. Furniture covered in plastic laminate is extremely appropriate for heavily used, high-activity areas, such as kitchens and children's rooms.

Plastic laminate can create an enormous variety of decorative effects. It can pose as wood and look like the rest of a wooden piece. It is available in all kinds of colors and textures.

Plastic laminate is made of melamine plastic and is known by such brand names as Formica, Micarta, Parkwood, Pionite, Textolite, and Melmac.

Rigid Plastic Furniture Rigid plastics are MOISTURE-RESISTANT. They are the perfect choice for wet areas like the bathroom. Some plastics can withstand the weather and be left outdoors. They can be wet-washed. They can endure children's fingerprints and fingerpaints and the outrageous accidents of the pets.

Rigid plastics are soil- and stain-resistant, but they are susceptible to scratching. Avoid abrasive cleaners. Plastics that have a matte finish or a slightly uneven texture show scratches less than smooth, shiny plastics. Kits are available for buffing up scratches. You might even use toothpaste.

With rigid plastic furniture, the key to quality is the thickness of the material. Thin plastic will crack under stress and shatter into spikes that are dangerous, especially to children and pets. Make sure the plastic you select will be strong enough to stand up to its use. Good plastic furniture is comparable in price to good furniture made of other materials.

Clear plastics are a modern miracle. Like glass, they blend with anything and they serve their purpose without seeming to take any space, but they weigh less and are less breakable than glass. They also have a special esthetic quality. The edges of the plastic transmit light and seem to glow with their own illumination.

Clear and translucent plastics are made of acrylic. Some brand names are Plexiglas, Lucite, Acrylite, and Perspex (British). These see-through plastics are used to make cube and coffee tables, chairs, and étagères. They can be used as divider panels to identify areas without breaking up the seeming flow of space.

Opaque plastic furniture is molded in many exciting shapes and flowing forms. The selection of shapes ranges from pedestal chairs that look like tulips to shapes that look like your mother's molars. (Round-edged shapes are safe for children's use.) Since color is intrinsic to the material, it can't be washed or scratched or chipped off.

Rigid plastics have all kinds of uses, including tables, seating, shelving, and wall systems. Some are used as frames for upholstered furniture.

Opaque rigid plastic furniture may be made from a variety of materials including ABS, polyolefins, rigid polyurethane, and Fiberglas-reinforced polyester. These materials are basically resistant to the weather and to being knocked around, but they have different degrees of resistance. Ask your salesman to be sure.

Soft Plastic Seating *Polyurethane foam* has allowed designers to create exciting sculptural shapes for seating. Some foam upholstery may have a structure underneath made of hardwood or of rigid plastic. Foam is used in different densities to create the firmness or softness desired. The piece is usually finished with stretch upholstery.

Inflatable furniture (including water beds) is made of vinyl. Make sure the vinyl is thick and sturdy and won't spring a leak.

FURNITURE OF CANE, RUSH, RATTAN, WICKER, BAMBOO

The beauty of these natural materials is that they can be used in almost any room, TRADITIONAL or MODERN. Because they are natural, they convey a fresh feeling, and because most are light-looking, they contribute to a SPACIOUS or COOL effect.

CANE Cane is a slender and usually flexible reed woven into airy open-work designs. It is most often used for chair seats and backs. The material is absolutely timeless. You'll find cane seats on LOUIS XV chairs, VICTORIAN bentwood chairs, and Marcel Breuer's MODERN Cesca chair. Cane is light-looking and permits the circulation of air. Because it is open-work, cane provides a subtle uneven texture—perhaps all the uneven texture you'd need in a SEMIFORMAL or FORMAL room.

RUSH Rush is used to make the seats of many COUNTRY/RUSTIC chairs. It is an interweaving of reeds or marsh plants with cylindrical, often hollow, stems. It has an earthy feeling and an uneven texture. Rush has been in use a long time. There are reports that Moses' crib was woven of such reeds.

RATTAN Rattan is a climbing palm with very long, round, tough, and pliable stems. Rattan furniture is formed from these stems. It is extremely DURABLE. It can stand up to the use it would get in a family room, for example.

Rattan has a natural, light-looking feeling. Because it creates a SPACIOUS and COOL effect, it is often used for porch or garden room furniture. However, the material has great versatility. It can be equally at home in a FORMAL living room. Because it is of Eastern origin, rattan can give an exotic Oriental accent to TRADITIONAL furnishings. It can give a back-to-nature accent to a MODERN room. Rattan is vastly adaptable. One firm I know offers a standard choice of twenty-six finishes.

WICKER   Wicker is a woven texture like a basket. It is often made of split rattan, but it may also be made of reed, willow, small pliant twigs, or even twisted paper.

Wicker furniture was once confined to the summer porch, but now its natural texture is welcomed into the living room. Wicker was the special on the VICTORIAN veranda, but now MODERNISTS appreciate its airiness, earthiness, and unevenness. They make much use of wicker in natural tones.

Wicker has incredible decorative versatility. It can be woven into almost any shape. Curved shapes are particularly appropriate in a room where you want a FEMININE feeling. Wicker can serve all kinds of purposes: tables, chairs, storage pieces, lamps, planters. Wicker may be left in its natural earth-tone light brown, or it may be painted any color in the rainbow.

A boon for the budget-minded, wicker is relatively inexpensive.

BAMBOO   Bamboo is a tropical woody grass. Its hollow stems have subtle curves and distinctive ridges. Bamboo stalks may be made into furniture. However, much of what we call bamboo furniture is actually wood shaped to imitate bamboo. (Wood is more likely than bamboo to survive life in steam-heated rooms without warping or splitting.) Imitation bamboo furniture has been popular ever since the eighteenth century. Its light natural look mixes

well with all sorts of styles.

FURNITURE OF GLASS, MARBLE, CERAMIC TILE

All these materials are used for tabletops. They are all the same sort of texture: smooth, slick, COOL to the touch. They are all DURABLE, hard-wearing, and EASY TO CLEAN. When should you choose which?

GLASS   Glass resists stains and cigarette burns. It is moisture-resistant. It is DURABLE, EASY TO CLEAN. The danger is that a sharp blow might break it. The thicker the glass, the safer (and more expensive) it is. When shopping, make sure the glass doesn't wobble. Glass is usually more secure when it is set into a frame.

Glass creates a SPACIOUS effect. See-through glass disappears visually. Colored glass, such as bronze glass or smoked glass, is less transparent; opaque glass, such as black or white glass, isn't transparent at all, but still the reflective surface will give a sense of space.

Glass can go with anything—any formality level, any style. Glass can cover any tabletop. Steel-and-glass tables are especially popular in MODERN rooms. However, glass tables are heavy. They should not be put in a position where they need to be moved often. For example, avoid using them in front of sofa beds.

MARBLE   Marble is luxurious and expensive; it can create a FORMAL feeling. Natural marble comes in different color families. You can choose a color coordinated to your room. There are different natural patterns in marble, due to the veining, clouds, mottlings, and shadings.

Marbles are generally DURABLE and hard-wearing, but different marbles have different degrees of resistance to wear. Some marbles can be stained; make sure yours is treated so that it is impervious to water and stains.

Marble can be TRADITIONAL or MODERN. Modernists are naturalists. They love marble's sleek elegance and natural graining. People in French LOUIS XV's era chose marble tabletops in pastel tints color-coordinated to their rooms. The Italians grow marble at home; they have been using it forever. The VICTORIANS also fancied marble tabletops.

Marble is heavy. You wouldn't put it on a piece of furniture you want to move often.

CERAMIC TILE Ceramic tile is DURABLE. It is impervious to water; it can be wiped clean. Once it is laid, it creates a very sturdy surface.

Ceramic tiles can suit all sorts of styles, depending on the design of the tiles. They are available in an enormous range of patterns and colors. They can suggest anything from a Spanish hacienda to a Delft Dutch windmill.

24

BUYING FABRICS

What are you choosing fabrics for? A wall-covering? A window treatment? Furniture? Accessories? The fabric must suit your purposes. It must have the appropriate esthetic characteristics and the right maintenance qualities at the price you want to pay. What is there to choose about a fabric?

OPAQUE OR SEE-THROUGH?

See-through fabrics are appropriate only for windows. They include sheers, glass curtains, and open-weave casement cloths. They serve to soften and filter the light and fuzz the view. For everything else, use opaque fabrics.

WEIGHT

Lightweight fabrics are only appropriate for windows. Light can come through lightweight fabrics and make them seem translucent. If you want them to look more substantial, you can line them.

Medium- or heavyweight fabrics may be used for drapery; they are required for upholstery. Medium- or heavyweight fabrics at the window block the view and darken the room.

Heavyweight fabrics, such as velvets and corduroys, create a WARM, even a sensuous, effect.

WEAVE

Loose-weave fabrics are appropriate for casement curtains at the windows. Unfortunately, many loose-weave fabrics are subject to snagging and shrinking and stretching.

Firmly woven fabrics are appropriate for everything else. The tighter the weave, the longer-lasting the fabric. This is especially true of upholstery. Fabrics used as wallcoverings, too, must be tightly woven to keep their shape.

TEXTURE

Texture is a great determinant of formality. Shiny fabrics are appropriate for FORMAL rooms. Think of the magic lights of silk and satin. Synthetics of acetate or rayon can simulate the sheen of silk, and they are cheaper and easier to care for.

Polished fabrics of less expensive fibers—polished cotton and chintz—can go anywhere. They create a cool, crisp effect.

Dull-finished fabrics (that don't shine) are

appropriate for INFORMAL rooms. Wool, acrylic, dull cottons are examples.

Every room requires some uneven texture. Do you want this fabric to provide the room's uneven texture? Do you want the FORMAL slubs of silk? Or MODERN nubby natural weaves? Or INFORMAL or MASCULINE tweeds? Or do you want the fabric to be smooth and simple?

COLOR

The color you choose must be practical. Where there is strong sunlight and danger of fading, avoid dark or bright solids. Light or muted colors will fade more gracefully. New easily washed synthetics and stain-resistant finishes make light colors more practical than ever before.

The colors must work well in the composition. Colors must be compatible with the wood tones in the room and they should suit the style of your furniture. Colors should be chosen according to what you want to emphasize or underplay. (See Chapters 18 and 19.)

PATTERNED OR PLAIN?

Patterned fabrics can hide dirt and stains more readily than plain fabrics. Patterns might fade more gracefully than plains. However, every room needs a nice balance between patterned and plain materials. To learn when to use which, and how to mix patterns together, see Chapter 20.

FIBER AND FINISH

The fiber you choose controls price, durability, and maintenance factors. Natural fibers—wool, cotton, linen, silk—are more beautiful, more long-lasting, and more expensive than synthetic fibers. They are worth the investment if you want consistent good looks for a period

of years. Natural fibers fade before they deteriorate through sun and chemical action.

Synthetics are less expensive and easier to care for than natural fibers. Many are washable at home. Some don't need to be ironed. The majority are mothproof and mildewproof. Synthetic fibers deteriorate before they fade.

Most synthetics are used for curtains and draperies. The list includes acetate, acrylic (including Orlon), modacrylic (including Ravana-Verel), glass fiber, nylon, polyester, rayon, and saran.

Rayon and nylon are the synthetics most often used in upholstery. Many times they are mixed in upholsteries of natural fibers to make the fabrics less expensive or stronger. Olefin fiber (such as Herculon) makes a DURABLE, heavy-duty upholstery. Acrylic wears moderately well as upholstery. Acetate is sometimes used, but only mixed with other fibers.

Don't go overboard for some new fiber or combination of fibers in upholstery. The manufacturer is using you as a guinea pig. Save your money for the selections that are a proven success. You won't regret it.

Read the label or hangtag. The label or hangtag is required by law to list the fiber content of the fabric. If the fabric is made from a combination of fibers, the fiber used in the greatest amount will be listed first; the fiber used in the second greatest amount will be listed second, and so on down. Percentages are often given. The fiber content will indicate what kind of performance you can expect from the fabric.

The label or hangtag will also tell you if any special finishes have been used. This will give you a further indication of how the fabric will perform. Spot- and soil-resistant finishes make a fabric more resistant to dust and dirt, and enable you to blot up spills or sponge them away. Most of these finishes will withstand a number of dry-cleanings and launderings, but it depends on the fiber and the finish used.

Spot- and soil-resistant finishes may be applied to the fabric before you buy it. If so, the tag will tell you. You may apply a soil-resistant finish yourself at home (Scotchgard or Zepel, for example), but BEWARE. Make sure the finish is recommended for all the fibers in the fabric, otherwise you might have a dreadful disaster. Some synthetics can't take spot-resistant finishes.

The fabric might be treated to eliminate shrinking or stretching, making the fabric what is called "dimensionally stable." Sanforization is the most popular method to reduce shrinkage, but there are others. Cotton, linen, and rayon should be treated against shrinkage. Wool may also be treated. Most synthetics are heat-treated to be dimensionally stable. You, yourself, must be careful not to apply too much heat to them for too long or you will undo the treatment. Follow directions when laundering!

Fibers may be treated against fading after they are woven into cloth. "Vat Dyed" fibers have a high degree of colorfastness. These fibers are colored before they are woven into cloth.

Wool should be mothproofed.

Other finishes might make the fabric permanent press or even water-repellent.

The label may also tell you how to care for the fabric. It may give you washing or cleaning instructions. Don't throw the label away. Leave it where you can find it on laundry day.

NATURAL FIBERS

Wool   *Texture.* Wool is warm to the touch. (It is good to use in cold climates.) Wool can be soft or itchy. Wool has a dull, unshiny surface. For that reason, it is used in INFORMAL interiors. Wool may be woven with either a smooth or a nubby, uneven texture. It is often used for tweedy effects.

Color. Wool has great depth and richness of color. Strong colors come out vivid and vibrant. Also, colors retain their character in night light. Natural wools range from off-white through all the browns to black.

Price. Wool is expensive, even more expensive than linen. There may be more sheep in your dreams than on the market.

Care and Maintenance. Wool wears extremely well. Its endurance is worth the invest-

ment if you want a fabric that will last a long time. Wool must be mothproofed. It may be treated against shrinkage. It must be dry-cleaned by professionals.

Uses. Open-weave wools, especially mohairs, are used for casement curtains, lightweight wools for draperies, and medium- and heavyweight wools for upholstery. Wool yarns are often mixed with cotton, rayon, and other fibers.

Cotton   *Texture.* Cotton is cooler to the touch than silk or wool, but less cool than linen or rayon. Usually the surface is dull, not shiny. Dull-finished cottons are not particularly dressy. Polished cottons have a shiny surface; they look crisp and cool and can be dressy. Cottons are usually smooth, but they can be woven with uneven textured effects.

Color. Cotton takes color well, except in the strongest hues.

Price. Cottons range in price. They are affordable.

Care and Maintenance. Cotton is a very serviceable fabric. It must be treated against shrinkage. Most cottons are washable at home. Cotton is slow to deteriorate—so slow, in fact, that cotton is used for drapery linings.

Uses. Cottons can be used for just about anything. Over two hundred kinds of cloth are made from cotton. Lightweight cottons may be used for draperies or shade cloths. Medium- or heavyweight cottons for upholstery. For an especially strong upholstery fabric, choose cotton mixed with rayon.

Linen   *Texture.* Linen is crisp and cool to the touch—even cooler than cotton. Linen is great in a hot climate. Linen has an uneven texture that gives it special richness and interest. When linen is on the smooth side and shiny, it is FORMAL and dressy. It can have a silky luster. When linen is rough and heavy, it is most INFORMAL (downright gutsy).

Color. Linen does not take dye well, and it is quick to fade. For this reason, it is often used in its natural color or bleached white. A printed pattern on upholstery might actually rub right off! Pattern is often embroidered on linen—that way, it stays.

Price. Linen is expensive.

Care and Maintenance. Linen has some assets: Strong linens may be washed. Linen is not subject to rotting. Humidity or heat won't make it lose its shape (so it's particularly good for loose-weave casements). That's the good news; now the bad news: Linen needs to be treated against shrinking. Linen wrinkles easily. (You know this if you've ever had a linen suit or dress.) We've already mentioned that it fades, so it is best to keep it light or white. Linen in upholstery shows weakness where it is bent, say at a sofa's edge or where it is made into a welt for a seam.

Uses. Linen makes wonderful casement cloths. The fiber lends itself to intricate designs. For longer-wearing upholstery, linen might be blended with cotton. Linen is often combined with synthetic fibers to create a dressy, lustrous fabric.

Silk *Texture.* Silk is warmer to the touch than either cotton or linen. Silk has a wonderful luster. It is highly luxurious and FORMAL as all get-out. It may be smooth or have slight slubs.

Color. Silk gives color a radiance and shimmer that no other fiber can duplicate. (Gold really looks like gold, not mustard.)

Price. The look is out of this world, and so is the price. Silk is the most expensive fiber there is. (Silk's dressy, shiny quality can be found in less expensive synthetics like acetate and rayon.)

Care and Maintenance. Silk is delicate and perishable, costly to care for. It stains easily. It rots in strong sunlight, so it always must be lined when used as draperies. It must be dry-cleaned by a good cleaner.

Uses. Silk draperies must be lined. For upholstery, silk may be combined with other fibers to make it stronger.

SYNTHETIC FIBERS

Acetate Acetate is shiny. It looks like silk. It is soft to the touch. It is not a strong enough fiber to go it alone; it is usually combined with other fibers. Acetate and rayon create a soft, silklike effect. When washing, do not expose it to too much heat for too long; you will ruin its treatment against shrinkage.

Acrylic (including Orlon) Acrylic looks like wool. It is soft and warm to the touch. It can be washed, although it might be preferable to dry-clean. It resists wrinkles, mildew, moths, and fading, and it drapes well. However, it burns like a torch. Other fibers (like modacrylic) should be woven with it to make it safer. Acrylic has other faults too. It pills and it isn't resistant to abrasion. Acrylic is used mainly for lightweight sheer draperies. For example, Orlon comes in a great variety of sheer fabrics. (They may yellow a bit with age.)

Modacrylic (including Ravana-Verel) Modacrylic is similar to acrylic, except it is *fire resistant* and it resists abrasion. It is washable, no-iron, and it hangs well. However, it might pill, shrink, or stretch. Modacrylic is used in drapery and casement fabrics.

Glass Fiber Glass fiber is used to make sheer curtains and casement cloths. It has good wash-and-wear qualities. It is DURABLE and it is *fire resistant.* You can wash glass fiber curtains at home. But don't put them in a washing machine, unless the instructions say you can. Agitation might bend and break the glass fibers. They dry rapidly and need no ironing. They resist sun, moths, and mildew, and they will not shrink or stretch.

Most glass fibers are unpleasant to the touch and you might get little glass particles in your hands. They don't cooperate with pinch-pleats. Draperies may not hang well. Glass fiber has poor resistance to abrasion. Also, some people have allergies to glass fibers.

Nylon Nylon comes in a variety of sheer fabrics that can be used for curtains. (Sometimes they yellow a bit with age.) Because of its great strength and durability, nylon is often used for upholstery. (The fabric is more beautiful if the nylon is combined with other fibers.) Nylon can be washed or dry-cleaned. It is colorfast and "dimensionally stable." It may fade, wrinkle, soil, and pill, but it pleats well.

Olefin (including Herculon) This is an upholstery for heavy-duty installations. It resists soil and stains. Soil stays on the surface and washes or dry-cleans easily. The fiber is quick-drying and it resists moths and mildew. Its only liability is that it can melt at high temperatures.

Polyester If you've ever had a polyester suit or shirt, you know how it behaves. It is washable, drip dry, and no-iron. It resists fading, moths, and mildew and it drapes well. Its

faults are that it pills and it doesn't resist oily stains. In home furnishings, polyester is used in drapery fabrics.

Rayon Rayon is shiny. It looks like silk. As a matter of fact, rayon was first known as "artificial silk." It is soft and cool to the touch. Rayon drapes well. It is wrinkle-resistant and relatively durable. It tends to rot, but it does so less quickly when mixed with other fibers. An all-rayon drapery would shrink if hung over a heating vent. Rayon should be treated against shrinkage. It is safer in a mix. A heavyweight rayon upholstery would wear well.

Saran Saran is used in drapery. It is easy-care, wrinkle-resistant, durable, unaffected by sunlight, and it drapes well.

25

BUYING THE FLOORCOVERING

Most floorcoverings cost a lot when you add up all those yards, but don't let them eat up too much of your budget pie. Leave room for your other expenses. However, because floorcovering *is* a large expense, you should decide on your choice in the early planning stages.

The real cost of any floorcovering is the purchase price, plus the cost of installation, plus the cost of maintenance, divided by its days of usefulness. Once installed, most floorcoverings are relatively permanent. Be sure to choose something that you will be happy living with for quite a while.

Masonry floors, such as concrete, brick, ceramic tile, are hard, permanent, and require the services of a professional mason to install. Some, such as marble, are expensive.

Wood floors are usually there when you move in. New wood floors are available in a wide price range. For most it's best to get a professional to install, but there are some prefinished wood floors you can install yourself.

Resilient floors, such as vinyl, cork, rubber, and linoleum, range in price, can be changed, and can be installed by you.

Rugs and carpets range in price. In determining what to spend, you should figure out how long you plan it to last. The longer you want it to last, the more you should spend.

Wall-to-wall carpeting is best installed by professionals. Carpeting with foam-rubber backing saves the separate expense of underlay or padding.

MASONRY FLOORS

Masonry floors create a COOL, SPACIOUS, architectural effect. They can run from outdoors in, linking the inside of the house with the outside. Because of their weight, they require a concrete subfloor. (If you don't have a concrete subfloor and you want masonry indoors, you can select a vinyl tile that looks like masonry.)

Masonry floors run into money, but they are a one-time-only expense. Because they are permanent, they should be completely compatible with the existing architecture. They should be installed by a professional mason.

Because masonry floors are hard, dropped china or glass is likely to break on them. Masonry floors are a safety hazard for small children, and they are tiring to stand on for long periods of time. Since sounds reverberate from them, they are more often used in the front hall than in the den.

CONCRETE Concrete is very DURABLE. It can be used in precast form indoors. Concrete is cold and uncomfortable underfoot, but it can be painted to improve its appearance. Paints for concrete now wear much longer than they used to.

BRICK Brick is inexpensive, DURABLE/EASY TO CLEAN, and it can run INDOOR/OUTDOOR. Brick needs to be coated with a sealer for protection against stains and scratches. After that it will wear well.

Appearance depends on the size and color of the bricks and on the pattern in which they are laid. You can create interesting effects by combining a variety of patterns in one floor, or by varying the thickness of the mortar joints or the color of the mortar.

Brick can be combined with other materials. For example, brick can be laid in sets defined at intervals by strips of marble. This not only gives the floor pattern and a variety of textures, but it can be laid in a way to define areas.

SLATE Slate is DURABLE, but slippery when wet. It is especially suitable for use in heavy-traffic areas. However, it has to be waxed for protection against stains and scratches. It is usually laid in a setting bed of portland cement about one-fourth inch thicker than the thickness of the slate. Slate floor tiles are usually about six inches square, but they can range up to twenty-four by eighteen inches. The natural colors of slate are gray, blue, black, purple, red, and green.

Slate has a natural grain which gives subtle pattern interest. If adjacent pieces have grain going in the opposite directions, the effect is the same as a wood parquet floor. You can use slate in two colors, say green and gray, to form a two-tone INFORMAL design.

MARBLE Marble is FORMAL—luxurious, gorgeous, glamorous. It is expensive—truly a luxury item. Because of its cost, you might prefer to use marble in a limited area such as an entrance or hall. You could use it as an accent with less expensive materials.

Marble should be laid only by a marble contractor or subcontractor, or under his direct supervision. Although generally DURABLE, marbles vary in their hardness, abrasion-resistance, and ability to withstand severe wear. They can be stained by certain liquids (watch out for wines and liqueurs). For protection, marble needs regular cleaning, sealing, and polishing. It is worth taking precautions; refinishing a marble floor is costly.

There are many colors and types of marble. Some of the color families are black-gray, blue-gray, brown-yellow, green, pink, white, white-blue, white-brown. Some types are calcite, dolomite, serpentine, onyx, and travertine, all with their own veining, clouds, mottlings, and shadings. Of the different surface finishes, the two most suitable for floors are the honed finish and the sand and/or abrasive finish.

TERRAZZO Terrazzo combines the beauty of marble with the strength and economy of concrete. It is composed of marble and onyx chips mixed up in concrete. It looks a lot like marble, but saves a whopping wad of money. It is usually divided into geometric sections by thin metal strips. Terrazzo may be installed indoors and outdoors. It can be bought in precast squares and installed like slate, but it is more often poured on the job and then polished when set. This is certainly a job to trust to the professionals. Terrazzo needs little maintenance. It is ideal for heavy-traffic areas. The only caution is to avoid contact with acids or strong alkaline concentrations.

When the chips are run through the crusher, great care is taken to run one color at a time. Therefore you can choose to have chips of a specific color, or a specific combination of colors. To produce special effects, the cement matrix may have colored pigments added.

POURED FLOORS Poured floors (also called formed-in-place, seamless floors, or floors from cans) are composed of a matrix (binding material) and fillers and/or decorative additives. The flooring materials, after application, form a seamless coating. The finished effects can be highly decorative. Some poured floors have a marblelike finish similar to terrazzo.

Poured floors can cover up foundation cracks and uneven floor surfaces when the right matrix is used. All poured floors are prepared at the time of installation and they should be installed by qualified operators.

Poured floors are relatively inexpensive and quite DURABLE. For maintenance, just wash.

AGGREGATE Aggregate is INFORMAL and rough. Basically, it's just smooth, black pebbles set in concrete. It is installed on site by a professional. It can be cleaned with a broom and a mop.

Aggregate has natural variety in color, pattern, and texture. Since it is so rough and lumpy underfoot, it is often combined with other, smoother materials such as slate, brick, terrazzo, wood, or concrete. When combined with other materials, it makes possible an infinite variety of pattern.

QUARRY TILE Quarry tiles are unglazed tiles made from clay and kiln-fired. Because the clay is used just as it comes from the earth (or quarry), all the colors are earth tones. Natural clay colors include red, rose, slate blue, buff, and a surprising number of other shades.

Quarry tile is really rugged. It can be used in heavy-duty areas indoors and out. It resists oil, grease, and moisture. Because its surface is irregular, it has good slip resistance. (Many people like quarry tile in the kitchen.)

Quarry tiles are usually a half inch thick. The most popular size is six by six inches. There are a variety of shapes available: diamonds, hexagons, and ovals, as well as squares and oblongs.

CERAMIC TILE Ceramic tiles are available in a wide range of colors. They are made from clay or a mixture of clay and organic materials, and fired in kilns at red-hot temperatures.

Unglazed ceramic tiles are popular for INDOOR/OUTDOOR use. They are made in a range of soft earthy shades, but they will spot easily unless coated with a protective sealer. Glazed ceramic tiles have a jewellike richness of color—the brilliant depths of rubies, emeralds, and sapphires. The effects are stunning.

You can find almost any kind of pattern you want in ceramic tile—geometrics, florals, Spanish styles, Dutch Delft styles, you name it.

In addition to all the varieties of colors and patterns, ceramic tiles come in a wide variety of sizes and shapes. The design possibilities are unlimited!

Ceramic tiles are WATERPROOF and highly DURABLE. Because they can withstand extremely cold temperatures, you can use them over floors that sit directly on the ground (such as the basement). For maintenance, just wash with water.

WOOD FLOORS

Wood is one of the oldest and most traditional of floorings. It's easy to live with. It makes a natural, neutral background. It has richness and character of its own. It wears well. It can even look nice and lived-in with a few scratches. It has a little give, so it is more comfortable to stand on than masonry. Because it is smooth, sounds bounce off a wood floor. To absorb sound, you might want to put something soft somewhere in the room—say an area rug, a tapestry wall hanging, or curtains.

A wood floor must blend with the wood tones of your furniture. It can be stripped or stained to achieve a compatible color. You can paint it. To protect your wood floor, you can polish and wax it, or you can cover it with polyurethane to make it impervious to water. If you don't like or want to see your wooden floor, you can cover it with any resilient or soft floorcovering. The only thing you cannot do is to put masonry over it.

THE TYPE OF FLOORING   Wood flooring is typically laid in one of three ways. *Strip flooring* is composed of long, uniformly narrow boards about two and a half inches wide. This type of flooring is in wide general use.

Random plank flooring is composed of boards ranging from three to twelve inches wide. The boards are not of uniform size. Random planks are typical of the early days before things were mass manufactured (or rather mass processed—who manufactures trees?). EARLY AMERICAN interiors featured random planks secured with wooden pegs. Random planks suggest a RUSTIC or INFORMAL feeling.

Block flooring is made of six- or nine-inch-square blocks. Popular *parquet flooring* is block flooring made of short strips of wood laid in geometrical patterns. The most common patterns are herringbone, checkerboard, basketweave, and *parquet de Versailles* (named after French King Louis XIV's sumptuous palace, where it is widely used). Parquet flooring is expensive and FORMAL. After all, would King Louis have anything less?

If the floor you have is in bad condition, or if you want to raise the floor level to create a platform, you can use *plywood* sheets as a new subfloor. Construction-grade plywood sheets are available at your local lumber yard. They are usually covered over with carpet or vinyl. If you want the floor uncovered, you can buy plywood with a good wood veneer surface.

THE COLOR   Most people today begin with oak hardwood floors, but through staining or bleaching, you can make your floor virtually any tone you want. The process is messy, but the results are worth it. The effect will last and last.

Painting the floor is advisable if your floor looks awful, if you are saving money, and if your landlord won't object. Painting a floor is inexpensive, but the surface will wear away

rapidly unless protected by coats of polyurethane. You can, however, achieve interesting effects. Think of how dramatic a white, black, or bright floor might be. If you are ambitious, you could even stencil a design on the floor.

THE FINISH   Wood floors must have their pores sealed or they will deteriorate rapidly. A finished or sealed floor will last a long, long time.

You can take off an old finish by either sanding or stripping. Sanding is a messy process. You will probably wake up in the morning with sawdust in your ears, but the results are well worth the agony. Put drop cloths over all your furniture. Stripping is done with certain liquid mixtures that will take off all the old wax and dirt. Ask at your hardware store.

When your floor is clean and beautiful and the color you want, you will want to seal it. New synthetic sealers give the floor a tough, wear-resistant film and make a good base for varnish or wax. A couple of coats of polyurethane will seal the floor and make it impervious to water. You can choose a high-gloss shine or something softer.

MAINTENANCE   Except for floors protected with polyurethane, woods and water don't mix. Water makes wood buckle and warp. You can clean with a damp mop, but avoid a big wet wash.

Burns are troublesome. You can sand them out, restain the spot, then wax.

RESILIENT FLOORS

The most common kinds of resilient flooring are vinyl and vinyl-asbestos. Others used less frequently are rubber, cork, asphalt, and linoleum. Essentially, resilient floorings are materials that are smooth and hard, but bouncy.

Resilient floors are comfortable. Because of their "give," resilient floors are easy on the feet. They are also warmer to the touch than masonry.

Resilients are ridiculously EASY TO CLEAN. An occasional washing and waxing is all that's required. A little cleansing powder will remove more stubborn stains.

Most resilients can be laid on any floors from basement to attic. Most can be installed over concrete or wood flooring. Installation is easy. You can do it yourself. Some resilients are even self-adhesive. If you change your mind, you can easily remove a resilient floor and replace it.

Resilient floors are available at a variety of prices, and you can achieve a fantastic variety of decorative effects with them. Some resilients are designed to look like masonry. Unlike genuine masonry work, they can be installed over wood floors. Masonry effects include: mosaics, travertine and carrara marble, wood, Spanish-style tiles, Delft tiles, brick. Resilients are available in almost limitless colors and patterns, and in a wide variety of sizes (including squares, oblong borders, and inserts). The variety available allows you to create a custom-design look without a custom-design price.

Because resilient floors are smooth and slick, they generally give a COOL and SPACIOUS effect. However, this effect is moderated if the colors are warm, dark, or bright or if the floor is patterned. Generally, resilient floors are INFORMAL. However, marblelike vinyl set with brass dividing lines is no slouch for sophistication.

Although not a vast aid to soundproofing, resilients are less resonant than hard floors. Cork, vinyl, and rubber are the quietest. Asphalt and linoleum are close behind.

Resilient floors come in two forms: tiles and rolls. Precut pieces, like vinyl tiles, usually come in nine- or twelve-inch squares. The yard goods, like rolls of linoleum, come in sheets of varying widths. Precut pieces have the advantage if you want to do the installation yourself. They are packed flat so it's not hard to get them to lie down on the floor. (Rolled yard goods have a nasty tendency to keep curling back into a roll.) Tiles can be cut to fit irregularly shaped areas with a minimum of waste, and later, if individual squares become damaged or worn, they are easily replaced.

ASPHALT TILE Asphalt is the least expensive of the resilients, but there is not much variety of design. Colors range from black and dark red to green, gray, sand, and off-white. Asphalt is usually used only in the most utilitarian areas. It is often used in basements and recreation rooms, installed over concrete. Because it is harder than other resilients, it is not as comfortable to walk on and it is the least noise-absorbing.

Asphalt can't withstand extremes of temperature. It tends to melt at high temperatures, and it tends to become very brittle and crack at low temperatures.

Asphalt is fireproof and skidproof. It resists alkalis, but it is not grease-resistant unless specially treated. It shows scuff marks and is prone to scratching. Rigid maintenance and waxing are recommended.

VINYL-ASBESTOS TILE Vinyl-asbestos tile is now said to outsell all other types of floor tiles. It is low in cost. It is similar to asphalt tile in appearance, but it is much more flexible and resilient.

Colors and designs in vinyl-asbestos are not quite as plentiful as in other vinyls, but texture has now been added to give design interest. There is enough variety in vinyl-asbestos tile to make it suitable for almost any interior.

Vinyl-asbestos is a good insulator; it withstands great extremes of temperature. It is exceptionally DURABLE. It withstands moisture and abrasion. It is resistant to chemicals, oil, and grease. It is hygienic, highly resilient, and easy to maintain. It is less noisy to the tread than asphalt tile.

VINYL Vinyl is one of the most practical and decorative of all the resilients. It wears extremely well. It resists grease, abrasion, acid, and bleaches. It is the easiest to clean. Some vinyls require no waxing, and all are washable—all you need is warm water and a light detergent. Vinyl is highly resilient and comfortable underfoot.

Vinyl has limitless design dimensions. It

can go with almost any style and fit in almost any room. It can pose as masonry—marble, brick, ceramic tile, for example. It can pose as wood; it can even look like old planks. It comes in a wide variety of solid colors. It can be matched to the background color of your wallpaper or upholstery pattern. You can choose subtle or neutral colors if you want to underplay the floor, or bold bright colors if you want to emphasize the floor.

You can buy, or make, almost any pattern your heart desires. There is a wide variety of patterned styles to choose from. (There seem to be new designs daily.) If you want, you can make your own pattern by choosing a variety of tiles in different sizes, shapes, or colors. You might make a border around the edge of the floor. You might place a design in the center of a solid-colored floor. You might create a checkerboard, stripes—whatever your imagination suggests.

If you want a textured effect, there are vinyls available with flecked patterns and other designs that will create that effect for you too.

Vinyls can give you a lot of pizzazz for your decorating dollar. They are the most expensive of the resilients, but even so, they come in a wide range of prices.

In addition to vinyl tiles, there are sheet vinyls and felt-backed printed vinyls. All vinyls can be installed on floors above ground level (above grade). Regular vinyl can be installed on floors on or below ground level if special adhesives are used, but felt-backed vinyls cannot (there would be a problem with dampness).

Vinyl sheet usually comes in widths of six feet, nine feet, and twelve feet. Because it is bigger and bulkier, vinyl sheet is less easy to remove than vinyl tile. You will probably be cementing it down for a long-term installation. That's okay; it's durable enough to be worth the investment.

Vinyl sheet is made in several thicknesses. It is made in a wide range of patterns, some with no-wax finishes. It is made with various backings. A more expensive cushion-backed form is sound-absorbing and especially comfortable to walk on.

Felt-backed printed vinyls are sold in standard rug sizes or by the yard. This flooring can be cemented down, loose-laid, or cemented only at certain points. It cannot be laid on floors that are on grade or below grade. Felt-backed printed vinyls are available in many colors and patterns.

RUBBER Rubber tile is a good performer, but it doesn't have vinyl's sense of style. Its repertory is limited. Its generally uninspiring colors are best for underplayed backgrounds. Since it is available in black and white, you can use rubber tile to make a stunning checkerboard.

Rubber is a good insulator, and it remains resilient in very hot and in very cold conditions. It cushions footsteps and it absorbs sound. It is durable, flexible, nonporous, and stainproof, but it is damaged by grease, oil, and strong alkaline cleaners. It is less expensive than vinyl, but higher priced than other resilients.

Rubber tiles can be installed over almost any level floor that is moisture-free. *Caution:* Smooth rubber tile is as slippery as a banana peel when wet. To avoid this problem, you might want to choose a rubber tile with an embossed surface.

CORK Cork is the most comfortable resilient to walk on, and it is the quietest. It is a great insulator. It gives protection from both heat and cold. It is not slippery when wet.

In terms of style, cork tile is not very versatile, but it is terrific in the right circumstances. It is best in INFORMAL MODERN rooms. It has the rich texture and warm earth tones that are preferred there. (Colors come in varying shades of tan and brown.) As a matter of fact, it is often used as a substitute for wood. Because of its distinctiveness, cork tile does not combine well with other flooring materials. It is most effective when used wall-to-wall. If pattern interest is desired, light tiles might be alternated with dark ones.

Cork costs less than vinyl, more than asphalt. It is in the middle range of the resilients. It may not be used on below-grade floors.

Cork is extremely porous. It must be sealed to wear well. There are four types of cork tile, sealed in different ways.

Natural cork tile is treated after installation. It is sanded smooth and then sealed. After sealing, it is waxed and buffed, waxed and buffed, however many times you want.

Factory-waxed cork tile is impregnated with a molten wax composition at the factory which makes it more stain- and wear-resistant. It does not require additional finishing.

Resin-reinforced-waxed cork tile gets plastic mixed in with the wax at the factory. The addition of the resin makes the tile tougher.

Vinyl cork tile or *"custom cork"* is a cork tile covered with a coating of vinyl. This makes the tile tougher still and comparable to easy-care vinyl-asbestos or linoleum. It will withstand heavy traffic and have more resistance to oils, grease, and staining.

LINOLEUM Linoleum is one of the oldest forms of resilient floorcovering. For that reason, some people generally refer to all resilient floorcoverings as "linoleum." Actual linoleum was the rage in the 1930s. Unfortunately, linoleum was more "with it" in the 1930s than it is now. The material hasn't kept up with the times. Choices are limited. There are mottled, striped, and embossed designs and a selection of colors. You could cut pieces to make simple geometric designs of different colors.

Linoleum is one of the least costly resilients. It is more comfortable to walk on than asphalt tile or vinyl asbestos. It is a good insulating material, and highly resistant to temperature changes.

Linoleum is highly sensitive to moisture. It should not be used for below-grade installations or for humid areas. Linoleum is less sound-absorbing than cork, rubber, or vinyl.

Linoleum is fairly DURABLE and easy to maintain. Waxing will add years to its life. Linoleum resists oil and grease stains, but it can be damaged by heavy weights, strong alkaline cleaners, and abrasives.

RUGS AND CARPETS

Soft flooring provides a feeling that is entirely different from any other type of flooring. It suggests calmness, ease, and comfort. It is the most comfortable underfoot. It conveys a feeling of luxury (without necessarily costing more). It keeps the floor from feeling cold and can make the room feel warmer. It absorbs noise. (The thicker the rug or carpet, the warmer it will make the room feel and the more sound it will absorb.)

THE SIZE Your choice of size depends on the size of your room and on whether you want to unify the room to make it seem more SPACIOUS, or break it up to make it seem more COZY.

Wall-to-wall carpeting unifies spaces. It gives a comfortable furnished look, and it has an amazing capacity to absorb noise. It can cover wood floors in poor condition, and with the proper underlay, it can cover concrete floors. It is fairly permanent; it might be hard to take with you when you go.

Originally, carpeting was woven in twenty-seven-inch widths. When the looms were expanded to accommodate carpeting of wider widths, the carpeting itself came to be known as "broadloom." Today 95 percent of the carpets sold are tufted, not woven, but they are still known as "broadloom." Most tufted carpets. are available in twelve-foot or fifteen-foot widths. If your room is wider than twelve feet, or fifteen feet, the carpet will have to be seamed. If your room is narrower than twelve or fifteen feet, you'll have to pay for some waste. Usually your carpet dealer will help you figure out the yardage you need, and provide the installation service. Proper installation is important because faulty installation can reduce the life of the carpet. Cleaning normally has to be done on location. To equalize wear in different areas, you can rearrange your furniture from time to time.

Carpet is also available in easily installed, interchangeable squares or tiles that have an adhesive backing. Carpet tiles come precut in twelve- or eighteen-inch squares. Carpet tiles provide a money-saving way to achieve the effect of wall-to-wall. You can dispense with professional installation, since you can do it yourself. You can dispense with an underlay, since the tiles already have a high-density foam backing. Maintenance is simplified. Worn areas can be replaced without disturbing the rest. Worn tiles may also be rotated to less obvious areas.

Room-sized rugs have much of the same unified, SPACIOUS effect as wall-to-wall carpeting. They should have only about a foot of the natural floor showing around the outside edges. The advantage of rugs over wall-to-wall is that they are portable. You can take them with you when you move. You can rotate them to distribute wear. You can send them out to the cleaners. You can even take them up in the summer for a cooler look.

Room-sized rugs that are smooth and unpatterned often look best with a mitered border. For a particularly handsome effect, you might have several borders. The first two might contrast with the center of the rug. The final outside border might repeat the center color. When rugs are cut from broadloom carpeting, you can specify any size or shape you want.

Area rugs are great in a large room. They break up that endless prairie of the floor into islands of interest. The room has to be big enough to break up into areas. An area rug would be ridiculous in a tiny room.

The area rug got its name because it is used to define a specific area of activity. Choose a rug of a size that fits your furniture grouping. Furniture must be squarely on the rug, or entirely off. If you are placing an area rug on top of a wall-to-wall carpet, don't make the mistake of thinking you can get away with something smaller just because you have so much carpet. An area rug still has to be of a size to define the area.

Scatter or accent rugs are small and are used in strategic places to add a spot of warmth or color. They might be by a bed or in front of a fireplace. Although usually used on bare floors, they may be placed over plain carpet.

PATTERN OR PLAIN? This choice depends on the role you want your floorcovering to play in your decorative scheme. A plain floorcovering should coordinate with the colors you use elsewhere in the room. In a muted or neutral color, it will stay in the background, and not compete for attention. In a strong or bright color, it will command attention.

Most patterned floorcoverings command attention and make a room seem smaller. Multicolored patterns can camouflage spills.

THE COLOR Again, this depends on the role you want your floorcovering to play in your decorative scheme. Muted, dull, or neutral colors will camouflage dirt and allow the floor to be underplayed. Bright colors will give emphasis to the floor. Pale colors will make the room seem larger; dark colors will make the room seem smaller. (Carpeting is usually at least one shade darker than the walls.) Reds and oranges will create a WARM effect; blues and greens a COOL effect.

THE TEXTURE The thicker the floorcovering, the more luxurious it will feel, the warmer it will seem, and the more it will absorb sound. The more uneven the surface of the floorcovering (imagine a wild shag), the more INFORMAL it will feel. The smoother the surface of the floorcovering (imagine an Oriental), the more FORMAL it will feel.

Uneven pile is on the IMFORMAL side. Smooth pile that is carved or cut out is SEMIFORMAL; it can go either way. Smooth cut pile can go anywhere. Looped pile is a bit uneven, so it tends toward tailored informality. Flat smooth tapestry weaves tend to be cool and FORMAL.

Looped pile wears far longer than cut pile

when loops are short and closely packed together.

THE FIBER AND THE CONSTRUCTION

This depends on how long you want the floorcovering to last and on what you have to spend. Soft flooring can be expensive, but you shouldn't spend more than you need to. There is no point in buying a wall-to-wall carpet that will last thirty years if you're going to move out of the house in five. The most expensive floorcoverings are made of wool and are densely packed. This high end represents only about 2 percent of the residential market. Less expensive floorcoverings are made from synthetics and/or have less material per square inch.

Although all the fiber producers are working mightily toward the day when each can offer the world the "perfect" fiber, that day has not yet dawned. You must select the best fiber in terms of your needs.

Price Wool is the most expensive fiber. Polyester and nylon are next. Olefin is low cost. Price is also affected by construction. The thicker and denser the carpet, the more fiber is needed and the greater the cost. It's a good idea to get the densest carpet your budget can stand.

Performance A good dense carpet will wear well. A cheap, sparse one won't. If the construction is identical, nylon is the strongest, most durable fiber. Polyester next. Acrylic after polyester. Wool after acrylic. But remember: A thick wool carpet will outlast a skimpy nylon one. Olefin or polypropylene in lower grades crushes easily. For that reason it is used mostly in a flat needlepunch construction.

Looks Wool is the most beautiful fiber—the softest, warmest, most luxurious. Acrylic is the prettiest synthetic. It comes the closest to wool. Polyester is soft, sort of downy. It, too, looks like wool and has a luxurious feel. Nylon feels a little more rugged. Some nylons show

an undesirable shininess. Olefin is used mostly in needlepunch indoor/outdoor carpet. It is not a sophisticated look.

Wool, along with most man-made fibers, dyes up into almost limitless colors. However, a sheep is off-white, not pure white, so if you want a pure white carpet or a very brilliant color, look to the synthetics. Acrylic, polyester, and nylon are good for white and brilliant colors. With olefin, colors are usually less bright and the choice much smaller.

Allergy Is there a serious allergy in your family? Then don't get a natural fiber like wool. The man-made fibers are nonallergenic.

Suitability to Your Climate Do you have a lot of sunlight? Wool can fade, especially in dark or very bright colors. Acrylic is resistant to sunlight. Polyester has good color retention. Olefin is fantastically resistant to fading.

Do you live by the sea or in a very wet climate? Wool absorbs moisture; you might find that wool carpet feels permanently damp. Man-made fibers don't absorb moisture. Olefin is the most moisture-resistant of all. Wool can be treated to be mildew-resistant, and all synthetics are mildewproof.

If you live in a dry climate, you might get annoying sparks from a nylon carpet unless it's been antistatic treated. Except in very dry places, other fibers are fine. Several processes have been developed to avoid static build-up in carpets. A treatment may be applied as part of the finishing process at the mill. Alternatively, after the carpet has been manufactured, it may be treated with antistatic sprays, powders, or liquids. This does not offer permanent protection, and it may cause the carpet to soil more rapidly. A third option is yours. You can buy a humidifier.

Maintenance Many carpets fuzz and pill when new. You have to keep hauling out the vacuum cleaner. Wool carpets fuzz when new. Nylon in staple form (that means short fibers) may tend to fuzz or pill with wear. Unlike nylon, acrylic resists pilling.

The fibers slowest to show dirt are wool and

nylons that are especially engineered to hide dirt. Then come most other nylons, together with polyester and acrylic. Medium colors show dirt less than light or dark ones. Color mixtures—tweeds, florals, patterns—are best of all. When it comes to ease of cleaning, the type of fiber is much less important than dealing with spills and stains right away—before they have a chance to set.

Carpets can get crushed down by the traffic of passing feet and by the weight of heavy furniture. Vacuuming will help the fibers stand up and look fresh again, but you might want to choose a fiber that bounces back on its own. Wool is excellent. It has a natural crimp that makes it bounce back after you step on it. Acrylic is also very good. Polyester and nylon are next. A twist or a low, tight-loop carpet of any fiber will show traffic lanes much less than a shag or a plush.

Flame-resistance is an important aspect of maintenance, as well as of safety. A lighted match will char wool carpet, but the charred fibers can be brushed away, leaving little or no change in appearance. Flame melts nylon, leaving a permanent spot. However, you can repair the damage by carefully cutting away the melted ends. If needed, a patch can be cut in. Acrylic is combustible unless other chemicals have been added. Flame melts surface areas, just as it does with nylon, leaving a scar or spot. (Some acrylic carpets are blended with modacrylics to increase their flame-resistance.)

Moths are more likely to get to rugs in storage than rugs in use. Many wool carpets are permanently mothproofed (see the label). All synthetics are mothproof.

Fiber Identification The Textile Fiber Products Identification Act requires that all textile fiber products show fiber content by generic name. Fibers must be listed in order of their predominance in the fabric and the percentage of each must be given. Still, just as you know you are nothing like your black-sheep cousin, there are a lot of differences within families of fibers.

Licensed Trademarks Sometimes the carpets are additionally marked with licensed trademarks. Although confusion is compounded by the over fifty carpet-fiber trade names, many a new trade name represents a specific technological improvement. The real advantage of a licensed trademark is its implied guarantee of quality. Anyone who licenses a trademark must control the quality of the product that carries that trademark.

GENERIC NAME	TRADE NAME
Wool	The Woolmark
Nylon	Anso
	Antron
	Cadon
	Caprolan
	Cumuloft
	Enkalure
	Enkaloft
Acrylic	Acrilan
	Creslan
	Orlon
	Sayelle
	Zefran
	Zefkrome
Polyester	Avlin
	Dacron
	Fortrel
	Encron
	Kodel
	Trevira
Olefin	Vectra
	Herculon
	Marvess
	Polycrest

Jute and Hemp Rugs Jute and hemp rugs have a straw summer feeling. Their natural texture creates a light, COOL effect. These rugs are inexpensive and earthy. They are DURABLE, not easily destroyed by the elements. They are often found on outside summer porches, basement family rooms, bedrooms, summer dining rooms, even living rooms.

Jute and hemp are available not only in the natural flaxen color, but also in pretty reds, golden yellows, blue, and green, and brown-and-black mixtures.

Their drawback is that some are prickly on bare feet.

THE CARPET UNDERLAY   A carpet that already has a foam-rubber backing usually doesn't require an underlay, but other carpets do. Carpet underlay is well worth the expense. It will make your carpet or rug last longer, look better, and feel better underfoot. It can even help absorb sound, often improving the acoustics of the room.

Carpet underlay may be made of hair or a combination of hair and jute. It may be made of flat or rippled sponge rubber, or it may be made of polyurethane. All types are made in various weights and thicknesses.

It is important to choose an underlay that will complement your floorcovering. If your carpet has a tendency to stretch or ripple, choose a felted underlay of hair and jute. Under flat rugs, such as Orientals, you will want a flat, not a rippled, underlay, so the rug sits flat. Under stair carpeting, a firm cushion would give you the best footing. In rooms where comfort is emphasized, such as living rooms and bedrooms, you might want a luxurious bouncy underlay of heavy sponge rubber.

The thickness should be suitable to your carpet too. You can't compromise. A thick underlay can't make a skimpy carpet seem thick. A skinny cushion will be felt even under a thick carpet. Cheap pads shorten the life of a carpet, so even though you don't see it, buy a good one. When in doubt, ask your carpet salesman's advice.

(Design by William Turner Associates; photo by Hans Van Ness.)
The walls are papered with old Chinese money!

26

BUYING THE WALLCOVERING

Paint is the least expensive treatment. You can do it yourself. Wallpaper need not be expensive, but it is more expensive than paint. You can do it yourself. Fabric-covered walls are more expensive than paper. Wood paneling is rather expensive, but maybe not as costly as you think.

BUILDING MATERIALS

Building materials such as stone, brick, concrete blocks, rough plaster, give architectural dimensions, textured interest. The rougher the materials, the more INFORMAL the feeling. Colors are usually natural, although some building materials may be painted. Pattern is achieved by the way the materials are laid.

Maintenance Even when you plan not to cover these materials, they may need some special care. To bring out their beauty, you may have them cleaned and treated. The treatment will fill their pores and reduce the future accumulation of dust and dirt.

Wall Ornamentation Some of these walls have so much texture and color interest that they need little or no further ornamentation. However, if you want to give them an accent or two, choose something that won't be overwhelmed. Wall accents or accessories need to be strong or vigorous in character. Try wrought iron, wood carvings, rough or bold wall hangings, vigorous oil paintings in strong simple frames, or plants and vines.

BRICK Whether in the city or the country, brick introduces a rather RUSTIC feeling, so be sure your other furnishings are compatible.

If you decide to face a wall with brick, the work must be done by a builder. You must first make sure that your floor will not collapse under the weight.

To achieve the effect of brick without the weight, there are kits of thin bricks that you can use to face the walls.

Brick may be left in its natural state, be treated with oils, or painted. White paint is popular; so are various reddish tones.

ROUGH PLASTER Unsmooth plaster, showing the workman's trowel marks, conveys a rather RUSTIC, primitive feeling. It is compatible with INFORMAL, SPANISH, or EARLY ENGLISH furniture. Its disadvantage is that it might crack.

It can be left in its natural state, white-washed, or painted.

TEXTURED CEMENT A wall surface of tex-tured cement creates an INFORMAL atmosphere, and it can give a room a lot of character.

The surface is usually created by mixing powder or cement with water or chemicals and applying it to the wall with a terry-cloth towel, a natural sponge, or a trowel. The surface should be applied with care and subtlety. If applied with too heavy a hand, the texture will not be attractive. It is best to treat all four walls the same, unless the other three walls are paneled.

PAINT

Paint is the least expensive wall treatment. It is easy to apply; you can do it yourself. It is changeable, therefore good for rentals. It is dust-free, EASY TO CLEAN. Paint is available in every conceivable color. You certainly can find one suitable to your scheme.

The texture of paint is usually smooth, but there are a variety of finishes from flat to glossy. Paint with sand in it makes an uneven (and permanent) texture. Overglazes can give an antiqued texture.

Paint is usually used to make a plain solid-colored surface, but it can be painted to make patterns as well as scenics and murals. (Sten-cils are useful in making patterns.)

Certain paints can seal the walls to keep moisture from seeping through. You can even change the apparent size and shape of your room by painting the walls advancing and/or receding colors (see Chapters 18 and 19).

If you want to emphasize the walls, you can do it with a warm, dark, or bright color. If you want to underplay the walls, you can do it with a pale or neutral color.

Selecting the Proper Paint Choose a store that is service-oriented. It will make your life a lot easier if the people are gracious enough to be concerned with your problems.

Tell your paint dealer the following:

1. What sort of surface you're covering.
2. What sort of use it will get.
3. The lighting conditions of the room, including the exposure, the amount of light, and possible reflections of other things in the room.
4. What you want the walls to go with. Bring in samples of your flooring and fabrics. If you have a swatch of something that is the color you want on your walls, show it to your dealer. He will tell you how the color might have to be adjusted to achieve the proper effect.

With your dealer's guidance, select sam-ples to take home and try in the actual setting. Choose only from the well-respected brands of paint. They will be more reliable, and cheaper in the long run.

What the Room Can Do to the Color You Select In order to avoid disaster, it's impor-tant to know what the room will do to the color you select.

Colors are likely to seem brighter and darker on walls than in small samples. A color on a swatch looks about three times brighter when it is spread all over the wall. That's be-cause there's a lot of wall. It's the largest area in the room. Because their area is so large, walls by themselves have a strong impact. They intensify the impact of whatever is on them. Light also bounces the color of one wall against the other walls, which intensifies the effect. Off-whites are the exception. They will seem lighter on the walls than on the swatch.

To get a good idea of how the color will ac-tually look on the wall, ask to see the paint chip for the next darker shade than the one you selected.

Paint changes color as it dries. If you want to test out an area, wait till the paint dries before you make a judgment. Dark color paints may dry light. Light colored paints may dry dark or light.

The exposures of the room affect the color

of the walls. Warm colors in a room with a southern or western exposure will seem hot. Cool colors in a room with a northern or eastern exposure will seem cold.

Reflections of other colors in the room will affect the walls. A terra-cotta patio outside sliding glass doors will reflect a red-orange color on your walls. A lot of grass and trees on the other side of the window will reflect a green color on your walls. Test any colors you're considering in the room itself to see how they are affected. Shadows can give a purplish cast to your walls. When you select a color sample, shade part of it with your hand to get an idea of how the color will look in shadow.

Blue is the most unpredictable of colors. Be careful with it. Buy it toned down.

What the Paint Finish Can Do to the Room *Glossy paint* draws attention and reflects light. Glossy paint highlights every imperfection in a wall, so make sure your walls are perfect before you consider using glossy paint.

If you want to emphasize a particular architectural feature or piece of furniture, glossy paint will draw attention to it.

Because glossy paint reflects light in a bright room, it might cause an unpleasant glare. Dark colors look best in a glossy finish. It makes them seem rich, not gloomy.

Enamels and glossy paints can stand washing better than flat paint. They are appropriate to use where fingerprints might gather.

Flat paint does not draw attention to itself and it absorbs light. Paler colors, reflecting light, usually look best in a flat finish. Dark flat colors in dark rooms would be dreary. Walls are most often covered in light-colored flat paint.

Semigloss paint is a compromise between the extremes. It has a soft shine. Woodwork, windows, and doors are most often covered in semigloss paint, both for emphasis and for washability.

Types of Paint *Alkyd-resin paints,* often incorrectly called oil paints, are more DURABLE

than latex. Alkyd-resins will usually cover old paint or paper in one coat.

Latex paints, which are water-emulsified paints, are popular because of their fast-drying quality. For example, two coats can be applied in one day, enabling you to finish painting all four walls quickly. Latex paints are particularly easy for you to apply yourself. Cleaning is simple. (Latex paint cannot be successfully applied over some bare woods.)

Vinyl paints are very easy to apply, with either a brush or a roller. There is no need for primers, sealers, or thinners. One coat covers most surfaces. Vinyl paint dries in minutes. The finish is satiny and the surface is scrubbable.

Enamel creates a high-gloss finish. It holds up well under frequent cleaning, even scrubbing, but it is harder on the eyes than a semigloss or a satin finish. A variety of new paints can create special effects. The wrinkle-finish enamels are sprayed on to create an interesting metallic texture. They can be applied to wood, metal, and all other surfaces. The effect is striking. Be warned that enamel paints are difficult for the amateur to apply successfully. They are likely to show overlaps and touchups.

Lacquer paints have a high-gloss finish and come in rich jewel colors.

Beautiful glazes and exotic antiquing effects suggest there is no limit to the ways a wall can be painted. These processes usually require talent as well as patience.

Stencils Stencils can help you paint in patterns. Check your paint store. You can buy something from the store's stock of stencil designs, or buy a stencil kit that will provide all the equipment and allow you to cut your own design.

Stenciled borders can draw attention to special features in your room, while giving a TRADITIONAL effect. You might want to emphasize some structural element, like an alcove or a doorway. But don't get carried away. Remember you must balance your areas of interest. Simple motifs are best—like leaves, fleurs-de-lys, or scrollwork.

Murals or Scenics Murals or scenics may be painted on the wall by you, if you're clever, by an artist friend if you have one, or by a student at the local art school if you trust him or her. Scenics and murals are more often bought, already painted, on a wallcovering.

WALLPAPER AND OTHER WALLCOVERINGS

Wallpaper and other wallcoverings are usually chosen to give some sort of emphasis to the wall. The emphasis can be through texture or pattern; it can be strong or subtle.

Although wallcoverings are more expensive than paint, you get a lot for the money. Wallcoverings can make a room feel furnished when there's not much furniture. They can warm up a cold and impersonal room instantly. They provide sufficient interest, so you don't have to spend much money elsewhere.

Patterned wallcoverings can pull the room together, unite the color scheme. Certain patterns can visually improve the proportions of the room. A wallcovering in a defined area can supply a focal point without eating up space. A wallcovering can conceal cracked walls.

If you're patient, you can save money by installing the wallcovering yourself.

The Wallcovering Scheme *Wallcovering on all four walls* will achieve a balanced interest all around the room.

Wallcovering on one wall will make that wall into a focal point. Choose an appropriate wall or else it will look weird. The room's major piece of furniture might be against this wall. It might be the sofa wall in a living room, the buffet wall in the dining room, or the bed wall in the bedroom. (You could cover the bed in a matching pattern for a look of unity.)

If you put a wallcovering on one wall, what do you do with the other three walls? It is usual to match the other walls to the background color of the wallcovering. You must try to balance the wall opposite the focal point with something heavy or interesting, but noncompetitive.

Wallcovering part of the walls. A wallpaper dado (on the bottom third of the wall) or frieze (a band around the wall at the ceiling line) is an inexpensive way of giving a room TRADITIONAL architectural finesse. The dado and frieze are often applied over a compatible companion paper. In a small room such as a dressing room, this treatment would provide all the interest the room would need.

A colorful dado of scrubbable vinyl in a child's room is useful. The child's art and fingerprints can be washed off, and you're saved the expense of covering the whole wall.

Wallpaper cutouts can define or emphasize certain areas of the room. You can frame architectural features. Paper borders can be put around doors and windows, around the wall just below the ceiling line, or around the wall just above the baseboard.

Certain architecturally defined areas may be emphasized. You may put a paper pattern or scenic on the wall over the mantel or in special alcoves or niches; you may put a pattern inside cabinets or cupboards.

You can define certain areas within a room. You may have a cutout garland of vines above each headboard in the guest room.

Caution: Neither overuse nor underuse cutouts within a single room. If you underuse, your efforts will look half-hearted, insecure, and incomplete. If you overuse, the room will look "cutesy"—heaven forbid. Use cutouts to make your point and then stop.

The Materials of the Wallcovering This choice involves the durability you require, your budget, the wall you have to begin with, and possibly your choice of textures.

The Backing: Regular wallpaper can be applied to smoothly plastered walls and to almost any other kind as well.

Fabric-backed wallcoverings are great for covering cracked plaster and other uneven surfaces. They have an added advantage.

Fabric-backed wallcoverings are easily stripped from the walls without soaking or scraping.

Paper surfaces. Plain paper can be damaged. Washable or colorfast papers are much less susceptible to dirt, and they can be scrubbed. The colors are made of oil-based paints, and the paper stock is treated for washability.

Plastic surfaces are DURABLE and EASY TO CLEAN. They have great wearing qualities.

Plastic-coated paper wallcoverings are immune to soiling. They are colorfast and keep their freshness for years. They are ideal for high activity areas, such as the kitchen, the family room, and the children's rooms.

Vinyl wallcoverings are even more heavy-duty than vinyl-coated paper. They are immune to soiling and are scrubbable. Heavyweight materials wear like iron. Some vinyls have embossed textured effects.

Foils and other metallic wallcoverings must be put on perfectly smooth walls. They provide a shiny, reflective surface that seems dressy.

Flocked wallcoverings have the look and feel of cut velvet. Flocking is usually applied in patterns. Today's papers are usually flocked with nylon, which makes them wearable. This soft, uneven texture should be reserved for rather FORMAL rooms.

Grasscloth wallcoverings can easily be damaged. They provide an interesting uneven texture.

Cork materials may require delicate care. They provide an interesting texture with a MODERN feeling.

What the Room Will Do to the Wallcovering You Select—How to Avoid Disaster Patterns look very different in a sample book than they do on the wall. The trouble is that you look at a small piece up close in the sample book and you will be looking at a large piece at a distance when it's on the walls. There is a great optical difference. For example, a bug may seem huge when it is flying two inches from your nose, but you hardly bother about it when it is winging its way around the room.

To be sure of your choice, hang a roll of each of the wallcoverings under consideration in the actual room for several days. It is almost impossible to make a good decision at the store while you are surrounded by so many samples.

Try to imagine the design multiplied a hundred times. If it is already very lively, beware! When I was a little girl I fell in love with a wallpaper design of red roses. When it got on the wall, it looked like chicken pox!

Remember too that colors are likely to seem brighter and darker on the walls than in small areas, and that the room's lighting conditions will affect your perceptions of color (see "Paint," preceding).

How To Figure the Number of Rolls of Wallcovering You Need Measure the distance around your four walls. This is the perimeter of your room. Measure the height of your walls—the distance between the baseboard and the ceiling line. Multiply the two figures together. This will give you the total square footage of your walls.

Now, you must measure the areas you won't be covering with wallcovering to find out how much square footage they take. For each area—window or door—multiply its width by its height. Add up the total square footage of these areas. Subtract this figure from the total square footage of the walls. The result will be the actual square footage you will want to cover with wallcovering.

Divide this figure by 30. This will give you the approximate number of wallcovering rolls you will require. (There are actually thirty-six square feet of wallcovering in a roll, but you have to allow at least six feet for cutting and waste.) You also need to consider the size of the design, and the problems the wallpaper hanger will have in matching the panels. A pattern with a large repeat will require more extra wallcovering than a pattern with a small repeat.

Installation It can be expensive to hire

someone to hang your wallcovering. You can save money by doing it yourself—that is, if you have the patience. Manufacturers have designed some wallcoverings especially for do-it-yourselfers.

Pretrimmed and prepasted papers are relatively easy to hang. You simply cut them, wet the dried paste on the back, and apply them to the walls.

Do-it-yourself wallpapering kits include the necessary materials, tools, and instructions. (You might start by practicing in the closet first.)

MURALS AND SCENICS Murals or scenics can create a focal point. They can emphasize or define some particular area—say an overmantel, a panel, a single wall, or a single section of a wall.

Murals and scenics create interest without taking up floor space. As a matter of fact, their deep perspectives can make a small room seem larger.

They are good for a room without much furniture—such as a dining room, a foyer, or a hall. A scenic is meant to be seen, so you won't want to obstruct the view with furniture. As a matter of fact, in a room where the furniture is low, such as a dining room, scenics are often put on the upper two-thirds of the wall with wood (or wallpaper—cheaper) dadoes or wainscoting below. Then the buffet and chairs can be pushed up against the dado without obstructing the view. Wood dadoes or wainscoting covering the bottom third of the wall provide a defined base for murals and scenics. They create a TRADITIONAL effect, but because they chop up the walls they are best in large rooms with high ceilings.

Murals and scenics provide a theme. It can be a theme of the same style as your furniture. You can pick a design from the same historical period as your furniture. To mention a few, there are EARLY AMERICAN designs, GEORGIAN designs, Roman designs (for straight-lined classic furniture styles), and Oriental designs (to go with your Oriental or Chinese Chippendale furniture).

You can suit your interests or the location of your home. The subject can be the hunt, or the activities in a fishing village, or even the antics of clowns at the circus.

Avoid the tired old sappy subjects. Sugary, sticky, oversentimentalized subjects might give your guests indigestion. Select something that reflects your interesting personality. The scene shouldn't be too lifelike, or you'll have people walking into the walls.

Scenics and murals can bring together a color scheme. The scene might repeat colors found elsewhere in the room.

The lines of the design should repeat the dominant line of the room. If most of the room's furnishings are curved, the design should emphasize curved shapes. If most of the room's furnishings are straight-lined, the design should emphasize straight-lined shapes of the same kind. If the emphasis in the room is on low, relaxing horizontal lines, do not choose a design with strong vertical lines. It would have the effect of a fire-alarm. (It would inspire you to stand up and get going.) If the emphasis in the room is on dignified vertical lines, a design emphasizing horizontal forms would seem like a guest with his shirt out at a black-tie party.

Wallcovering scenics are available in both paper and vinyl materials. Vinyl is more durable and washable than paper.

Wallcovering scenics come in strips or panels. Designs might cover from four to eight panels. Depending on the space you want to cover, you can buy as many panels as you want.

Placing a Scenic on the Walls Identify the section of wall that you want to be the center of interest. Put the most interesting and dominant part of the scenic design there. Then arrange the rest of the design around on either side of this center.

Make sure that a window or door won't interrupt the design at a crucial point. At noncrucial points, you can fudge.

If you place a scenic on one wall or on part of a wall, the other walls should match the background of the scenic. Wallcovering scenics usually come with a companion paper for the other walls. Cut-out motifs from the scenic could also be used in other areas to complement the main panel. Woodwork and doors should be painted the chief light color in the scenic.

FABRIC

A fabric covering for the walls is more expensive than paper, but it has some distinct advantages. Fabric is excellent for covering badly cracked or damaged walls that are too far gone for wallpaper. Fabric is easy to remove and take with you when you move—especially if it is not glued to the wall.

It offers insulation. Back in the Middle Ages when castles were drafty and damp, people hung tapestries, velvets, and brocades on the cold stone walls. It was not the work of some dippy decorator; it made solid sense. The fabrics not only gave beauty and color to the room, but they kept the wind from wafting through. Today fabrics are still hung for their beauty and for their powers of insulation.

It offers soundproofing. All fabrics on the walls will suck up sound. The thicker the fabric, the more sound it will absorb. A layer of cotton padding underneath the fabric will further increase soundproofing.

Like wallpapers, fabrics are usually chosen to give textural or patterned interest to the walls. The difference is that fabrics provide a comfortable sense of softness.

Fabric-covered walls can lend a rich elegance to the decor, but the definite decorative effect depends on the fabric and method of installation you choose.

INSTALLATION Fabrics can be applied flat like wallpaper. They can be stretched on panels. They can be hung loosely—draped, gathered, or swagged—for an especially soft effect.

Method #1: Attached Flat to the Wall with Adhesive *Caution:* You must choose the adhesive very carefully to avoid staining the ma-

terial. Read the small print on the label.

The fabric must be heavy and tightly woven. Suitable fabrics include: felt, burlap, denim, ticking, calico, chintz, canvas, linen, leathers, vinyls.

Certain fabrics *require* a layer of cotton padding underneath so that the adhesive won't injure them. These fabrics include delicate damasks and silks.

You can have fabrics especially prepared for hanging on the wall. You can have them backed with paper, or some other firm material, so that they are no more difficult to hang than wallpaper.

Some fabrics are already prepared for hanging on the wall. Felt is available already backed for hanging. It can make sound-absorbing, colorful walls. (In green it could match the pool table.) Some new materials come with glue on the back.

Method #2: Attached to the Wall with Staples or Small Tacks *Caution:* Be careful the staples or tacks don't show. Usually you can hide them with a narrow wooden molding or a border trim.

For a tight effect you can attach the fabric at the ceiling and at the baseboard. You could tack a narrow wooden lath around the space, and stretch or pleat the fabric over this, attaching it with small tacks. With this method the fabric is relatively easy to remove for cleaning.

For a loose effect, you could attach the fabric to the wall only at the ceiling line. Fabrics can be gathered, pleated, or just eased on, depending on the look you like and the stiffness of the fabric. Almost any firmly woven material is usable. The foremost benefit of this method is that the fabric is easily removed. This is a perfect idea for a rental space where the landlord doesn't want you to change the dingy paint on the walls. You can take your home improvement with you when you move.

Method #3: Attached to a Curtain Rod at the Ceiling and Baseboard *Caution:* Choose an inconspicuous curtain rod. You won't want to see it.

A curtain rod has some advantages over staples or tacks. You make fewer holes in the wall; it is easier to achieve a gathered effect, and it is easier to keep everything even. This method will hold the fabric firmly in place, but still give you all the flexibility of being able to take up your tent and go.

If you want a tight effect, you can stretch a fabric between rods at the ceiling and baseboard. If you want a loose effect, you can simply hang the fabric at the ceiling line.

PANELING

Paneling is a good cover-up for damaged walls. It can hide unsightly pipes and similar fixtures. Much of it can be applied right over plaster. Paneling is a marvelous insulator against heat, cold, and noise. Paneling, especially wood paneling, introduces a sense of architecture.

Paneling of all sorts is easy to maintain, DURABLE. Prices range all over the ballpark, depending on the material, the style, and the manner of installation. Paneling can save you money elsewhere. It makes a room feel furnished so you can get away with very few pieces of furniture.

The Paneling Scheme *Paneling all four walls* is no problem.

Paneling the lower third of all walls is a treatment called a dado or a wainscot. It gives a room a TRADITIONAL sense of architecture. It can provide a defined base for murals and scenic wallpaper, and it can seem to lower a too-high ceiling. The dado is topped by a chair rail, a strip of molding placed at the height of the top of a chair to protect the wall from being scraped.

Paneling one wall can make that wall into the focal point of the room. If you have a long skinny room, it's a good idea to panel the short far wall. Then that wall will seem to come closer, thereby improving the proportions of the room.

If you're doing a TRADITIONAL room and want to spend the money for matching period wood-

work, one wall would probably be enough to blow the budget. (However, it might be well worth it. One wall will be enough to achieve elegant authenticity.)

Paneling at repeated regular intervals will make a large room seem smaller. Your eye will move from panel to panel and seem to take tucks in the wall.

The Method of Mounting Paneling mounted vertically will seem to raise the height of the ceiling. Paneling mounted horizontally will seem to lower the height of the ceiling. Paneling mounted diagonally will seem to push out the walls. It is INFORMAL and STIMULATING.

For added decorative impact, paneling may be spaced by grooves, beadwork, or by slim shafts of other materials. For example, you might have rosewood panels spaced by slim shafts of ebony or chrome.

WOOD PANELING Wood paneling gives a room architectural and textural dimensions. It is available in all the natural wood tones and it may be painted if you wish. It is expensive, but maybe not as costly as you think. In terms of maintenance, avoid contact with water unless the wood has been treated against it.

For a rough, INFORMAL effect, you could use barnsiding. For a smooth, FORMAL effect, you could use polished fine woods. For a MODERN effect, you could use plain paneling. For a TRADITIONAL effect, you could use period woodwork. (It will cost an arm and a leg, but it will create a gracious, dignified atmosphere. If you are blessed by the stars, you might find some period paneling through a wrecker who has stripped it from the walls of some expensive estate he has demolished.)

Veneers Almost every type of wood—from rare and exotic zebrawood to EARLY AMERICAN planking—can be found in veneers at relatively modest cost. Veneers come in sheets large enough to cover almost any area you have in mind. If you are handy, you can install the simpler styles yourself.

Plywood Paneling Plywood paneling is the least expensive wood paneling. It simulates many types of woods and finishes and is ready-cut to be installed by the do-it-yourselfer.

Woods include FORMAL mahogany and Brazilian rosewood, SEMIFORMAL walnut, and INFORMAL knotty pine and weathered cypress. (Cypress may be enhanced by a light wash of paint in white or another pale color.)

Many manufacturers supply complete instructions and materials required for installation.

PLASTIC-LAMINATE PANELING Plastic-laminate paneling is DURABLE, immune to soiling, EASY TO CLEAN. It is washable with water.

It can cover imperfect walls while giving decorative overtones. It is available in all kinds of colors, patterns, and textures. It can even simulate building materials.

Installation Elaborate paneling should be installed by a professional. Who wants to mess around with such a large investment? Less complex paneling is often easily installed by the do-it-yourselfer.

TILES

Tiles are WATERPROOF, EASY TO CLEAN, DURABLE, and COOL. They create a SPACIOUS feeling because of their sleek texture.

Ceramic tiles are permanent. They are usually limited to bathrooms and kitchens and to the outdoors, except in Mediterranean or SPANISH homes.

Vinyl tiles are changeable. They might be used in children's rooms or in game rooms. They are softer and more cushiony than ceramic tile.

You can achieve an enormous variety of decorative effects with tiles. Tiles are available in all sorts of sizes and shapes. The size and shape of the tiles alone will give a slight pattern to the walls.

Tiles are available in an incredible range of colors. You can choose a one-color treatment, or mix colors. You may decide on a contrasting border, or a stripe or checkerboard design.

There are plentiful patterns to suit all sorts of styles. Designs with scrollwork suit SPANISH or Mexican homes. Delft tiles look at home in a country kitchen. You could mix patterned tiles with plain.

Some tiles even have textured surfaces.

With this serviceable surface, the choice is huge.

CARPETED WALLS

For centuries, people have been hanging rugs on the walls as decorative wallhangings. Today, carpeting can cover entire walls and be attached permanently. A number of carpet manufacturers make special products for this purpose.

Carpeted walls absorb sound and light. They make a place feel WARM, CALM, and COZY. They create a soft atmosphere where you could bounce against the walls without hurting yourself. (Carpeted walls can be rather sensuous and SEXY.)

What do you have to choose? You have to choose the texture, the color, whether to have patterned or plain, and if patterned, what kind of pattern. Many of the same rules for carpeting the floor apply to carpeting the walls. Look up "Rugs and Carpets" in Chapter 25. Remember, however, that the walls have more visual impact than the floor. You should be careful with strong decorative effects.

MIRRORED WALLS

A mirrored wall will stretch space, make the most of the light, and make the wall seem to disappear. It will double the impact of whatever is in front of it.

Installation The mirrored area should be defined by some architectural feature, or by furniture. Mirror can cover a complete wall, cover the complete overmantel, or completely face a niche. Otherwise, it can be framed by moldings, half-columns, or bookcases. If a large mirror is just tacked up on part of a wall, it will look unfinished.

One or two walls can be mirrored—usually not more. If you were to mirror three or four walls, people would lose their bearings and get confused by the multiple images. The room would seem like a no-fun fun house.

There are exceptions. If the mirror is clouded or divided by conspicuous lines so that people are aware that the mirror is there, you can cover all four walls with mirror. I've seen it done in a bathroom—complete to the ceiling. (Talk about being self-conscious!)

The Size Mirror comes in large sheets or in precut shapes such as squares and dia-monds. A large sheet can give you a clear, slick expanse. Precut shapes can be laid in patterns. The dividing lines between the pieces will help people realize that the area is not a passageway.

Colors and Effects Mirrors come tinted in various tones. Choose one that would best blend with your room. Frankly, I like the clear ones and the steely gray ones. Those tinted pink and yellow remind me of smelly bathrooms in cheap saloons. Mirrors can also be smoked or antiqued (rippled with gold and shadows). Both give the mirror a textured effect and soften its shine.

Price Be prepared to pay the price for the best. Cheap mirrors give distorted reflections and don't last long.

(Photo courtesy of Thayer Coggin, Inc.; design by Milo Baughman; photo by Alexandre Georges.)

27

BUYING THE WINDOW TREATMENT

Your window treatment has a big job to do. It should flatter your window and your room. And it should give you the right kind of control over the lighting and the view. It might also have to cope with or conceal radiators and air-conditioners.

If you have a good view and privacy, and like a lot of light and an airy open feeling, you might leave your windows naked. (That certainly is an inexpensive answer!) To minimize the glare on the windows at night, light up the area outdoors.

For all other window treatments there are three rules to follow:

All window treatments should start and stop (or seem to start and stop) at architectural features. Short draperies or curtains should be long enough to reach the windowsill. Alternatively, the treatment should extend to the bottom of the apron. (The apron is the part of the window frame that's under the windowsill.) Short treatments tend to be INFORMAL.

Long draperies should extend to within an inch or less of the floor. The inch or less allows them to hang free and protects them from the dust (there's dust?) on the floor. Long treatments tend to be more FORMAL.

Windows should look okay from the outside of the house. For this reason, you might want to line patterned draperies.

The size of the treatment should suit the size of the window and the size of the room.

For almost any window treatment, you will need accurate measurements of your windows. Write down the following dimensions:

1. The width of your windows (include the window frame if it will be covered)
2. The height of your windows (again, include the window frame if it will be covered)
3. The measurement from your windowsill to the floor
4. The measurement from the top of your window to the ceiling

CURTAINS AND DRAPERY

Curtains and draperies are soft-textured. They can absorb noise. If the room is entirely furnished in hard surfaces, you will probably need something soft at the windows to absorb sound. Curtains and draperies can make the atmosphere seem relaxed and comfortable. Soft textures are quieting and CALM.

Depending on the fabric, curtains and draperies can filter the light and fuzz the view or block the light and shut out the view.

Curtain and drapery fabrics vary widely in price. You can buy bedsheets or luxurious silks.

Price also depends on how the curtains or draperies are made. Of course, you can save money by making your own. Ready-made curtains and draperies are available at most department stores. Generally, they are inexpensive. You can buy them and hang them quickly. They are good for conventional windows. They are available in about a dozen lengths and about a half a dozen widths. There is a good choice of fabrics, but the designs and colors are somewhat limited. The more expensive ones are made of finer quality fabrics and often are better constructed. Consider the cost of upkeep. It might be worthwhile to spend more on a low-maintenance fabric.

You might have draperies or curtains made to measure. You measure your windows yourself and take the measurements to a store that offers the made-to-measure service. This is good for any type or size of window, but it takes a little while to have them made. Made-to-measure lines are usually confined to straight panels with pleated headings. Fabric selection is usually good, but the patterns are limited. Prices vary according to the fabric, size, and style. Made-to-measure curtains are more expensive than ready-mades, but less expensive than custom-mades.

Custom-made curtains and draperies are the expensive way to treat your windows, but generally the only way to achieve elaborate or unusual effects. A representative of the decorator shop or retail store will come to your home, measure your windows, and show you a selection of fabrics. The choice of fabrics is extensive. Later the shop or store will send someone to install the hardware and hang the draperies. They will take responsibility for the draperies fitting perfectly, and guarantee the quality of the workmanship.

The Length They can be of sill, apron, or floor length, although floor length is the most popular. Draperies that reach practically to the floor can be mounted at the top of the window or at the ceiling line. Apron-length curtains are usually hung from the top of the window frame. Sill-length curtains are usually hung from inside the window frame.

Overdraperies used with sheer or glass curtains should be matched in length. The only exception might be if a cabinet or a radiator jutted out below the windowsill—then the sheer curtains might be shorter. However, if the radiator juts out only slightly (four inches or less), the better solution might be to move the whole arrangement out farther into the room so it can all hang straight.

The Width Draperies (before pleating) should be approximately twice the width of the space they are to cover so that they don't look skimpy. Never skimp on the amount of fabric. If you must skimp somewhere, it's better to buy a cheaper material.

Draperies or curtains just at the sides of the window can frame the view and give the window more importance. (If the view is bad, you can fuzz it by hanging glass curtains, shades, or blinds in back of the draperies.) To improve the proportions of the window, you can hang draperies out over the wall to give the illusion of a window of the proper proportions, in the proper position. (You can conceal the actual position of the window by hanging shades or blinds in back of the drapery.)

Drapery fabric normally comes in fifty-inch widths. This is wide enough for a side drapery for a normal window. If the window is extra wide, you would need more material to frame it.

Draw draperies that completely cover the window demand more fabric. If the draperies are of a see-through material (such as a casement cloth), they will fuzz the view while letting in light. If the draperies are of opaque (or non-see-through) material, they will shut out the outside world. They will create warmth, darkness, quiet, and privacy. (These draw draperies might be used in combination with sheer curtains, shades, or blinds).

Draperies covering a complete wall can camouflage windows of awkward appearance and give the room a unified look. If hung out far enough into the room, they can conceal radiators and air-conditioners. However, this treatment requires *a lot* of fabric. If the fabric is heavy and opaque, the treatment might look hot.

The Style *Curtains or draperies hanging straight* are a timeless treatment. If the treatment is from floor to ceiling, it will create a strong vertical line that will seem to push up the ceiling height.

To soften a bad view and to filter sunlight, you could combine draperies hanging straight with sheer curtains, shades, blinds, or shutters.

Tied-back curtains or draperies are also a timeless treatment. Gently tied-back draperies make a curved shape. They create a gracious, graceful, FEMININE feeling. Severely pulled back draperies create a diagonal line which may be unpleasant.

For a FORMAL effect you can use rich fabrics. For an elegant TRADITIONAL effect, you can combine tiebacks with ornate swag valances. These were used in eighteenth-century interiors.

For an INFORMAL effect, use common fabrics. For an especially FEMININE or RUSTIC effect, you can use tied-back curtains with ruffles.

To soften a bad view and to filter sunlight, you could combine tied-back draperies with sheer curtains, shades, blinds, or shutters. To hide an ugly radiator or air-conditioner, you could combine them with a lower cafe curtain.

Cafe curtains are a treatment in tiers. They are rather INFORMAL, but they are adaptable. You could have a double tier, a triple tier, a single tier with a ruffle valance above, or a single lower tier combined with tied-back draperies. The style is often associated with EARLY AMERICAN interiors (rough, heavy printed linens and documentary prints of the period would be appropriate fabrics).

Cafe curtains save space. They can be hung entirely within the window frame. They are a good idea for dormer windows or other windows where there isn't much space to the side of the window.

Cafe curtains give flexible control of light, air, and the view—you can open the top tier for

light and air while closing the bottom for privacy.

Shirred curtains are curtains gathered on rods attached above and below the glass. They are usually sheer and light in weight so that they filter light and fuzz the view.

They save space. Because they are held close to the glass, they do not intrude into the space in the room. They also can show off the shape of the window. They are a tidy treatment for tall thin windows, French doors, fan-shaped windows, and transoms. For a fan-shaped window, the top rod may be curved around the window's arch to shape the shirred curtains into a sunburst.

Shirred curtains are not appropriate for double-hung windows. How would you open the window? However, you could use shirred curtains on the bottom sash for privacy, combined with something else—perhaps draperies framing the window. If used with casement windows, make sure that the treatment is not in the way of the control crank.

The Fabric *See-through fabrics* let in the light; they just filter out its glare. In the daytime they allow you to observe, without being observed. Because they allow the free circulation of light and air, they make a room feel COOL and SPACIOUS. See-through curtains are available in styles that range from simple weaves to elaborate laces.

Sheer or glass curtains can be the complete window treatment, or they can be combined with side or draw draperies. They usually hang close to the window glass itself. Sheers may be hung completely within a window frame for a light look, or to show off the window moldings. You can find glass curtains ready-made that will fit most window sizes.

Glass curtains are very light in color, usually white, so that you can see through them. There is a wide selection of light colors.

Most glass curtains are practical and long-lasting. Most can be washed easily at home and rehung in a day. Some do not require ironing. The fiber is usually a nylon, Orlon, or Fiberglas in a smooth voile or organdy. Fiberglas stands out for its fire resistance and durability. Nylon and Orlon sometimes yellow a bit with age, but come in a greater variety of sheer fabrics. Lightweight sheers are made in new synthetics and combinations every day.

Open-weave casement curtains provide an interesting texture through the play of light. They are a good answer for a window wall in a MODERN room. Usually they are a solo treatment, but they may be combined with shades or blinds. If you will occasionally want a sun screen or total privacy, you can put a blackout lining on separate traverse tracks.

Opaque fabrics when drawn across the window will block out the light and the view and give complete privacy. They will also make the room seem warmer and cozier. (Thick, soft textures are particularly sexy.) Opaque fabrics are often used for draperies that are drawn at night.

Opaque fabrics are also appropriate for draperies that sit at the sides of windows, framing the view.

What Can Happen to a Fabric When You Hang It at the Windows? *Fabrics can fade or rot in strong sunlight.* There is no perfect fiber. To balance strengths and weaknesses, many curtain and drapery fabrics are a blend of synthetic and natural fibers.

Since eventual fading and rotting is inevitable, what will seem to make the process go slowly? Mixtures fade in a more mellow way than plain solids. After all, the changes may be seen as part of the pattern or texture. Some colors fade more gracefully than others. Gray, brown, green, yellow, and orange simply get more subtle. Maybe you'll even like them better in their old age. Dark solid colors die young. Their character is soon compromised. Drapery linings protect against fading and rotting.

In changeable humidity, some fabrics rise and fall with the weather. Casement cloths, because they are loosely woven, are the most susceptible to stretching and shrinking. If necessary, you can always rehem them, but better—look for fabrics that are "dimensionally stable."

When a design hangs in folds, you lose a lot of detail. An exquisitely delicate design or weave may seem to lose its refinement. You can't see the subtleties. They get lost in the folds or the shadows. Something less expensive and less subtle may be just as effective. Bold designs, too, change character when they hang in folds. Be sure to drape the fabric you're considering, so you'll have some idea of what you're getting.

Inside or outside light sometimes affects the design you see. A casement cloth with a horizontal slub may look fine at night with the inside light shining on it, but with light from behind during the day, that slub may seem like a stripe. A light background will sit back at night, but during the day it will shine and seem more important than the design.

To Line or Not to Line? Lining gives added insulation against heat and cold. It protects the fabric from fading or rotting in strong sunlight. It makes windows look uniform from outside. It can give an inexpensive fabric more weight and body so that it hangs better. For room darkening, special blackout linings can either be attached to the draperies or hung on a separate track.

All printed or highly colored draperies should be lined. Draperies made of fibers that are subject to rotting, like silk, should always be lined. And so should inexpensive, insubstantial drapery fabrics.

You should never line sheer curtains or casement cloths. Their beauty is their see-through quality. White or off-white draperies don't need to be lined either.

Drapery lining material must be opaque and of tight weave. The best colors to use are beige or white. Drapery lining is usually of cotton. (Cotton is slow to rot.) Metallic and thermal linings are especially designed for insulation.

Some linings pin or clip into place. Some are sewn onto the drapery fabric. Some (called "self linings") are applied directly to the back of the drapery fabric. There's even a relatively new backing made of acrylic foam. Self linings are less cumbersome than other linings.

The Mounting: Headings and Hardware The heading should be appropriate to the curtain or drapery style you select. Any type of curtain or drapery looks attractive with a heading of wide pinch pleats. Door windows, or large windows that open out, look nice with box pleats or scallops. Cafe curtains often have scalloped headings. Sheer curtains usually have shirred (or gathered) headings.

The drapery hardware must be appropriate to the style of your treatment. (The store salesperson will advise you.)

Traverse rods are appropriate for draw draperies. Traverse rods fit any window and they come complete with cord, pulley, extension strips, and plastic slides. They may be hung on the wall above the window or on the ceiling. (The ceiling type is especially appropriate if you want to hang the draperies out in the room far enough to conceal a radiator or an air-conditioner.) Choose one-way adjustable traverse rods when you want to draw the draperies just in one direction, two-way adjustable traverse rods when you want to draw draperies together in the center. Choose a combination traverse rod and valance rod when you want to combine draw draperies with an over-the-top-of-the-window valance.

Single curtain rods are fine for curtains or draperies you won't be moving as well as those you'll be moving by sliding them by hand. "Baton pulls" ease movement by hand.

On *double curtain rods,* you can combine glass or sheer undercurtains with swagged tied-back overdraperies.

Spring-tension cafe rods are appropriate for light curtains you want to hang within the window frame.

Cafe-traverse rods with matching ring slides give you decorative hardware as well as movement you can control with a cord.

There are rods that fit around corners, in case you have that need.

Swinging brackets are especially useful for casement and French doors that open inward. You can swing the draperies out of the way when you want to open the window or get to the control crank.

The drapery hardware may be underplayed, even concealed, or it can be chosen to add pizzazz to your window treatment. Rods and rings come in all kinds of materials and colors. For example, there's brass, bronze, iron, and various woods as well as a variety of colors. Decorative finials (those things that poke out at the ends of the rod) and tiebacks (a piece of hardware that sticks out so you can bunch the drapery behind it) come in all sorts of styles. Ask the salesperson which one would be suitable to your window treatment and style of furniture.

Trims You might want to trim your draperies or curtains to add interest, or to make an inexpensive fabric look like something more. Many TRADITIONAL styles are authentic with braid or fringe trim and decorative tiebacks with tassels. If the trim repeats a color found elsewhere in the room (say the color of the carpet), it will create a unified effect.

TREATMENTS ACROSS THE TOPS OF WINDOWS

Treatments across the tops of windows have several uses. They can make the window treatment look finished. They can hide hardware. They can complete an authentic period treatment. They can conceal artificial lighting. (A fluorescent tube may be hidden behind a valance to give the illusion of sunlight or to focus attention on the window treatment.)

They can make a too-high ceiling seem lower. A wider-than-usual valance in an inconspicuous color can seem to bring down the ceiling height. Interest along the bottom edge of a valance will attract your attention so you see no higher. The bottom edge might be carved into an interesting shape or decorated with trim.

RUFFLES AND BOX PLEATS Ruffles and box pleats belong to INFORMAL styles, including

EARLY AMERICAN. You can put them on a simple upper curtain rod. They can be combined with a bottom cafe curtain or a lower tier of shutters.

VALANCES A valance is a flat projection at the top of the window which covers the drapery hardware and should be coordinated to complement the rest of the window treatment.

A valance must be in the proper proportion to the room and window. How do you determine the proper size?

A valance covering the space from the ceiling to the top of the window casing will in most cases measure about twelve to fourteen inches in depth. The depth is determined by dividing the ceiling height by 6. For example, if you have a twelve-foot ceiling in your living room, a valance for the windows in that room should be two feet at its deepest point. If you have a room with a more standard eight-foot ceiling, a valance should be approximately fourteen inches at its deepest point.

A valance may be hung from the top of the window instead of from the ceiling line. To determine the proper depth of a valance hung from the top of the window, divide your *window* height by 6. The shallowest part of your valance should be at the frame of the window; only the deepest points in the shape of the valance will cover the window's glass portion. A valance of this type is, of course, mounted on the wall above the window.

To see if what you have in mind will look right, first make a facsimile out of wrapping paper and hang it up. Then you can look at it from a distance.

Fabric Valances Fabric valances can be INFORMAL or FORMAL and elaborate, depending on the fabric. Fabric valances are usually made to match the draperies. You can use a contrasting fabric if you wish, but make sure the two are compatible. The fabric should never be lighter in weight than the draperies.

Fabric valances are often stitched to a backing of buckram. Buckram, like crinoline, is a stiff material that will keep the fabric evenly stretched and taut. It won't sag or fall out of place. A buckram valance is removable for cleaning.

Fabric valances can be bought ready-made to match ready-made draperies, or ordered with made-to-measure and custom-made draperies.

Swag Valances A swag is a shaped width of fabric draped over the top of the window. Swag valances tend to be dressy and FORMAL.

Ornate swag valances combined with tied-back draperies of rich fabrics spell TRADITIONAL elegance. The GEORGIAN period was characterized by elaborate draperies hung with valances, swags, and jabots with elaborate fringes and tiebacks. The ENGLISH REGENCY, FRENCH LOUIS XV and XVI, and EMPIRE styles used swag valances. The VICTORIAN period was characterized by heavy draperies with swags, jabots, and heavy fringes (and sheer lace curtains underneath).

Swag valances can be used alone as well as with curtains or draperies. Swag valances can have tails so long on both sides that draperies aren't needed. The effect is TRADITIONAL and light-looking.

Swag valances can be combined with a lower tier of shutters for a light, dressy look, say in a dining room.

Valances Made of Plywood, Sometimes Called Cornice Boards Wooden cornices are for sale in most department stores, and they can be painted or covered with fabric, wallpaper, cork, mirror, leather, or whatever inspires you. Depending on the material covering them, they can coordinate with almost any room. Fabric applied to plywood must be completely removed for cleaning—a tedious process.

Shaped Valances. Valances made of plywood or composition board can be cut out in shapes. Shaped valances of covered plywood can go with almost any decor. They are TRADITIONAL to American Colonial and eighteenth-century English periods.

LAMBREQUINS Lambrequins are structures that go across the top of the window and down the sides as well. See them under "Structural Treatments," following.

WINDOW SHADES

There's hardly a window alive that can't be covered by a window shade. Shades can fit any window size or shape. Shades don't take up much space, and they are unobtrusive when rolled up. Roller shades on tracks might be convenient for awkwardly placed windows or ones that slant.

Shades can be completely open to expose the view, or pulled completely down to cover the view and give you privacy. Roller shades that pull up from the bottom provide privacy, or block the view, while still allowing light and air to enter the room. Bamboo or matchstick shades obscure the view while letting in light and air, and so do sheer austrian shades.

Opaque shades will block the light and darken the room. To filter and soften the light, you could use translucent shades, bamboo or matchstick shades, or austrian shades in a sheer material.

Window shades are generally inexpensive.

Shades used alone, with no additional draperies, are definitely INFORMAL. (Austrian shades are the exception.) Shades used alone create a SPACIOUS and COOL effect. Because they are contained within the window casing and are close to the glass, shades alone do not intrude into the space in the room.

Shades alone can have decorative interest. The bottom of a roller shade might be shaped in an interesting way. The shade could provide interesting texture. Bamboo, matchstick, and woven wood shades have an appealing uneven texture. Vinyl shades are available in a variety of textures. Roman shades and other fabric shades may be made of textured materials. The shade may be an interesting color or pattern. It may match drapery, wallpaper, or upholstery. A shade the same as the wall will play down an awkwardly shaped window. A shade the same as a pattern elsewhere in the room will tie the room together. When there is little pattern elsewhere, a shade can provide the pattern interest for the room. You could decorate plain vinyl shades, or make a shade of a patterned fabric.

Shades Used Together with Draperies When draperies do not provide privacy and light control, shades can. When used in combination with draperies and curtains, shades should not attract undue attention. Generally, the subtler and plainer they are the better.

If shades are to be covered by sheer curtains at all times, the shades should be as inconspicuous as possible. You don't want to see big square blots in back of your curtains. Shades should be neutral in color, smooth or subtle in texture, and unpatterned.

Sometimes when you want to create a heavier, or more dramatic, window treatment you can match your shade to the draperies, or give the shade a subtle textural treatment.

Shades in Other Combinations Shades look handsome in combination with shutters, louvers, or lambrequins. This is a rather clean architectural treatment. (See "Structural Treatments.")

ROLLER SHADES When the tops of roller shades are to be exposed, it is attractive to reverse the way they are usually hung to avoid seeing those ugly rolls at the top. That is, turn the roll to the outside instead of inward.

If you want a shade permanently down to block the view, the shade itself should have some decorative interest. It might be hand-painted.

Vinyl roller shades are generally inexpensive and simple to sponge clean. They come in different degrees of opacity, from light-filtering to room-darkening strengths. They come in a variety of textures—from a linen look to puckered seersucker-looking material. The selection of colors tends toward muted neutrals that will blend with almost any color scheme.

A decorated shade can be the complete window treatment in an INFORMAL room. The addition of a braid or a fringed trim that blends with the color scheme can give the shade a custom look at very little cost. Shades can be appliquéd with fabric or paper to reiterate the pattern of fabrics or wallpaper. (It is best to do this on the bottom of the shade, where it won't be rolled.) If you are handy with paints and stencil, you can create a shade with character. Certain shades take stencil designs easily. Ask your salesman. You could cover the complete shade with Contact Paper, or just add a border. If you use this device in a bedroom, you might also cover the bed wall and the walls in the bathroom with the same Contact Paper.

Fabric roller shades are slightly more expensive than vinyl shades, but they are worth their price in pizzazz.

You can laminate almost any fairly lightweight, closely woven fabric to a shade. This makes the possible variations of textures, colors, and patterns almost endless. Buy a shade that is adhesive-coated and heat-sensitive. Then you can iron on your fabric.

If, for a light look, you want to make a loosely woven fabric into a shade, it can be done. You can glue a loosely woven fabric to an ordinary roller shade, dip it into a stiffening solution, and add weights at the bottom.

If you wish, you can finish your fabric shade with a trim. The bottom of the shade may also be shaped in interesting ways. For a final touch, you can have your fabric shade vinyl-coated for easy maintenance.

MATCHSTICK, BAMBOO, OR WOVEN WOOD SHADES

Matchstick, bamboo, or woven wood shades give a textural treatment to your windows. They can help you achieve a SPACIOUS look, because they are light-looking and they don't take up any floor space.

You can achieve a wide range of esthetic effects with these shades. Natural bamboo colors have a COOL, earthy effect. White bamboo shades have a gardeny or FEMININE feeling. Dark woven woods convey a MASCULINE mood.

The more uneven the texture of the shades, the more INFORMAL the feeling.

The loosely woven shades filter and soften the sunlight, but do not provide a complete blackout. Other shades are specifically designed and woven to block out the light.

Matchstick bamboo shades are available, cheap, at many Japanese import stores. Woven wood shades are more expensive. They may be designed to custom order and feature woven yarns color-coordinated to your room. Matchstick and bamboo shades may also be made to custom size and color.

AUSTRIAN SHADES OR "POUFS"

Austrian shades are also called "poufs," balloon shades, and festoon blinds (by the English). They are pulled by a cord and gather up in scalloped puffs. They are traditionally made of a sheer, unpatterned white material like organdy or voile. Contemporary designers are making them of other materials.

Their esthetic effect is soft and delicate. In TRADITIONAL white, austrian shades are often seen in FORMAL ballrooms and fancy restaurants, all decorated with fringes and tassels. They have a cool, airy, graceful look. Because of their softness and curved shape, austrian shades can convey a FEMININE feeling. In a colorful cotton or a spring-flower chintz, austrian shades would do well in a daughter's bedroom. In a more sophisticated fabric, they would create a RELAXING restful mood in other rooms. Depending on the material, austrian shades can be contemporary. For a delicate, earthy ambience, one might even be made of strands of twine.

Austrian shades can be a problem to maintain. With their scalloped folds, they are dust-catchers. To look their best, they must be sparkling clean, dusted carefully, and hanging in full folds.

What do they cost? If you want them in a sheer, white, unpatterned material, you can buy them ready-made at your local department store at a reasonable price. If you want some other material—a dark color, or a print—you'll either have to make them yourself or have them custom-made.

ROMAN SHADES Roman shades are solid fabric shades, which, when raised, accordion up and fold in layers. The fabric is firm, or slightly stiffened. In back, the fabric is divided at regular intervals by rigid horizontal slats. As the shade is raised, the slats pile up on each other like venetian blinds, bringing the fabric into equally spaced accordion folds. Colored bands often run vertically on the outside of the shade to conceal mechanical parts. The esthetic effect is clean and crisp and tailored. Roman shades are adaptable to any style, depending on the fabric used. They are fresh-looking because they are not used too often. In a dark or textured fabric, they can be MASCULINE looking.

The fabric for a roman shade should be opaque so you can't see the mechanism. It therefore would cut out a certain amount of light when down.

Roman shades need not be expensive, but it depends on the fabric, and on who makes the shades.

With their flat accordion folds, roman shades run the danger of bunching up if they are moved very often.

BLINDS

Blinds give you absolute control of the light and the view. The slats on blinds can be adjusted to let in the amount of light you want. Blinds can filter light or darken the room. Blinds can be completely closed to block out the view and give you privacy, or they may be tilted to obscure the view and give you privacy while still letting in light and air.

In dusty locations, blinds are difficult to keep clean.

Blinds are often used behind draperies to control the light and the view. In this case the blinds are an inconspicuous color.

Blinds alone have a COOL, SPACIOUS effect. Because they are architectural in appearance, they blend with almost any decor. Vertical blinds are usually used alone. Horizontal blinds used alone often have special decorative interest—color or pattern. Horizontal blinds within a lambrequin look clean, neat, architectural.

Choosing Blinds You can choose standard venetian blinds, the elegant new skinny-slat tapeless blinds, or vertical blinds.

Standard *venetian blinds* in white or off-white are often used behind draperies. They look a bit bare used alone unless they are decorative. They are available in a variety of colors and textures. Some simulate wood. Others can be laminated with fabric for decorative effects. Slats are available in a variety of widths.

The new *skinny-slat tapeless blinds* have grace and elegance and an architectural ambience. They have the light airy look favored in MODERN interiors, but they are neutral enough to blend beautifully with TRADITIONAL decor. In bright or bold colors (or stripes) they are the right lively touch for an INFORMAL room. In a glistening metallic finish they are as FORMAL as you could wish. These blinds are available in an incredible range of colors and finishes. There is something to suit almost any room. Less expensive than a drapery treatment, these blinds will enjoy a long life. Unlike venetian blinds, they don't have big tapes to get dirty. They look fine alone, or framed by a lambrequin. The slender slats are easy to see between to enjoy the view.

Vertical blinds are like venetian blinds, except the slats run up and down, instead of across. Vertical blinds are used wall-to-wall, floor-to-ceiling. Like draperies, they may be drawn across the window, or totally to the side. They create a vertical line which seems to push up the ceiling height. They have a clean, architectural effect. They are a good understated treatment for a window wall in a MODERN room. And they are an especially effective treatment at long windows. They can be hung out into the room far enough to conceal a radiator or air-conditioner. Vertical blinds come in a variety of colors and textures. For other decorative effects, fabric may be laminated to them.

SHUTTERS

Shutters give a SPACIOUS feeling because they are clean and neat and don't take up floor space. They are more architectural than decorative. Open to the sides of a window, shutters can make a window look larger. They are timeless. They can create an old-world atmosphere, or a modern one. They can be informal or formal. They last forever. Because of their endurance, they are certainly worth their price.

Shutters give you great control of light, air, the view, and privacy. Any treatment in tiers gives you special control of the window. You can close the bottom tier to give yourself privacy or to obstruct the view, while leaving the upper tier open for light and air. To darken the room, you can close the shutters completely. To filter light, you can adjust the slats of the shutters accordingly.

To conceal unsightly air-conditioners or radiators, you can extend the shutters down below the windowsill.

Shutters are especially appropriate to EARLY AMERICAN and SPANISH styles. In dark wood tones, shutters can seem MASCULINE. In light wood tones or colors, shutters can help create a garden effect.

And now the bad news: Shutters are costly and difficult to install. In dusty locations they are difficult to keep clean. In wet conditions, wood shutters may warp unless the wood is sealed.

Choosing Shutters Shutters are most often made of wood, but they are available in metal and in plastic. Will you want the wood stained or painted? Stained shutters are INFORMAL, except when they match the wood paneling in an eighteenth-century room. Make sure the wood stain coordinates with the other wood tones in the room. (You will probably want some furniture of other materials—say upholstery or metal—so you don't get an excessively woody feeling.) Shutters painted in light or pale colors can seem FORMAL. Bold or bright colors seem INFORMAL. They can match a jolly scheme

in bedroom or bath. Lacquer paint would seal the wood against water.

How will you hang them? Two tiers take care of most windows, but you may need more. As noted, shutters may be repeated below the windowsill to hide radiators.

A single lower tier of shutters with a pretty ruffled valance above is very INFORMAL—fine for a kitchen. A single lower tier of shutters with a swag valance above is FORMAL—fine for a dining room. The shutters should be a pale color. The swag valance might be combined with jabots hanging down the sides of the window casing.

A single lower tier of shutters might be combined with a cafe curtain or a shade above. For a window above a kitchen sink, a lower tier of shutters painted with lacquer will withstand splashing. A curtain wouldn't last so long.

Shutters might be combined with draperies, but *caution:* Unless the shutters can fold neatly and completely within the window casing, they will interfere with the draperies.

STRUCTURAL TREATMENTS

Structural treatments are wooden frames for your window. They are usually made from plywood, cut out in suitable shapes, and covered with fabric, wallpaper, or paint.

They give a structural, architectural effect. They look like an extension of the interior architecture. They may actually come down from ceiling beams or connect with wood wall paneling. This architectural look may have a MODERN feeling.

Structural treatments give an ordinary window more importance. Framing a window with anything gives it a greater sense of dimension.

Structural treatments can camouflage the size or the position of your windows. They can be placed where you wish your windows were, with a camouflaging curtain or drapery behind. They can make windows of different sizes seem the same. They can correct the proportions and positions of windows that seem awkward or unbalanced. With fluorescent tube lighting behind, they can even create windows where there are none!

Structural treatments are, of course, great for hiding air-conditioners or radiators. If the structural treatment is built out from the wall, it might contain roller shades that pull up from the bottom to cover the air-conditioner or radiator.

What are the disadvantages? The price of plywood has been going up. Wood can warp in wet conditions. Built out into the room, structural treatments take space; they may make the room seem smaller.

Choosing Structural Treatments   There are many variations of structural treatments. You may simply frame the window with wooden boards for an INFORMAL, architectural effect. For an airy, garden effect, you may choose an openwork treatment such as a grille or latticework.

A *lambrequin* is a wooden frame that goes across the top of the window and down the sides to the floor. The frame may be straight-lined or cut into curved shapes. It may be covered with wallpaper, fabric, or paint. It may match the walls, the window shade, or upholstered pieces in the room. It may be built out from the wall, so that shades, blinds, or curtains hung within can clear radiators or air-conditioners.

Plywood frames can be constructed in any size or shape. You might just have a big circular opening in front of the window. Draperies, shades, or blinds behind will conceal the actual size and position of the window. The frame can be covered in a multitude of materials.

DECORATIVE SCREENS

Treatments to the sides of the window can make the window seem more important, and frame the view. Vertical panels to the sides of the window create a vertical line that seems to push up the height of the ceiling.

Decorative screens can be put on ceiling tracks to slide in front of the windows to provide privacy and filter the light or darken the room.

The material of the screen must suit the style of the room. Oriental shoji screens have a light look appropriate for a room with Oriental furniture or light low furniture. Filigree screens of wood (or Masonite) with cut-out designs also have a light look. Wrought-iron screens might have a SPANISH flavor. Plexiglas screens give a distinctly MODERN, SPACIOUS feeling. Floor-length wood structures covered with fabric are versatile; they simulate draperies. Rattan or wicker screens give a fresh garden feeling.

Choosing Screens   You can obtain information on decorative screens from your local carpentry shop, hardware store, or lumberyard.

OTHER

Glass shelves mounted within the window frame can convert a window into an illuminated cupboard for glass, plants, or pottery. This idea provides privacy and distracts attention from the view while still making the most of the light and air. Because it doesn't intrude on the room, it is a SPACIOUS treatment.

A *stained-glass* panel in front of a window lets in streams of colored light while concealing the view in and out. It might be suspended on chains in front of the window. Alternatively, it might be installed within the window casing. Attach screw eyes to the underside of the upper window jamb. Attach screw eyes to the top of the stained-glass frame, and then attach the two with fine wire.

A *wood carving* can be suspended in front of a window or installed within the casing. It can close up a window with an ugly view, where you don't need light and air.

A *tapestry* (or even a decorative beach towel) might be wrapped around a wooden frame and installed within the window casing. You can take it with you when you go and leave not a mark. This is a good idea for a window with an ugly view, where you don't need light or air.

A curtain of *beads* can bring out the gypsy in you. Beaded window curtains and doorways were a Hollywood favorite in the movies of the thirties and forties. Threaded bead curtains can be installed on traverse rods to pull open and shut.

Mirror along the insides of the window casing can emphasize a beautiful view, particularly of city lights. It gives a glamorous glisten.

CONCLUSION

The end of this story is, I hope, that you will have the home you want—a home that reflects your needs, your wishes, your own special personality.

I felt all along that you would have the right answers if only you were asked the right questions! This book raises all the questions that you should consider while decorating your home and exposes you to all your options. It explains the design principles that help you to orchestrate your options and refine your design. Finally, it helps you get through the nitty-gritty of purchasing the parts.

You *can* express yourself in the language of design. You *do* have a lot to say to a naked room!

GLOSSARY

Adam Robert and James Adam were the most forceful taste-makers of the late Georgian era in England. Their style was light-looking and classical. (See Chapter 12.)

Adobe A building material traditional to the southwestern United States and other arid regions, adobe brick is composed primarily of sun-dried clay.

Arcade An architectural term, describing a covered passageway constructed with a series of adjoining arches.

Armoire A piece of furniture that functions as a movable closet. It was originally conceived to store armor. Typically an armoire has long double doors. It may be carved or painted with decorations.

Art Deco (also Art Moderne) A style dating from about 1923 to 1939 that celebrated the excitement of contemporary life. Modern technology had recently offered the inventions of the radio, car, airplane, steamship. It promised a better life for all. To do honor to the machine many objects of the era were created in austere geometrical shapes (to look machine-made), but made of luxurious materials (to convey a this-is-the-ultimate image). Another element of the era was a romantic attraction to objects of exotic cultures: Mayan temples, Egyptian art, East European folk art. The style takes its name from the 1925 Paris Exposition Internationale des Arts Decoratifs et Industriels.

Art Nouveau A style born of a protest against the 19th century's historical hodgepodge of inspirations. Believing that nature is a constant, always fresh source of inspiration, the movement took up the asymmetrical, curvilinear shapes of flowers and vines. The style made use of new materials, especially iron, to express its linear, floral forms. Art Nouveau started in the 1890s and lasted less than three decades, but in its search for relevancy and its use of new materials, it made way for Art Deco and the modern movement.

Asymmetrical A kind of arrangement that achieves balance with unlike objects that have about the same visual impact. Asymmetrical balance gives an easy, offhand air of informality. (See Chapter 15.)

Austrian shades Austrian shades are also called puff shades, balloon shades, and festoon blinds (by the English). They are pulled by a cord to gather up in soft, scalloped puffs. They are traditionally made of a sheer white and unpatterned material like organdy or voile. Contemporary designers are making them of other materials.

Bachelor chest A low three- or four-drawer chest introduced during the Queen Anne period (early 18th century) to house a man's haberdashery. It usually has a top that pulls out to serve as a work surface. Because of their storage capacity and small size, bachelor chests are often used today as end tables.

Banister-back chair A late 17th-century American chair with a high back constructed with upright supports similar to those on the banister of a staircase.

Baroque A style born in Italy in the 16th century that dominated Europe until the beginning of the 18th century. Characterized by grand scale, sweeping curves, and heavy ornamentation, the style expresses wealth and power. It was the style of French Louis XIV who lived in the Palace of Versailles and was known as the Sun King.

Bauhaus The Bauhaus is the name of a school founded in Weimar, Germany, in 1919. Its objective was to make a marriage between art and technology. Its leader, Walter Gropius, brought together architects, artists, furniture designers, graphic designers and industrial designers and challenged them to use technology to create useful and beautiful objects for everyday life. The Bauhaus crystalized and focused the modern movement. Such expressions as "form follows function" and "less is more" were born there.

Bay window A bay window is a small-windowed recess set off from the main part of the room. When the windows meet at angles, they are called *bay*.

Beading A decorative molding that looks like a string of beads.

Bergère A deep armchair with a carved frame and upholstered seat, back, and sides. An invention of 18th-century France, the chair takes its name from the French word for shepherdess, lover, nymph. Was it designed to accommodate the shepherdess's skirts or the lover's languor? Who knows? The style is still comfortable today.

Biedermeier A provincial German adaptation of the French Empire style, popular during the first half of the 19th century. (See Chapter 12.)

Block-front The front of a chest designed in three equal parts, the side parts protruding past the recessed center part. This design is typical of fine furniture made in Newport, Rhode Island, in the 18th century. Often the three-part panels were decorated with a scallop-shell shape. The shell would be convex on the protruding side panels and concave in the center—to give further impact to the in-out imagery.

Bombé A description of the rounded shape of a chest that bulges out in the center and/or sides. Characteristic of the French Louis XV style, the voluptuous curving form reflects the era's sensuousness as well as the artistry of its craftsmen.

Breakfront A large cabinet so named because its front is a broken surface. The center panel protrudes beyond the two side panels. Typically a breakfront is constructed with a bottom storage section enclosed by doors. The upper section, intended for display, may either be open or have glass doors.

Brocade A fabric woven in a way that causes the pattern to be raised from the background surface. Brocade offers subtle textural variety. It is usually thought to be formal and traditional and is often used for upholstery and draperies.

Broken pediment A pediment is a triangular structure often used to give a finished feeling to the top of a doorway, cabinet, or bookcase. A broken pediment is one wherein the parts of the triangle are parted in the center to allow more decorative play.

Cabriole A curved leg for furniture, inspired by the shape of an animal's leg. It flares out at the knee, tapers in at the ankle, and ends in an ornamental foot. This leg is a distinguishing feature of 18th-century Queen Anne, early Chippendale, and Louis XV furniture.

Carved pile Rug pile that is cut at varying heights in order to produce a pattern. Sometimes a patterned rug has its pile carved in order to emphasize the design.

Case goods If a case is a box or receptacle to contain something, case goods are all furnishings meant for storage—at least that's how the term is used in the furniture industry. It refers to desks, bookcases, hutches, cabinets—practically anything that isn't upholstery.

Casements: window, cloth, curtain A casement window is hinged on the sides and swings in or out. A casement cloth takes its name from the window it was designed to dress. It is a cloth with an open, airy weave that filters light and can cover a large expanse of windows without creating a heavy effect. A casement curtain is, naturally enough, a curtain made from casement cloth.

Chair rail A strip of molding placed along the wall at the height of the top of the chairs, designed to prevent the chairs from scraping the wall.

Chaise longue Literally a long chair designed so you can put your feet up and relax. The chaise longue may be in one piece or two. The French 18th-century version consisted of an upholstered chair, plus a matching abutting ottoman. Sometimes two facing armchairs shared an ottoman between them.

Chinese Chippendale In 18th-century England Thomas Chippendale was not only a master craftsman, but an ingenious inventor. To fashion his furniture he interpreted influences from all over the world. His "Chinese" styles featured chairbacks with fretwork designs, chair and table legs with dragon feet, beds and cabinets with pagoda tops, and furniture finished with lustrous lacquer.

Chippendale (1740–99) Thomas Chippendale II was the dictator of style in the early and middle Georgian period. A prolific designer, Chippendale created furniture inspired by Gothic, Chinese, French rococo, and classic sources. His sketchbook of furniture designs inspired a host of imitators both in the British Isles and in America.

Classic, Classicism Inspired by the styles of ancient Greece and Rome. Math more than nature is its impetus. Lines generally are straight rather than curved. Ornament is symmetrical; decorative motifs are urns, medallions, scrolls, wreaths. The 18th-century rediscovery of ancient Roman cities through archaeological excava-tion encouraged a return to classicism. It inspired the delicate styles of English Adam, Sheraton and Hepplewhite, French Louis XVI, and American Federal. Later in the 18th century classical motifs were handled in a heavier, more dramatic way in the French Empire and English Regency styles.
The word *classic* is also used to denote a standard of excellence.

Claw-and-ball foot A type of carved foot at the end of a furniture leg. Thought to be an adaptation of the Chinese "dragon foot" in which a scaled claw grasps "the pearl of wisdom." The claw-and-ball foot is found on some Queen Anne and Chippendale furniture.

Commode French word for a low chest of drawers. The Victorians in their delicacy used the term to refer to the chamberpot.

Console table The word *console* sometimes means a bracket, so the term *console table* meant a table attached to the wall with brackets. Now the term is used more broadly to mean a table placed up against the wall, or even up against the back of a sofa.

Cornice The word has many meanings. A cornice molding is a decorative molding placed along the walls at the ceiling line. The word *cornice* used in connection with a window treatment means a horizontal structure—usually plywood—over the top of the window, used to conceal curtain rods or the other mechanics of the window treatment. A cornice can also refer to a decorative structure atop a cabinet, used to give the piece of furniture a finished feeling. In general a cornice is high and horizontal.

Dado Refers to the lower part of the wall when the lower part is treated differently from the upper part. For instance, the lower part of the wall may be paneled with wood while the upper part is wallpapered, or the lower part may be wallpapered while the upper part is painted. The dado also refers to the molding or chair rail typically used to separate the upper and lower parts of the wall.

Damask A flat-surfaced reversible fabric with a pattern created by the weave. It is usually of only one color and often made of dressy lustrous fibers.

Directoire A transitional French style bridging the gap between Louis XVI and Napoleon. After Louis XVI was executed in the revolution of 1789 and before Napoleon was named emperor in 1804, the country was run by a directorate. Craftsmen of the time kept the delicacy of forms of the Louis XVI period but looked for new ornamental motifs not associated with the old aristocracy. They used military and agricultural themes—drums, trumpets, stars, ploughs, scythes, sheaves of wheat—to tout the new power elite. Later in the period (anticipating Empire), the forms of ancient Greece became an influence.

Documentary design A design or pattern that is a copy of an older original. The official original is known as the *document*. The copy is known as a *documentary design*.

Dormer Those structures that stick out from a sloping roof to house vertical windows are dormers. Both the window and the structure are called *dormers*.

Eclectic A style of decorating that involves combining furnishings from different periods or places. To succeed, an eclectic interior must observe some coherence of size, shape, texture, and color. (See Chapter 15.)

Elizabethan Part of what I call the "Early English" style (see Chapter 12), Elizabethan furnishings combine Gothic and Italian Renaissance influences. Elizabethan furnishings can be identified by the bulbous melon shape of furniture legs and supports.

English Regency The style after Georgian, before Victorian. Greatly influenced by the French Empire and the Prince Regent's sense of the exotic. (See Chapter 12.)

Entablature According to classical architectural orders, the entablature is the name for the structure stacked vertically atop a supporting column. It consists of three parts: first the architrave, then the frieze, then the cornice for the final topping.

Étagère Free-standing open shelves, usually over six feet in height, used to display art objects, collections, or books. Étagères are made in many materials including wood or steel and glass.

Festoon Derived from the word for festival, a festoon is a decorative chain looped between two points of support. It could be a chain of greens at Christmas; a garland of flowers in the spring; or a carved, molded, or painted ornament for furnishings in any season. It may also be a loop of fabric draped above a window.

Flocked wallpaper A wallpaper with a design that feels like cut velvet, achieved by gluing short fibers to the paper.

Fluting Parallel vertical channels cut into a column or furniture leg. When the parallel lines are raised instead of sunken, the treatment is called *reeding*.

Formica A trade name for a rigid plastic laminate surface that is wonderfully easy to maintain. Available in all kinds of colors and patterns to blend with almost any decor.

French door A door of two vertical halves, featuring glass within the door frames. The doors are hinged on the sides (like casement windows) to swing in or out. French doors are often used to enter onto balconies or terraces.

French Empire Napoleon's furniture style (1804–15) was created specifically to communicate the message of his power and prestige. Using Roman motifs, he allied himself with the Holy Roman Empire. Using Egyptian motifs, he broadcast his military conquests. Bright color, heavy weight, and gilt ornamentation added to the impact. (See Chapter 12.) The Empire style influenced English Regency and Victorian, American Federal and Greek Revival, and German Biedermeier.

French Provincial Country versions of court styles throughout the years. The more remote the area from the city center, the cruder the copy. (See Chapter 12.)

French Régence Transitional style between the imperial grandeur of Louis XIV and the intimate small scale of Louis XV, the French Regency style (1700–1730) kept the large scale of Louis XIV, but introduced the free curves that became characteristic of Louis XV.

Fretwork A geometric border design of interlocking straight lines. (Imagine a border design at the hem of a Greek toga.) Fretwork designs are sometimes called *key* patterns. Fretwork can also refer to latticework, cutout patterns in wood or metal.

Gabled roof A pointed roof composed of two slanting sides. The triangular areas under the eaves at the ends of the building are known as *gables*.

Georgian During the reigns of George I, II, and III, throughout the 18th century, English furnishings achieved a high degree of elegance and refinement. The best-known craftsmen of the era are Chippendale, Hepplewhite, Sheraton, and the Adam brothers. Although incorporating a number of influences, the style is generally formal. (See Chapter 12.)

Glass curtains Sheer curtains, usually hung close to the glass, used to filter light, provide privacy, and soften the look of the window. Glass curtains are smooth in texture, light in color. They are usually made of nylon, orlon, or Fiberglas.

Gothic Gothic is a style of the Middle Ages (1150–1500). Best known in church architecture, the style features soaring ceilings, pointed arches, a general vertical thrust pointing heavenward. Gothic furnishings were adaptations in oak of architectural forms. The mid-19th-century hunger for novelty precipitated a Gothic Revival.

Hadley chest A type of Early American chest decorated with crude, incised carving. It stood on four short legs and usually had one drawer below the chest proper. Actually originating in Connecticut, the Hadley chest was misnamed for a Massachusetts town.

Hepplewhite George Hepplewhite was a London cabinetmaker of great influence in the late Georgian era. He led a trend toward a more delicate, lighter look. He introduced the use of satinwood and painted finishes and he invented the sideboard. (See Chapter 12.)

Highboy A tall chest of drawers on legs, usually finished on top with a decorative pediment, characteristic of 18th-century furniture of English inspiration. A highboy may be constructed in one part or two. If divided, the lower section, called a *lowboy*, may be either a low chest or a table with one drawer. The English call this a "chest on chest."

Hunt table Designed to help serve a buffet after the hunt, the hunt table is high and semicircular, allowing one person to stand behind it to offer all the dishes. The table often has drop leaves to augment the serving surface. The style makes a convenient wraparound desk.

Inlay Decoration achieved by laying contrasting materials into another surface. English and French cabinetmakers of the 18th century used inlays of wood, metal, ivory, and shell to enrich their furnishings.

Jacobean Part of the Early English period (see Chapter 12), the Jacobean style followed the Elizabethan. Chairs became more comfortable with the addition of upholstery nailed to their rectangular seats and backs. Straight or spiral dwarf columns and the motif of the twisted rope gradually replaced the bulbous ornamentation of the Elizabethan era.

Kas A type of primitive cupboard typical of the Dutch-American colonists who settled in New York State and the Delaware Valley. Generally tall and wide, the cupboard was usually hand-painted with engaging designs of birds, flowers, and fruit.

Ladder-back chair A chair with ladderlike rungs on its back, a simple country conception used in Early America. The style is also called a *slat-back* chair.

Lambrequin A wooden frame that goes across the top of the window and down the sides to the floor. Usually made of plywood, it may be straight-lined or cut into curved shapes. It may be covered with paint, wallpaper, or fabric.

Laminating A process of bonding together thin layers of material—usually by applying a resin and compressing with heat. Plywood is made by laminating thin layers of wood. Formica and Micarta are made by laminating a thin layer of plastic to plywood. Fabric may be laminated to certain window shades.

Lattice Strips of wood or metal attached together (often at right angles) to form an open network. For example, a trellis used to train ivy is a construction of latticework.

Lawson A reference to a type of fully upholstered piece—sofa, love seat, or chair—that has classically simple lines. The back is square and the arms are midway between the seat and back in height.

Louis Philippe With the short restoration of the monarchy after Napoleon came a revival of the style of Louis XV. However, now much of it was poorly made by machine. Following Paris fashions, Americans of this mid-19th-century Victorian era made fantastic interpretations of the Louis Philippe revival of the Louis XV style.

Louis Quatorze (XIV) The Baroque style of the 17th century Sun King who built the Palace of Versailles. Furnishings were grand, gilded, curved, and symmetrical.

Louis Quinze (XV) The Rococo style of the first half of the 18th century. During Louis XV's reign, rooms and their furnishings diminished in size; curves became free instead of symmetrical; colors became pastel; and decorative patterns became pastoral or sentimental. (See Chapter 12.) This era also witnessed the introduction of Oriental influences.

Louis Seize (XVI) The Neo-Classic style of the latter part of the 18th century. Louis XVI restored classical order, symmetry, simplicity, and the straight line. The scale of furnishings remained small and pastel colors remained popular. (See Chapter 12.)

Louvers Fixed or movable slats that allow the flow of air, can soften the light, deflect rain, and provide privacy. Shutters, for example, have louvers.

Lowboy A short storage piece of 18th century English invention. It may be either a low chest or a table with a drawer or so. It may be used alone or as the base of the *highboy*, or chest on chest.

Lyre A stringed musical instrument related to the harp used by the ancient Greeks to accompany recitation and song, the lyre is a motif adopted by Americans after the Revolution to affirm affinity with ancient self-governing Greece. Duncan Phyfe, the most influential designer of the American Federal period, used the lyre as a motif for table bases and chairbacks. (See Chapter 12.)

Marquetry An elaborate technique for decorating furniture with patterns of contrasting materials, such as different woods, ivory, or mother of pearl. Instead of laying the contrasting materials into a surface carved out to fit them (inlay), marquetry involves creating the complete surface to affix to the furniture. It is a thin, flush, flat composition of veneers and contrasting materials.

Matte finish Having a smooth, even surface that is not shiny. The term often refers to paint.

Medallion A circular or oval frame containing an ornamental motif, painted or in relief. Sheraton used medallions of classical subject matter to decorate some of his furnishings.

Mission An American style of the turn of the century born as a revolt against the machine age. Mission furnishings are made by hand of local materials (often white oak), and are designed with clean and simple lines. The style was inspired by Shaker furnishings, the Arts and Crafts movements in England, Austria and Scotland, and the Franciscan missions of the American West. In its emphasis on functional forms, the style anticipates the modern movement.

Moiré A lustrous fabric of one color that has a subtle wavy design suggestive of a watermark.

Molding A contoured and continuous strip of wood, plaster, stone, metal, or other material used to grace architecture or furniture. For example, a baseboard is a molding at the bottom of the wall where it meets the floor. (Moldings are often used at points of joinings.)

Neo-Classic The 18th-century excavation of the ancient Roman city of Pompeii inspired a revival of classical forms in pacesetting England and France. The style is known as *Neo-Classic* or new classic. The Adam brothers in England were its primary instigators. Chippendale, Hepplewhite, Sheraton, Louis XVI, and American Federal furnishings all reflect its taste for the light look and the straight line.

Ormolu Invented by Boulle for Louis XIV, ormolu is an ornamentation for furniture made of cast bronze, finished by hand, and coated in gold. Although the scale and style changed, ormolu was a feature of all the French-court styles of the 18th century.

Ottoman A low, backless, armless, cushioned seat, an idea borrowed by 18th-century Europe from the Ottoman Empire. The ottoman is also used in conjunction with a chair as an upholstered footrest.

Paisley A pattern, typically with a curved teardrop motif, originating in Kashmir, India, as embroidery on scarves and copied in Paisley, Scotland, on woven cashmere shawls. Now paisley patterns may be printed as well as woven.

Parapet A railing or low wall placed at the edge of a roof, bridge, or platform to provide protection.

Parquet floor A wood flooring made up of patterned squares rather than plain straight strips. The pattern is composed of straight, short lengths of wood arranged in a geometrical configuration such as a checkerboard, a herringbone design, or a basketweave.

Pedestal table Table with a support in the center instead of legs at the ends.

Pediment The term originally referred to the triangular shape (gable) under the roof line at the end of a Greek temple. It was often carved or decorated—the building's crowning glory. The idea of the pediment was adapted for decorative use in interior architecture and furnishings. It crowned doorways and tall cabinets. Because in these uses it was not functioning as a structural support, the shape could be varied. The basic triangle is sometimes rounded, sometimes separated in the center with an ornament inserted and with the sides straight or scrolled.

Pembroke table Designed in the 18th century for the Earl of Pembroke, this versatile table has one drawer and two wide drop leaves that double its size. It is often used as a lamp or end table.

Phyfe, Duncan The most outstanding cabinetmaker in America in the early 19th century, Phyfe was influenced by the classic revival. His initial designs, inspired by Sheraton, show refinement of line and delicacy of detail. His later work has the heavier look of French Empire and English Regency. (See Chapter 12.)

Pilaster A decorative architectural element attached to a wall, posing as a column. It does not offer the building structural support, but it does give architectural interest. It is usually fully equipped with a base and a capital.

Plastic laminate An easy-maintenance surface of rigid plastic over plywood. Formica and Micarta are examples. (See *laminating* above.)

Porcelain A fine ceramic ware, fired at an extremely high temperature, that is hard, nonporous, and translucent.

Portico A porch, often at the entrance of a building, with its roof supported by a series of columns. Porticos are characteristic of the Greek Revival style of architecture.

Queen Anne The reigning English monarch at the beginning of the 18th century, Queen Anne is noted for furniture of walnut wood made in graceful curved shapes with unornamented, simple surfaces. A characteristic piece is a dining chair with curved cabriole legs and the vertical splat back. An American Colonial interpretation is the *fiddle-back* chair, so named because the back splat is carved into the silhouette of a violin.

Raked legs Sloping legs, inclining from the perpendicular. Also called splay legs. Such slanting legs are characteristic of Early American Windsor chairs.

Relief A type of decoration in which the monotony of a plane, flat surface is relieved by raising some figures above the surface. Figures in *high relief* are raised a good deal above the surface, making them almost three-dimensional. Figures in *low relief* are raised only slightly from the surface.

Renaissance A *rebirth* of humanism and classical culture after the Dark Ages. The movement began in Italy in the 14th century, spread throughout Europe, and lasted well into the 17th century. As in the previous Gothic period, furnishings were inspired by the shapes and ornament of architecture. Scale was large; lines were straight; forms were borrowed from antiquity.

Rococo A small-scale, curve-legged, asymmetrical style invented during the reign of Louis XV, named after the *rocailles* and *coquilles* (rocks and shells) that were its prominent decorative motifs. A radical change from the previous Baroque period of grandeur and symmetry, Rococo furnishings suggest intimacy and informality.

Roman shade A window shade made of fabric designed to fold up in accordion pleats when drawn. The Roman shade has a neat, tailored appearance.

Rosette An ornament resembling a rose, usually contained within a square, round, or oval frame and carved in relief. Characteristic of French 18th-century furnishings.

Satin A smooth, dressy fabric with a lustrous front and a dull back, often woven of silk or a synthetic fiber simulating silk.

Sawbuck table A sawhorse. A surface over two X-shaped supports. Originally rough and rustic and made of wood, today the simple style has been dressed up with steel or chrome supports and tops of glass, Lucite, or marble.

Secretary A tall, slim piece of furniture with a drop-down desk leaf, shelves behind doors above and drawers below.

Semainier Clean underwear for each day of the week. (*Semaine* means week in French.) A semainier is a tall, narrow bedroom chest with seven drawers meant to store lingerie.

Serpentine Describes a snaky shape, an undulating curve—maybe on the top of a Chippendale chair or the front of a chest or table.

Settle A place to settle down and rest yourself, a settle is a wooden bench with arms used in Colonial times. It has a high, solid back (to eliminate drafts) and an enclosed foundation that can be a storage chest.

Shaker A Christian sect of "shaking Quakers," the Shakers believed in purity. The furnishings they created in the early 19th century in America are noteworthy for their purity of line and functional form. (See Chapter 12.)

Sheraton Thomas Sheraton was the last of the great furniture designers of 18th-century Georgian England. He and Hepplewhite used the same woods and often the same chair legs, but Sheraton furnishings are distinguished by a greater emphasis on straight lines. Sheraton had a mechanical mind and a genius for invention. He designed furniture that could fold to change its identity and perform a different service—for example, a table that could turn into library steps. He also is known for creating cabinets with secret compartments.

Sideboard A board on the side, specifically when *board* means a table spread with a meal. An extra place to put food or the accoutrements of a meal. A dining-room piece used as a surface and for storage.

Slat-back chair Same as a *ladder-back* chair. A chair with a back composed of horizontal slats or rungs placed between vertical uprights.

Sleigh bed A bed shaped like a sleigh, with a high headboard and footboard rolling outward at the top. Popular in America during the first half of the 19th century, the sleigh bed was a domestic interpretation of a French Empire bed.

Slub A heavy area in an unevenly spun yarn.

Splat, Splat-back chair A thin, flat piece of wood centered vertically in the back of a chair. The splat may be shaped on its sides. For example, the *fiddle-back* chair has a back splat shaped to the silhouette of a violin. In more sophisticated styles the center splat may not be flat, but carved.

Stretcher A brace stretching horizontally from furniture leg to furniture leg, connecting them and thereby strengthening the structure. Stretchers are used on chairs and tables of many styles.

Stucco A cement or plaster used as a covering for walls. Most often the texture is rough, showing the irregular impressions of the plasterer's trowel.

Swag Something hanging in a curve between two points, like a festoon. A swag often refers to a cloth draped in a loop over the top of a window.

Symmetrical, Symmetry A kind of arrangement that achieves balance by placing identical objects in an equidistant position. Symmetrical balance inspires a formal—sometimes stiff—feeling.

Taffeta A crisp fabric that is smooth and lustrous on both sides, taffeta used in home furnishing gives a room a dressy look.

Tambour Ever wonder what to call the top of a rolltop desk? Those thin wood strips are glued onto canvas so they can have the flexibility to roll along a grooved track and follow a curved shape. All this ingenuity is called a tambour. There are tambour tops, rolling up and down, and tambour doors, rolling from side to side.

Toile, Toile de Jouy Toile is the French word for a plain and simple twill weave fabric, often woven of cotton or linen. Toile de Jouy is the name of a particular type of pattern printed on this fabric. It is usually a sentimental scene printed in one color on a light, often off-white, ground. It was introduced in Jouy, France, in the 18th century and is still popular today.

Tole, Tolework Derived from the French word for sheet metal, tole is decorated metal, usually painted or enameled tin, made into useful household objects such as lamp bases or shades, boxes, and trays.

Tree-of-life pattern A pattern that dates back to the ancient Assyrians, the tree-of-life design is truly a classic. It consists of a tree or vine with branches, leaves, flowers, and birds and animals lurking about. It was introduced in England during Henry VIII's reign, having been brought back by British ships from East India. The design became enormously popular. It was reproduced in painted patterns, crewel embroidery, hand-blocked prints, and even weaves. The pattern remains popular today.

Valance A valance is a horizontal treatment over the top of a window designed to conceal drapery hardware and to give interest and importance to the window. It may be made of fabric, wood, or metal.

Venetian blinds A window covering composed of horizontal slats connected on each side to a vertical tape. The slats may be turned up or down to control the amount of light entering the room. A newer incarnation is the skinny-slat, tapeless blind, which is easier to keep clean and more elegant in proportion. A favorite of contemporary designers, these skinny-slat blinds are available in an enormous variety of colors and metal finishes.

Vertical blinds Blinds whose slats run vertically instead of horizontally. Clean, light, and architectural in feeling, vertical blinds are often used floor to ceiling, wall to wall. The slats can be adjusted to allow the circulation of air while concealing the view.

Victorian Victoria was the queen of England from 1837 to 1901. During her time the industrial revolution engaged people's minds more than the arts. Pure—even prissy—social behavior did not extend its scruples to the arts. The Victorian era is noted for its indiscriminate revival of all sorts of styles and its often indelicate treatment of those styles. (See Chapter 12.)

Vitrine A French word for shop window or showcase, a vitrine is a glass case with shelves designed for displaying objects.

Voile A fine, soft, sheer fabric often used for curtains or the "glass curtains" described above.

Wainscot Usually a paneled, wooden lining of an interior wall. The term wainscot is also used interchangeably with the term *dado* to refer to a treatment of the lower wall when it differs from the treatment of the upper wall.

William and Mary William of Orange brought a Dutch influence to England when he married Mary Stuart and became King of England (1689–1702). William and Mary furnishings are characterized by bracing with flat stretchers, legs in spiral or trumpet shapes, and feet shaped like flattened balls (called bun feet). The era introduced the highboy, and the widespread use of walnut wood. William and Mary styles inspired emulation in Colonial America.

Windsor chair Early America's most common chair, the chair named after Windsor Castle first appeared in England during Queen Anne's reign. Conceived by wheelwrights, the chair has a hoop-shaped back supported by spindles; a saddle-shaped seat; and raked, splayed legs. Variations of the style look like their names and include: the loop, the comb, the fan, the bow.

Wing chair An upholstered armchair with a high, solid back and projecting sides or *wings* that provide protection from drafts as well as corners for nestling the head.

INDEX